Toscani Giovanni, Giovanni Toscani

Italian Conversational Course

A New Method of Teaching of Italian Language, Both Theoretically and Practically.

Fifth Edition

Toscani Giovanni, Giovanni Toscani

Italian Conversational Course
A New Method of Teaching of Italian Language, Both Theoretically and Practically. Fifth Edition

ISBN/EAN: 9783337084042

Printed in Europe, USA, Canada, Australia, Japan

Cover: Foto ©Suzi / pixelio.de

More available books at **www.hansebooks.com**

ITALIAN

CONVERSATIONAL COURSE.

A NEW METHOD OF

TEACHING THE ITALIAN LANGUAGE, BOTH THEORETICALLY AND PRACTICALLY.

BY

GIOVANNI TOSCANI,

PROFESSOR OF THE ITALIAN LANGUAGE AND LITERATURE
IN QUEEN'S COLLEGE, LONDON.

Fifth Edition.

LONDON:
TRÜBNER & CO., 58, LUDGATE HILL.

1875.

LONDON:

PRINTED BY C. F. HODGSON & SON

GOUGH SQUARE, FLEET STREET.

PREFACE TO THE FIRST EDITION.

LONG experience in the teaching of his native tongue has enabled the Author of this ITALIAN CONVERSATIONAL COURSE to judge of the practical utility of the Italian grammars commonly used in this country. Meritorious as some of these are, he is not acquainted with any one which embodies the modern principles of instruction so successfully applied in the teaching of other modern languages. The aim of the author has therefore been to supply to students of Italian advantages of method heretofore almost exclusively enjoyed by students of French and German.

The main feature, then, of this Work is, that it unites grammatical theory with conversational practice; and that the pupil, thus combining the study of words with their immediate application, is enabled to form complete sentences from the very commencement of the course.

To this end, the author has given the study of the Verb the first place in his work. This Chapter, which gives the complete accidence and syntax of the Verb, comprises twelve Exercises; each Exercise being followed by a series of simple questions in Italian, which serve chiefly the purpose of exciting intellectual activity on the part of the pupil.

The theory of the other parts of speech, which are comprehended in separate chapters, is intended to be

studied concurrently with the Verb; and afterwards
the Practical Exercises, which accompany these parts of
speech, to be worked out in the same manner as the
preceding exercises on the Verb. A Chapter is also
devoted to an explanation of the different modes of
address in Italian. When this has been mastered, the
student is to return to the Exercises on the Verbs, and
re-work them, applying the directions given in the text.

The different parts of the course having been thus
repeatedly brought before the student, will remain per-
manently impressed on the memory.

The rules have been for the most part illustrated by
quotations from Italian classics; and the Conversational
Exercises have been made the vehicle of useful information about Italy.

The Author may mention that the tables of irregular
and exceptional forms in the various parts of speech
are here given more comprehensively and exactly than
in any Italian grammar that has fallen under his notice.

GIOVANNI TOSCANI.

January, 1867.

PREFACE TO THE SECOND EDITION.

To add to the utility of the work, and in accordance
with the advice of practical teachers, the Author has
supplemented the English-Italian vocabulary of the
former Edition by an Italian-English one of all the
words used in the questions on the exercises, and elsewhere.

G. T.

May, 1867.

PREFACE TO THE THIRD EDITION.

THE rapid sale of two editions of this work affords a sufficient indication that such a compilation was really wanted; and the favourable comments of the press, as well as of practical teachers, convince the author that the plan he has followed in its construction is found in the hands of others as effective as he has found it in his own.

The plan, the general order and arrangement, of the work has been preserved in this as in the former editions; but many additions and improvements have been made in each division of the book.

There have been given, at the outset of the work, complete tabulated forms of the inflected parts or speech, which generally precede the verb; these will be found sufficient to explain such inflected words as are met with in the exercises.

The practical exercises, which in the former editions consisted only of English sentences to be translated into Italian, have each of them been preceded by a Reading Exercise in Italian, consisting of phrases, passages, and extracts, chiefly chosen from the best writers, to be translated into English; and the Questions following the exercises are made to refer to both.

The use of the different Moods and Tenses of the Verb, as also the mode of their formation, have been

carefully explained, and a Table has been added, showing the conjugation of all verbs, regular and irregular,
which will be found greatly to facilitate the learning of
the verbs, and to aid in retaining them in the memory.

Observations have been appended to all the chapters,
on the orthography of the different parts of speech; and
throughout the work great care has been taken to point
out differences of idiom and construction between the
Italian and English languages.

In conclusion, the author desires to acknowledge the
assistance he has received from Mr. E. Grosvenor, to
whose knowledge of the language, and literary skill,
he is indebted for several improvements in matters of
detail.

GIOVANNI TOSCANI.

QUEEN'S COLLEGE, HARLEY STREET, W.
January, 1870.

CONTENTS.

CHAPTER I.

CHAPTER II.

VERBS.

CHAPTER III.

NOUNS.

CHAPTER IV

ARTICLES.

CHAPTER V.

ADJECTIVES.

CHAPTER VI.

CHAPTER VII.

CHAPTER VIII.

PRONOUNS.

CHAPTER IX

ADVERBS.

CHAPTER X.

PREPOSITIONS.

CHAPTER XI.

CONJUNCTIONS.

CHAPTER XII.

INTERJECTIONS.

CHAPTER XIII.

CHAPTER XIV.

List of the Abbreviated Names of Authors and Works quoted in this book.

ALB., Alberto.
ARI., Ariosto.
BEM., Bembo.
BEN. C., Bentivoglio, Cardinale.
BOC., Boccaccio.
BUONAR., Buonarotti.
CAS., Della Casa.
CES., Cesari.
DAN., Dante.
DA RIP., Da Ripalta.
FIOR., Fiorentino.
GUA., Guarini.
GUI., Guicciardini.

G. VIL., Giovanni Villani.
LEOP., Leopardi.
MAC., Machiavelli.
MAF., Maffei.
MANZ., Manzoni.
MET., Metastasio.
PET., Petrarca.
PROV., Proverbio.
SAC., Sacchetti.
S. CONC., San Concordio.
S. GREG., San Gregorio.
SEGN., Segneri.
TAS., Tasso.

List of Abbreviations.

Abl., Ablative.
Acc., Accusative.
Adj., Adjective.
Cond., Conditional.
Dat., Dative.
Dem. or Demons., Demonstrative.
Ex., Example.
Excep., Exception.
F. or Fem., Feminine.
Fut., Future.
Gen., Genitive.
Imp. or Imperf., Imperfect.
Indef., Indefinite.
Indic., Indicative.
Inter., Interrogative.

M. or Masc., Masculine.
Nom., Nominative.
No., Number.
Obs., Observation.
P., Page.
Perf., Perfect.
Pers., Person.
Pers. Pron., Personal Pronoun.
Pl. or Plur., Plural.
Poss., Possessive.
Pres., Present.
Pron., Pronoun.
Relat., Relative.
Sg. or Sing., Singular.
Subj., Subjunctive.
Voc. or Vocab., Vocabulary.

Explanation of the Marks employed in the Exercises.

1. A word within parentheses ( ) is not to be translated.
2. An Italian word placed under a dash — shows that the word is wanting in English.
3. English words between brackets [ ] indicate the literal translation of the Italian words to be used.
4. The small figures affixed to English words denote the order of the words in Italian.
5. A figure under an English word refers to a corresponding sentence in the same Exercise.
6. The numbers which follow some of the questions refer to sentences in the Reading and Translation Exercises immediately preceding.

CHAPTER I.

PRONUNCIATION.

THE ALPHABET.

THE Italian Alphabet consists of twenty-two letters, which are pronounced as follows :—

A	B	C	D*	E	F	G	H	I
ah	bee	chee	dee	ay	ef-fay	jee	ak-kah	ee

J*	L	M	N	O	P	Q	R
ee loon-go	el-lay	em-may	en-nay	o	pee	koo	er-ray

S	T	U	V	Z*
es-say	tee	oo	vee	dsay-tah.

Of these letters, *a, e, i, o, u* are vowels, and the rest, consonants.

VOWELS.

A has only one sound in Italian—that of the English *a* in 'father'; as, *fato*, fate.

ᵃ It should be observed that it is in Tuscany that the letters *b, c, d* are pronounced *bee, chee, dee ;* in other parts of Italy they are sounded *bay, chay, day.*

ᵇ *j*, called in Italian *i-lungo*, having the same sound as *i*, is by modern grammarians no longer reckoned among the letters of the Italian alphabet. But as in books we occasionally meet with words in which *j* is used instead of *i* or *ii ;* as, in *jeri*, for *ieri*, yesterday ; in *noja*, for *noia*, vexation ; and in *tempj*, for *tempii*, temples, &c., it was thought necessary to give it in this work.

ᶜ The student will observe that K, W, X, Y are not found in the Italian alphabet.

B

E has two sounds, the *open* and the *close*. The *open* is that
of the English *ai* in 'fair'; as, *erba*, grass; and the
close is that of the English *a* in 'fate'; as, *bene*, well.

I is always pronounced like *e* in 'be'; as, *vino*, wine.

O, like *e*, has two sounds, one *open*, the other *close*. The
first is that heard in the English word 'not'; as
notte, night; and the second is that of the *o* in the
word 'note'; as, *pomo*, apple.

U has invariably the sound of *oo* in the English word
'root'; as, *uno*, one.

CONSONANTS.

The Italian consonants are pronounced like the English, except the following: *c, g, h, q, r, s, z*.

H in Italian is never sounded.   (1.) It is used at the beginning of the following words to distinguish them
from others:—

ho, I have.	*o*, or.
hai, thou hast.	*ai*, to the.
ha, he has.	*a*, to.
hanno, they have.	*anno*, year.

(2.) It prolongs the sound of the vowels *a, e, i, o, u*,
in the interjections *ah*, ah; *deh*, alas; *ih* (interjection of abhorrence), shame; *oh*, oh; *uh* (interjection of pain), oh.

(3.) It is also used to harden the sound of *c* or *g*
before the vowels *e, i*.

The following arrangement will show the pronunciation of *c, g, q, r, s, z*, in combination with other letters[a]:—

C soft before *e, i*, like *ch* in 'cherry,' 'chilly.'

COMBINATION.	PRONUNCIATION.	EXAMPLES.
ce	*chay*	*céna*, supper
ci	*chee*	*cibo*, food
cia	*chee-ah*	*ciálda*, wafer
cie	*chee-ay*	*ciélo*, heaven
cio	*chee-o*	*cióttolo*, pebble
ciu	*chee-oo*	*ciúffo*, forelock

---

[a] In the examples which follow, the accent has been given merely
as a guide to their correct pronunciation.

SC soft before *e, i,* like *sh* in ' shell,' ' ship.'

COMBINATION.	PRONUNCIATION.	EXAMPLES.
sce	shay	scéna, scene
sci	shee	scímia, monkey
scia	she-ah	sciálle, shawl
scie	she-ay	sciénza, science
scio	shee-o	scióne, whirlwind
sciu	shee-oo	sciupóne, spendthrift

CC like *t-ch* in ' hatchet.'

cce	t-chay	accénto, accent
cci	t-chee	láccio, tie
ccia	t-chee-ah	fáccia, face
ccio	t-chee-o	lúccio, pike
cciu	t-chee-oo	pacciúme, sweepings

C hard before *a, o, u,* like *k.*

ca	kah	cása, house
co	ko	cóllo, neck
cu	koo	cúna, cradle

CH hard, like *k.*

che*	kay	chéto, quiet
chi	kee	chíno, bent

G soft before *e, i,* like *j* in ' jest,' ' jig.'

ge	jay	gélo, frost
gi	jee	gíro, turn
gia	jee-ah	giállo, yellow
gio	jee-o	giórno, day
giu	jee-oo	giúdice, judge

GG like *d-j* in ' adjust.'

gge	d-jay	légge, law
ggi	d-jee	óggi, to-day
ggia	d-jee-ah	pióggia, rain
ggio	d-jee-o	fággio, beech-tree
ggiu	d-jee-oo	aggiúnta, addition

G hard before *a, o, u,* as in English.

ga	gah	gátto, cat
go	go	góla, throat
gu	goo	gústo, taste

* See 3, p. 2.

B 2

GH hard before *e*, *i*, like *g* in 'gamut.'

COMBINATION.	PRONUNCIATION.	EXAMPLES.
ghe[a]	*gay*	*sghémbo*, crooked
ghi	*ghee*	*ghíro*, dormouse

GL before *i*, liquid sound, like *ll* in 'million.'

gli	*l-yee*	*égli*, he
glia	*l-yah*	*fóglia*, leaf
glie	*l-yay*	*móglie*, wife
glio	*l-yo*	*cíglio*, eye-brow
gliu	*l-yoo*	*figliuólo*, child

GN like *ni* in 'companion.'

gna	*n-yah*	*magágna*,[b] blemish
gne	*n-yay*	*agnéllo*, lamb
gni	*n-yee*	*incógnito*, unknown
gno	*n-yo*	*bisogno*, need
gnu	*n-yoo*	*cagnúccio*, little dog

Q (which is always accompanied by *u*) like *qu* in 'question.'

qua	*qu-ah*	*quánto*, how much
que	*qu-ay*	*quéllo*, that
qui	*qu-ee*	*quí*, here
quo	*qu-o*	*quóta*, share

R a rolling sound.

ere	*ayr-ray*	*áere*, air
ori	*or-ree*	*oriuólo*, watch
oro	*or-ro*	*óro*, gold
uro	*oor-ro*	*futúro*, future

S sibilant (sharp) at the beginning of a word or syllable, like *s* in 'saint.'

sa	*sah*	*sála*, hall
se	*say*	*sénso*, sense
si	*see*	*sídro*, cider
so	*so*	*rósso*, red
su	*soo*	*súgo*, juice

[a] See 3, p. 2.
[b] *g* does not form one syllable with the letter preceding it, except in a word where there is a double *g*; *magagna*, e.g. = *ma-ga-gna*.

S flat between vowels, like *z* in ' doze,' or *s* in ' easy.'[a]

COMBINATION.	PRONUNCIATION.	EXAMPLES.
ese	ay-zay	*inglése*, English
iso	ee-zo	*viso*, visage
osa	o-zah	*rósa*, rose

Z sharp, like *ts* in ' benefits,' before *i* followed by a vowel.

zi	tsee	{ *zío*, uncle { *grázia*, grace

Z flat, like *ds* in ' Windsor,' generally at the beginning of a word, or after a consonant.

za	dsah	*sénza*, without
zo	dso	*zóna*, zone

ZZ sometimes like *ts*, and sometimes like *ds*.

zza	tsah	*bellézza*, beauty
zzo	dso	*rózzo*, rough

OBSERVATIONS. — 1. In Italian every letter is pronounced. Two or more vowels coming together in a word are articulated separately, even when two or three form but one syllable ; as, *ciò*, that ; *miei*, my.

2. Double consonants are pronounced with double emphasis. The mute consonants *b, p, d, t, v* with two distinct and somewhat separate sounds ; as, *babbo*, papa; *addio*, good-bye; *zappa*, hoe; *atto*, act; *avventura*, adventure. The liquids *l, m, n, r*, and the *f* and *s*, are pronounced with a continued sound ; as, *fallo*, fault; *mamma*, mamma; *canna*, reed; *serra*, hot-house ; *offesa*, offence ; *osso*, bone.[b]

ACCENTS.

There are two accents in Italian, the *grave* (`) and the *acute* ('). The *grave accent* is placed over the final vowel of such words as have the accent on the last syllable ; as, *sarò*, I shall be ; *beltà*, beauty ; and is also used as a sign of distinction between certain words spelt alike, but differing in signification ; as, *dì*, day—*di*, of ; *sì*, yes, so—*si*, one's self ; *è*, is—*e*, and ; *là*, there—

---

[a] In the reflective form of the verb, the *s* of the *si* is always sibilant.

[b] See double *c* and *g*, p. 3, and double *z* above.

la, the, her; *lì,* there—*li,* the, them; *dà,* he gives, give thou—*da,* from; *però,* therefore—*pero,* a pear tree; *nè,* neither, nor—*ne,* of it, us; *testè,* just now—*teste,* heads; *costà,* there—*costa,* shore; *tè,* tea—*te,* thee.

The *acute accent* is only placed over the vowel *i* in the terminations *ia, io,* when the two vowels are to be pronounced in two distinct syllables; as, *magía,* magic; *desío,* desire.

OBS.—Although every Italian word bears an accent, it is only in cases like the above that it is written. The position of the accent must therefore be learned by practice. The greater number of Italian words have the accent on the penultimate, or last syllable but one; fewer on the antepenultimate, or last syllable but two; and very few on the last but three. Peculiar stress is laid on the accented vowel; as, *párlo,* I speak; *párlano,* they speak.

For the convenience of the student, the accent has been given throughout the conjugations of verbs in this book.

THE APOSTROPHE.

In Italian the apostrophe (') is frequently used to mark the elision of a vowel or syllable; thus, *la,* the, or her; *il,* the, or him; *egli,* he; *poco,* little; are often written *l', 'l, e', po'.* But some words are shortened without requiring the apostrophe; as, *bel,* for *bello,* fine.

N.B.—In the course of the work, rules will be given for determining when this elision should take place, and the apostrophe be used.

USE OF CAPITALS.

Capital letters are not so frequently employed in Italian as in English. Their use is restricted to the following cases:—

1. The first word of a sentence.
2. The first word of every line in poetry.
3. All proper names, and names of rank and dignity, but not the adjectives derived from proper names; as, *Alessandria è così chiamata da Alessandro, Pontefice romano,* Alexander is so named from Alexander, a Roman Pontiff.

TABLES OF INFLECTIONS, &c., FOR REFERENCE.

INFLECTIONS OF NOUNS.

TERMINATIONS.		EXAMPLES.		
Singular.	Plural.	Sing.		Plural.
a {fem.	e	f. *sorella,*	sister,	*sorelle.*
a {masc.	i	m. *poeta,*	poet,	*poeti.*
o masc. or fem.	i	m. *libro,*	book,	*libri.*
		f. *mano,*	hand,	*mani.*
e "	i	m. *padre,*	father,	*padri.*
		f. *madre,*	mother,	*madri.*
i "		m. *lunedì,*	Monday,	*lunedì.*
		f. *crisi,*	crisis,	*crisi.*
		m. *bambù,*	bamboo,	*bambù.*
u "		f. *virtù,*	virtue,	*virtù.*
ie "		m. *treppiè,*	tripod,	*treppiè.*
mono-syllables } "		f. *effigie,*	image,	*effigie.*
		m. *Re,*	king,	*Re.*
accented } "		f. *gru,*	crane,	*gru.*
vowels } "		m. *falò,*	bonfire,	*falò.*
		f. *carità,*	charity,	*carità.*

(The bracket joining these plural forms is labelled **Invariable.**)

EUPHONIC MODIFICATIONS OF PLURAL NOUNS.

TERMINATIONS.		EXAMPLES.		
Singular.	Plural.	Sing.		Plural.
ca {fem.	che	f. *monaca,*	nun,	*monache.*
ca {masc.	chi	m. *monarca,*	monarch,	*monarchi.*
ga {fem.	ghe	f. *bottega,*	shop,	*botteghe.*
ga {masc.	ghi	m. *collega,*	colleague,	*colleghi.*
co masc.	chi and ci	m. *tedesco,*	German,	*tedeschi.*[a]
		m. *amico,*	friend,	*amici.*
go masc.	ghi and gi	m. *asparago,*	asparagus,	*asparagi.*
		m. *lago,*	lake,	*laghi.*
.cia {fem. } with i	ce	f. *faccia,*	face,	*facce.*
gia } not ac-	ge	f. *frangia,*	fringe,	*frange.*
io masc. } cented.	i	m. *specchio,*	mirror,	*specchi.*

IRREGULAR PLURALS.

m. *dio,*	god,	*dei.*		f. *moglie,*	wife,	*mogli.*
m. *uomo,*	man,	*uomini.*		m. *bue,*	ox,	*buoi.*

Also several nouns ending with the masculine termination o, of which some form their plural in a, and become feminine; as, *paio,* pair, *paia;* and others which have two terminations in the plural, one in *i* regular masculine, the other irregular in *a* feminine; as, *dito,* finger, *diti* and *dita.*

[a] See No. 3, page 6.

INFLECTIONS OF ARTICLES.

	DEFINITE ARTICLE.				INDEFINITE.		
	Masculine.		Feminine.		Masc.	Fem.	
	Sing.	Plur.	Sing.	Plur.			
Before a consonant	*il*	*i*	*la*	*le*	*un*	*una*	
Before *s* followed by a consonant	*lo*	*gli*	–	– } the	*uno*	– }	the
Before a vowel	*l'*	*gli*	*l'*	*le*	*un*	*un'*	

PREPOSITIONS IN COMBINATION WITH THE DEFINITE ARTICLE.

	with *il*.	with *i*.	with *lo*.	with *gli*.	with *la*.	with *le*.	with *l'*.
di = of	*del*	*dei* or *de'*	*dello*	*degli*	*della*	*delle*	*dell'*
a = to	*al*	*ai* or *a'*	*allo*	*agli*	*alla*	*alle*	*all'*
da = from	*dal*	*dai* or *da'*	*dallo*	*dagli*	*dalla*	*dalle*	*dall'*
in = in	*nel*	*nei* or *ne'*	*nello*	*negli*	*nella*	*nelle*	*nell'*
con = with	*col*	*coi* or *co'*	*collo*	*cogli*	*colla*	*colle*	*coll'*
su = on	*sul*	*sui* or *su'*	*sullo*	*sugli*	*sulla*	*sulle*	*sull'*
per = for	*pel*	*pei* or *pe'*	*per lo*	*per gli*	*per la*	*per le*	*per l'*
tra = among	*tra'l*	*trai* or *tra'*	*tra lo*	*tra gli*	*tra la*	*tra le*	*tra l'*

INFLECTIONS OF ADJECTIVES.

	Sing.	Plur.	EXAMPLES.		
Masculine	*o*	*i*	*antico,*	ancient,	*antichi.*[a]
Feminine	*a*	*e*	*buona,*	good,	*buone.*
Both genders {	*e*	*i*	*felice,*	happy,	*felici.*
	i	*i*	*pari,*	equal,	*pari.*

INFLECTIONS OF PRONOUNS.

PERSONAL PRONOUNS.

Singular.

io, I; *me, mi*, me.

tu, thou; *te, ti*, thee.

masc. *egli* or *esso*, he it; *lui, ne, gli, lo, il*, him, it.

fem. *ella* or *essa*, she, it; *lei, ne, le, la*, her, it.

reflective: *se, si*, himself, herself, itself, oneself.

Plural.

noi, we; *ci, ne*, us.

voi, you; *vi*, you.

eglino or *essi*, they; *loro, ne, li, gli*, them.

elleno or *esse*, they; *loro, ne, le*, them.

se, si, themselves.

[a] The plurals of adjectives are subject to the same euphonic modifications as the plurals of nouns, see p. 7.

POSSESSIVE PRONOUNS.

Singular.		Plural.		
Masc.	Fem.	Masc.	Fem.	
mio	*mia*	*miei*	*mie*	my, mine.
tuo	*tua*	*tuoi*	*tue*	thy, thine.
suo	*sua*	*suoi*	*sue*	his, her, hers, its.
nostro	*nostra*	*nostri*	*nostre*	our, ours.
vostro	*vostra*	*vostri*	*vostre*	your, yours.
loro	*loro*	*loro*	*loro*	their, theirs.

DEMONSTRATIVE PRONOUNS.

(*For Things.*)

Singular.			Plural.		
Masc.	Fem.		Masc.	Fem.	
questo	*questa*	this.	*questi*	*queste*	these.
cotesto	*cotesta*	} that.	*cotesti*	*coteste*	} those.
quello, quell', or *quel*	*quella*, or *quell'*		*quelli, quegli*, or *quei*	*quelle*, or *quell'*	

ciò (invariable), this, that.

(*For Persons.*)

Singular.				Plural.	
Masc.		Fem.		Masc. & Fem.	
questi *costui* }	this man.	*costei*,	this woman.	*costoro* {	these men. these women.
cotesti *cotestui* }	that man.	*cotestei*,	that woman.	*cotestoro* {	those men. those women.
quegli *colui* }	that man.	*colei*,	that woman.	*coloro* {	those men. those women.

RELATIVE PRONOUNS.

For Persons or Things.

Invariable.	Singular.	Plural.	
che, cui,	m. *il quale,* f. *la quale,*	*i quali,* *le quali,* }	who, that, which.

INTERROGATIVE PRONOUNS.

Invariable.		For Persons or Things.		
For Persons.	For Things.	Sing.	Plural.	
chi ? who?	*che ?* what?	*quale ?*	*quali ?*	which?

B 3

INDEFINITE PRONOUNS.

Used Substantively

For Persons.		For Things.
altri	other, some-other.	*checchè* } whatever,
altrui	other *or* others.	*checchessia* } whatsoever.
chi	he who, some one who, some person who. } invariable.	*checchesivoglia* }
chiunque	whoever.	*nulla, niente,* nothing.
tutti	all, everybody.	*tutto,* everything.
si	one, they, people.	

For Persons and Things.

Singular.		Plural.		
			uno	one
			altro	other
chicchesia } whosoever *or*		*chicchesiano*	*ciascuno* } each one
chisivoglia } whomsoever.		*chisivogliano*	*ciascheduno* }
			alcuno { anybody, { some one
m. *veruno,* f. *veruna* } no one,		No plural.	
m. *nessuno,* f. *nessuna* } nobody.			*qualcheduno* } some one
m. *niuno,* f. *niuna* }			*qualcuno* }
			taluno some one
m. *taluno* } a certain person.		*taluni*	*ognuno* every one
f. *taluna* }		*talune*	*tale* such a one } pl. *tali*
m. *qualcuno* } some one,		*qualcuni*	*quale* some } *quali*
f. *qualcuna* } somebody.		*qualcune*	*cotale* such a one } *cotali*

fem. una, altra, &c., but no plural.

Used Adjectively, for Persons and Things.

uno	one, a, an } fem. *una,* &c.		*alcuno*	some, *pl.* a few	
un altro	another }		*ciascuno*	each	
ogni	every } invariable,		*tanto* } so much		with
qualche	some } and used		*cotanto* }		their
qualunque	any, what- } only in the		*alquanto*	somewhat	feminines
	ever } singular.		*altrettanto*	as much	and
qualsisia } any what- } pl. *qualsisiano,*		*medesimo* } same		plurals
qualsivoglia } ever } *qualsivogliano.*		*stesso* }		*alcuna,*
veruno }		*poco*	little	*alcuni,*
nessuno } no one { fem. *veruna,* &c.,		*molto*	much	*alcune,*
niuno } { but no plural.		*troppo*	too much	&c.
nullo }		*tutto*	all	
		certo	certain	
		altro	other	

tale or *tal* } such { for both genders, with their plurals *tali, cotali,*
cotale or *cotal* } { or poetically, *tai, cotai.*
parecchi, m., *parecchie,* f., several } used in plural only.
più (invariable) several }
ambo, or *ambe,* or *ambi*
ambeduo, or *ambedue,* or *ambedui* } both { for both genders, used in the
entrambi { plural only.

CHAPTER II.

VERBS.

PREVIOUSLY to entering upon the conjugation of the Verb, it is necessary to mention that the personal pronouns, which are the subjects of the verb, are—

SINGULAR.	PLURAL.

1st pers. *io*, I.   1st pers. *noi*, we.

2nd „ *tu*, thou.   2nd „ *voi*, you.

3rd „ $\left.{egli \atop esso}\right\}$ (m.), he, it. 3rd „ $\left.{eglino \atop essi}\right\}$ (m.), they.

  „ $\left.{ella \atop essa}\right\}$ (f.), she, it.[a]   „ $\left.{elleno \atop esse}\right\}$[a] (f.), they.

These pronouns are only expressed in Italian—(i.) when they are necessary for the perspicuity of the sentence; (ii.) when a particular stress is laid on the pronouns; and (iii.) when two nominative pronouns are placed in contrast.

In all other cases, they are generally understood, the termination of the verb being sufficient to indicate the person and number of the subject of the sentence. For this reason, the verbs are to be conjugated without them.

AUXILIARY VERBS.

The Auxiliaries are — *éssere*, to be, and *avére*, to have.[b]

---

[a] *esso, essa, essi, esse*, may be used for beings both animate and inanimate; but *egli, ella*, &c. only for animate beings.

[b] The compound tenses of all verbs (whether regular or irregular) must be conjugated with the help either of *essere*, to be, or *avere*, to have, which are therefore called *auxiliaries*, and it is for this reason they precede the regular conjugations.

CONJUGATION OF THE VERB *ESSERE.*[a]

Infinitive—*éssere,* to be.

Indicative Mood.

PRESENT TENSE.
	Singular.		*Plural.*
sóno,	I am.	*siámo,*	we are.
séi,	thou art.	*siéte,*	you are.
è,	he, she, *or* it is.	*sóno,*	they are.

IMPERFECT.
éra or éro,[b]	I was, *or* used to be.	*eravámo,*	we were.
éri,	thou wast.	*eraváte,*	you were.
éra,	he was.	*érano,*	they were.

PERFECT *or* PAST.
fúi,	I was.	*fúmmo,*	we were.
fósti,	thou wast.	*fóste,*	you were.
fu,	he was.	*fúrono,*	they were.

FUTURE.
sarò,	I shall be.	*sarémo,*	we shall be.
sarái,	thou wilt be.	*saréte,*	you will be.
sarà,	he will be.	*saránno,*	they will be.

Conditional Mood.
saréi,	I should be.[c]	*sarémmo,*	we should be.
sarésti,	thou wouldst be.	*saréste,*	you would be.
sarébbe,	he would be.	*sarébbero,*	they would be.

Imperative Mood.
No first person singular.		*siámo,*	let us be.
sii or *sía,*	be (thou).	*siáte,*	be (you).
sía,	let him be	*siano,*	let them be.

---

[a] *Essere* being used to form its own compound tenses, is the first auxiliary to be learnt. The English student will thus practically appreciate the difference between the Italian *essere* and the verb *to be.* *Avere* is never used as an auxiliary to *essere.*

[b] The termination *o* is used in common conversation, but in composition *a* should be employed.

[c] Also, 'I could or might be,' &c.

Subjunctive Mood.

PRESENT TENSE.

ch' io sia,[a]	that I may be.[b]	*che siámo,*	that we may be.
che tu sia	that thou mayest	*che siáte,*	that you may be.
or *sii,*	[be.	*che siano,*	that they may be.
ch'e egli sia,	that he may be.		

IMPERFECT.

s'c io fóssi,	if I might be.[d]	*se fóssimo,*	if we might be.
se tu fóssi,	if thou mightest be.	*se fóste,*	if you might be.
se fósse,	if he might be.	*se fóssero,*	if they might be.

Present Participle—*esséndo*, being.

Past Participle—*státo*, been.

COMPOUND TENSES.

Infinitive—*essere stato,*[e] to have been.

Indicative Present.

sono stato, or *stata,* I have			*siamo stati,* or *state,* we have		
sei stato	„	thou hast	*siete stati*	„	you have
è stato	„	he or she has	*sono stati*	„	they have

(been.)

[a] As, from a similarity in the verb-forms, some ambiguity might arise, it is often better to employ the personal pronouns in the three persons singular of the present tense of the subjunctive, and in the first and second persons singular of the imperfect of the same mood.

[b] Also, 'if I be,' &c.

[c] *che*, that, and *se*, if, drop the final *e* before *e* and *i*, the elision being marked by an apostrophe.

[d] Also, 'if I were,' *or* 'were I,' &c.

[e] The reader will observe that the compound tenses of the auxiliary *essere* are not formed, as in English, by the help of *avere*, to have, but of *essere* itself; so that, instead of saying *I have been, I had been*, &c., the Italians say, *sono stato, era stato*, &c.; literally, *I am been, I was been*, &c.

[f] The past participle of any verb conjugated with the auxiliary *essere* (see Note *b*, p. 11) agrees always, like an adjective, in gender and number with the subject of the verb, so that for the first person masculine singular of the compound Ind. Pres. of *essere* we must say *sono stato;* feminine, *sono stata;* for the first person masculine plural, *siamo stati;* feminine, *siamo state*, and so for the remaining persons, singular and plural. The same of course takes place in the other compound tenses.

Indicative Imperfect .... *era stato,* I had been.
    ,,   Perfect or Past... *fui stato,* I had been.
    ,,   Future .... *sarò stato,* I shall have been.
Conditional .... *sarei stato,* I should have been.
Subjunctive Present .... *ch' io sia stato,* that I may have been.
    ,,   Imperfect ...... *s' io fossi stato,* if I might have been.

         Participle—*essendo stato,* having been.

CONJUGATION OF THE PRESENT INDICATIVE:—

Interrogatively.

sono ?[a]	am I ?	*siamo ?*	are we ?
sei ?	art thou ?	*siete ?*	are you ?
è ?	is he ?	*sono ?*	are they ?

Negatively.

non sono,[b]	I am not.	*non siamo,*	we are not.
non sei,	thou art not.	*non siete,*	you are not.
non è,	he is not.	*non sono,*	they are not.

Interrogatively and Negatively.

non sono ?	am I not ?	*non siamo ?*	are we not ?
non sei ?	art thou not ?	*non siete ?*	are you not ?
non è ?	is he not ?	*non sono ?*	are they not ?

N.B.—All the other moods and tenses are to be conjugated in the same way, except the *imperative*[c] and *subjunctive,* which take the negative, but do not admit the interrogative forms.

---

[a] A verb is conjugated *interrogatively,* both in English and Italian, by placing its subject after it; but as the Italians generally omit the pronoun (p. 11) when speaking, the inflection of the voice ought to indicate whether it be an affirmation or a question which is expressed.

[b] When a verb is conjugated *negatively,* the negative particle is in English placed after the verb, but in Italian it always precedes the verb.

[c] After a negative particle, the infinitive mood is substituted for the second person singular of the imperative; as, *non essere,* be not (thou).

PHRASES.

essere vispo,	to be lively.		*essere sano,*	to be healthy.
„ *diligente,*	„ diligent.		„ *ghiotto,*	„ greedy.
„ *mesto,*	„ sad.		„ *sobrio,*	„ sober.
„ *allegro,*	„ merry.		„ *lieto,*	„ glad.
„ *laborioso,*	„ industrious.		„ *solo,*	„ alone.
„ *sgarbato,*	„ rude.		„ *meschino,*	„ miserable.
„ *sdegnato,*	„ angry.			

VOCABULARY.

Roma, Rome.	*tutto,* all.	*vero,* true.
ora, now.	*tempo,* time.	*ieri,* yesterday.
capitale (f.), capital.	*in,* in.	*oggi,* to-day.
Italia, Italy.	*che,* that.	*domani,* to-morrow.
quando, when.	*campagna,* country.	*domenica,* Sunday.
ragazzo, boy.	*perchè,* because.	*lunedì,* Monday.
a, at, *or* to.	*madre,* mother.	*martedì,* Tuesday.
scuola, school.	*appena che,* as soon as.	*mercoledì,* Wednesday.
ogni, every.	*quì,* here.	*giovedì,* Thursday.
giorno, day.	*ma,* but.	*venerdì,* Friday.
mattina, morning.	*e,* and.	*sabbato,* Saturday.
sera, evening.		

READING EXERCISE.

[N.B.—At the *end of the book* will be found a Vocabulary of all the words contained in the Exercises.]

1. Roma è ora la[a] capitale d'[b] Italia. 2. Quando egli[c] era ragazzo, era[d] vispo. 3. A scuola noi eravamo[d] diligenti[e] ogni giorno. 4. Ieri fui[f] mesto dalla[a] mattina alla[a] sera. 5. Tutto il[a] tempo che[g] noi fummo in campagna fummo[f] allegri[e]. 6. Oggi sono stato[h] laborioso.

---

[a] See Table of Articles, p. 8.

[b] The preposition *di,* of, drops the *i* before words beginning with a vowel. [c] See p. 11.

[d] The *Imperfect Indicative* points to a state or action present in relation to another which is past. It is also used in speaking of a continuous state or action, without fixing the time of its duration, as in the case of an habitual or repeated action. (Compare Nos. 2 and 3 above.) [e] See Adj., p. 8.

[f] The *Perfect* is an historic tense, *i.e.* the tense in which events or experiences are related. It points to a fact which has happened at a certain definite or limited time, and completely over at the time it is related. (Compare Nos. 4 and 5 above.)

[g] See Relative Pronouns, p. 9.

[h] The *Compound Present* denotes a fact which has happened at a time past not specified, or in a time specified but not completely past.

7. Perchè egli era stato[a] sgarbato, sua[b] madre fu sde-
gnata.　8. Appena ch' io fui stato[c] in campagna, fui sano.
9. Sarò quì domani.　10. Non essere[d] ghiotto, ma sii
sobrio e sarai sano.　11. Non è vero ch' io sia[e] lieto.
12. S'[f] io fossi solo, sarei meschino.

VOCABULARY.

Italian, *italiano*.	France, *Francia*.	one, *uno*.
English, *inglese*.	Rome, *Roma*.	two, *due*.
German, *tedesco*.	Germany, *Germania*.	three, *tre*.
French, *francese*.	hour, *ora*.	four, *quattro*.
a long time, *un pezzo*.	or, *o*.	five, *cinque*.
that, *che*.	how much { *quanto*. *quanta*. }	six, *sei*. seven, *sette*.
in *or* into, *in*.		
Italy, *Italia*.	how many { *quanti*. *quante*. }	eight, *otto*. nine, *nove*.
year, *anno*.		
here, *quì*.		ten, *dieci*.
where, *dove*.		eleven, *undici*.
England, *Inghilterra*.		twelve, *dodici*.

TRANSLATION EXERCISE.

　1. Are[g] you[h] (a)[i] native of Italy?　2. No; I am not
　　　　　　　　[Italian]　　　　　　　*No*

---

[a] The *Compound Imperfect* denotes that a fact was already past
when another fact, also past, was taking place.

[b] See Poss. Pron., p. 9.

[c] The *Compound Perfect* denotes a fact which took place prior to
another fact also past. It is used chiefly after such expressions as
appena che, or *tosto che*, or *subito che*, as soon as; *dopo che*, or
posciachè, after that.

[d] Note *c*, p. 14.

[e] When the verb of a dependent sentence does not express a
certainty, it must be in the subjunctive mood, with the conjunction
che, after all verbs used negatively.

[f] *Se*, if, when used in a doubtful sense, and pointing to a supposed fact which will not take place, requires the Imperfect of the
subjunctive mood after it, the dependent verb being in the Conditional.

[g] There are three modes of address in Italian:—the 2nd person
singular, the 3rd person singular, and the 2nd person plural. The
latter, which agrees with the English mode, will be used for the
present. When the student has learnt all the personal and possessive pronouns, and the rules which will be found in this book for
addressing persons in these different modes, he may practise them
by changing the first one through all the translation exercises.

[h] See p. 11.

[i] See explanation of the marks and abbreviations employed in
this work, facing p. 1.

(an) Italian; I am (a) native of England. 3. Of what
                     [English]   *Di che*

country is your uncle? 4. He is (a) German, and
paese   vostro   zio   *e*

my grandfather is (a) Frenchman. 5. How long
mio   nonno   [French]   [Is (it) a long

have you been in Italy? 6. I have been here two years.
time that you are[a]]   [They are two years[b] that

           7. Where were[c] you two years[b] ago?
I am here.]   [they are]

8. I was[c] in England. 9. Were you in that
                     [Have[d] you been[e]] *quel'*

country a long time? 10. Not long, as I was[g]
                    lungo tempo siccome

five years[b] in France with my brother. 11. Has he been[h]
              con mio fratello

in Italy? 12. Yes; he and our[i] grandmother have[2] been[3]
          sì egli   la   nonna

here[1] three times. 13. My uncle will be in Rome during
ci   tre   volte   Mio zio   *durante*

the seasons of – spring and – summer. 14. I
le stagioni della primavera   della   state

shall be in Germany next[4] – autumn[1] and[2] – winter[3].
                 prossimi l' autunno e   l' inverno

Is (it) true that – your parents are in (the) country?
    vero che i vostri genitori   *campagna*

---

[a] In speaking of a state or action which has not yet ceased, the present tense, and not the past, is used in Italian.

[b] See Pl. of Nouns, p. 7.   [c] Note *d*, p. 15.

[d] Notes *e* and *f*, p. 13.

[e] The verb which has for its subject the pronoun *you*, expressed or understood, addressing one person only, is to be in the second person plural, but the past participle preceded by *essere* must be in the singular, and agree with the person represented by the same pronoun. See Note *f*, p. 13.

[f] See Demons. Pron., p. 9.   [g] Note *f*, p. 15.

[h] Note *h*, p. 15, and Note *f*, p. 13.

[i] The definite article is substituted for the possessive pronoun, when the noun which follows refers to the subject of the sentence,

15. It is not true that they are[a] in (the) country. They
were[2b] there[1] – last[2] month[1], and will be[2] there[1] –
       vi *il passato mese*   *vi* *la*

next[2] week[1], but now they are in town. 16. I
prossima settimana, *adesso*   *città*

should be happy, if[c] I were now in Naples with my aunt.
  felice   *Napoli con mia zia*

17. Naples is at-present the largest· city in Italy.
        [now] *la più grande città d'*

18. What o'clock is (it)? 19. It is – ten (o'clock).
[what[d] hour]   *sono[e] le*

20. I shall be late home.
    in ritardo a casa

QUESTIONS.[f]

[N.B.—The numbers which follow some of the questions refer to
sentences in the Reading and Translation Exercises *immediately
preceding.*—Numbers referring to the *Reading Exercise* are dis-
tinguished by an asterisk attached to the number.]

Di che paese siete? 3.—E vostro nonno francese o
tedesco? 4.—Dove eravate otto anni sono? 7.—Quante
volte siete stato (*or* stata) in Francia? 12.—Vi siete
stato (*or* stata) un pezzo? 5.—Quando sarete a casa?—
Quali sono le stagioni dell' anno? 13 & 14.—Qual[g] è la
più grande città d' Italia? 17.—Che ora è? 19.—Quanti
giorni vi sono in una settimana?—Quanti mesi vi sono
in un anno?—Qual[g] è la capitale d' Italia? 1*.—Quando
sarete quì? 9*.—Che giorno è oggi?—Che giorno era
ieri?—Che giorno sarà domani?

---

[a] Note *e*, p. 16.   [b] Note *d*, p. 15.
[c] Note *f*, p. 16.   [d] See Inter. Pron., p. 9.

[e] Observe that the verb must be in the plural number with a
plural subject, whether that subject precede the verb or follow it.
In the above instance, the word *ore*, hours, is understood with *sono*.

[f] The above questions must be answered by the student in
Italian, taking care to answer with a full sentence.

[g] *Quale* is not used with an apostrophe, but it may be contracted
into *qual* before vowels and consonants, except *s* followed by a
consonant.

CONJUGATION OF THE VERB *AVERE*.

Infinitive—*avére*, to have.

Indicative Mood.

PRESENT TENSE.

Singular.		*Plural.*	
ho,[a]	I have.	*abbiámo,*	we have.
hái,	thou hast.	*avéte,*	you have.
ha,	he, she, *or* it has.	*hánno,*	they have.

IMPERFECT.

avéva,[b]	I had.	*avevámo,*	we had.
avévi,	thou hadst.	*aveváte,*	you had.
avéva,	he had.	*avévano,*	they had.

PERFECT *or* PAST.

ébbi, ·	I had.	*avémmo,*	we had.
avésti,	thou hadst.	*avéste,*	you had.
ébbe,	he had.	*ebbero,*	they had.

FUTURE.

avrò,	I shall have.	*avrémo,*	we shall have.
avrái,	thou wilt have.	*avréte,*	you will have.
avrà,	he will have.	*avránno,*	they will have.

Conditional Mood.

avréi,	I should have.[c]	*avrémmo,*	we should have.
avrésti,	thou wouldst have.	*avréste,*	you would have.
avrébbe,	he would have.	*avrébbero,*	they would have.

Impérative Mood.

No first person singular.		*abbiámo,*	let us have.
ábbi,	have (thou).	*abbiáte,*	have (you).
ábbia,	let him have.	*ábbiano,*	let them have.

Subjunctive Mood.

PRESENT TENSE.

ch' io ábbia,[d]	that I may have.	*che abbiámo,*	that we may have.
che tu ábbi,	that thou mayest	*che abbiáte,*	that you may have.
or *ábbia,*	have.	*che ábbiano,*	that they may
ch' egli ábbia,	that he may have.		[have.

---

[a] See, concerning *h*, p. 2. [b] Or *avévo*. See Note *b*, p. 12.
[c] Also, 'I would, could, or might have,' 'thou couldst have,' &c.
[d] Note *a*, p. 13.

IMPERFECT.

s' io avéssi,	if I might have.[a]	*se avéssimo,*	if we might have.
se tu avéssi,	if thou mightest	*se avéste,*	if you might have.
	[have.	*se avéssero,*	if they might have.
se avésse,	if he might have.		

Present Participle $\begin{Bmatrix} avéndo \\ avénte \end{Bmatrix}$ having.[b]

Past Participle—*avúto,* had.

COMPOUND TENSES.

Infinitive—*avere avuto,* to have had.

Indicative Present.

ho avuto, I have had.	*abbiamo avuto,*[c] we have had.
hai avuto, thou hast had.	*avete avuto,* you have had.
ha avuto, he has had.	*hanno avuto,* they have had.

Indicative Imperfect,	*aveva avuto,* I had had.
" Perfect,	*ebbi avuto,* I had had.
" Future,	*avrò avuto,* I shall have had.
Conditional	*avrei avuto,* I should have had.
Subjunctive Present,	*ch' io abbia avuto,* that I may have had
" Imperfect,	*s' io avessi avuto,* if I might have had.
Participle—	*avendo avuto,* having had.

All verbs are conjugated *interrogatively* and *negatively* in the same way.[d]

---

[a] Also, If I should have, had I, &c.   [b] Note *e,* p. 26.

[c] The *Past Participle* of any verb conjugated with the auxiliary *avere* (see Note *b,* p. 11) does not agree with the subject of the verb, but it agrees in certain cases with the object :—(i.) It remains invariable in its masculine termination *o* when it is a neuter verb, or is followed by an Infinitive. (ii.) It agrees in gender and number with the object when preceded by it, or when used absolutely, *i.e.,* without the Auxiliary. (iii.) It may either remain invariable, or agree with the object (by changing its final vowel *o* into *a, i,* or *e*), when the object follows the verb ; as,

> *Ho avuto* (or *avuta*) *una serva in casa.*
> I have had a maid-servant in the house.

> *Ho avuto* (or *avute*) *delle serve in casa.*
> I have had some maid-servants in the house.

[d] Notes *a, b,* and *c,* p. 14.

CONJUGATION OF THE PRESENT INDICATIVE:—

Interrogatively.

ho ?	have I ?	*abbiamo ?*	have we ?
hai ?	hast thou ?	*avete ?*	have you ?
ha ?	has he ?	*hanno ?*	have they ?

Negatively.

non ho,	I have not.	*non abbiamo,*	we have not.
non hai,	thou hast not.	*non avete,*	you have not.
non ha,	he has not.	*non hanno,*	they have not.

Interrogatively and Negatively.

non ho ?	have I not ?	*non abbiamo ?*	have we not?
non hai ?	hast thou not ?	*non avete ?*	have you not ?
non ha ?	has he not ?	*non hanno ?*	have they not ?

PHRASES.

avere cura, to take care.	*avere premio,* to obtain a reward.
„ *lettera,* to receive a letter.	„ *pena,* to incur punishment.
„ *nuove,* to receive news.	„ *animo,* to have courage.
„ *danaro,* to receive money.	„ *agio,* to be comfortable.
„ *visite,* to receive visits.	„ *compagnia,* to have com-
„ *grandi pretese,* to have great	pany.
expectations.	

VOCABULARY.

bambinaia, nursemaid.	*tredici,* thirteen.	*gennaio,* January.
bambino, child.	*quattordici,* fourteen.	*febbraio,* February.
babbo, papa.	*quindici,* fifteen.	*marzo,* March.
zia, aunt.	*sedici,* sixteen.	*aprile,* April.
perchè, because.	*diciasette,* seventeen.	*maggio,* May.
buono, good.	*diciotto,* eighteen.	*giugno,* June.
cattivo, bad.	*dicianove,* nineteen.	*luglio,* July.
più, more.	*venti,* twenty.	*agosto,* August.
bramoso, desirous.	*vent' uno,* twenty-one.	*settembre,* September.
pericolo, danger.	*venti due,* twenty-two.	*ottobre,* October.
faccenda, business.	*trenta,* thirty.	*novembre,* November
	trent' uno, thirty-one.	*dicembre,* December.
	trenta due, thirty-two.	

READING EXERCISE.

1. La[a] bambinaia ha cura dei[a] bambini[b].   2. Dove

---

[a] See Table of Articles, p. 8.   [b] See Pl. of Nouns, p. 7.

eravate[a] due anni sono[b]? 3. Ieri ebbi[c] lettera dal[d] babbo. 4. Io non ho avuto mai[e] buone nuove dalla[d] zia. 5. Egli fu allegro, perchè aveva avuto[f] del[d] danaro. 6. Tosto ch' ebbe avuto[g] grandi pretese, fu meschino. 7. Avrò premio se sarò buono, e pena se sarò cattivo. 8. Abbi animo nei[d] pericoli. 9. Se[h] avessimo più agio, saremmo più lieti. 10. È vero che avete avuto molte visite oggi? 11. Non sarei stato in casa, se non avessi avuto molte visite; sono bramoso d'[i] avere[j] compagnia perchè non ho nessuna[e] faccenda.

VOCABULARY.

what? *che?* or *che cosa?*	Albert, *Alberto.*	need, *bisogno.*
name, *nome* (m.)	street, *via.*	pen, *penna.*
John, *Giovanni.*	cold, *freddo.*	paper, *carta.*
looks, *cera* (sing. only)	warm, *caldo.*	inkstand, *calamaio.*
fear, *paura.*	hunger, *fame* (f.)	right, *ragione* (f.)
cold, *infreddatura.*	thirst, *sete* (f.)	wrong, *torto.*
air, *signore.*	sleep, *sonno.*	wisdom, *giudizio.*
toothache, *mal di denti*	lesson, *lezione* (f.)	happy, *felice.*
headache, *mal di capo.*	shame, *vergogna.*	

TRANSLATION EXERCISE.

1. What is your name?   2. My name is John.
[What have you name?]   [I have name John.]

3. How old are you?   4. I am ten years old.
[How many[k] years[l] have you?]   [I have ten years.]

5. You do not look well;   I am afraid you have
[You have not good[m] looks; I have fear that you may have]

---

[a] Note *d*, p. 15.   [b] See No. 7, p. 17.
[c] Note *f*, p. 15.   [d] See Table of Articles, p. 8.
[e] When *mai*, never, *nulla* or *niente*, nothing, *niuno, nessuno, veruno*, no one, nobody, come after the verb, the negative *non* must be put before the verb. When the above words precede the verb, they are generally used without the negative; as, *Nessuno era in casa*, nobody was at home.
[f] Note *a*, p. 16.   [g] Note *c*, p. 16.
[h] Note *f*, p. 16.   [i] Note *b*, p. 15.
[j] After a preposition, the infinitive mood is always used in Italian.
[k] See Vocab., p. 16.   [l] See Pl. Nouns, p. 7.
[m] *cera* being feminine, the adjective must end in *a*. See Adj., p. 8.

a cold. 6. No, Sir; but I have the toothache and the
un' No il il

headache. 7. Albert, what was the matter with that boy
[— what had —]ᵃ *quel*
che

− in the street ? Was he cold or warm ? 8. He was
ch' era per la [had] [He had*

hungry, thirsty, and sleepy. 9. Where will you have
hunger, thirst, and sleep.] (fut. of *avere*)

yourᵇ lesson to-day ? 10. I and my brother will have
la mio

our Italian lesson in the dining-room; and − my
la lezione d' italiano nella stanza da mangiare le mie

sisters will have their music-lesson in the ante-room.
sorelle la lezione di musica nell' anticamera

11. How manyᶜ lessonsᵈ have you had,ᵉ John ? 12. I

have already had twenty lessons. 13. Have you beenᵉ
già

to school ? 14. Yes; but I was late.ᶠ 15. I should be
[I should have

ashamed of beingᵍ late at − school. 16. Do you want
shame] *alla* [Have you need of

pen, ink, and paper ? 17. We do not want anything.
pen, paper, and inkstand?] [We have not need of nothingʰ,]

18. What day is to-day? 19. It is Monday. 20. No;

it is Tuesday. 21. Yes; you are right, and I am wrong.
[youᶦ have right, and I have wrong]

22. Be wise and you will be happy.
[Have wisdom]

ᵃ Note *d*, p. 15.   ᵇ Note *i*, p. 17.
ᶜ See Vocab., p. 16.   ᵈ See Pl. of Nouns, p. 7.
ᵉ Note *h*, p. 15.   ᶠ See No. 20, p. 18.
ᵍ Note *j*, p. 22.   ʰ Note *e*, p. 22.
ᶦ See iii., p. 11.

QUESTIONS.[a]

Che ha nome vostro fratello ? 1.—Quanti anni ha ? 3.
Che avete ? 7.—Che aveva quel ragazzo ch' era per la
via ? 7.—Dove avrete la lezione d' italiano ? 10.—Quante
lezioni avete avute[b] ?—Ho io ragione o torto ? 21.—In
che giorno avrete lezione di musica ? 10.—Di che avete
bisogno ? 16.—Da chi avete avuto lettera ieri ? 3*.—
Quanti giorni ha febbraio ?—Quali mesi hanno trenta
giorni ?—Chi ha cura dei bambini ? 1*.—Da chi avete
avuto nuove ? 4*.—Avevate caldo o freddo ieri ? 7.

REGULAR VERBS.

All Italian verbs end in the Infinitive in one or other
of the terminations, *are, ere, ire,* and are divided into
three conjugations. Verbs ending in *are,* as *parlare,* to
speak, belong to the 1st conjugation ; those ending in *ere,*
as *credere,* to believe, to the 2nd ; and those ending in
ire, as *sentire,* to feel, to the 3rd.

The verb *parl-are,*[c] to speak, will serve as a model for
the 1st conjugation.

---

[a] Note *f*, p. 18.

[b] Note *c*, p. 20.

[c] In every Italian verb a distinction must be made between the
root and the *termination.* That part of the verb which is before the
termination (are, ere, or *ire*) of the Infinitive, is called the *root,* and
in regular verbs it remains unchanged throughout the conjugation.
The *termination* changes for every *mood, tense, number,* and *person.*

Infinitive—*parláre*, to speak.

Indicative Mood.

PRESENT TENSE.

Singular.	*Plural.*
párl-o, I speak.[a]	*parl-iámo*,[b] we speak,
párl-i, thou speakest.	*parl-áte*,[c] you speak.
párl-a, he speaks.	*párl-ano*,[d] they speak.

IMPERFECT.

parl-áva,[e] I was speaking.[f]	*parl-avámo*, we were speaking.
parl-ávi, thou wast speaking.	*parl-aváte*, you were speaking.
parl-áva, he was speaking.	*parl-ávano*, they were speaking.

PERFECT or PAST.

parl-ái, I spoke.	*parl-ámmo*, we spoke.
parl-ásti, thou spokest.	*parl-áste*, you spoke.
parl-ò, he spoke.	*parl-árono*, they spoke.

FUTURE.

parl-erò, I shall speak.	*parl-erémo*, we shall speak,
parl-erái, thou wilt speak.	*parl-eréte*, you will speak.
parl-erà, he will speak.	*parl-eránno*, they will speak.

Conditional Mood.

parl-eréi, I should speak.	*parl-erémmo*, we should speak,
parl-erésti, thou wouldst speak.	*parl-eréste*, you would speak.
parl-erébbe, he would speak.	*parl-erébbero*, they would speak.

---

[a] Also, 'I do speak,' or 'am speaking,' &c. Simple tenses are always formed in Italian by inflections, therefore the English *to do, to be, will, shall, may*, &c., are never to be translated in Italian when used to form simple tenses.

[b] The 1st person plural of the Present Indicative of all verbs ends in *iamo*, and is used also for the first person plural of the Imperative and of the Present Subjunctive. (See *essere* and *avere*.)

[c] The 2nd person plural of the Present Indicative of all verbs, except *essere*, is formed by changing the Infinitive terminations *are, ere, ire* respectively into *ate, ete, ite*.

[d] The 3rd person plural of the Present Indicative of all verbs of the 1st conjugation is formed by adding *no* to the 3rd singular of the same tense. The *n* must be doubled when the singular is a monosyllable, or has the final vowel *a* accented.

[e] The termination *vo*, instead of *va*, may be used in conversational language, in the 1st pers. sing. of the Imperfect of all verbs.

[f] Or, 'I used to speak'; also sometimes 'I spoke,' or 'did speak,' &c.

Imperative Mood.

No first person singular.
párl-a, speak (thou).
párl-i, let him speak.

parl-iámo, let us speak.
parl-áte, speak (you).
párl-ino,[a] let them speak.

Subjunctive Mood.

PRESENT TENSE.

ch' io párl-i, that I may ⎫
che tu párl-i, that thou mayest ⎬ speak.
ch' egli párl-i,[b] that he may ⎭

che parl-iámo, that we may ⎫
che parl-iáte,[c] that you may ⎬ speak.
che párl-ino,[d] that they may ⎭

IMPERFECT.

s' io parl-ássi, if I might speak.
se tu parl-ássi, if thou mightest
[speak.
se parl-ásse, if he might speak.

se parl-ássimo, if we might speak.
se parl-áste, if you might speak.
se parl-ássero, if they might
[speak.

Present Participle ⎰ *parl-ándo*[e] ⎱ speaking.
                    ⎱ *parl-ánte* ⎰

Past Participle, *parl-áto*, spoken.

---

[a] The Imperative mood of all verbs is taken from the Present Indicative and the Present Subjunctive. In the 1st conjugation, for the 2nd pers. sing. and 1st and 2nd pers. plur. we take the 3rd sing. and 1st and 2nd plur. of the Indicative; for the 3rd sing. and plur., the same persons of the Subjunctive.

[b] The termination of the singular of the Present Subjunctive is the same for all the three persons. In the 1st conjugation it is *i* for all regular verbs, and is the 2nd sing. of the Present Indicative.

[c] All verbs have the termination *iate* in the 2nd pers. plur. of the present subjunctive. (See *essere* and *avere*.)

[d] The 3rd pers. plur. of the Present Subjunctive of all verbs is formed by adding *no* to the singular of the same tense.

[e] In this work the name of *Present Participle* is given to both the real Present Participle and to what is in Italian generally called the *Gerund*, and this is done in order that the pupil may not be embarrassed with the latter grammatical term. It is, however, to be observed that, of these two participles, the one in *ndo* is always used in a verbal capacity, and the other in *nte* in that of an adjective and a noun, but very seldom in that of a verb; in the latter case, the pronoun *che* with the *Present Indicative* being generally substituted. Notice the following examples:—

essendo il re buono,   the king being good,
un animale parlante,   a talking animal.
un amante,   a lover (one who loves).
guardo un fanciullo che balla,   I look at a child dancing.

It is further to be remarked that the Participle in *nte* is wanting in

Compound Tenses.

Infinitive—*avere parlato,*[*] to have spoken.

Indicative Present... *ho parlato,* I have spoken.
   „   Imperfect, *aveva parlato,* I had spoken.
   „   Perfect, *ebbi parlato,* I had spoken.
   „   Future, *avrò parlato,* I shall have spoken.
Conditional............ *avrei parlato,* I should have spoken.
Subjunctive Present, *ch' io abbia parlato,* that I may have spoken.
   „   Imperfect, *s' io avessi parlato,* if I might have spoken.

Participle—*avendo parlato,* having spoken.

Conjugation of the Present Indicative :—

Interrogatively.

parlo ? do I speak ?	*parliamo ?* do we speak ?
parli ? dost thou speak ?	*parlate ?* do you speak ?
parla ? does he speak ?	*parlano ?* do they speak ?

Negatively.

non parlo, I do not speak.	*non parliamo,* we do not speak.
non parli, thou dost not speak.	*non parlate,* you do not speak.
non parla, he does not speak.	*non parlano,* they do not speak.

Interrogatively and Negatively.

non parlo ? do I not speak ?	*non parliamo ?* do we not speak ?
non parli ? dost thou not speak ?	*non parlate ?* do you not speak ?
non parla ? does he not speak ?	*non parlano ?* do they not speak ?

Obs. 1.—Verbs ending in the Infinitive in *care* or *gare,* take *h* after *c* or *g,* when those letters are followed by *e* or *i,* in order to

---

many verbs (see *essere*); but when used, it must always agree in gender and number with the person or thing to which it relates; as,   *due animali parlanti,* two talking animals.
          due amanti,   two lovers (two who love).

The Participle in *ndo* is invariable, ending always in *o.* It is never used with a preposition or article, the Infinitive being usually substituted; as,
    Gli scolari studiando imparano, or ⎫
    Gli scolari collo studiare imparano, ⎬ Scholars learn by studying.

[*] Note *c,* p. 20.

preserve the hard sound; as, *cerchi*, thou searchest, from *cercare*, to search; *paghèrò*, I will pay, from *pagare*, to pay.

OBS. 2.—Verbs ending in *ciare* or *giare*, drop the *i* before another *i* or *e*, for the sake of euphony; as, *mangi*, thou eatest, from *mangiare*, to eat; *ciancerò*, I will chat, from *cianciare*, to chat.

OBS. 3.—Verbs ending in *gliare*, *chiare*, or *sciare*, drop the *i* only before another *i*; as, *pigliamo*, we take, from *pigliare*, to take; *invecchi*, thou growest old, from *invecchiare*, to grow old; *lasci*, thou leavest, from *lasciare*, to leave.

OBS. 4.—The verbs *giocare*, to play (game), *sonare*, to play (music), *rinnovare*, to renew, *rotare*, to wheel, and a few others, take *u* before *o* when the accent falls upon the *o* of the root; that is, in the singular and 3rd person plural of the Present Indicative and Present Subjunctive, and in the singular and 3rd person plural of the Imperative; as, *giuóco*, I play (game); *suónano*, they play (music), &c.

PHRASES.

giocare agli scacchi, to play chess.
legare l' involto, to tie a parcel.
sonare il pianoforte, to play upon the piano.
fabbricare una casa, to build a house.
viaggiare di giorno (di notte), to travel by day (by night).

trovare una cosa, to find a thing.
girare attorno a, to revolve round.
bramare una cosa, to wish for a thing.
sprecare il tempo, to waste one's time.
pigliare degli uccelli, to catch (some) birds.

VOCABULARY.

spago, cord.
muratore, mason.
Copernico, Copernicus.
terra, earth.
sole (m.), sun.
divertimento, amusement.
rete (f.), net.
quaranta, forty.
cinquanta, fifty.

sessanta, sixty.
settanta, seventy.
ottanta, eighty.
novanta, ninety.
cento, a hundred.
Londra, London.
Parigi, Paris.
Firenze, Florence.
Venezia, Venice.
Genova, Genoa.

Milano, Milan.
Livorno, Leghorn.
Edimburgo, Edinburgh.
Pietroburgo, St. Petersburg.
Madrid, Madrid.
Berlino, Berlin.
Vienna, Vienna.

READING EXERCISE.

1. Io giuoco[a] agli[b] scacchi. 2. Tu leghi[c] l' involto collo[b] spago. 3. Quando io era in campagna sonava[d] il pianoforte ogni mattina. 4. I[b] muratori[e] fabbricheranno[e]

---

[a] Obs. 4, above.
[b] See Table of Articles, p. 8.
[e] See Plural of Nouns, p. 7.

[c] Obs. 1, p. 27.
[d] Note *d*, p. 15.

una casa. 5. Non viaggeremo[a] di giorno, ma di notte.
6. Copernico ha[b] trovato che la terra gira attorno al sole.
7. Non bramo ch' egli sprechi[c] il tempo in divertimenti.
8. Se avessimo delle reti, piglieremmo[d] degli uccelli.

VOCABULARY.

to speak, *parlare*.
to study, *studiare*.
to learn, *imparare*.
to find, *trovare*.
to sing, *cantare*.
to dine { *pranzare* { *desinare.*
to eat, *mangiare*.
to call, *chiamare*.
to ask, *domandare*.
to order { *ordinare* { *comandare.*
to invite, *invitare*.
to lay the cloth, *apparecchiare la tavola.*

to bring, carry, *portare*.
to wish (something to any one), *augurare*.
to salute, take one's leave, *salutare.*
at what o'clock? *a che ora?*
letter, note, *lettera.*
post, *posta*.
man-servant, *servo*.
maid-servant, *serva.*
well, *bene*.
very well, *benissimo*.
much, *molto*.
very much, *moltissimo*.
table, *tavola.*

TRANSLATION EXERCISE.

1. Do[e] you speak English? 2. No, Sir; but I speak
French and German. 3. Does[e] Mr.[f] Dolci speak English?
francese tedesco inglese

4. Mr.[f] Dolci speaks Italian[g] only[1]; but — my sisters
italiano le mie sorelle

speak English very well. 5. How long have you
[Is it a long time[g] that you

studied the English[g] language[1]? 6. I have studied
study[h]] *la inglese lingua* [They are two months[f]

---

[a] Obs. 2, p. 28.
[b] *Avere* is used to form the compound tenses of all active verbs.
[c] Obs. 1, p. 27.   [d] Obs. 3, p. 28.   [e] Note *a*, p. 25.
[f] Before *Signor*, Mr., *Signora*, Mrs., and *Signorina*, Miss, when not used in the vocative case, the definite article must be used. Thus we say, *Il Signor Neri*, Mr. Neri, *La Signora Magri*, Mrs. Magri, *La Signorina Loti*, Miss Loti. Notice that the word *Signore* drops the final when followed by a *noun*.
[g] See No. 5, p. 17.   [h] Note *a*, p. 17.
[i] See Plural of Nouns, p. 7.

English two months now.   7. Did you study[a] much now that I study the English.]

when you were learning[b] – French ?   8. I used to study[c]
                il

two hours a day.   9. Did you find[a] – German difficult ?
             il   *il*   *difficile*

10. Yes; I found[a] – German more difficult than
           il   *più*   *di*

any   other language.   11. My nephew and —
qualunque altra   *Mio nipote*   *mia*

niece have found[c] – Italian easy.   12. Where have you
nipote   *l'*   *facile*

learnt the French[2] language[1] ?   13. I learnt[d] – French
   la francese   *lingua*   *il*

in Paris, and – German in Berlin.   14. Will you sing
      il

to-night ?   15. I would sing with pleasure, but I have
stasera[e]   *volentieri*

a cold.   16. Perhaps your sister will sing a   song.
              vostra sorella   *una canzone*

17. She is not at home, and she never[f] sings, because she

has not (a) good voice.   18. Have you dined[a] ?   19. I
       buona voce

have[2] not[1] eaten[4] anything[5] yet[3].   20. You shall dine
          [nothing] *ancora*

with-me : Albert, call John, to[g] ask if – dinner is
meco   *il pranzo*

---

[a] Note *h*, p. 15, and Note *b*, p. 29.   [b] Note *d*, p. 15.
[c] Note *d*, p. 15, and Note *f*, p. 25.   [d] Note *h*, p. 15.
[e] The pronoun *questa*, this, is generally abridged before the words *notte*, night, *mane* or *mattina*, morning, and *sera*, evening, and united with them, as follows : *stanotte*, this night, *stamane* or *stamattina*, this morning, *stasera*, this evening.
[f] Note *e*, p. 22.
[g] *to*, before an Infinitive, in the sense of *in order to*, or *with the design of*, is rendered in Italian by *per*.

ready. 21. Do not order – dinner for me, because
pronto il *per me*

I have been invited elsewhere. 22. The servant is laying[b]
[I am[a] invited] *altrove*

the cloth, and in two minutes dinner will be on table.
fra minuti [they will bring in table]

23. Had I not been invited elsewhere, I would dine with
[If[c] I were not invited] 21 *con*

you with pleasure, but to-day (I) wish[2] you[1] a good
voi 15 *vi*[d] *un buon*

appetite, and take my leave.
appetito [(I) salute[2] you[1]]

QUESTIONS.

Perchè[c] non cantate? 15.—Quante lingue parla vostra
zia?—È un pezzo (*or* quanto tempo è) che studiate
l'italiano? 5.—Quante ore il giorno studiavate quando
eravate in campagna? 8.—Imparerete la vostra canzone
domani o lunedì? — A che ora pranzerà vostro fratello martedì prossimo?—Trovate il tedesco difficile?—
Chi porterà la lettera alla posta?—Perchè chiamate
Giovanni?—Chi ha apparecchiato la tavola?—A che
ora porteranno in tavola? 22.—Con chi giocherete agli
scacchi? 1*.—Chi fabbrica le case? 4*.—Quando viagge-
rete? 5*.—Che ha trovato Copernico? 6*.— Che cosa
legherete collo spago? 2*.—In quali città siete stato (*or*
stata)?

The verb *crédere*, to believe, will serve as a model for
the 2nd Conjugation.

---

[a] *Essere* is employed as an auxiliary with *passive verbs.*
[b] Note *a*, p. 25.
[c] Note *f*, p. 16.
[d] See Personal Pronouns, p. 8,
Observe that *perchè* has both the meaning of *because* and *why.*

Infinitive—*crédere*, to believe.

Indicative Mood.

PRESENT TENSE.

Singular.	*Plural.*
créd-o, I believe.	*cred-iámo*,[a] we believe.
créd-i, thou believest.	*cred-éte*,[b] you believe.
créd-e, he believes.	*créd-ono*,[c] they believe.

IMPERFECT.

cred-éva, I was believing.	*cred-evámo*, we were believing.
cred-évi, thou wast believing.	*cred-eváte*, you were believing.
cred-éva, he was believing.	*cred-évano*, they were believing.

PERFECT *or* PAST.

cred-éi, (or *cred-étti*), I believed.	*cred-émmo*, we believed.
cred-ésti, thou believedst.	*cred-éste*, you believed.
cred-è (or *cred-étte*), he believed.	*cred-érono* (or *cred-éttero*[d]), they [believed.

FUTURE.

cred-erò, I shall believe.	*cred-erémo*, we shall believe.
cred-erái, thou wilt believe.	*cred-eréte*, you will believe.
cred-erà, he will believe.	*cred-eránno*, they will believe.

Conditional Mood.

cred-eréi, I should believe.	*cred-erémmo*, we should believe.
cred-erésti, thou wouldst believe.	*cred-eréste*, you would believe.
cred-erébbe, he would believe.	*cred-erébbero*, they would believe.

Imperative Mood.

No first person singular.	*cred-iámo*, let us believe.
créd-i, believe (thou).	*cred-éte*, believe (you).
créd-a, let him believe.	*créd-ano*,[e] let them believe.

---

[a] Note *b*, p. 25.   [b] Note *c*, p. 25.

[c] The 3rd person plural of the Present Indicative of verbs of the 2nd and 3rd conjugations is formed by adding *no* to the 1st person singular of the same tense. *Essere*, to be, *avere*, to have, and *sapere*, to know, are the only verbs that do not follow this rule.

[d] *Dipendere*, to depend on, *fremere*, to fret, *gemere*, to groan, *godere*, to enjoy, *pendere*, or *impendere*, to hang, *perdere*, to lose, *premere*, to press, *propendere*, to incline, *ricevere*, to receive, *risplendere* or *splendere*, to shine, *stridere*, to scream, *temere*, to fear, and *vendere*, to sell, have the double terminations shown in the 1st and 3rd singular, and 3rd person plural of the Perfect tense. All other regular verbs of the 2nd conjugation have only the first of these two terminations.

[e] The Imperative mood is taken from the Present Indicative and

Subjunctive Mood.

PRESENT TENSE.

ch' io créd-a, that I may believe. *che cred-iámo*, that we may be-
che tu créd-a, that thou mayest &c. *che cred-iáte*, that you &c. [lieve.
ch' egli créd-a,[a] that he may &c. *che créd-ano*,[b] that they &c.

IMPERFECT.

s' io cred-éssi, if I might believe. *se cred-éssimo*, if we might believe.
se tu cred-éssi, if thou mightest &c. *se cred-éste*, if you &c.
se cred-ésse, if he might &c. *se cred-éssero*, if they &c.

Present Participle $\left\{ \begin{array}{l} cred\text{-}éndo \\ cred\text{-}énte \end{array} \right\}$ believing.[c]

Past Participle, *cred-úto*, believed.

COMPOUND TENSES.

Infinitive—*avere creduto*, to have believed.

Indicative Present... *ho creduto*, I have believed.
  „   Imperfect *aveva creduto*, I had believed.
  „   Perfect... *ebbi creduto*, I had believed.
  „   Future... *avrò creduto*, I shall have believed.
Conditional............ *avrei creduto*, I should have believed.
Subjunctive Present *ch' io abbia creduto*, that I may have believed.
  „   Imperfect *s' io avessi creduto*, if I might have believed.

Participle—*avendo creduto*, having believed.

CONJUGATION OF THE PRESENT INDICATIVE:—

Interrogatively.

credo? do I believe? *crediamo?* do we believe?
credi? dost thou believe? *credete?* do you believe?
crede? does he believe? *credono?* do they believe?

Present Subjunctive (see Note *a*, p. 26). In the 2nd and 3rd conjugations, for the 2nd singular and 1st and 2nd persons plural, we
take the same persons of the Indicative; and for the 3rd persons,
those of the Subjunctive. Only *essere*, to be, *avere*, to have, *sapere*,
to know, and *volere*, to be willing, have the 2nd person Imperative,
both singular and plural, different from the same persons of the
Present Indicative. *Dire*, to say, is contracted in the 2nd singular
of the Imperative *di'*.

[a] The singular of the Present Subjunctive of all verbs of the
2nd and 3rd conjugations is formed by changing the final *o* of the
1st person singular of the Present Indicative into *a*; *essere*, *avere*,
and *sapere* being the only exceptions to this rule. (See Note *b*, p. 26.)

[b] Note *d*, p. 26. [c] Note *e*, p. 26.

c 3

Negatively.

non credo, I do not believe.	*non crediamo*, we do not believe.
non credi, thou dost not believe.	*non credete*, you do not believe.
non crede, he does not believe.	*non credono*, they do not believe.

Interrogatively and Negatively.

non credo ? do I not believe ?	*non crediamo ?* do we not believe ?
non credi ? dost thou not believe ?	*non credete ?* do you not believe ?
non crede ? does he not believe ?	*non credono ?* do they not believe ?

OBS.—Verbs ending in *cere* and *scere*, that have the Past Participle regular in *uto*, take *i* between *e* and *u* for the sake of preserving the root-sound; as, *taciuto*, from *tacere*, to be silent; *pasciuto*, from *pascere*, to feed, &c.

PHRASES.

vendere } *una cosa*,   to sell } a thing.
credere }   to believe }

combattere in una battaglia, to fight in a battle.
pascere alcuno, to feed any one.
mietere il grano, to reap the corn.
cominciare a piovere, to commence raining.
ricevere con bella grazia uno, to receive a person kindly.
perdere il tempo in inezie, to lose one's time in trifling.
ripetere una cosa, to say a thing again.
narrare una cosa, to relate a thing.

VOCABULARY.

fornaio, baker.	*pastore*, shepherd.	*qualunque*, any.
pane (m.), bread.	*pecora*, sheep.	*persona*, person.
erba, grass.	*contadino*, countryman.	*per favore*, if you
antico, ancient.		[please.

READING EXERCISE.

1. Il fornaio vende il pane.   2. Gli antichi[a] credevano che il sole girasse[b] attorno alla terra.   3. Dante Alli-

---

[a] Note *a*, p. 8.
[b] When the verb of a dependent sentence does not express a certainty, it is put in the Subjunctive mood, with the conjunction *che* expressed or understood, after all verbs that denote *asking*, as *chiedere*, to ask; *entreating*, as *pregare*, to pray; *suspecting*, as *sospettare*, to suspect; *wondering*, as *maravigliarsi*, to wonder; *rejoicing*, as *rallegrarsi*, to rejoice; *grudging*, as *rifiutare*, to refuse; *supposing*, as *supporre*, to suppose; *hoping*, as *sperare*, to hope; *imagining*, as *figurarsi*, to imagine; *conjecturing*, as *conghietturare*, to conjecture; *intimating*, as *intimare*, to intimate; as well as after all verbs expressing *desire*, as *bramare*, to long for; *fear*, as *temere*, to fear; *belief*,

ghieri combattè[a] in due battaglie. 4. Il pastore ha pasciuto[b] d' erba le sue pecore. 5. Subito che i contadini ebbero mietuto[c] il grano, cominciò a piovere. 6. Ricevete con bella grazia qualunque persona. 7. Se aveste più giudizio, non perdereste il tempo in inezie. 8. Per favore, ripetete quel che[d] avete narrato.

Vocabulary.

to knock at the door, *battere alla porta.*	to prolong, *prolungare.*
to ring, *sonare.*	to enjoy, *godere.*
to think (believe), *credere.*	to feed (neut.), *pascolare.*
to receive, *ricevere.*	to sell, *vendere.*
to write, *scrivere.*	to beat, *battere.*
to hope, *sperare.*	to yield, *cedere.*
to tap at a door, *bussare all' uscio.*	to leave, abandon, *abbandonare.*
to be afraid, *temere.*	to gain, *guadagnare.*
to arrive, *arrivare.*	to pour out (wine into a glass), *mescere.*
to shine, *splendere.*	to pour out (anything), *versare.*

Translation Exercise.

1. Somebody knocks[e] at the door.   2. They are
      alcuno

knocking[f] and ringing.[g]   3. John, who has knocked and rung[e]?   4. I believe (it) is[h] Mr.[i] Bianchi.

5. Certainly I received[j] (a) letter from his brother
      Certamente   da   suo

yesterday in which[k] he writes that he hoped[l] to dine
      in   cui   che   ▲   di

with us to-day.   6. Somebody taps at the door.
con noi   1

---

as *credere*, to believe; *will*, as *volere*, to wish; *command*, as *ordinare*, to order; *permission*, as *permettere*, to allow; *prohibition*, as *proibire*, to forbid; *doubt*, as *dubitare*, to doubt; and *ignorance*, as *ignorare*, to ignore. (See also Note *e*, p. 16.)

[a] Note *f*, p. 15.   [b] Obs., p. 34.   [c] Note *c*, p. 16.

[d] *che*, preceded by the demonstrative pronouns *quello*, or *quel*, or *ciò*, that, has the meaning of the English *what* or *that*, in the sense of *that which*.

[e] Attention must be paid not to confound conjugations 1 and 2.

[f] Note *a*, p. 25.   [g] Obs. 4, p. 28.   [h] Note *b*, p. 34.
[i] Note *f*, p. 29.   [j] Note *f*, p. 15.
[k] See Relat. Pron., p. 9.   [l] Note *d*, p. 15.

7. Come-in.   8. Madam, your[2] servant[1].
Avanti (*literally,* forward).   *Signora vostro*

9. I was afraid you would not arrive[a] in time for –
                               a tempo per il

dinner.   10. Madam, the sun was shining[b] so
                   il   *sole*   *cosi*

beautifully this morning,[c] that I prolonged[d] – my
a maraviglia   *la mia*

walk (too far).   11. You have,[2] no doubt,[1] enjoyed[e]
passeggiata   *senza dubbio*

– your walk.   12. Yes, very much; the country is
la vostra   *moltissimo*   *là*   [has

now looking   very beautiful, and there are many sheep
now an aspect]   *bellissimo*   *molte pecore*
     un aspetto

feeding[f]   in the meadows.   13. Have you sold[e] –
[which feed]   *nei*   *prati*   *la*

your country-house?   14. I have not yet sold[e] – my
vostra casa di campagna   *ancora*   *la mia*

country-house.   15. Have you received any news
                            delle   *nuove*

about the war?   16. Yes; the enemy have been
intorno alla guerra   *i*   *nemici*

beaten,[g] and the general yielded disgracefully, aban-
       il generale   *vergognosamente*

doning all – his troops.   17. Then we have gained
      tutti i suoi soldati   *Allora*

a decisive[3] victory[1].   18. Yes, Madam, the enemy
una assoluta vittoria   16

have lost all.   19. The[3] dinner[3] is[4] now[1] ready, so
        tutto   *il*   *cosi*

let us begin.   20. I have a good appetite after – my
              un buon appetito dopo la mia

---

     [a] Note *b*, p. 34.   [b] Note *a*, p. 25.   [c] Note *e*, p. 30.
     [d] Note *f*, p. 15.   [e] Note *h*, p. 15.   [f] Note *e*, p. 26.
     [g] Note *a*, p. 31, and Note *f*, p. 13.

long walk.   21. Charles, have you poured out[a] (a glass
lunga   10   *Carlo*

of wine) for Mr.[b] Bianchi?   22. Yes; and I shall pour

out   a   glass   of   port wine   for you.
un   bicchiere   di   vino d'Oporto   per   voi

QUESTIONS.

Chi vende il pane? 1[*].—Che cosa credevano gli[c] antichi
del[c] sole e della[c] terra? 2[*].—In quante battaglie ha com-
battuto Dante Allighieri?—Dove pascoleranno le pecore? 12.—Da chi avete avuto lettera ieri? 5.—In che
mese dell'[c] anno mietono il grano in Inghilterra? 5[*].—
Perchè non mescete? 21.—Avete goduto la vostra
passeggiata? 11.—Quando avete cominciato a studiare la
musica? 5[*].—Avete battuto o sonato quando siete arrivato a casa? 3.

The verb *sentíre*, to feel, to hear, will serve as a model
for the 3rd Conjugation.

Infinitive—*sentíre*, to feel.

Indicative Mood.

PRESENT TENSE.

Singular.	*Plural.*
sént-o, I feel.	*sent-iámo*,[d] we feel.
sént-i, thou feelest.	*sent-íte*,[e] you feel.
sént-e, he feels.	*sént-ono*,[f] they feel.

IMPERFECT.

sent-íva, I felt.	*sent-ivámo*, we felt.
sent-ívi, thou feltest.	*sent-iváte*, you felt.
sent-íva, he felt.	*sent-ívano*, they felt.

PERFECT or PAST.

sent-íi, I felt.	*sent-ímmo*, we felt.
sent-ísti, thou feltest.	*sent-íste*, you felt.
sent-í, he felt.	*sent-írono*, they felt.

---

[a] Obs., p. 34.   [b] Note *f*, p. 29.   [c] See Articles, p. 8.
[d] Note *b*, p. 25.   [e] Note *c*, p. 25.   [f] Note *a*, p. 32.

FUTURE.

sent-irò, I shall feel.   *sent-irémo*, we shall feel.
sent-irái, thou wilt feel.   *sent-iréte*, you will feel.
sent-irà, he will feel.   *sent-iránno*, they will feel.

Conditional Mood.

sent-iréi, I should feel.   *sent-irémmo*, we should feel.
sent-irésti, thou wouldst feel.   *sent-iréste*, you would feel.
sent-irébbe, he would feel.   *sent-irébbero*, they would feel.

Imperative Mood.

No first person singular.   *sent-iámo*, let us feel.
sént-i, feel (thou).   *sent-íte*, feel (you).
sént-a, let him feel.   *sént-ano*,[a] let them feel.

Subjunctive Mood.

PRESENT TENSE.

ch' io sént-a, that I may feel.   *che sent-iámo*, that we may feel.
che tu sént-a, that thou mayest   *che sent-iáte*, that you may feel.
              [feel.   *che sént-ano*,[c] that they may feel.
ch' egli sént-a,[b] that he may feel.

IMPERFECT.

s' io sent-íssi, if I might feel.   *se sent-íssimo*, if we might feel.
se tu sent-íssi, if thou mightest   *se sent-íste*, if you might feel.
              [feel.   *se sent-íssero*, if they might feel.
se sent-ísse, if he might feel.

Present Participle $\left\{ \begin{matrix} sent\text{-}éndo^d \\ sent\text{-}énte^e \end{matrix} \right\}$ feeling.

Past Participle, *sent-íto*, felt.

COMPOUND TENSES.

Infinitive—*avere sentito*, to have felt.

Indicative Present... *ho sentito*, I have felt.
    „   Imperfect *aveva sentito*, I had felt.
    „   Perfect... *ebbi sentito*, I had felt.
    „   Future... *avrò sentito*, I shall have felt.
Conditional............ *avrei sentito*, I should have felt.
Subjunctive Present *ch' io abbia sentito*, that I may have felt.
    „   Imperfect *s' io avessi sentito*, if I might have felt.

Participle—*avendo sentito*, having felt.

---

[e] Some verbs of the 3rd conjugation have the termination *iente* instead of *ente*, in the Present Participle; as, *finire*, to finish, *finiente*; others have both terminations; as, *dormire*, to sleep, *dormente* and *dormiente*, &c.

CONJUGATION OF THE PRESENT INDICATIVE :—

Interrogatively.

sento ? do I feel ?	*sentiamo ?* do we feel ?
senti ? dost thou feel ?	*sentite ?* do you feel ?
sente ? does he feel ?	*sentono ?* do they feel ?

Negatively.

non sento, I do not feel.	*non sentiamo,* we do not feel.
non senti, thou dost not feel.	*non sentite,* you do not feel.
non sente, he does not feel.	*non sentono,* they do not feel.

Interrogatively and Negatively.

non sento ? do I not feel ?	*non sentiamo ?* do we not feel ?
non senti ? dost thou not feel ?	*non sentite ?* do you not feel ?
non sente ? does he not feel ?	*non sentono ?* do they not feel ?

OBS.—The most regular form of the 3rd Conjugation, in its analogy with the other two conjunctions, is that of *sentire;* but the only verbs which are always completely conjugated like *sentire* are—

bollire, to boil.	*pervertire,* to pervert.
divertire, to divert.	*servire,* to serve.
dormire, to sleep.	*sortire,* to sally out.
fuggire, to flee.	*sovvertire,* to subvert.
partire, to depart, start.	*vestire,* to clothe, dress.
pentire, to repent.	

—and their derivatives. All the other verbs in *ire,* with the exception of some which will be found in the table of the irregular verbs of the 3rd conjugation, take *isc* before the person-ending, throughout the singular number, and in the 3rd person plural of the Present Indicative, Present Subjunctive, and Imperative.

MODEL.

Infinitive—*finire,* to finish.

Indicative Mood.

PRESENT TENSE.

fin-isco, I finish.	*fin-iámo,*[a] we finish.
fin-isci, thou finishest.	*fin-ite,*[b] you finish.
fin-isce, he finishes.	*fin-iscono,*[c] they finish.

[a] Note *b,* p. 25.   [b] Note *c,* p. 25.   [c] Note *e,* p. 32.

Imperative Mood.

No first person singular.   *fin-iámo*, let us finish.
fin-ísci, finish (thou).   *fin-íte*, finish (you).
fin-ísca, let him finish.   *fin-íscano*,ᵃ let them finish.

Subjunctive Mood.

PRESENT TENSE.

ch' io fin-ísca, that I may
che tu fin-ísca, that thou mayest } finish.
ch' egli fin-ísca,ᵇ that he may

che fin-iámo, that we may
che fin-iáte, that you may } finish.
che fin-íscano,ᶜ that they may

All the other moods and tenses not given in the above Model are conjugated like *sentire*.

N.B.—The following verbs in *ire* are conjugated indifferently either like *sentire*ᵈ or like *finire :*—

abborrire, to abhor.   *mentire*, to lie.
applaudire, to applaud.   *muggire*, to bellow.
avvertire, to warn.   *nutrire*, to nourish.
inghiottire, to swallow.   *ruggire*, to roar.

PHRASES.

fiorire nella primavera, to flower in spring.
inaridire per mancanza di pioggia, to wither for want of rain.
finire il lavoro, to finish one's work.
guarire l' ammalato, to cure the patient.
inghiottire la medicina, to swallow the medicine.
guarire da una malattia, to recover from an illness.
fuggire i cattivi compagni, to shun bad companions.
pulire lo spazzo della camera, to clean (sweep up) the floor of the
obbedire gli ordini, to obey orders.   [room.
adempire i suoi doveri, to fulfil one's duties.

VOCABULARY.

margheritina, daisy.   *passato*, last.   *esattezza*, precision.
state (f.), summer.   *fiore* (m.), flower.   *tutti*, all.
padrone, master.   *medico*, doctor.

READING EXERCISE.

1. La margheritina fiorisceᵉ nella primavera. 2. La state passata i fiori inaridivano per mancanza di pioggia. 3. Ieri non finiiᶠ il mio lavoro. 4. Il medico non ha

---

ᵃ Note *e*, p. 32.   ᵇ Note *a*, p. 33.   ᶜ Note *d*, p. 26.
ᵈ A few verbs are inflected like *sentire* only in poetry; as, *assorbire*, to absorb, *languire*, to languish, &c.
ᵉ Obs., p. 39.   ᶠ Note *f*, p. 15.

guarito l' ammalato. 5. S' egli avesse inghiottito la medicina, sarebbe guarito della sua malattia. 6. Fuggiamo i cattivi compagni. 7. Desidero che la serva pulisca[a] lo spazzo della mia camera. 8. Obbedite gli ordini dei padroni. 9. Adempirò con esattezza tutti i miei doveri.

VOCABULARY.

to understand, *capire.*	to take, *prendere.*
to prefer, *preferire.*	to leave, depart from, *partire da*
to sleep, *dormire.*	or *di.*
to suffer, *soffrire.*	to serve, *servire.*
to want, *avere bisogno di.*	to hear of, *sentire parlare di.*
to boil, *bollire.*	to take place, *avere luogo.*

TRANSLATION EXERCISE.

1. Good morning, Sir; do[b] you understand – English?
Buon   giorno   l'

2. A little; but I prefer[c] speaking Italian.   3. How did
Un poco   [to speak]   Come

you sleep[d] –   last[2] night[1]?   4. Not well, for I suffered[e]
la passata notte   perchè

from toothache the[3] whole[1] night.   5. Do[b] you want   a
del   la   tutta   notte   una

cup   of coffee?   6. Thank you, I do not want
chicchera di caffè   Grazie

anything[f].   7. The water boils, and in ten minutes the
[nothing]   L' acqua   fra   minuti il

coffee will be ready.   8. Indeed I should not sleep if I
Davvero

took[g] a cup of coffee now.   9. When do you leave
5   [shall you leave[h]]

---

[a] Note *b*, p. 34.   [b] Note *a*, p. 25.   [c] Obs., p. 39.
[d] Note *h*, p. 15.   [e] Note *f*, p. 15.   [f] Note *e*, p. 22.
[g] Note *f*, p. 16.
[h] In Italian the *Future* is generally employed instead of the English *Present* when speaking of a future time; even when two or three verbs are used, they must all be in the future; as, *meglio diventerai se alla morte* PENSERAI (Prov.), thou wilt become better if thou *thinkest* of death

England?   10. I shall leave – England to-morrow.
11. Have you had good attendance during – your
        [Have you been well served*]   *durante il vostro*
residence in this country?   12. In England there are
soggiorno   questo

good hotels.   13. Have you heard of the death of –
buoni alberghi   *della   morte del*
Mr. B.?   14. Yes; I have heard of – his death, which
                                    della sua

took place yesterday at two (o'clock).
                    alle

QUESTIONS.

Che lingua preferite parlare? 2.—Quando fioriscono
le margheritine? 1*.—Quando partirete da Londra? 9.—
Prendete una chicchera di caffè la mattina o la sera? 8.
—Chi ha pulito lo spazzo della camera? 7*.—Perchè
inaridiscono i fiori? 2*.— Quali ordini obbedisce il
servo? 8*.—Chi ha guarito l' ammalato? 4*.—Di che
avete bisogno? 5.—Capisce vostra zia l' italiano?

REFLECTIVE VERBS.

OBSERVATIONS.

1. In conjugating *reflective* verbs, the Italians employ
the conjunctive pronouns—

    mi,[b] me, *or* to me;   *ci*, us, *or* to us;
    ti, thee, *or* to thee;   *vi*, you, *or* to you;

answering to the English myself, thyself, ourselves,
yourselves;

    and *si*, himself, herself, itself, oneself, themselves.

---

* Note *a*, p. 31.   b See Table of Pers. Pron., p. 8.

2. The above Italian pronouns either follow or precede the verb.

(i.) They follow the verb and are united to it—

In the Infinitive used affirmatively, its final *e* being dropped; as, *scaldarsi*, to warm one's self.

In the Present Participle; as, *scaldandosi*, warming one's self.

In the Past Participle, when elliptically used with the auxiliary verb understood; as, *vestitosi*, i.e. *essendosi vestito*, having dressed himself.

In the second person singular and first and second persons plural of the Imperative used affirmatively.

(ii.) In the Infinitive and Imperative used negatively, and in all other persons and tenses, both simple and compound, the above pronouns generally precede the verb[a]; as may be seen from the following model of a reflective verb:—

Model.

Infinitive—*scaldársi*, to warm one's self.

Indicative Mood.

Present Tense.

Singular.	*Plural.*
mi scáldo,[b] I warm myself.	*ci scaldiámo*, we warm ourselves.
ti scáldi, thou warmest thyself.	*vi scaldáte*, you warm &c.
si scálda, he warms himself.	*si scáldano*, they warm &c.

---

[a] It may be useful to add here,—(1) That the above rules respecting the placing of the pronouns are to be applied, not only in conjugating reflective verbs, but also, generally, with any other verb; and that what has been said in respect of *mi, ti, ci, vi, si*, is likewise applicable to the other conjunctive pronouns, *lo, li, la, le, gli*, and *ne* (see Pers. Pron., p. 8). (2) That the pronouns *lo, la, gli, le*, are subject to the same elisions as the same words when articles (see Articles, p. 8). (3) That *mi, ti, si, vi, ne* may suffer elision before any vowel; *ci* only before *e* and *i*.

[b] The words *stesso* or *medesimo*, plural *stessi* and *medesimi*, (see Indef. Pron., p. 10,) which have the meaning of *self* or *selves*, are sometimes used in Italian with the *reflective verb*, but this is done only in cases where the English *self* or *selves* is intended to be emphatic; as, *Non vedo voi, vedo me stesso*, or *me medesimo*, I do not see you, I see myself. The other persons would, in such cases, be formed as follows: *te stesso*, thyself; *sè stesso*, himself, herself, itself; *noi stessi*, ourselves; *voi stessi*, yourselves; *sè stessi*, themselves.

IMPERFECT.

mi scaldáva, I warmed myself.	*ci scaldavámo*, we warmed our-
ti scaldávi, thou warmedst thyself.	*vi scaldaváte*, you &c. [selves.
si scaldáva, he warmed himself.	*si scaldávano*, they &c.

PERFECT *or* PAST.

mi scaldái, I warmed myself.	*ci scaldámmo*, we warmed our-
ti scaldásti, thou warmedst thyself.	*vi scaldáste*, you &c. [selves.
si scaldò, he warmed himself.	*si scaldárono*, they &c.

FUTURE.

mi scalderò, I shall warm myself.	*ci scalderémo*, we shall warm our-
ti scalderái, thou wilt &c.	*vi scalderéte*, you will &c. [selves.
si scalderà, he will &c.	*si scalderánno*, they will &c.

Conditional Mood.

mi scalderéi, I should warm [myself.	*ci scalderémmo*, we should warm [ourselves.
ti scalderésti, thou wouldst &c.	*vi scalderéste*, you would &c.
si scalderébbe, he would &c.	*si scalderébbero*, they would &c.

Imperative Mood.

No first person singular.	*scaldiámoci*, let us warm our-
scáldati, warm thyself.	*scaldátevi*, warm &c. [selves.
si scáldi, let him warm himself.	*si scáldino*, let them &c.

Subjunctive Mood.

PRESENT TENSE.

ch' io mi scáldi, that I may warm [myself.	*che ci scaldiámo*, that we may [warm ourselves.
che tu ti scáldi, that thou &c.	*che vi scaldiáte*, that you &c.
ch' egli si scáldi, that he &c.	*che si scáldino*, that they &c.

IMPERFECT.

s' io mi scaldássi, if I might [warm myself.	*se ci scaldássimo*, if we might [warm ourselves.
se tu ti scaldássi, if thou &c.	*se vi scaldáste*, if you &c.
se si scaldásse, if he &c.	*se si scaldássero*, if they &c.

Present Participle $\left\{ \begin{array}{l} \textit{scaldándosi} \\ \textit{scaldántesi} \end{array} \right\}$ warming one's self.

Past Participle, *scaldátosi*, warmed one's self.

COMPOUND TENSES.

Infinitive—*essersi*[a] *scaldato*, to have warmed one's self.

Indicative Present... *mi sono scaldato* or *scaldata*,[b] I have warmed myself.
    ,,   Imperfect *mi era scaldato*, I had warmed myself.
    ,,   Perfect... *mi fui scaldato*, I had warmed myself.
    ,,   Future ... *mi sarò scaldato*, I shall have warmed myself.
Conditional............ *mi sarei scaldato*, I should have warmed myself.
Subjunctive Present *ch' io mi sia scaldato*, that I may have warmed myself.
    ,,   Imperfect *s' io mi fossi scaldato*, if I might have warmed myself.

Participle—*essendosi*[c] *scaldato*, having warmed himself,

CONJUGATION OF THE PRESENT INDICATIVE :—

Interrogatively.

mi scaldo ? do I warm myself?
ti scaldi ? dost thou &c.
si scalda ? does he &c.

ci scaldiamo ? do we warm our-
vi scaldate ? do you &c. [selves?
si scaldano ? do they &c.

Negatively.

non mi scaldo, I do not warm
        [myself.
non ti scaldi, thou dost not &c.
non si scalda, he does not &c.

non ci scaldiamo, we do not
        [warm ourselves.
non vi scaldate, you do not &c.
non si scaldano, they do not &c.

Interrogatively and Negatively.

non mi scaldo ? do I not warm
        [myself?
non ti scaldi ? dost thou not &c.
non si scalda ? does he not &c.

non ci scaldiamo ? do we not
        [warm ourselves?
non vi scaldate ? do you not &c.
non si scaldano ? do they not &c.

OBS.—*Reflective verbs* are conjugated in the same way

---

[a] *Essere* is always used to conjugate the compound tenses of reflective verbs.

[b] The past participle of a reflective verb agrees with the subject, when *mi, ti, si*, &c. are direct objects, or are used with a neuter verb (see Note *i*, p. 47). It may remain invariable in its masculine termination *o*, or agree with the object of the sentence, when *mi, ti,* &c., are indirect objects, that is, have the signification of *a me*, to me, *a te*, to thee, &c. (see Obs. 1, p. 42); as,

      Quel uomo si è conservato (or *conservata*) *la sanità,*
      That man has preserved his health.

[c] When, in the compound tenses, the Auxiliary is in the Infinitive or Participle, the conjunctive pronoun follows the Auxiliary, and is united to it.

as other verbs, so far as regards their terminations; that is, those ending in *are*, like *parlare;* those in *ere*, like *credere;* those in *ire*, like *sentire* or *finire.*

The student should now, therefore, conjugate *credersi*, to believe one's self; and *divertirsi*, to amuse one's self, in order to become well acquainted with the reflective forms.

RECIPROCAL VERBS.

OBS.—These are conjugated in the same way as Reflectives, but only in the *plural* of their tenses, both simple and compound; as,

> *ci parliamo,* we speak to one another.[a]
> *vi parlate,* you speak to one another.
> *si parlano,* they speak to one another, &c.

PHRASES.

vestirsi alla moda, to dress (one's self) after the fashion.
adattarsi a tutto, to accommodate one's self to everything.
accompagnarsi[b] colla chitarra, to accompany one's self on the guitar.
cavarsi i guanti, il cappello,[c] &c., to take off one's gloves, one's hat, &c.
allungarsi la vita, to lengthen one's life.
ridersi[d] di uno, to laugh at one.

---

[a] The English *one another* or *each other*, in cases similar to those above, is sometimes expressed in Italian by *uno* and *altro*, accompanied by the definite article, or by such words as *scambievolmente*, mutually; *reciprocamente*, reciprocally; as,

> *noi ci amiamo l' un l' altro*, or } we love one another.
> *noi ci amiamo scambievolmente* }

[b] An Italian reflective verb is rendered in English by another reflective verb, when the words *mi, ti,* &c. are direct objects, and have in Italian the meaning of *me*, me, *te*, thee, &c. (Obs. 1, p. 42); as, *L' uomo vano si loda,* a vain man PRAISES HIMSELF.

[c] An Italian reflective verb is rendered in English by an active verb and a possessive pronoun before the object of the sentence, when *mi, ti,* &c. are indirect objects, and have in Italian the meaning of *a me*, to me, *a te*, to thee, &c.; as,

> *Io mi allaccio le scarpe*, I LACE MY shoes.

[d] By a divergence of English and Italian idiom, an Italian reflective verb is often Englished by a neuter verb; as,

> *Io mi pento del passato*, I REPENT of the past.

abusarsi della bontà di uno, to take advantage of any one's kindness.
alterarsi facilmente, to get easily excited.
pentirsi d'aver parlato, to repent of having spoken.
ferirsi in un duello, to wound one another in a duel.

VOCABULARY.

sempre, always.   *guanto,* glove.
ieri sera, last night.   *ragazza,* girl.
                    nessuno, no one.

READING EXERCISE.

1. La Signora B. si veste sempre alla moda. 2. Quando io era ragazza, mi adattava a tutto. 3. Ieri sera Mongini cantò una canzone, e s' accompagnò[a] colla chitarra. 4. Ella s' è cavati i guanti[b] per sonare il pianoforte. 5. Vi allungherete[c] la vita se sarete[d] sobrii. 6. Non vi ridete[e] mai di nessuno. 7. Sperava ch' egli non s' abusasse[f] della mia bontà. 8. Non ti alterare[g] facilmente. 9. Ti sei pentito d' avere parlato? 10. Si sono feriti[h] in un duello.

VOCABULARY.

to wonder, *maravigliarsi.*
to be ashamed, *vergognarsi di.*
to rise, get up $\begin{cases} alzarsi, \\ levarsi. \end{cases}$
to feel $\begin{Bmatrix} well, \\ unwell, \end{Bmatrix}$ *sentirsi* $\begin{cases} bene, \\ male. \end{cases}$
to awake $\begin{cases} svegliarsi, \\ destarsi. \end{cases}$
to go to rest, *coricarsi.*
to enjoy one's self, *divertirsi.*
to get tired, *stancarsi.*

to fall asleep, *addormentarsi.*
to get ill, *ammalarsi.*
to rest, *riposarsi.*
to get angry $\begin{cases} adirarsi, \\ arrabbiarsi. \end{cases}$
to remember, *ricordarsi di.*
to be glad, *rallegrarsi di.*
to behave well, *diportarsi bene.*
to forget $\begin{cases} dimenticarsi di, \\ scordarsi di. \end{cases}$

TRANSLATION EXERCISE.

1. I wonder[i] – my son is not ashamed[j] to get up
   che mio figlio

---

[a] Note *b*, p. 46; and Note *a* (3), p. 43.   [b] Note *c*, p. 46.
[c] Note *d*, p. 46.   [d] Note *h*, p. 41.   [e] Obs. ii., p. 43.
[f] Note *b*, p. 34.   [g] Note *c*, p. 14.   [h] Obs., p. 46.
[i] Observe that many *neuter verbs* are conjugated in the *reflective* way in Italian, though they are not so in English. The pronoun *si* suffixed to the Infinitive in the vocabulary will indicate to the student that the verb is *reflective.* (See Note *d*, p. 46.)
[j] Note *b*, p. 34.

so late.   2. Sir, he felt[a] unwell last night, but he will
così tardi   *ieri sera*

be here immediately.   3. Why[b] did you awake[c] so late
         subito   1

this morning?   4. Because I went to rest late last

night.   5. Did you enjoy yourself[c] at the concert?
                                    al   *concerto*

6. On-the-contrary; I got tired[c], and did not fall asleep
    Anzi

till this morning.   7. You will get ill[d] if you do not rest
che

enough.   8. Do not get angry,[e] and I will remember
abbastanza

     your advice.   9. I am glad[d] to hear that you will
del vostro avviso

behave well in future, and I hope you will not forget
                       futuro

–   your promise.
della vostra promessa

Questions.

Che s'[f] allunga l' uomo sobrio? 5*.—Chi s' ammala? 7.
—A che ora v'[f] alzavate quando eravate in campagna? 1.
—Che vi siete cavato per sonare il pianoforte? 4*.—Con
che s' è accompagnata quella signora che cantò ieri
sera? 3*.—Quando si coricheranno i fanciulli? 4.—Vi
siete divertito più in città o in campagna? 5.—Vi ri-
cordate in che giorno siete arrivato a Londra? 9.—Vi
sentite bene o male? 2.

---

[a] Note *d*, p. 15.   [b] Note *e*, p. 31.
[c] Note *h*, p. 15; and Note *i*, p. 47.   [d] Note *i*, p. 47.
[e] Obs. (ii.), p. 43.   [f] Note *a* (3), p. 43.

PASSIVE VERBS.

OBSERVATIONS.

1. An *active verb* is rendered *passive* in Italian in the same way as in English, that is, by a combination of the verb *essere*, in all its moods, tenses, and persons, and the Past Participle of the active verb; as,

(Active.) *Il padre* PUNISCE *il figlio*, the father punishes the son.

(Passive.) *Il figlio* È PUNITO[a] *dal*[b] *padre*, the son is punished by the father.

2. In Italian, however, the passive meaning is very often, in the 3rd person of both numbers, obtained by the reflective construction; *i.e.*, by employing *si*[c] in all moods and tenses, using the auxiliary *essere* for the compound tenses. In this case, the verb must be in the *singular* or *plural* number, according to the number of the noun with which the *si* is employed; as,

Lo scolare si castiga, the pupil is punished (*literally*, the pupil punishes himself).

Le perle si trovano nel mare, pearls are found in the sea (*literally*, pearls find themselves in the sea).

3. There is another manner of using the active verb reflective along with the little word *si*, which is very remarkable. This word *si*, which, as above noticed, represents all the English pronouns *oneself, himself, her-*

---

[a] *Venire*, to come, is frequently used instead of *essere*, to form the simple tenses of *passive* verbs. Thus, we may say, *Il figlio viene punito*, instead of *è punito;* but in compound tenses, *essere* only can be used; as, *Il figlio è stato punito*, the son has been punished.

[b] The preposition which follows the Passive Past Participle is *da*, and sometimes *per*.

[c] The passive meaning is generally obtained by the reflective construction with *si*, when we wish to point to the action received by the object in an indeterminate manner, without reference to the subject; as,

Nelle scuole si ammaestra la gioventù, youth is taught in schools. To use *essere* in such a case, and say, *Nelle scuole la gioventù è ammaestrata*, would denote merely an accomplished fact, and not a subsisting state.

D

self, itself, themselves, is constantly used with the reflective verb in the third person of both numbers to express the meaning of the English words *one, you, they,
people*[*] (in the sense of *the world in general*) ; as,

one praises virtue ⎫
they praise virtue   ⎬ SI *loda la virtù.*
people praise virtue ⎪
we praise virtue ⎭

one loves one's friends ⎫
we love our friends   ⎬ SI *amano gli amici.*
people love their friends ⎪
they love their friends ⎭

That is, literally, *virtue praises itself; friends love themselves.*

4. This idiomatic use of *si* with the *reflective verb* is of
the most constant occurrence in Italian. It must however be observed, that the words *we* and *they*, as used
in the above examples, may also be turned into Italian
by employing the verb in the 1st and 3rd persons
plural ; as,

    Amiamo gli amici, we (*indef.*) love our friends.
    Lodano la virtù, they (*indef.*) praise virtue.

5. Sometimes also the pronoun *uno,* or the word
uomo, man, may be used to represent the English *one,* as
above employed ; as,

    Uno (or *l'uomo*) *si avvezza facilmente alla vita oziosa,*
    One easily accustoms one's self to an idle life ;

but these forms are very seldom employed.

IMPERSONAL VERBS.

OBSERVATIONS.

There are in Italian two classes of impersonal verbs,—
(1.) The true impersonals, which have no subject, and
only the forms of the 3rd person singular in all tenses, as

---

[*] As *si* may have different meanings, the student must pay
attention in future not to mistake one for the other. (See also
Obs. 2 and 3, and Note *c*, p. 49.)

in English, with this difference, that in Italian they are generally used without a pronoun; as, *piove*, it rains, from *piovere*; *gelerà*, it will freeze, from *gelare*.

(2.) Quasi-impersonal verbs, which are used in the 3rd person, both singular and plural,* and may have a subject expressed. Such verbs, though not properly impersonals, may, in certain cases, be used impersonally. Thus *importare*, to import, concern, is used impersonally in the following sentence :—

> *Quelle cose nè a me nè a voi importano,*
> Those things concern neither me nor you.

Observations on the use of the Auxiliaries *Avere* and *Essere* in the conjugation of other verbs.

1. It has been already said that *avere* is used to form the compound tenses of all *active* verbs, and that *essere* is employed as an auxiliary with *reflective* and *passive* verbs. It remains, therefore, to speak only of *neuter* and *impersonal* verbs.

2. *Neuter* and *impersonal* verbs are conjugated, some of them with *avere*, and some with *essere;* but no certain rules can be given.

3. However, special attention must be paid to the following verbs, which in Italian are conjugated with *essere*, whereas in English they are generally conjugated with ' to have ' (*avere*) :—

accadere,	to happen.	*partire*,	to set out, depart, start.
accorrere,	to run up to.		
andare,	to go.	*passare*,	to pass.
arrivare,	to arrive.	*pervenire*,	to arrive.
avvenire,	to happen.	*restare*, }	to remain, stay.
cadere,	to fall.	*rimanere*, }	
discendere,	to come down.	*riuscire*,	to succeed.
divenire, }	to become.	*salire*,	to come up, go up.
diventare, }		*stare*,	to stay, stand.
entrare,	to enter, walk in.	*tornare*,	to return.
giungere,	to reach, arrive at.	*uscire*,	to go out.
morire,	to die.	*venire*,	to come.

* *Ricordarsi, rimembrarsi,* and *sovvenirsi,* to recollect, are sometimes used impersonally in the singular; as,

> *Ancor mi ricorda essere in Pisa una torre pendente,*
> I still remember that there is a leaning tower in Pisa.

Notice the following examples :—

Io SONO *andato*, I *have* gone.
Egli È *arrivato*, He *has* arrived.

4. There is also a distinction to be made with respect to the use of *avere* and *essere*, when the verb is one of those which may, according to the sense in which it is employed, be either a verb *neuter* or *active;* for then in the first instance *essere* is employed, but in the second *avere;* as,—

SONO *fuggito dai miei nemici,*	I have fled from my enemies.
Ho *fuggito i miei nemici,*	I have escaped my enemies.
Egli È *morto,*	He is dead.
Egli HA *morto il nemico,*	He has killed his enemy.

5. The verbs *potere*, to be able, *volere*, to be willing, *dovere*, to be obliged, followed by another verb in the Infinitive, may take before them the auxiliary of the second verb; as,

Non mi son potuto ritenere,
I have not been able to restrain myself.

PHRASES.

combattere di notte, to fight by night.
esser * *abbagliato dalla luce del sole*, to be dazzled by the light of the sun.
esser battuto col coreggiato, to be threshed with the flail.
esser divorato dal lupo, to be devoured by the wolf.
esser allagato dalle pioggie, to be inundated by the rains.
toccare ad uno (used impersonally), to be one's turn, one's duty, one's business; or, to fall to one's lot.
accadere una disgrazia (used impersonally), to happen a misfortune.
annottare ad un' ora, to become night at the same time.

VOCABULARY.

occhio, eye.	*agnello,* lamb.
una volta, once.	*campo,* field.
grano, corn.	*continuo,* continual.
generalmente, generally.	*mondo,* world.

READING EXERCISE.

1. Di notte non si combatte. 2. I nostri occhi sono abbagliati dalla luce del sole. 3. Una volta il grano si batteva più generalmente col coreggiato. 4. Ieri

---

* The Infinitive of all Italian verbs may drop the final vowel *e* before all words, excepting those beginning with *s* followed by a consonant.

l'agnello fu divorato dal lupo. 5. I campi sono stati alla-
gati dalle continue pioggie. 6. Quando toccherà a me,
comincerò u parlare. 7. Si crede che sia accaduta una
disgrazia al Signor P. 8. Mai non annotta in tutto il
mondo ad[a] un' ora.

VOCABULARY.

to wear, *portare.*	to freeze, *gelare.*
to found, *fondare.*	to thaw, *digelare.*
to be necessary, *bisognare.*	to hail, *grandinare.*
to thunder, *tuonare.*	to be enough, *bastare.*
to rain, *piovere.*	to mind, *badare.*
to snow, *nevicare.*	to drop, *cadere.*

TRANSLATION EXERCISE.

1. Where is – coral found[b] ? 2. In the Mediterranean[2]
   il corallo   *Nel mediterraneo*

Sea[1], and many ornaments of coral were formerly
mare   *molti ornamenti*   *altre volte*

worn[b] by Italian[2] ladies[1]. 3. By whom was Rome
   dalle italiane Signore   *Da chi*

founded ? 4. It is generally believed that it was

founded[c] by[d] Romulus. 5. What language was spoken
     Romolo

by the ancient Romans ? 6. – Latin. 7. Would it be
dagli antichi Romani   *Il latino*

necessary[e] to study much to learn – Italian ? 8. One
        per   *l' italiano*

learns[f] Italian more quickly than – German. 9. It
     più presto del

---

[a] The preposition *a*, to, and the conjunctions *o*, or, *e*, and, generally, though not necessarily, take a *d* after them when followed
by a word beginning with a vowel.
 [b] Obs. 2, p. 49.   [c] Note *b*, p. 34.   [d] Note *b*, p. 49.
 [e] The verbs *bastare*, to be enough; *bisognare* or *convenire*, to be
necessary; *desiderare*, to wish; *dovere*, to be obliged; *fare*, to do,
make; *lasciare*, to leave, allow; *parere*, to seem, appear; *potere*, to
be able; *sapere*, to know; *sentire*, to feel, hear; *solere*, to be accustomed; *udire*, to hear; *vedere*, to see; when followed by an Infinitive, take no preposition after them; as, *Bisogna studiare tutti i
giorni*, it is necessary to study every day.   [f] Obs. 3, p. 49.

thunders,[a] perhaps it will rain. 10. It snowed last night.
ieri sera

11. Yes, and this morning[b] it froze[a]. 12. But it has
thawed already. 13. Does it rain often in Italy?
già   *spesso*
14. In Italy it does not rain so often, but it hails more
così
often than in England. 15. This is enough for to-day;
che   *Questo*
we shall speak more[2] Italian[1] to-morrow. 16. Mind,
di più

you have dropped   some papers.
[to you are dropped[c]] *delle carte*

QUESTIONS.

Da che sono abbagliati i nostri occhi? 2*.—Con che si
batteva generalmente il grano? 3*.—Da chi fu divorato
l'agnello? 4*.—Dove si trova il corallo? 2.—Da chi si
crede che sia stata fondata Roma? 4.—Che lingua si
parla in Germania? 5.—Pioveva ieri?—È nevicato
molto l'inverno passato?—In che stagione gela?—Che
vi è caduto? 16.

IRREGULAR VERBS.

OBSERVATIONS ON IRREGULAR VERBS.

1. Italian verbs are always *regular*[d] in the following
five tenses, which are thus formed:—

The IMPERFECT INDICATIVE, by changing the Infinitive
terminations—

are into *ava* or *avo, avi, ava ; avamo, avate, avano.*
ere „ *eva* or *evo, evi, eva ; evamo, evate, evano*[e].
ire „ *iva* or *ivo, ivi, iva ; ivamo, ivate, ivano*[f].

---

[a] Obs (1), p. 50.   [b] Note *e*, p. 30.
[a] See Obs. (2) and Obs. 3, p. 51.   [d] Note *c*, p. 24.
[e] Except *essere*. The forms of *essere* are not reducible to rule;
and it must be regarded as an exception to the scheme here given.
[f] The first vowel of the Infinitive termination, *a* for the 1st

The FUTURE, by changing the Infinitive terminations—

are into	*erò,*	*erai,*	*erà ;*	*eremo,*	*erete,*	*eranno*[a].
ere „	*erò,*	*erai,*	*erà ;*	*eremo,*	*ereto,*	*eranno.*
ire „	*irò,*	*irai,*	*irà ;*	*iremo,*	*irete,*	*iranno.*

The CONDITIONAL, by changing the Infinitive terminations—

are into	*erei,*	*eresti,*	*erebbe ;*	*eremmo,*	*ereste,*	*erebbero*[a].
ere „	*erei,*	*eresti,*	*erebbe ;*	*eremmo,*	*ereste,*	*erebbero.*
ire „	*irei,*	*iresti,*	*irebbe ;*	*iremmo,*	*ireste,*	*irebbero.*

The IMPERFECT SUBJUNCTIVE, by changing the Infinitive terminations—

are into	*assi,*	*assi,*	*asse ;*	*assimo,*	*aste,*	*assero*[b].
ere „	*essi,*	*essi,*	*esse ;*	*essimo,*	*este,*	*essero.*
ire „	*issi,*	*issi,*	*isse ;*	*issimo,*	*iste,*	*issero.*

The PRESENT PARTICIPLE, by changing the Infinitive terminations—

are into $\begin{cases} ando^c \\ ante \end{cases}$ *ere* into $\begin{cases} endo \\ ente \end{cases}$ *ire* into $\begin{cases} endo^d \\ ente^e \end{cases}$

2. All the irregularities of verbs, therefore, are confined to the Present and Perfect of the Indicative, the Imperative, the Present Subjunctive, and the Past Participle. But a verb may be irregular in only one, two, or

---

conjugation, *e* for the 2nd, and *i* for the 3rd, is called the *characteristic*. It generally constitutes the only difference between the conjugations in the terminations of all those tenses and persons which are always regular. In the 1st conjugation, *e* is substituted instead of the characteristic *a* throughout the Future and Conditional; and in the 3rd, *e* instead of *i* is used in the Present Participle.

[a] The Future of all verbs has invariably the terminations *rò, rai,* &c.; and the Conditional *rei, resti,* &c. We shall, however, find, in the irregular verbs, that these two tenses are subject to contraction.

[b] Except *dare,* to give, and *stare,* to stand, which make *dessi,* &c., and *stessi,* &c.

[c] Note *a,* p. 26.   [d] Note *f,* p. 54.   [e] Note *e,* p. 38.

three of these tenses; and even when it is so in all, the irregularities do not extend to all the persons.

3. When a verb is irregular in the Perfect tense, it is so in three persons only, the other three being always regular.

The three irregular persons are the 1st and 3rd persons singular and the 3rd person plural. The two last are invariably formed in the following manner: the 1st person singular always ends in *i*, as, *lessi*, I read; by changing this *i* into *e* we have the 3rd person singular, *lesse*, he or she read; and by adding *ro* to the 3rd person singular, we have the 3rd person plural, *lessero*, they read.

The three persons which are always regular, therefore, are the 2nd singular, which is formed from the Infinitive by changing *are* into *asti*[a], *ere* into *esti*, and *ire* into *isti*; the 1st plural, which is formed by changing *are* into *ammo*[b], *ere* into *emmo*, *ire* into *immo*; and the 2nd plural, which is formed by changing *are* into *aste*[c], *ere* into *este*, and *ire* into *iste*[d]. Thus, from *leggere*, to read, which has *lessi* in the Perfect, we shall have—

Singular.	Plural.
lessi, I read.	*leggemmo*, we read.
leggesti, thou didst read.	*leggeste*, you read.
lesse, he read.	*lessero*, they read.

N.B.—These observations are of great utility in conjugating irregular verbs; for, having learnt the 1st person singular of the Perfect, the Past Participle, and the singular and 1st person plural of the Present Indicative of any verb, the student will be able to conjugate all the other tenses and persons, by referring to Notes *b, c, d*, p. 25, and *a, b, c, d*, p. 26, for the 1st conjugation; and to Notes *c, e*, p. 32, and *a*, p. 33, for the 2nd and 3rd conjugations.

---

[a] Except *dare*, to give, and *stare*, to stand, which make *desti* and *stesti*.

[b] Except *dare* and *stare*, which make *demmo* and *stemmo*.

[c] Except *dare* and *stare*, which make *deste* and *steste*.

[d] Note *f*, p. 54.

Obs.—The irregular verbs of the 1st conjugation are : *andare*, to go; *dare*, to give; *fare*[a], to do, make; *stare*, to stand, stay ; and some of their derivatives, which are conjugated like them.

IRREGULAR VERBS—FIRST CONJUGATION.

CONJUGATION OF THE VERB *ANDARE*.

Infinitive—*andáre*, to go.

Indicative Present.

Singular.	Plural.
vo or *vaddo*,[b] I go.	*andiámo*,[c] we go.
vái, thou goest.	*andáte*, you go.
va, he goes.	*vánno*,[d] they go.

Indicative Imperfect... *andáva*,[e] I was going.
    „   Perfect...... *andái*, I went.
    „   Future ...... *andrò*,[f] I shall go.
    Conditional—*andréi*, I should go.

Imperative Mood.

No first person singular.	*andiámo*, let us go.
va', go (thou).	*andáte*, go (you).
váda, let him go.	*vádano*, let them go.

Subjunctive Present.

ch' io váda, that I may go.	*che andiámo*, that we may go.
che tu váda, that thou mayest go.	*che andiáte*, that you may go.
ch' egli váda, that he may go.	*che vádano*, that they may go.

---

[a] *Fare* is in many grammars classed with the verbs of the 2nd conjugation, because it is contracted from *facere*, which is now obsolete. On account of its similarity in the terminations with the other three irregular verbs above mentioned, it is here considered as belonging to the 1st conjugation. The Imperfect Indicative and Subjunctive, as well as the Present Participle and the regular persons of the Perfect of this verb, are conjugated regularly, like *facere*. Some persons also of the Present Indicative and Subjunctive, and of the Imperative, are formed according to *facere*.

[b] *Vado* comes from the Latin verb *vadere*, to go; and this form is used in forming the Imperative and the Present Subjunctive, according to the rules given for the 2nd conjugation.

[c] See N.B., p. 56.

[d] The singular and 3rd person plural of the Present Indicative of *andare*, *dare*, *fare*, and *stare*, are all identical with the same persons of the verb *avere*, except that the first letter *h* is changed respectively into *v*, *d*, *f*, or *st*. (See Present Indicative of *avere*, p. 19.)

[e] Obs. 1., p. 54.   [f] Note *a*, p. 55.

Subjunctive Imperfect—*s' io andássi*, if I might go.

Present Participle $\left\{ \begin{array}{l} andándo \\ andánte \end{array} \right\}$ going.

Past Participle—*andáto*, gone.

COMPOUND TENSES.

Infinitive—*essere andato*[a], to have gone.

Indicative Present—*sono andato* or *andata*[b], I have gone.
&c.   &c.   &c.

OBS.—The compounds of *andare*[c], *riandare*, to go again, repass, and *trasandare*, to pass over, are conjugated like *andare*; but *riandare*, to reconsider, *trasandare*, to neglect, are regular, like *parlare*.

CONJUGATION OF THE VERB *DARE*.

Infinitive—*dáre*, to give.

Indicative Present.

Singular.	*Plural.*
do, I give.	*diámo*, we give.
dái, thou givest.	*dáte*, you give.
dà, he gives.	*dánno*, they give.

Indicative Imperfect—*dáva*, I was giving.

Perfect or Past.

diédi or *détti*, I gave.	*démmo*, we gave.
désti, thou gavest.	*déste*, you gave.
diéde or *détte* or *diè*, he gave.	*diédero* or *déttero* or *diéro*[d], they [gave.

Future—*daró*[e], I shall give.

Conditional—*daréi*, I should give.

---

[a] Obs. 3, p. 51.   [b] Note *f*, p. 13.

[c] The verb *andare* has sometimes the meaning of the English *must*, and sometimes that of the English *to be*, implying motion, continuation; as,

Le buone assuefazioni VANNO *prese nella prima età*, (SEGN.)
Good habits *must* be acquired at an early age.

Il fanciullo VA *cogliendo fiori pel giardino*,
The child *is* gathering flowers in the garden.

[d] Obs. 3, p. 56.

[e] Notice that the verb *dare* has in the Future *aró*, *arai*, *ará*, *aremo*, *arete*, *aranno*, instead of *eró*, *erei*, &c.; and in the Conditional, *arei*, *aresti*, *arebbe*, *aremmo*, *areste*, *arebbero*, instead of *erei*, *eresti*, &c. *Fare* and *stare* have the same terminations as *dare* in these tenses. (See Note *a*, p. 55.)

Imperative.

No first person singular.   *diámo*, let us give.
da', give (thou).   *dáte*, give (you).
dia, let him give.   *diano* or *dieno*, let them give.

Subjunctive Present.

ch' io dia, that I may give.   *che diámo*, that we may give.
che tu dia, that thou mayest give.   *che diáte*, that you may give.
ch' egli dia, that he may give.   *che diano* or *dieno*, that they may
        [give.

Imperfect.

s' io déssi, if I might give.   *se déssimo*, if we might give.
se tu déssi, if thou mightest give.   *se déste*, if you might give.
se désse, if he might give.   *se déssero*, if they might give.

Present Participle $\begin{Bmatrix} dándo \\ dánte \end{Bmatrix}$ giving.

Past Participle—*dáto*, given.

COMPOUND TENSES.

Infinitive—*avere dato*, to have given.

Indicative Present—*ho dato*, I have given.
    &c.   &c.   &c.

OBS.—Only *ridare*, to give again, and *addarsi*, to perceive, are conjugated in the same way as *dare*.

CONJUGATION OF THE VERB *FARE*.

Infinitive—*fáre*[a], to do, make.

Indicative Present.

Singular.   *Plural.*
fo or *fáccio*, I do.   *facciámo*, we do.
fái, thou doest *or* dost.   *fáte*, you do.
fa, he does.   *fánno*, they do.

Imperfect—*facéva*, I was doing.

Perfect or Past.

féci, I did.   *facémmo*, we did.
facésti, thou didst.   *facéste*, you did.
féce, he did.   *fécero*, they did.

Future—*farò*, I shall do.
Conditional—*faréi*, I should do.

---

[a] Note *a*, p. 57.

Imperative Mood.

No first person singular.	*facciámo*, let us do.
fa', do (thou).	*fáte*, do (you).
fáccia, let him do.	*fácciano*, let them do.

Subjunctive Present.

ch' io fáccia, that I may do.	*che facciámo*, that we may do.
che tu fáccia, that thou mayest do.	*che facciáte*, that you may do.
ch' egli fáccia, that he may do.	*che fácciano*, that they may do.

Imperfect—*s' io facéssi*, if I might do.

Present Participle $\left\{ \begin{array}{l} facéndo \\ facénte \end{array} \right\}$ doing.

Past Participle—*fátto*[a], done.

COMPOUND TENSES.

Infinitive—*avere fatto*, to have done.

Indicative Present—*ho fatto*, I have done.
&c.   &c.   &c.

OBS.—The compounds of *fare*—*affarsi*, to suit; *assuefare*, to accustom; *confarsi*, to agree; *contraffare*, to counterfeit; *disfare*, to undo; *liquefare*, to melt; *misfare*, to do wrong; *rifare*, to do again; *sopraffare*, to overpower; *soddisfare*, to satisfy; *stupefare*, to stupify; *strafare*, to do more than is necessary, &c., are conjugated like *fare*[b].

CONJUGATION OF THE VERB *STARE*[c].

Infinitive—*stáre*, to stand.

Indicative Present.

sto, I stand.	*stiámo*, we stand.
stái, thou standest.	*státe*, you stand.
sta, he stands.	*stánno*, they stand.

Imperfect—*stáva*, I was standing.

---

[a] *Fare* and its compounds are the only verbs of the 1st conjugation that are irregular in the Past Participle.

[b] *Fare*, followed by a name of profession or trade, means to 'exercise,' 'practise,' and is rendered in English by the verb *to be*; as, *Io farò il medico*, I *shall be* a doctor. *Fare*, immediately followed by an Infinitive, has the meaning of the English 'to have,' 'cause,' or 'let,' in phrases like the following:—*Farò fabbricare una casa*, I shall have a house built.

[c] *Stare* is conjugated like *dare*, by simply changing *d* into *st*. *Stare* has but one form in the Perfect, *stetti*, &c.

Perfect *or* Past.

stétti, I stood.	*stémmo*, we stood.
stésti, thou stoodest.	*stéste*, you stood.
státte, he stood.	*stéttero*, they stood.

Future—*starò*,[a] I shall stand.

Conditional—*staréi*, I should stand.

Imperative.

No first person singular.	*stiámo*, let us stand.
sta', stand (thou).	*státe*, stand (you).
stía, let him stand.	*stíano*, let them stand.

Subjunctive Present.

ch' io stía, that I may stand.	*che stiámo*, that we may stand.
che tu stía, that thou mayest [stand.	*che stiáte*, that you may stand.
ch' egli stía, that he may stand.	*che stíano* or *stíeno*, that they [may stand.

Imperfect.

s' io stéssi, if I might stand.	*se stéssimo*, if we might stand.
se tu stéssi, if thou mightest stand.	*se stéste*, if you might stand.
se stésse, if he might stand.	*se stéssero*, if they might stand.

Present Participle $\left\{ \begin{array}{l} \textit{stándo} \\ \textit{stánte} \end{array} \right\}$ standing.

Past Participle—*státo*, stood.

. COMPOUND TENSES.

Infinitive—*essere stato*, to have stood.

Indicative Present—*sono stato* or *stata*,[b] I have stood.
    &c.   &c.   &c.

OBS.—*Ristare*, to stop, *distare*, to be distant, *soprastare*, to temporise, *contrastare*, to stand close against, are conjugated like *stare*.[c] *Soprastare* or *sovrastare*, to impend, to rule, *contrastare*, to dispute, and all other verbs derived from *stare*, are regular, like *parlare*.

N.B.—All the verbs which are conjugated like *andare*, *dare*, *fare*, and *stare*, have their final vowel accented in the first and third

---

[a] Note *e*, p. 58.

[b] Observe that the compound tenses of *stare* are identical in form with those of *essere*. The reason of this is, that *essere* having lost its own Past Participle (which was *suto*) has borrowed the Past Participle of *stare*, which likewise forms its own compound tenses with *essere*.

[c] *Stare* and *essere*, followed by the preposition *per*, have the meaning of 'to be on the point of'; as,

$\left. \begin{array}{l} \text{Sto} \\ \text{Sono} \end{array} \right\}$ *per partire*, I am on the point of leaving.

persons singular of the Present Indicative; as, *rivò*, I go again;
ridà, he gives again; *rifà*, he does again; *ristò*, I stop.   The compounds of *andare* and *fare*, however, do not require any accent
when the forms *rado* and *faccio* are used; as, *rivado*, I go again;
rifaccio, I am doing again.

PHRASES.

andare carponi, to go on all fours.   *andare a piedi*, to go on foot.
  „ *in barca*, to go in a boat.   „ *a cavallo*, to go on horseback.
  „ *a caccia*, to go a-hunting.   „ *per vapore*, to go by steamboat.
  „ *a pescare*, to go a-fishing.   „ *per strada ferrata*, to go by railway
      fare una girata in carrozza, to go out for a drive.
      andare giù di tavola, to leave the table.
      stare composto a tavola, to sit properly at table.
      fare colazione, to breakfast.
      dare il buon giorno, to say good morning.
      andare d' accordo, to agree.
      dare retta, to heed, lend an ear to.
      andare in collera, to put one's self in a passion.

VOCABULARY.

prima di, before.   *Carlino*, (little) Charles.
camminare, to walk.   *suggerimento*, advice.
ritornare, to return.

READING EXERCISE.

1. I fanciulli prima di camminare vanno carponi.[a]
2. In campagna io andava spesso in barca, a caccia ed
a pescare.   3. Siete[b] andato in città a piedi od[a] a cavallo?   4. Andai per vapore, e ritornai a casa per strada
ferrata.   5. Domani farò una girata per la città in carrozza.   6. Signor Carlino, non andate giù di tavola,
state composto, e quando avrete fatto colazione andrete
a[c] dare il buon giorno al babbo.   7. Bramo che andiate[d]
d' accordo coi fratelli; se deste[e] retta ai miei suggeri-
menti, non andreste in collera per niente.

---

  [a] Note *a*, p. 53.   [b] Obs. 3, p. 51.
  [c] Verbs denoting *teaching*, as *insegnare*, to teach; *learning*, as
imparare, to learn; *attaining*, as *pervenire*, to reach; *insisting*, as
insistere, to insist; *remaining*, as *stare*, to stay; *continuing*, as
seguitare, to follow on; *helping*, as *aiutare*, to help; *engaging*, as
impiegare, to employ; *accustoming*, as *abituarsi*, to accustom one's
self; *encouraging*, as *incoraggiare*, to put in heart; *obliging*, as *costringere*, to compel, as well as all verbs denoting *motion*, require
the proposition *a* before the Infinitive coming after them.
  [d] Note *b*, p. 34.   [e] Note *c*, p. 56.

Vocabulary.

to do, make, *fare*.
to get ready, *allestirsi*[a].
to be right \} of a thing done \{ *andare male*,
to be wrong \}   \{ *andare bene*.
to go for a walk, *andare a spasso*.
to pay a visit, *fare una visita*.
to live, reside, *stare, abitare*.
to be well \} of health \{ *stare bene*,
to be unwell \}   \{ *stare male*.
to intend, *fare conto di*.
to be fine weather, *fare bel tempo*.
to be bad weather, *fare cattivo tempo*.
to start. *partire*.

Translation Exercise.

1. What are[b] you doing? 2. I am[c] getting ready
for a walk. 3. Was –[3] your[4] translation[5] wrong[2]?
        la   *la vostra traduzione*

4. No, it was right; I only[2] made[1] two mistakes.
                                     sbagli

5. Has[d] your brother gone for a walk? 6. No, he
has gone to[e] pay a visit to – Mrs. G., who lives in
                      alla Signora   *che*

(the) country. 7. How do you   do,   my[2] friend[1]?
            Come   [stand] *mio amico*

8. I am   very well: how have you been?
  [I stand]   [have you always been[f] well?]

9. I was   unwell yesterday, but to-day   I am
  [I stood]   [I stand]

---

[a] Note *i*, p. 47.   [b] Note *a*, p. 25.

[c] *Stare* may be used to render the English verb *to be*, used with
the Present Participle of another verb, but this can only be done
with verbs denoting rest; as, *sto leggendo*, I am reading; *sto
pensando*, I am thinking. To use *stare* to translate *to be* in sentences like *I am running, I am walking*, would be nonsense, for
stare means to stay in one spot, and not to move from it while
acting. This peculiar construction should be used sparingly by
beginners. *Mi allestisco*, I get ready, is simpler than *sto allestendomi*,
and is equally correct.

[d] Obs. 3, p. 51   [e] Note *c*, p. 62.   [f] Note *b*, p. 61.

better.   10. When do you intend going to Italy?
meglio   *in*

11. I intend going to Italy next autumn, should the
                                      [if it shall
weather be fine.   12. Even   should it be   bad
make* fine weather]   *Anche*   [if it might make]
weather, you would do well   to start (all)
                    meglio (*lit.* better)
the same, because when   it is   bad weather in
lo stesso   [it makes]
England, it   is   often fine in Italy.
      [makes]   *bello*

QUESTIONS.

Come vanno i fanciulli prima di camminare? 1*.—
Come sta vostra sorella? 7.—Che tempo faceva ieri? 11.
—Come andrete a casa? 4*.—A che ora avete fatto colazione? 6*.—E andato vostro padre in città a piedi od in
carrozza? 3*.—Dove fate conto d' andare domani? 10.
—Quante visite farete?—Che avete fatto, quando eravate in campagna? 2*.—Come bisogna stare a tavola? 6*.
—Andava bene la vostra traduzione? 4.—Quanti sbagli
avete fatti? 4.

IRREGULAR VERBS—SECOND CONJUGATION.

OBSERVATIONS.

1. In order that the irregularity of verbs of the
second conjugation may be perfectly understood, it is
necessary to observe that they differ in the accenting of
their Infinitives, some being pronounced *long*, that is,
with the accent on the penultimate, or last syllable but
one; as, *temére, godére,* &c.; and others *short*, viz., with
the accent on the antepenultimate, or last syllable but
two; as, *crédere, véndere,* &c.
2. The following, with their derivatives, are the only
verbs which have the Infinitive in *ére* long:—

* Note A p. 41.

avére, to have.	*potére*, to be able.
cadére, to fall.	*rimanére*, to remain.
calére, to care for.	*sapére*, to know.
dissuadére, to dissuade.	*sedére*, to sit.
dolére, to pain, ache.	*solére*, to be accustomed.
dovére, to owe, be obliged.	*tacére*, to be silent.
giacére, to lie down.	*tenére*, to hold, keep.
godére, to enjoy.	*temére*, to fear.
parére, to appear, seem.	*valére*, to be worth.
persuadére, to persuade.	*vedére*, to see.
piacére, to please, like.	*volére*, to be willing.

3. As the above verbs occur very frequently, both in speaking and writing, and, with the exception of *temére* and *godére* (which are conjugated like *crédere*), are all of them irregular, it is very necessary that the student should begin by learning these practically. We shall therefore give three exercises upon them, and afterwards proceed to explain the irregularities of the verbs in *ere* short.

I.—CONJUGATION OF IRREGULAR VERBS IN *ÉRE* (long).

[N.B.—We have chosen *potére*, *volére*, *dovére*, and *sapére* for the first Exercise, they being of greater importance than the other verbs in *ére* long.]

Potére, to be able.

Infinitive — *potére*, to be able.

Indicative Present.

Singular.	Plural.
pósso, I can, *or* am able.	*possiámo*, we can.
puói, thou canst.	*potéte*, you can.
può, he can.	*póssono*,[a] they can.

Indicative Imperfect ... *potéva*, I could, *or* was able.
  „   Perfect ...... *potéi*, I could.
  „   Future ...... *potró*,[b] I shall be able.

---

[a] Note *c*, page 32.

[b] The Future and Conditional of *potére* are contracted, in order that they may not be confounded with *poteró* and *poterei*, which are the Future and Conditional of *potare*, to prune. See Note *a*, p. 55.

Conditional—*potréi*, I should be able.

No Imperative Mood.

Subjunctive Present.

ch' io póssa,[a] that I may be able.	*che possiámo*, that we may be able.
che tu póssa, that thou &c.	*che possiáte*, that you &c.
ch' egli póssa, that he &c.	*che póssano*, that they &c.

Subjunctive Imperfect—*s' io potéssi*, if I might be able.

Present Participle $\left\{ \begin{array}{c} poténdo \\ poténte^b \end{array} \right\}$ being able.

Past Participle—*potúto*, been able.

COMPOUND TENSES.

Infinitive—*avere potúto*, to have been able.
    &c.   &c.   &c.

Obs.—The verb *ripotere*, to be able again, is conjugated like *potere*.

Volére, to be willing, to want, will, wish.

Infinitive—*volére*, to be willing.

Indicative Present.

Singular.	Plural.
vóglio or *vo'*, I will or am willing.	*vogliámo*, we are willing.
vuói, thou art willing.	*voléte*, you are willing.
vuóle, he is willing.	*vógliono*,[c] they are willing.

Imperfect—*voléva*, I was willing.

Perfect or Past.

vólli,[d] I was willing.	*volémmo*, we were willing.
volésti, thou wast willing.	*voléste*, you were willing.
vólle, he was willing.	*vóllero*, they were willing.

Future.

vorrò,[e] I shall be willing.	*vorrémo*, we shall be willing.
vorrái, thou wilt be willing.	*vorréte*, you will be willing.
vorrà, he will be willing.	*vorránno*, they will be willing.

---

[a] Note *a*, p. 33.   [b] *Potere* has also the form *possente*.
[c] Note *c*, p. 32.   [d] Obs. 3, p. 56.

[e] Verbs ending in the Infinitive in *lere* and *nere*, and the verb *venire*, to come, with its derivatives, take a double *r* throughout the Future and the Conditional; as, *volere*, to be willing, makes in the Future *vorrò* &c., and in the Conditional *vorrei* &c.; *tenere*, to hold, makes *terrò* &c., and *terrei* &c.; and *venire*, to come, makes *verrò* &c., and *verrei* &c. See Note *a*, p. 55.

Conditional.

vorréi, I should be willing.	*vorrémmo*, we should be willing.
vorrésti, thou wouldst be willing.	*vorréste*, you would be willing.
vorrébbe, he would be willing.	*vorrébbero*, they would be willing.

Imperative Mood.

No first person singular.	*vogliámo*, let us be willing.
vógli, be (thou) willing.	*vogliáte*, be (you) willing.
vóglia, let him be willing.	*vógliano*, let them be willing.

Subjunctive Present.

ch' io vóglia, that I may be wil-	*che vogliámo*, that we may be wil-
che tu vóglia, that thou &c. [ling.	*che vogliáte*, that you &c. [ling.
ch' egli vóglia, that he &c.	*che vógliano*, that they &c.

Subjunctive Imperfect—*s' io voléssi*, if I might be willing.

Present Participle $\left\{ \begin{array}{l} voléndo \\ volénte \end{array} \right\}$ being willing.

Past Participle—*voluto*, been willing.

COMPOUND TENSES.

Infinitive—*avere voluto*, to have been willing.
    &c.   &c.   &c.

OBS.—*Disvolere*, to refuse, to say no, and *rivolere*, to wish again, are conjugated like *volere*.

Dovére,[a] to owe, to be obliged (ought, must).

Infinitive—*dovére*, to owe.

Indicative Present.

Singular.	*Plural.*
dévo or *débbo*, I owe.	*dobbiámo*, we owe.
dévi, thou owest.	*dovéte*, you owe.
déve or *débbe*, he owes.	*dévono* or *débbono*, they owe.

Indicative Imperfect... *dovéva*, I owed.
       „   Perfect...... *dovéi* or *dovétti*[b], I did owe.
       „   Future...... *dovrò*, I shall owe.
           Conditional—*dovréi*, I should owe.

---

[a] *Dovere* = 'to owe,' in the sense of 'to be indebted,' and 'to be obliged,' when it denotes duty or necessity. *Dovere* may be used in all persons, instead of the impersonal verb *bisognare* = to be necessary.
[b] *Dovere* has two forms in the Perfect, like *credere*. See p. 32.

No Imperative Mood.

Subjunctive Present.

ch' io débba, that I may owe.   *che dobbiámo*, that we may owe.
che tu débba, that thou &c.   *che dobbiáte*, that you may owe.
ch' egli débba, that he &c.   *che débbano*, that they may owe.

Subjunctive Imperfect—*s' io dovéssi*, if I might owe.

Present Participle— $\begin{Bmatrix} dovéndo \\ dovénte \end{Bmatrix}$ owing.

Past Participle—*dovúto*, owed.

COMPOUND TENSES.

Infinitive—*avere dovuto*, to have owed.
&c.   &c.   &c.

N.B.—The verb *dovere* has, besides the forms above given,—

In the Indicative Present,

déggio,   *deggiámo*,
déi,
dée or *dé*,   *déggiono* or *déono* or *dénno*.

And in the Subjunctive Present,

ch' io déggia,
che tu déggia,
ch' egli déggia,   *che déggiano*.

OBS.—The verb *ridovere*, to be obliged again, is conjugated like *dovere*.

Sapére,[a] to know, to be acquainted with.[b]

Infinitive—*sapére*, to know.[c]

Indicative Present.

Singular.	Plural.
so, I know.	*sappiámo*, we know.
sái, thou knowest.	*sapéte*, you know.
sa, he knows.	*sánno*, they know.

---

[a] *Sapere* is conjugated like *avere*, the only change being the substitution of *s* for *h* and *p* for *b* and *v*.

[b] *Sapere* = 'to know' through the mind. When we wish to express 'to know' through the senses, we use *conoscere*. Thus we say, *conoscere una persona, una città, un fiore*, &c., to know a person, a city, a flower, &c.; and *sapere un verbo, una storiella, la lezione*, &c., to know a verb, a story, the lesson, &c.

[c] *Sapere* has often the meaning of *to be able*, in expressions like the following :—*Ella sa sonare*, she can play. *Egli non mi ha saputo dire niente*, he could not tell me anything. *Non vi saprei dire come fosse*, I could not possibly tell you how it was.

Indicative Imperfect—*sapéva*, I did know.

Perfect *or* Past.

séppi,[a] I knew.	*sapémmo*, we knew.
sapésti, thou knewest.	*sapéste*, you knew.
séppe, he knew.	*séppero*, they knew.

Future—*saprò*, I shall know.

Conditional—*sapréi*, I should know.

Imperative Mood.

No first person singular.	*sappiámo*, let us know.
sáppi, know (thou).	*sappiáte*, know (you).
sáppia, let him know.	*sáppiano*, let them know.

Subjunctive Present.

ch' io sáppia, that I may know.	*che sappiámo*, that we may know.
che tu sáppia, that thou &c.	*che sappiáte*, that you &c.
ch' egli sáppia, that he &c.	*che sáppiano*, that they &c.

Subjunctive Imperfect—*s' io sapéssi*, if I might know.

Present Participle—*sapéndo*,[b] knowing.
Past Participle—*sapúto*, known.

COMPOUND TENSES.

Infinitive—*avere sapúto*, to have known.
&c.   &c.   &c.

OBS.—*Risapere*, to come to know again, is conjugated like *sapere*.

PHRASES.

potere vedere, to be able to see.
volere bene ad uno, to be fond of a person.
si vuole[c] che la pace sia fatta, it is believed that peace is made.
ci vuole[d] tempo a fare una cosa, it requires time to do a thing.

VOCABULARY.

stella, star.	*prima che*, before.
a cagione, in consequence.	*da*, for.
alcuni, some.	*un ignorante*, an illiterate man.

READING EXERCISE.

1. Di giorno non si[e] possono vedere le stelle a cagione della luce del sole. 2. Io voglio bene a mia madre.

---

[a] Obs. 3, p. 56.   [b] No other form.
[c] *volere*, used impersonally with *si*, means 'to be believed'.
[d] *volere*, used impersonally with *ci*, means 'to require'.
[e] Obs. 3, p. 49.

3. Si* vuole che la pace sia fatta. 4. Ci vorranno*
alcuni mesi prima ch'*io possa parlare italiano. 5. Che
vorreste* da colazione ?   6. Io non devo* niente a mio
fratello. 7. Si deve* studiare* per imparare. 8. Gl' igno-
ranti non sanno* scrivere.

VOCABULARY.

to make one's self understood,
  farsi capire.
to forget, *dimenticare.*
to be able (can), *potere.*
to wish, *volere.*
to be obliged (must), *dovere.*
to smell, *sapere.*

to have a good smell, *sapere di
  buono.*
to have no smell, *non sapere di
  niente.*
to be very tired, *non ne potere più.*
to mean, *voler dire.*

TRANSLATION EXERCISE.

1. Can you speak Italian ?   2. I (can) speak it* a
   [Do you speak]   *lo   un*

little.   3.   Once   I could make* myself understood*
poco   Una volta

---

* Note *c*, p. 69.   b Note *d*, p. 69.
  c The following pronouns and conjunctions require the Subjunctive after them:—

ansi che ⎫	*purchè* ⎫
avanti che ⎪	*qualora* ⎬ providing.
dinanzi che ⎬ before.	*solo che* ⎭
innanzi che ⎪	*per tema che*, for fear that.
davanti che ⎪	*ove* ⎫
prima che ⎭	*dove* ⎬ if.
acciochè ⎫	*quando* ⎭
affinchè ⎬ in order that.	*come* ⎰ as if.
chè or *perchè* ⎭	*quasi* ⎱
chiunque, whoever.	*senza che*, without, unless.
qualunque, whatever.	*ovunque*, wherever.
ogniqualvolta, whenever.	*ancorchè*, although.
dato che ⎫	*benchè* ⎫
caso che ⎪	*sebbene* ⎪
supposto che ⎬ admitting that.	*quantunque* ⎬ though, although.
posto che ⎭	*tuttochè* ⎭
se mai ⎰ if ever.	*come che*, however.
se pure ⎱	*avvegnachè*, inasmuch as.

  d *Volere* alone, in the sense of 'to wish,' is rendered in English by
the verb 'to have' with 'will' or 'would.'   e Note *a*, p. 67.
  f The verb that follows *potere, volere, dovere, fare*, and *sapere*,
when signifying 'to be able,' is almost always in the Infinitive.
See also Note *e*, p. 53.
  g Note *c*, p. 68.   h Note *a* (1), p. 43.

in Italian, but now I have forgotten that beautiful
 quella bella

language.   4. I am studying – Italian, and hope
 l'

  to be able   to speak it* again.   5. Do you know[b]
[I shall be able]   *lo ancora*

Mr.[c] A. by reputation or by sight ?   6. I know him*
 di fama   *di vista*

personally.   7. Do you know[b] the verbs by heart ?
di persona   *i verbi a mente*

8. I do not know them* now, but I shall know them*
 li

– next[2] week[1].   9. Whoever wishes[d] to speak   a
la   *Chiunque*   *una*

language   'fluently,   must[e] have the verbs at (his)
 correntemente   [know]   *a*

fingers' ends.   10. Has[f] the[2] camelia[3] a good smell[1]?
mena dito   *la*

11. It has no smell.   12. I have been to the end of the
 [in] *fondo delle*

Cascine[g], and I am very tired.   13. What does *specchio*
 Che

mean[h] ?   14. It means *looking-glass*.

QUESTIONS.

Perchè di giorno non si possono vedere le stelle ? 1*.—
Volete bene a vostra madre ? 2*.—Che bisogna fare per
imparare la lingua italiana ? 9*.—Quanto ci vorrà avanti
che possiate parlarla ? 4*.—Quanto vi devo ? 6*.—Può
vostra zia farsi capire in italiano ? 3.—Conoscete la Signora B. di persona o di fama ? 5.—Avete dimenticato i
verbi ? 8.—Che si deve fare per parlare correntemente
una lingua? 9.—Che vuol[h] dire, non ne posso più ? 12 & 14.

---

* Note *a* (1), p. 43.   [b] Note *b*, p. 68.   [c] Note *f*, p. 29.
[d] Note *c*, p. 70.   [e] 3rd pers. sing. Pres. Ind. of *dovere*.
[f] 3rd pers. sing. Pres. Ind. of *sapere*.
[g] *Le Cascine* is a fashionable and picturesque walk near Florence.
[h] All verbs which, in the 3rd pers. sing. Pres. Ind., end in *le, ne,*
or *re*, may drop their final vowel *e*.

Giacére, to lie down. ⎫
Piacére, to please.* ⎬ These three verbs are
Tacére, to be silent. ⎭ conjugated alike.

Indicative Present.

Singular.	*Plural.*
giáccio[b], I lie down.	*giacciámo*, we lie down.
giáci, thou liest down.	*giacéte*, you lie down.
giáce, he lies down.	*giácciono*, they lie down.

Imperfect—*giacéva*, I lay down.

Perfect *or* Past.

giácqui, I did lie down.	*giacémmo*, we did lie down.
giacésti, thou didst lie down.	*giacéste*, you did lie down.
giácque, he did lie down.	*giácquero*, they did lie down.

Future—*giacerò*, I shall lie down.

Conditional—*giaceréi*, I should lie down.

Imperative Mood.

No first person singular.	*giacciámo*, let us lie down.
giáci, lie (thou) down.	*giacéte*, lie (you) down.
giáccia, let him lie down.	*giácciano*, let them lie down.

Subjunctive Present.

ch'io giáccia, that I may lie down.	*che giacciámo*, that we may lie
che tu giáccia, that thou &c.	*che giacciáte*, that you &c. [down.
ch' egli giáccia, that he &c.	*che giácciano*, that they &c.

Subjunctive Imperfect—*s'io giacéssi*, if I might lie down.

Present Participle { *giacéndo* ⎱ lying down.
                    giacénte ⎰

Past Participle—*giaciúto*, lain down.

---

* *Piacere* and *dispiacere*, used with a dative of the object, are Englished by 'to like,' 'to be fond of,' &c., and, 'to dislike,' 'to be sorry,' &c., as,

Mi piace la musica ⎱ I like music.
To me pleases (the) music ⎰

Vi piacciono i fiori? ⎱ Are you fond of flowers?
To you please (the) flowers? ⎰

Mi dispiace il rumore ⎱ I dislike noise.
To me displeases noise ⎰

Mi dispiace di disturbarvi ⎱ I am sorry to trouble you.
It displeases me to trouble you ⎰

[b] *Tacere* has only one *c* in the 1st pers. sing. Pres. Ind., where it might otherwise be mistaken for *taccio*, from the verb *tacciare*, to accuse.

Compound Tenses.

Infinitive—*avere giaciuto*, to have lain down.

&c.   &c.   &c.

Obs.—The verbs *compiacere*, to please, *dispiacere*, to displease, *ripiacere*, to please again, and *soggiacere*, to succumb, are conjugated like *giacere*.

Cadére, to fall, to drop.

Infinitive—*cadére*, to fall.

Indicative Present.

Singular.	*Plural.*
cáddo or *cággio*, I fall.	*cadiámo* or *caggiámo*, we fall.
cádi, thou fallest.	*cadéte*, you fall.
cáde, he falls.	*cádono* or *cággiono*, they fall.

Imperfect—*cadéva*, I was falling.

Perfect *or* Past.

cáddi, I did fall, *or* I fell.	*cadémmo*, we did fall.
cadésti, thou didst fall.	*cadéste*, you did fall.
cádde, he did fall.	*cáddero*, they did fall.

Future—*cadrò* or *caderò*, I shall fall.

Conditional—*cadréi* or *caderéi*, I should fall.

Imperative Mood.

No first person singular.	*cadiámo* or *caggiámo*, let us fall.
cádi, fall (thou).	*cadéte*, fall (you).
cáda or *cággia*, let him fall.	*cádano* or *cággiano*, let them fall.

Subjunctive Present.

ch' io cáda or *cággia*, that I may [fall.		*che cadiámo* or *caggiámo*, that we [may fall.
che tu cáda	„ that thou &c.	*che cadiáte*, that you &c.
ch' egli cáda	„ that he &c.	*che cádano* or *cággiano*, that &c.

Subjunctive Imperfect—*s' io cadéssi*, if I might fall.

Present Participle $\begin{Bmatrix} \text{\textit{cadéndo}} \\ \text{\textit{cadénte}} \end{Bmatrix}$ falling.

Past Participle—*cadúto*, fallen.

Compound Tenses.

Infinitive—*essere*[a] *caduto*, to have fallen.

&c.   &c.   &c.

Obs.—*Accadere*, to happen, *decadere* or *scadere*, to fall off, *ri-*

---

[a] Obs. 3, p. 51.

E

cadere, to fall again, and other compounds of *cadere*, are conjugated in the same way; but in the Present Indicative, the Imperative, and the Present Subjunctive, they generally take only the regular form.

Dissuadére, to dissuade.
Persuadére, to persuade.

These two verbs are inflected alike, and are only irregular in the Perfect and Past Participle, the other moods and tenses being inflected like *credere*.[a]

Perfect *or* Past.

dissuási, I dissuaded.   *dissuadémmo*, we dissuaded.
dissuadésti, thou dissuadedst.   *dissuadéste*, you dissuaded.
dissuáse, he dissuaded.   *dissuásero*, they dissuaded.

Past Participle—*dissuáso*, dissuaded.

COMPOUND TENSES.

Infinitive—*avere dissuaso*, to have dissuaded.
   &c.   &c.   &c.

Sedére, to sit.

Indicative Present.

Singular.	Plural.
siédo or *séggo*, I sit.	*sediámo* or *seggiámo*, we sit.
siédi, thou sittest.	*sedéte*, you sit.
siéde, he sits.	*siédono* or *séggono*, they sit.

Indicative Imperfect ... *sedéva*, I was sitting.
     „   Perfect ...... *sedéi* or *sedétti*, I did sit, *or* I sat.
     „   Future ...... *sederò*, I shall sit.

Conditional—*sederéi*, I should sit.

Imperative Mood.

No first person singular.	*sediámo* or *seggiámo*, let us sit.
siédi, sit (thou).	*sedéte*, sit (you).
siéda or *ségga*, let him sit.	*siédano* or *séggano*, let them sit.

Subjunctive Present.

ch' io siéda or *ségga*, that I may sit.	*che sediámo* or *seggiámo*, that we
che tu siéda „ that thou &c.	*che sediáte*, that &c. [may sit.
ch' egli siéda „ that he &c.	*che siédano* or *séggano*, that &c.

Subjunctive Imperfect—*s' io sedéssi*, if I might sit.

---

[a] Obs. 2, p. 55.

Present Participle $\begin{Bmatrix} sedéndo \\ sedénte \end{Bmatrix}$ sitting.

Past Participle—*sedúto*, seated.

COMPOUND TENSES.

Infinitive—*essere seduto*, to be seated.

&c.   &c.   &c.

OBS.—*Risedere*, to reside, *presedere*, to preside, *possedere*, to possess, *soprassedere*, to temporize, are conjugated like *sedere*.

Vedére, to see.

Infinitive—*vedére*, to see.

Indicative Present.

Singular.	Plural.
védo, véggo, or *véggio,* I see.	*vediámo* or *veggiámo,* we see.
védi, thou seest.	*vedéte,* you see.
véde, he sees.	*védono, véggono,* or *véggiono,* they [see.

Imperfect—*vedéva,* I saw.

Perfect *or* Past.

vídi, I saw, *or* did see.	*vedémmo,* we saw.
vedésti, thou sawest.	*vedéste,* you saw.
víde, he saw.	*vídero,* they saw.

Future—*vedrò,* I shall see.

Conditional—*vedréi,* I should see.

Imperative Mood.

No first person singular.	*vediámo* or *veggiámo,* let us see.
védi, see (thou).	*vedéte,* see (you).
véda, végga, or *véggia,* let him see.	*védano, véggano,* or *véggiano,* let [them see.

Subjunctive Present.

ch' io véda, végga, or *véggia,* that [I may see.	*che vediámo* or *veggiámo,* that we [may see.
che tu véda, végga, or *véggia,* that [thou mayest see.	*che vediáte* or *veggiáte,* that you [may see.
ch' egli véda, végga, or *véggia,* that [he may see.	*che védano, véggano,* or *véggiano,* [that they may see.

Subjunctive Imperfect—*s' io vedéssi,* if I might see.

Present Participle $\begin{Bmatrix} vedéndo \\ veggéndo \\ veggénte \end{Bmatrix}$ seeing.

Past Participle—*vedúto* or *vísto,* seen.

E 2

COMPOUND TENSES.

Infinitive—*avere veduto*, to have seen.
&c. &c. &c.

Obs.—All the compound derivatives of *vedere*—as, *antivedere* or *prevedere*, to foresee *avvedere*, to perceive, *divedere*, to demonstrate, *provvedere*, to provide, *ravvedere*, to repent, *rivedere*, to see again, *travedere*, to see indistinctly, &c.—are conjugated in the same way. But *antivedere*, *divedere*, *ravvedere*, and *travvedere*, have only the Past Participle in *uto ;* while *divedere*, *prevedere*, *provvedere*, and *travvedere* are not contracted in the Future and Conditional: *divederò*, *divederei*, not *divedrò*, &c.

PHRASES.

giacere in letto, to lie in bed.
soggiacere a disgrazie, to succumb to misfortunes.
compiacersi di fare una cosa, to be pleased to do a thing.
bacchiare le noci, to bring down nuts with a stick.
cadere a terra, to fall to the ground.
persuadere uno a tacere, to persuade a person to be silent.
sedere all' ombra, to sit in the shade.
possedere molto, to have much property.
prevedere una cosa, to foresee a thing.
provvedere quanto occorre, to provide for contingencies.
rivedersi, to see one another again.

VOCABULARY.

tante, so many.
rispondere, to answer.
senza, without.
indugio, delay.
agricoltore, husbandman.

sovente, often.
albero, tree.
astronomo, astronomer.
ecclissi (m. & f.), eclipse.

READING EXERCISE.

1. Quando sono ammalato, io giaccio in letto. 2. Eglino soggiacquero[a] a tante disgrazie. 3. Ella si compiacque di[b] rispondere senza indugio alla mia lettera. 4. Le

---

[a] See Obs., p. 73.
[b] Verbs signifying *remembering*, as *ricordarsi*, to remember; *forgetting*, as *dimenticarsi*, to forget; *pleasing*, as *piacere*, to please; *displeasing*, as *dispiacere*, to displease; *rejoicing*, as *rallegrarsi*, to rejoice; *grieving*, as *rammaricarsi*, to grieve; *denying*, as *negare*, to deny; *permitting*, as *permettere*, to allow; *prohibiting*, as *proibire*, to forbid; *telling*, as *dire*, to tell; *declaring*, as *dichiarare*, to declare; *offering*, as *offrire*, to offer; *supposing*, as *supporre*, to suppose; *suspecting*, as *sospettare*, to suspect; *fearing*, as *temere*, to fear; *commanding*, as *comandare*, to order; *asking*, as *domandare*, to ask;

noci, non essendo state bacchiate dall' agricoltore, cad-
dero a terra. 5. Egli m'ha persuaso a tacere. 6. D'estate
siedo sovente all' ombra degli alberi. 7. Non credo
ch' egli possegga molto. 8. Gli astronomi previdero
l' ora dell' eclissi. 9. Io ho provvisto quanto occorre.
10. Ci* rivedremo domani.

Vocabulary.

to sit, be seated, *sedere.*	to burn down the house, *abbru-*
to seat oneself, sit down, *sedersi.*	*ciare la casa.*
to lie, *giacere.*	to be sorry, *dispiacere.*
to see, *vedere.*	to hear, *sentire.*
to happen, *accadere* (impers.)	to depart, *partire.*
	to see again, *rivedere.*

Translation Exercise.

1. What-a-number-of people there are in (the) gar-
   Quanta *gente* [there is[b]]

den! Some are sitting down, and many are lying
   Alcuni[c] *molti*

on the grass. 2. Let us sit down – also. 3. How
   sull' erba *noi pure*

did you like[d] – your journey – last[2] autumn[1] ?
   il vostro viaggio l' passato

4. I liked it very much. 5. When did you see[e] your
   moltissimo

brother ? 6. I saw[f] him[g] yesterday ; he had
   [to him[g] happened]

---

entreating, as *supplicare,* to supplicate ; *doubting,* as *dubitare,* to
doubt ; *promising,* as *promettere,* to promise ; *begging,* as *pregare,* to
pray ; *finishing,* as *finire,* to finish ; *proposing,* as *proporre,* to pro-
pose, and verbs implying 'desire' or 'aversion,' as *bramare,* to desire,
and *abborrire,* to abhor, require the preposition *di,* of, before the
Infinitive coming after them. (See also Note *e,* p. 53, and Note *c,*
p. 62.)

[a] Obs., p. 46.
[b] Collective nouns require the verb 'to be' in the singular number.
[c] Indef. Pron., p. 10. [d] Note *a,* p. 72. [e] Note *h,* p. 15.
[f] Note *f,* p. 15. [g] Note *a,* p. 43, and Note *f,* p. 15.

a great misfortune last Monday, a   fire
una gran   disgrazia   *un incendio* [to him[a]

burnt his house down.   7. I am sorry[b] to hear it.
has burnt down the house]

8. Who[c] is that officer who[d] sits near — Countess B.?
         quel militare   *vicino alla Contessa*

9. It is her uncle – Admiral B.; he arrived – last
      suo   *l' Ammiraglio*

week from – India, I saw him at the hotel yester-
      dall'   *all' albergo*

day.   10. Now I must   go.   Good-bye, Marquis.
                 [depart]   *Addio   Marchese*

11. Good-bye, Count, (I hope) soon[3] to[1] see you again[2].
                 presto a

QUESTIONS.

Vi piace più la lingua italiana o la francese?—Chi vi siede vicino a pranzo? 8.—Quando avete visto vostra zia? 9.— Perchè tacque vostro padre tutto il giorno ieri?— Qual paese vi piacerebbe di rivedere? 11.— Quando vi compiacerete di rispondere alla lettera che avete ricevuta? 3*.— Che cosa preveggono gli astronomi? 8*.—Perchè sono cadute a terra le noci? 4*.— Dove vi piace sedere d' estate? 6*.—Quando ci rivedremo? 10*.

Paróre, to appear, seem.

Infinitive—*paróre*, to seem.

Indicative Present.

Singular.	*Plural.*
páio, I seem.	*pariámo*, we seem.
pári, thou seemest.	*paréte*, you seem.
páre, he seems.	*páiono*, they seem.

Imperfect—*paréva*, I seemed.

---

[a] Note *a*, p. 43, and Note *h*, p. 15.
[b] Note *a*, p. 72, and Note *b*, p. 76.
[c] Inter. Pron., p. 9.   [d] Relative Pron., p. 9.

Perfect *or* Past.

párvi,[a] I did seem, *or* I seemed.	*parémmo*, we did seem.
parésti, thou didst seem.	*paréste*, you did seem.
párve, he did seem.	*párvero*, they did seem.

Future—*parrò*,[b] I shall seem.

Conditional—*parréi*, I should seem.

Imperative Mood.

No first person singular.	*pariámo*, let us seem.
pári, seem (thou).	*paréte*, seem (you).
páia, let him seem.	*páiano*, let them seem.

Subjunctive Present.

ch' io páia, that I may seem.	*che pariámo*, that we may seem.
che tu páia, thou thou &c.	*che paiáte*, that you may seem.
ch' egli páia, that he &c.	*che páiano*, that they may seem.

Subjunctive Imperfect—*s' io paréssi*, if I might seem.

Present Participle—*paréndo*,[c] seeming.
Past Participle—*párso* or *parúto*, seemed.

Compound Tenses.

Infinitive—*essere parso*, to have seemed.
&c.   &c.   &c.

Obs.—*Disparere*, to contest, a verb seldom used, is conjugated like *parere*.[d]

Dolére or *dolérsi*, to grieve, complain.

Infinitive—*dolérsi*,[e] to grieve.

Indicative Present.

Singular.	*Plural.*
mi dólgo or *dóglio*, I grieve.	*ci dogliámo*, we grieve.
ti duóli, thou grievest.	*vi doléte*, you grieve.
si duóle, he grieves.	*si dólgono* or *dógliono*, they &c.

---

[a] Obs. 3, p. 56.

[b] The Future and Conditional of *parere* are contracted in order that they may not be confounded with *parerò*, &c. and *parerei*, &c., the Future and Conditional of *parare*, to adorn, to ward off.

[c] Note *e*, p. 26.

[d] *Parere*, used impersonally with dat. pers. pron., means 'to think, believe'; as, *Mi pare che tu sia un po' fioco* (Pulci), I think thy voice is a little weak.

[e] *Dolere*, to complain, is always conjugated in the reflective way with *mi, ti, si, ci, vi*. In the signification of 'to grieve,' 'to ache,' 'to be ill,' *dolere* takes a dative of the object; as, *mi duole il capo*, I have the headache; *mi dolgono i denti*, I have the toothache; *mi duole di non poter rivedervi*, I am sorry not to be able to see you again. (See Obs. (2.), p. 51.)

Imperfect—*mi doléva*, I grieved.

Perfect *or* Past.

mi dólsi, I did grieve.	*ci dolémmo*, we did grieve.
ti dolésti, thou didst grieve.	*vi doléste*, you did grieve.
si dólse, he did grieve.	*si dólsero*, they did grieve.

Future—*mi dorrò*,[a] I shall grieve.

Conditional—*mi dorréi*, I should grieve.

Imperative Mood.

No first person singular.	*dogliámoci*, let us grieve.
duóliti, grieve (thou).	*dolétevi*, grieve (you).
si dólga or *dóglia*, let him grieve.	*si dólgano* or *dógliano*, let them [grieve.

Subjunctive Present.

ch' io mi dólga or *dóglia*, that I [may grieve.	*che ci dogliámo*, that we &c.
che tu ti dólga or *dóglia*, that &c.	*che vi dogliáte*, that you &c.
ch' egli si dólga or *dóglia*, that &c.	*che si dólgano* or *dógliano*, that [they may grieve.

Subjunctive Imperfect—*s' io mi doléssi*, if I might grieve.

Present Participle $\left\{ \begin{array}{l} doléndosi \\ doléntesi \end{array} \right\}$ feeling.

Past Participle—*dolútosi*, grieved.

COMPOUND TENSES.

Infinitive—*essersi doluto*, to have grieved.

Indicative Present—*mi sono doluto* or *doluta*, I have grieved.
&c.   &c.   &c.

OBS.—*Condolere*, to condole, *ridolersi*, to complain again, and other derivatives of *dolere*, are conjugated in the same way.

Valére, to be worth, to cost.

Infinitive—*valére*, to be worth.

Indicative Present.

Singular.	Plural.
válgo or *váglio*, I am worth.	*vagliámo*, we are worth.
váli, thou art worth.	*valéte*, you are worth.
vále, he is worth.	*válgono* or *vágliono*, they are &c.

Imperfect—*valéva*, I was worth.

---

[a] Note *e*, p. 66.

Perfect *or* Past.

válsi, I was worth.	*valémmo*, we were worth.
valésti, thou wast worth.	*valéste*, you were worth.
válse, he was worth.	*válsero*, they were worth.

Future—*varrò*, I shall be worth.

Conditional—*varréi*, I should be worth.

Imperative Mood.

No first person singular	*vagliámo*, let us be worth.
váli, be (thou) worth.	*valéte*, be (you) worth.
válga or *váglia*, let him be worth.	*válgano* or *vágliano*, let them &c.

Subjunctive Present.

ch' io válga or *váglia*, that I may [be worth.	*che vagliámo*, that we may be [worth.
che tu válga „ that thou &c.	*che vagliáte*, that you &c.
ch' egli válga „ that he &c.	*che válgano* or *vágliano*, that &c.

Subjunctive Imperfect—*s' io valéssi*, if I might be worth.

Present Participle— $\begin{cases} valéndo \\ valénte \end{cases}$ being worth.

Past Participle—*válso* or *valúto*, been worth.

COMPOUND TENSES.

Infinitive—*avere valso*, to have been worth.
&c.   &c.   &c.

OBS.—Conjugate in the same way *prevalere*, to prevail, *invalere*, to obtain, and all compounds of *valere*.[a]

Rimanére, to remain, stay.

Infinitive—*rimanére*, to remain.

Indicative Present.

Singular.	*Plural.*
rimángo, I remain.	*rimaniámo*, we remain.
rimáni, thou remainest.	*rimanéte*, you remain.
rimáne, he remains.	*rimángono*, they remain.

Imperfect—*rimanéva*, I was remaining.

---

[a] *Valersi di qualche cosa*, means to avail one's self of anything, to make use of it ; as *valetevi del cavallo* (Gozzi), make use of the horse.

Perfect *or* Past.

rimási, I did remain.
rimanésti, thou didst remain.
rimáse, he did remain.

rimanémmo, we did remain.
rimanéste, you did remain.
rimásero, they did remain.

Future—*rimarrò,*[a] I shall remain.

Conditional—*rimarréi,* I should remain.

Imperative Mood.

No first person singular.
rimáni, remain (thou).
rimánga, let him remain.

rimaniámo, let us remain.
rimanéte, remain (you).
rimángano, let them remain.

Subjunctive Present.

ch' io rimánga, that I may re-
[main.
che tu rimánga, that thou &c.
ch' egli rimánga, that he &c.

che rimaniámo, that we may re-
[main.
che rimaniáte, that you &c.
che rimángano, that they &c.

Subjunctive Imperfect—*s' io rimanéssi,* if I might remain.

Present Participle $\begin{cases} rimanéndo \\ rimanénte \end{cases}$ remaining.

Past Participle—*rimáso* or *rimásto,* remained.

COMPOUND TENSES.

Infinitive—*essere rimaso,* to have remained.

Indicative Present—*sono rimaso* or *rimasa,* I have remained.
&c. &c. &c.

OBS.—*Permanere,* to persevere, to last, which is seldom used, is conjugated like *rimanere.*[b]

Tenére, to hold, keep.

Infinitive—*tenére,* to hold.

Indicative Present.

Singular.
téngo, I hold.
tiéni, thou holdest.
tiéne, he holds.

Plural.
teniámo, we hold.
tenéte, you hold.
téngono, they hold.

Imperfect—*tenéva,* I was holding.

---

[a] Note *e,* p. 66.
[b] The verbs *rimanere* and *restare,* to remain, are sometimes used in the signification of *to be,* and are then followed by a Past Participle, which must agree with the subject of the verb; as, *egli rimase* (=*fu*) *maravigliato,* he was astonished.

Perfect *or* Past.

ténni, I held.   *tenémmo*, we held.
tenésti, thou heldest.   *tenéste*, you held.
ténne, he held.   *ténnero*, they held.

Future—*terrò*, I shall hold.

Conditional—*terréi*, I should hold.

Imperative Mood.

No first person singular.   *tenidmo*, let us hold.
tiéni, hold (thou).   *tenéte*, hold (you).
ténga, let him hold.   *téngano*, let them hold.

Subjunctive Present.

ch' io ténga, that I may hold.   *che teniámo*, that we may hold.
che tu ténga, that thou &c.   *che teniáte*, that you may hold.
ch' egli ténga, that he &c.   *che téngano*, that they may hold.

Subjunctive Imperfect—*s' io tenéssi*, if I might hold.

$$\text{Present Participle} \begin{cases} tenéndo \\ tenénte \end{cases} \text{holding.}$$

Past Participle—*tenúto*, held.

Compound Tenses.

Infinitive—*avere tenuto*, to have held.
&c.   &c.   &c.

Obs.—All compounds of *tenere*, as *appartenere*, to belong, *attenere*, to reach, &c., are conjugated like *tenere*.[*]

———

N.B.—The other irregular verbs in *ére* long are *avere*, to have, *calere*, to care for, and *solere*, to be accustomed. *Avere* has already been given, and its compound *riavere*, to have back, is conjugated like it. *Calere* and *solere* are wanting in certain tenses, and will be found among the Defective Verbs.

Phrases.

parere forestiero, to seem (look like) a foreigner.
dolersi della sua sorte, to bewail one's lot.
condolersi con un amico delle sue sventure, to condole with a friend on his misfortunes.
sostenere le sue perdite con fermezza, to bear one's losses with firmness.

———

[*] *Tenere* and *avere*, followed by the preposition *per*, mean ' to consider,' as, *Tenete il Signor D. per uomo dotto?* Do you consider Mr. D. a learned man?

mantenere la parola, to keep one's word.
ottenere più colle buone che colle cattive, to obtain more with mildness
    than with severity.
rimanere colla lettura, or } to leave off reading.
tralasciare di leggere }

VOCABULARY.

signore, gentleman.
assai, much.
lira italiana, Italian *lira.*

lira sterlina, a pound sterling.
pagina, page.

READING EXERCISE.

1. Quei[a] Signori mi paiono forestieri.   2. Io non mi dolgo mai[b] della mia sorte.   3. Gli duole[c] assai di non poter rivedervi più spesso.   4. Ieri vidi l' amico mio, e mi condolsi[d] seco[e] delle sue sventure.   5. Venti cinque lire italiane equivalgono[f] ad una lira sterlina.   6. Siete[g] rimasto in campagna un pezzo ?   7. Egli sostenne le sue perdite con molta fermezza.   8. Spero che manterrete[h] la parola.   9. S'[i] otterrebbe più colle buone che colle cattive.   10. Dove siamo rimasti[g] colla lettura ?   11. Abbiamo tralasciato di leggere alla pagina tre.

VOCABULARY.

to think (be of opinion), *parere*
    (impers.)
to be worth, *valere.*
turn, *giro.*
to ache, pain, *dolere.*
to seem, *parere* (impers.)
regimen, *igiene* (f.)
to keep (preserve), *mantenere.*
to take care of a thing, *tenere*
    conto di una cosa.

to remain, *rimanere.*
to stay (in one place), *trattenersi* (refl.)
to be obliged, *dovere.*
dog, *cane* (m.)
the means, *i mezzi.*
to belong, *appartenere.*
to keep, *tenere.*
baptism, *battesimo.*

TRANSLATION EXERCISE.

1. What do you think[j] of these singers ?   2. They
        di questi cantanti

are not worth a straw.   3. Let us take a stroll
     un' acca (lit. 'h')   [Let us make a turn]

---

[a] See Dem. Pron., p. 9.   [b] Note *e*, p. 22.
[c] Note *e*, p. 79, and Note *a*, p. 43.   [d] Obs., p. 80.
[e] *Meco, teco, seco,* are compound words for *con me,* with me, *con te,* with thee, and *con sè,* with him, her, it, them.
[f] Obs., p. 81.   [g] Obs. 3, p. 51.   [h] Note *e*, p. 66.
[i] Obs. 3, p. 49, and Note *a* (3), p. 43.   [j] Note *d*, p. 79.

through the garden;   I am not   well.   4. What is
    pel   *giardino* [I do not stand[a]]

the matter with you ?   Are you in pain ?   5. I have
             [What pains you[b] ?]   [To me

the tooth-ache.   6. I never have the tooth-ache.   7. You
ache the teeth.]

seem[c] never[d] to have[e] anything-the-matter-with-you.
                          [nothing]

8. My dear friend, – good regimen keeps – man
Mio caro amico la buona   *l' uomo*

in-good-health.   9. For this (reason) I also take care
 sano   *questo*   *io anche*

of –   myself.   10. Did you remain[f] in the country a
della [my health]

long time ?   11. I remained[g] there[i] two months, and I
                           vi

should have stayed[g] there[i] longer, had I[g] not been
               vi   *di più*

obliged[h] to return[i] to town on some important[2]
             in   *per qualche importante*

business[1].   12. Is this[3] dog[8] yours[1] ?   13. No, I do
affare   *questo*   *vostro*

not keep dogs, because   I cannot afford it.
                   [I have not of it[j] the means]

14. To whom does it belong, then?   15. It belongs to
   chi   *dunque*

Mr. D., the gentleman who yesterday stood godfather to
     il   *Signore*   *che*   [held at baptism]

my son.

---

[a] When the words *non*, no or not, *in*, in, *con*, with, *per*, for,
are followed by a word beginning with *s* followed by a consonant,
as *stare*, to stand, *strada*, road, &c., an *i* is generally prefixed to the
second word; as, *Non istò bene*, I am not well. (See N.B., p. 61.)

[b] Note *e*, p. 79.   [c] Note *d*, p. 79.   [d] Note *e*, p. 22.
[e] Note *b*, p. 34.   [f] Note *h*, p. 15, and Obs. 3, p. 51.
[g] Imp. of Subj. (See Obs. 3, p. 51.)   [h] Obs. 5, p. 52.
[i] Note *e*, p. 53.   [j] Note *a*, p. 43.

QUESTIONS.

A quante lire sterline equivalgono venti cinque lire italiane? 5*.—Di che vi dolete? 2*.—Credete che generalmente s' ottenga più colle buone o colle cattive? 9*.—Quando avete visto l'amico vostro? 4*.—Che vi duole? 4.—Che cosa mantiene l'uomo sano? 8.—Tiene vostra sorella conto dei suoi libri? 9.—Siete rimasto un pezzo in campagna? 11.—A chi appartengono le cose che sono in questa stanza? 15.—Quando si è data la parola di fare una cosa, che bisogna anche fare? 8*.

IRREGULAR VERBS IN *ERE* (*short*)ᵃ.

OBSERVATIONS.

1. The only verbs in *ere* short, which are conjugated entirely like *credere*, are

battere, to beat,	*ricevere*, to receive,
cedere,ᵇ to yield,	*riflettere*,ᵉ to reflect, think,
fremere, to fret,	*ripetere*, to repeat,
gemere, to groan,	*solvere*, to solve,
mescere,ᶜ to mix,	*splendere*, to shine,
mietere, to reap,	*stridere*, to shriek,
pascere, to feed,	*tessere*, to weave,
pendere, to hang,	*tondere*, to shear,
premere,ᵈ to press,	*vendere*, to sell,
prescindere, to prescind,	

with the derivatives of *battere*, *pendere*, *splendère*, *tessere*, and *vendere*; as, *combattere*, to fight, *dipendere*, to depend, &c.

2. Of all the other verbs ending in *ere* short, a few are

ᵃ Obs. 1, p. 64.

ᵇ *Cedere* has, in poetry, the Perfect *cessi;* and some of its derivatives, as *concedere*, to grant, &c., have also other forms, which will be given with the irregular verbs.

ᶜ *Mescere* has, in the Past Participle, two forms, *misto* and *mesciuto*.

ᵈ *Premere* signifies also 'to be anxious,' 'to have at heart'; but then is only used in the 3rd person with the dative of the subject; as, *Mi preme di finire quest' opera*, I am anxious to finish this work.

ᵉ The verb *riflettere*, in the sense of 'to reflect light,' has in the Perfect *riflessi*, and in the Past Participle *riflesso*.

irregular in the Present and Perfect of the Indicative, Imperative, Present Subjunctive, and in the Past Participle ; some have only one irregular form in three persons of the Perfect and in the Past Participle, while others have two forms in either or both the Perfect and Past Participle, one form being irregular and another generally regular. (See Obs. 2, p. 55.)

———

MODELS OF CONJUGATION OF VERBS IN *ERE* (*short*) IRREGULAR IN THE PRESENT AND PERFECT OF THE INDICATIVE, IMPERATIVE, AND PRESENT SUBJUNCTIVE, AS WELL AS IN THE PAST PARTICIPLE.

Addúrre (contracted from *adducere*), to bring.

Infinitive—*addúrre*, to bring.

Indicative Present.

Singular.	Plural.
addúco,ᵃ I bring.	*adduciámo*, we bring.
addúci, thou bringest.	*adducéte*, you bring.
addúce, he brings.	*addúcono*, they bring.

Imperfect—*adducéva*, I was bringing.

Perfect or Past.

addússi, I brought.	*adducémmo*, we brought.
adducésti, thou broughtest.	*adducéste*, you brought.
addússe, he brought.	*addússero*, they brought.

Future—*addurrò*,ᵇ I shall bring.

Conditional—*addurréi*, I should bring.

Imperative Mood.

No first person singular.	*adduciámo*, let us bring.
addúci, bring (thou).	*adducéte*, bring (you).
addúca, let him bring.	*addúcano*, let them bring.

———

ᵃ All verbs ending in *urre* are conjugated in the Present and Imperfect Indicative, Imperative, and Present and Imperfect Subjunctive, as well as in the regular persons of the Perfect, and in the Present Participle, according to the obsolete termination *ucere*.

ᵇ Any contraction in the Infinitive always runs through the Future and the Conditional ; thus, *addurre* makes in the Future *addurrò, addurrai*, &c.; and so with all other verbs in *urre*.

Subjunctive Present.

ch' io addúca, that I may bring.   *che adduciámo,* that we may &c.
che tu addúca, that thou &c.   *che adduciáte,* that you &c.
ch' egli addúca, that he &c.   *che addúcano,* that they &c.

Subjunctive Imperfect—*s' io adducéssi,* if I might bring.

Present Participle $\begin{Bmatrix} adducéndo \\ adducénte \end{Bmatrix}$ bringing.

Past Participle—*addótto,* brought.

COMPOUND TENSES.

Infinitive—*avere addotto,* to have brought.
    &c.   &c.   &c.

OBS.—All verbs ending in *urre,* as *tradurre,* to translate, *condurre,* to lead, &c., are conjugated like *addurre.*

Bévere or *bére,* to drink.

Infinitive—*bévere* or *bére,* to drink.

Indicative Present.

Singular.	*Plural.*
bévo or *béo,* I drink.	*beviámo* or *beiámo,* we drink.
bévi or *béi,* thou drinkest.	*bevéte* or *beéte,* you drink.
béve or *bée,* he drinks.	*bévono* or *béono,* they drink.

Imperfect—*bevéva* or *beéva,* I was drinking.

Perfect *or* Past.

bévvi, I drank.	*bevémmo* or *beémmo,* we drank.
bevésti or *beésti,* thou drankest.	*bevéste* or *beéste,* you drank.
bévve, he drank.	*bévvero,* they drank.

Future—*beverò* or *berò,*[a] I shall drink.

Conditional—*beveréi* or *beréi,* I should drink.

Imperative Mood.

No first person singular.	*beviámo* or *beiámo,* let us drink.
bévi or *béi,* drink (thou).	*bevéte* or *beéte,* drink (you).
béva or *béa,* let him drink.	*bévano* or *béano,* let them drink.

Subjunctive Present.

ch' io béva or *béa,* that I may [drink.]   *che beviámo* or *beiámo,* that we [may drink.]
che tu béva or *béa,* that thou &c.   *che beviáte* or *beiáte,* that you &c.
ch' egli béva or *béa,* that he &c.   *che bévano* or *béano,* that they &c.

---

[a] Note *b,* p. 87.

Subjunctive Imperfect—*s' io bevéssi* or *beéssi*, if I might drink.

Present Participle { *bevéndo* or *beéndo* } drinking.
                   { *bevénte* }

Past Participle—*bevúto*, drunk.

COMPOUND TENSES.

Infinitive—*avere bevuto*, to have drunk.
     &c.   &c.   &c.

OBS.—The compound *imbevere* or *imbere*, to imbibe, is conjugated like *bevere* or *bere*. The second form of these verbs is used chiefly in poetry.

Cógliere, to gather.

Infinitive—*cógliere* or *córre*, to gather.

Indicative Present.

Singular.	*Plural.*
cólgo, I gather.	*cogliámo*, we gather.
cógli, thou gatherest.	*cogliéte*, you gather.
cóglie, he gathers.	*cólgono*, they gather.

Imperfect—*cogliéva*, I was gathering.

Perfect *or* Past.

cólsi, I gathered, *or* did gather.	*cogliémmo*, we did gather.
cogliésti, thou didst gather.	*cogliéste*, you did gather.
cólse, he did gather.	*cólsero*, they did gather.

Future—*coglierò* or *corrò*[a], I shall gather.

Conditional—*coglierèi* or *corréi*, I should gather.

Imperative Mood.

No first person singular.	*cogliámo*, let us gather.
cógli, gather (thou).	*cogliéte*, gather (you).
cólga, let him gather.	*cólgano*, let them gather.

Subjunctive Present.

ch' io cólga, that I may gather.	*che cogliámo*, that we may gather.
che tu cólga, that thou &c.	*che cogliáte*, that you may &c.
ch' egli cólga, that he &c.	*che cólgano*, that they may &c.

Subjunctive Imperfect—*s' io cogliéssi*, if I might gather.

---

[a] The letter *o* of the root in *cogliere* has an open sound, which prevents any confusion between the Future and Conditional of this verb, and the contracted forms of the Future and Conditional of *correre*, to run, *corrò*, &c., sometimes used in poetry; the *o* of the root of this latter verb having a close sound. A similar distinction separates *colto*, gathered, from *colto*, cultivated. (See *O*, p. 2.)

Present Participle $\left\{ \begin{array}{l} \textit{cogliéndo} \\ \textit{cogliénte} \end{array} \right\}$ gathering.

Past Participle—*cólto,* gathered.

COMPOUND TENSES.

Infinitive—*avere colto,* to have gathered.
&c.   &c.   &c.

OBS.—All verbs ending in *gliere,* as *scegliere,* to choose, *sciogliere,* to loose, *togliere,* to take away, &c., are conjugated like *cogliere.*

Cuócere, to cook.

Infinitive—*cuócere,* to cook.

Indicative Present.

Singular.	*Plural.*
cuóco, I cook.	*cociámo,* we cook.
cuóci, thou cookest.	*cocéte,* you cook.
cuóce, he cooks.	*cuócono,* they cook.

Imperfect—*cocéva,* I was cooking.

Perfect *or* Past.

cóssi, I cooked.	*cocémmo,* we cooked.
cocésti, thou cookedst.	*cocéste,* you cooked.
cósse, he cooked.	*cósscro,* they cooked.

Future—*cocerò,* I shall cook.

Conditional—*cocceréi,* I should cook.

Imperative Mood.

No first person singular.	*cociámo,* let us cook.
cuóci, cook (thou).	*cocéte,* cook (you).
cuóca, let him cook.	*cuócano,* let them cook.

Subjunctive Present.

ch' io cuóca, that I may cook.	*che cociámo,* that we may cook.
che tu cuóca, that thou mayest &c.	*che cociáte,* that you may cook.
ch' egli cuóca, that he may cook.	*che cuócano,* that they may cook.

Subjunctive Imperfect.

s' io cocéssi, if I might cook.	*se cocéssimo,* if we might cook.
se tu cocéssi, if thou mightest &c.	*se cocéste,* if you might cook.
se cocésse, if he might cook.	*se cocéssero,* if they might cook.

Present Participle $\left\{ \begin{array}{l} \textit{cocéndo} \\ \textit{cocénte} \end{array} \right\}$ cooking.

Past Participle—*cótto*, cooked.

COMPOUND TENSES.

Infinitive—*avere cotto*, to have cooked.
    &c.   &c.   &c.

OBS.—The verb *cuocere*, and its compound *ricuocere*, to cook again, keep the *u* of the root in the singular and 3rd person plural of the Present Indicative and Subjunctive, and in the Imperative ; *muovere*, to move, *nuocere*, to hurt, *scuotere*, to shake, with all their derivatives, as *rimuovere*, to remove, *riscuotere*, to redeem, &c., are subject to the same anomaly. However, the Perfect and Past Participle of the latter verbs, though irregular, are not all conjugated like *cuocere ; muovere* has *mossi* and *mosso ; nuocere, nocqui* and *nociuto ;* and *scuotere, scossi* and *scosso.*

Pórre (contracted from *pónere*,* now obsolete), to put, place.

Infinitive—*pórre*, to put.

Indicative Present.

Singular.	Plural.
póngo, I put.	*poniámo* or *ponghiámo*, we put.
póni, thou puttest.	*ponéte*, you put.
póne, he puts.	*póngono*, they put.

Imperfect—*ponéva*. I was putting.

Perfect *or* Past.

pósi, I did put.	*ponémmo*, we did put.
ponésti, thou didst put.	*ponéste*, you did put.
póse, he did put.	*pósero*, they did put.

Future—*porrò*,[b] I shall put.

Conditional—*porréi*, I should put.

Imperative Mood.

No first person singular.	*poniámo* or *ponghiámo*, let us put.
póni, put (thou).	*ponéte*, put (you).
pónga, let him put.	*póngano*, let them put.

---

* The verbs ending in *orre* are conjugated according to their obsolete termination *onere* in the same tenses and persons in which verbs in *urre* are conjugated according to their obsolete termination *ucere.* (See note *a*, p. 87.)   [b] Note *b*, p. 87.

Subjunctive Present.

ch' io pónga, that I may put. *che poniámo* or *ponghiámo*, that
che tu pónga, that thou &c.   [we may put.
ch' egli pónga, that he may put. *che poniáte*, that you may put.
           che póngano, that they may put.

Subjunctive Imperfect—*s' io ponéssi*, if I might put.

Present Participle $\left\{\begin{array}{l}ponéndo\\ponénte\end{array}\right\}$ putting.

Past Participle—*pósto*, put.

COMPOUND TENSES.

Infinitive—*avere posto*, to have put.
 &c.   &c.   &c.

OBS.—Conjugate in the same manner all the derivatives of *porre*; as, *comporre*, to compose; *disporre*, to dispose, &c.

Spégnere, to extinguish.[a]

Infinitive—*spégnere* or *spéngere*, to extinguish.

Indicative Present.

Singular.	*Plural.*
spéngo[b] or *spégno*, I extinguish.	*spegniámo* or *spengiámo*, we ex-
spégni or *spéngi*, thou &c.	[tinguish.
spégne or *spénge*, he extinguishes.	*spegnéte* or *spengéte*, you &c.
	spéngono or *spégnono*, they &c.

Imperfect—*spegnéva* or *spengéva*, I extinguished.

Perfect *or* Past.

spénsi, I extinguished.	*spegnémmo* or *spengémmo*, we ex-
spegnésti or *spengésti*, thou ex-	[tinguished.
[tinguished.	*spegnéste* or *spengéste*, you &c.
spénse, he extinguished.	*spénsero*, they extinguished.

Future—*spegnerò* or *spengerò*, I shall extinguish.

Conditional—*spegneréi* or *spengeréi*, I should extinguish.

Imperative.

No first person singular.	*spegniámo* or *spengiámo*, let us
spégni or *spéngi*, extinguish	[extinguish.
[(thou).	*spegnéte* or *spengéte*, extinguish
spénga or *spégna*, let him &c.	[(you).
	spéngano or *spégnano*, let &c.

---

[a] *Spegnere* and *spegnersi*, speaking of light or fire, may mean 'to put out' and 'to go out.'

[b] Of the above two forms of *spegnere*, the first is the one most commonly used throughout all tenses.

Subjunctive Present.

ch' io spénga or *spégna*, that I [may extinguish.
che tu spénga or *spégna*, that &c.
ch' egli spénga or *spégna*, that &c.

che spegniámo or *spengiámo*, that [we may extinguish.
che spegniáte or *spengiáte*, that &c.
che spéngano or *spégnano*, that &c.

Subjunct. Imperf.—*s' io spegnéssi* or *spengéssi*, if I might extinguish.

Present Participle $\begin{Bmatrix} spegnéndo \\ spegnénte \end{Bmatrix}$ extinguishing.

Past Participle—*spénto*, extinguished.

COMPOUND TENSES.

Infinitive—*avere spento*, to have extinguished.
&c.   &c.   &c.

OBS.—The verbs *cingere*, to gird, *dipingere*, to paint, *piangere*, to weep, *tingere*, to dye, *ungere*, to grease, and all verbs ending in *angere*, *ingere*, or *ungere*, admit of the above double forms like *spegnere*. Some writers have also used an *h* after the *g* in the 1st and 2nd persons plural of the Present Subjunctive of *spegnere*, and have written *spenghiamo* and *spenghiate*.

Svéllere or *svérre*, to uproot, pluck up, tear up.

Infinitive—*svéllere* or *svérre*, to tear up.

Indicative Present.

Singular.	*Plural.*
svéllo or *svélgo*, I tear up.	*svelliámo*, we tear up.
svélli, thou tearest up.	*svelléte*, you tear up.
svélle, he tears up.	*svéllono* or *svélgono*, they &c.

Imperfect—*svelléva*, I was tearing up.

Perfect *or* Past.

svélsi, I did tear up.	*svellémmo*, we did tear up.
svellésti, thou didst tear up.	*svelléste*, you did tear up.
svélse, he did tear up.	*svélsero*, they did tear up.

Future—*svellerò*,[a] I shall tear up.

Conditional—*svelleréi*, I should tear up.

Imperative Mood.

No first person singular.	*svelliámo*, let us tear up.
svélli, tear (thou) up.	*svelléte*, tear (you) up.
svélla or *svélga*, let him tear up.	*svéllano* or *svélgano*, let them &c.

---

[a] The verb *svellere*, though contracted in the Infinitive, does not admit any contraction in the Future and Conditional. (See Note *b*, p. 87.)

Subjunctive Present.

ch' io svélla or *svélga*, that I may [tear up.
che tu svélla or *svélga*, that &c.
ch' egli svélla or *svélga*, that &c.

che svelliámo, that we may tear [up.
che svelliáte, that you &c.
che svéllano or *svélgano*, that they [may tear up.

Subjunctive Imperfect—*s' io svelléssi*, if I might tear up.

Present Participle $\left\{ \begin{array}{l} \textit{svelléndo} \\ \textit{svellénte} \end{array} \right\}$ tearing up.

Past Participle—*svélto*, torn up.

COMPOUND TENSES.

Infinitive—*avere svelto*, to have torn up.
&c.   &c.   &c.

OBS.—*Divellere*, which has the same meaning as *svellere*, is the only verb conjugated like *svellere*.

Trárre (contracted from *traere* or *trahere*, or *traggere*, now obsolete), to draw, take out.

Indicative Present.

Singular.
trággo, I draw.
trái or *trággi*, thou drawest.
tráe or *trágge*, he draws.

Plural.
traiámo or *traggiámo*, we draw.
traéte, you draw.
trággono, they draw.

Imperfect—*traéva*, I was drawing.

Perfect or Past.

trássi, I did draw.
traésti, thou didst draw.
trásse, he did draw.

traémmo, we did draw.
traéste, you did draw.
trássero, they did draw.

Future—*trarrò*, I shall draw.

Conditional—*trarréi*, I should draw.

Imperative Mood.

No first person singular.
trái, draw (thou).
trágga, let him draw.

traiámo or *traggiámo*, let us draw.
traéte, draw (you).
trággano, let them draw.

Subjunctive Present.

ch' io trágga, that I may draw.
che tu trágga, that thou &c.
ch' egli trágga, that he &c.

che traiámo or *traggiámo*, that [we may draw.
che traiáte, that you &c.
che trággano, that they &c.

Subjunctive Imperfect—*s' io traéssi*, if I might draw.

Present Participle $\left\{\begin{array}{l} \textit{traéndo} \\ \textit{traénte} \end{array}\right\}$ drawing.

Past Participle—*trátto*, drawn.

COMPOUND TENSES.

Infinitive—*avere tratto*, to have drawn.
&c.   &c.   &c.

OBS.—All the compounds of *trarre*, as *astrarre*, to abstract, *contrarre*, to contract, *sottrarre*, to subtract, &c., are conjugated like *trarre*.

PHRASES.

riprodurre la sua specie, to reproduce its species.
bevere il caffè col latte, to drink coffee with milk.
condurre al pascolo le pecore, to drive sheep to the pasture.
andare a trovare alcuno[a], to go to see any one.
accogliere benignamente alcuno, to receive any one kindly.
cuocere alcuna cosa, to cook something.
rimuovere alcuna cosa da un luogo, to remove anything from a place.
comporre la faccia, to compose one's countenance.
porsi in capo di fare una cosa, to take into one's head to do a thing.
porre in campo pretesti, to bring forward excuses.
trarsi d' impaccio, to get out of trouble.
spegnere la sete, to quench one's thirst.
sottrarre un numero da un altro, to subtract one number from
contrarre debiti, to contract debts.   [another.
condurre alcuno in prigione, to take any one to prison.

VOCABULARY.

seme (m.), seed.	*rosa*, rose,
di buon mattino, early in the morning.	*stelo*, stem of a flower or herb.
pentola, saucepan.	*bellezza*, beauty.
minestra, rice-soup.	*ilarità*, cheerfulness.
tegghia, earthen pie-dish.	*foglio*, a sheet of paper.
torta, tart.	*chiaro*, clear.
	fuggire, to flee.

READING EXERCISE.

1. I semi riproducono[b] la loro specie.   2. In Italia ogni mattina io beveva il caffè col latte.   3. Ieri il pastore condusse[b] di buon mattino al pascolo le sue pecore. 4. Quando vado a trovare il Signor e la Signora Guidi,

---

[a] Indef. Pron., p. 10.   [b] Obs., p. 88.

essi m' accolgono[a] sempre benignamente. 5. La serva
ha cotto nella pentola la minestra, e nella tegghia la
torta. 6. Quando la rosa è rimossa[b] dal suo stelo, essa
perde la sua bellezza. 7. Il curato compose[c] la faccia a
tutta quella ilarità che potè. 8. Quando egli s' è posto
in capo di fare una cosa, la fa certamente. 9. Quantunque
essi pongano[d] in campo pretesti, non si trarranno[e] d' impaccio. 10. I pastori spengono la sete nell' acqua chiara.
11. Se sottraggo[f] due fogli da cinque, ne rimarranno tre.
12. Roberto avendo contratto molti debiti è[g] dovuto
fuggire per non essere condotto in prigione.

VOCABULARY.

to introduce, *introdurre.*
to make acquaintance with any
  one, *fare la conoscenza di*
  alcuno.
to take (*meaning* to conduct),
  condurre.

to gather, *cogliere.*
to see home, *condurre a casa.*
to compose, *comporre.*
to translate, *tradurre.*
to draw, *estrarre.*

TRANSLATION EXERCISE.

1. Mamma, I introduce – Mrs. Botta to you[h].

2. Madam, I am glad[i] to make – your acquaintance.
  Signora   *la vostra*

Laura, have you taken[j] – Mrs. Botta to see the garden?
                            il giardino

3. Yes, mamma. 4. And has she gathered any flowers?
   mamma   *dei fiori*

5. Yes; she has gathered some violets and a few
                    delle viole   *dei*

pinks. 6. Who will see them home? 7. The servant.
garofani   *le*   *Il servo*

8. Who composed[k] that piece of music — you play?
            quel pezzo di   *che*

---

[a] Obs., p. 90.
[b] Obs., p. 91.
[c] Obs., p. 92.
[d] Note *c*, p. 70.
[e] Note *b*, p. 87.
[f] Obs., p. 95.
[g] Obs. 5, p. 52.
[h] Note *a*, p. 43.
[i] Note *b*, p. 76.
[j] Note *c*, p. 62.
[k] Note *h*, p. 15.

9. It was composed by[a] Rossini.   10. Have you trans-
   [is]

lated – your exercise ?   11. Yes ; I translated[2] it[1] this
   il vostro esercizio   *lo*

morning before – breakfast.   12. From where do – bees
         avanti la   *Da   dove   le api*

draw the honey ?   13. From – flowers.
   il   miele   *Dai*

QUESTIONS.

Chi vi conduce a spasso[b] ? 2.—Che si beve[c] generalmente la mattina in Italia? 2*.—Come siete stato accolto
dalla Signora Botta ? 4*.—Dove si cuocono la minestra
e la torta ? 5*.—Quando perde la rosa la sua bellezza ?
6*.—Sottraendo otto da nove, quanto rimane ? 11*.—
Che fiori avete colti in giardino ? 5.—A che ora ha spento
la serva il fuoco[d] ?—Da chi è composto ·il pezzo di
musica che avete da imparare ? 8.—Quando tradurrete
l' esercizio ? 10.—Che cosa estraggono le api dai fiori ?
12. — Come si traggono spesso d' impaccio coloro[e] che
hanno contratto molti debiti ? 9* & 12*

VERBS IN *ERE* (*short*) WHICH HAVE ONLY ONE IRREGULAR
FORM IN THREE PERSONS OF THE PERFECT (See Obs.
3, p. 56) AND IN THE PAST PARTICIPLE.

These verbs vary in the form of their Perfect and
Past Participle, according to the letter, or letters, preceding the infinitive termination *ere*. The following
Table, divided into seven groups, will show the formation
of the Perfect and Past Participle of these verbs :—

---

[a] Note *b*, p. 49.   [b] See Voc., p. 63.   [c] Obs. 3, p. 49.
[d] Note *a*, p. 92.   [e] See Demon. Pron., p. 9.

F

TABLE OF VERBS IN **ERE** (SHORT) WHICH HAVE ONLY IRREGULAR FORMS IN THREE PERSONS OF THE PERFECT (See Obs. 3, p. 56) AND IN THE PAST PARTICIPLE.

Infinitive Termination *ere*, preceded by	Change into		Examples			Observations
	Perfect.	Past Part.	Infinitive.	Perfect.	Past Participle.	
I. { -dere } { -ndere } { -rere }	-si	-so	chiu-dere spe-ndere cor-rere[2]	chiu-si spe-si cor-si	chiu-so[1] to shut spe-so to spend cor-so to run	1. *chiedere*, to ask, *rispondere*, to answer, *scindere*, to sever, and *spandere*, to spill, with all their derivatives, *richiedere*, to require, *corrispondere*, to correspond, &c., make in the Past Participle *chiesto*, *risposto*, *scinto*, *spanto*, &c.
						2. *occorrere*, to occur or require, and *soccorrere*, to succour, compounds of *correre*, are often contracted in the Future and Conditional; *occorrà*, it will require, *soccorrà*, it will succour, *occorrebbe*, it would be required, &c.
						3. Obs., p. 93.
II. { -gere } { -guere }	-si	-to	pian-gere[3] estin-guere	pian-si estin-si	pian-to[4] to weep estin-to to extinguish	4. *spargere*, to scatter, *rifulgere*, to shine, *stringere*, to press, *tergere*, to wipe, with their derivatives *cospargere*, to strew, *aspergere*, to besprinkle, *immergere*, to plunge in water, &c., make in the Past Participle *sparso*, *rifulso*, *stretto*, *terso*, &c. *Esigere*, to exact, and *negligere*, to neglect, with their derivatives, make in the Perfect *esigei* and *neglessi*, in the Past Participle *esatto* and *negletto*.

	Perfect	Past Part.			Meaning
III. { -gg|ere / -v|ere }	-ssi		-tto		
IV. -im|ere	-essi		-esso		
V. -um|ere	-unsi		-unto		
VI. -omp|ere	-uppi		-otto		

Infinitive	Perfect	Past Participle	Meaning
le-ggere[3]	le-ssi	le-tto	to read
scri-vere	scri-ssi	scri-tto	to write
oppr-imere	oppr-essi	oppr-esso	to oppress
espr-imere	espr-essi	espr-esso	to express
ass-umere	ass-unsi	ass-unto	to assume
r-ompere	r-uppi	r-otto	to break
assorbere	assorsi	assorto	to absorb
conoscere[6]	conobbi	conosciuto	to know
crescere[6]	crebbi	cresciuto	to grow
discutere[7]	discussi	discusso	to discuss
esistere[8]	esistei	esistito	to exist
espellere[9]	espulsi	espulso	to expel
mettere[10]	misi	messo	to put
nascere[11]	nacqui	nato	to be born
nuocere[11]	nocqui	nociuto	to hurt
torcere[12]	torsi	torto	to twist
vincere[12]	vinsi	vinto	to conquer

VII. Verbs which cannot be classified according to termination as above...

5. *suggere*, to suck, makes in the Perfect *suggi*, and has no Past Participle; *succhiato*, from *succhiare*, to suck, being used in its stead.

6. The compounds of *conoscere* and *crescere* are conjugated alike.

7. *concutere*, to shake, *genuflettere*, to bend the knee, *incutere*, to inculcate, strike, are conjugated like *discutere*.

8. All verbs ending in *istere* are conjugated in the same manner.

9. *impellere*, to impel, *convellere*, to cause distension, *repellere*, to repel, are conjugated like *espellere*.

10. All the compounds of *mettere*, as *permettere*, to allow, *rimettere*, to differ, are conjugated alike.

11. The compounds of *nascere* and *nuocere* are conjugated alike.

12. The compounds of *torcere* and *vincere* are conjugated alike.

PHRASES.

deludere le speranze del suo genitore, to disappoint one's father's hopes.
distinguersi agli esami, to distinguish one's self at the examinations.
corrispondere male alle cure di alcuno, to repay badly the care of anyone.
inchiudere lettere in un piego, to enclose letters in a parcel.
mettere un piego, o una lettera, nella buca,[a] to put a parcel, or letter, in the post-office letter-box.
fingere di avere qualche cosa, to pretend to have something the matter with one.
non occorrere niente, not to want anything.
esigere subito la paga della sua fatica, to require immediate payment of one's labours.
estinguersi (una lucerna) per mancanza d'olio, to go out (of a lamp) for want of oil.
accorgersi di qualche cosa, to perceive anything.
volgere le spalle ad alcuno, to turn one's back on anyone.
rivolgersi ad alcuno, to apply to any person.
riavere alcuna cosa, to have anything back.
esprimere un pensiero, to express a thought.
corrompersi (una materia), to go bad (of any substance).
espellere alcuno da un luogo, to eject any one from a place.
incutere spavento, to strike terror.
mettere in sesto le cose, to arrange things properly.
rimettere una cosa ad un altro tempo, to put a thing off to another time.
immergere una cosa nell' acqua, to plunge a thing into water.
mettere alte strida, to utter loud screams.

VOCABULARY.

Pietro, Peter.
Luigi, Lewis.
invece, instead.
paterno, fatherly.
ieri l' altro, the day before yes-
febbre, fever.   [terday.
vaccaro, cow-keeper.
latte, milk.
console, consul.

passaporto, passport.
adeguato, proper.
parola, word.
fermo, stagnant (of water).
vista, sight.
fuoco, fire.
lavandaia, laundress.
pannilini, (linen) clothes.

READING EXERCISE.

1. Ieri Pietro non deluse[b] le speranze del suo genitore, egli si distinse[c] agli esami. 2. Luigi invece ha mal corrisposto[d] alle cure paterne. 3. Spero che non abbiate letto[e] le mie carte. 4. Tosto che ebbi inchiuso[f] le lettere

---

[a] *buca* literally 'a hole.'   [b] Group I., p. 98, and Obs. 3, p. 56.
[c] Group II., p. 98.   [d] Obs. 1, p. 98.
[e] Group III., p. 99.   [f] Note e, p. 16.

nel piego lo misi[a] nella buca. 5. Ieri l' altro Carlo, per
non andar a scuola, finse[b] d' aver la fobbre '6. Il vaccaro ha spanto[c] il latte. 7. S' io fossi a casa' mia
non m' occorrebbe[d] niente. 8. Egli ha esatto[e] subito le
paga della sua fatica. 9. La lucerna s' estinso[b] per mancanza d' olio. 10. Io non m' accorsi ch' egli m' aveva
volto le spalle. 11. Ieri, bramando partire, mi rivolsi al
console, e riebbi[f] il mio passaporto. 12. Un pensiero
deve essere espresso[g] con adeguate parole. 13 Le acque
si sono corrotte[h] stando ferme. 14. Oggi il servo è stato
espulso[a] dalla casa. 15. La vista del fuoco incusse[i]
spavento alla serva, e mise alte strida. 16. Oggi ho
messo[a] in sesto tutte le mie cose. 17. Noi abbiamo
rimesso[j] la cosa ad un altro giorno. 18. La lavandaia
ha già immerso[e] i pannilini nell' acqua.

VOCABULARY.

to light, *accendere.*	to be born, *nascere.*
to break, *rompere.*	to ask, *chiedere.*
to spill, *spandere.*	to answer, *rispondere.*
to wipe, *tergere.*	to hide one's face, *nascondersi il*
to shut, *chiudere.*	to weep, *piangere.* [*volto.*
to arrive, *giungere.*	to overcome, *opprimere.*
to put, *mettere.*	to begin, *mettersi a.*
to read, *leggere.*	to laugh, *ridere.*
to write, *scrivere.*	to put on, *mettersi.*
to make one's self understood,	to warm up, *riscaldare.*
farsi capire.	

READING EXERCISE.

1. At what time did the servant light[k] the fire
    A   [hour]   *la*   *il fuoco*

in the drawing-room this-morning? 2. At – ten
nel   *Alle*

(o'clock). 3. Well done! you have broken[h] the cup,
            Bravo

---

[a] Group VII., p. 99.   [b] Group II., p. 98.   [c] Obs. 1, p. 98.
[d] Obs. 2, p. 98.   [e] Obs. 4, p. 98.   [f] N.B., p. 83.
[g] Group IV., p. 99.   [h] Group VI., p. 99.   [i] Obs. 7, p. 99.
[j] Obs. 10, p. 99.   [k] Group I., p. 98 ; and Note *h*, p. 15.

and spilt[a] all the coffee on the table-cloth.   4. Oh,
   tutto il   *sulla* *tovaglia*

there is everything wiped-up[b] again.   5. Have you
   tutto   *di nuovo*

shut the street door? 6. I shut it when my
  la porta della strada   *la*

father-in-law arrived.   7. Where have you put the
suocero   *la*

 Italian[4] letter[1] —[2] I wrote[3] last night?   8. I put
[in Italian] *che*   *ieri sera*

it on the table in the little room.   9. Have you read
la sulla   *nello stanzino*

many Italian[2] works[1]?   10. No; I have not read many
molte italiane opere

Italian works, but I have written many exercises;
           molti temi

and if I could[c] remember all the words contained
       tutte le parole [which they

in them, I should be able to speak Italian
contain]

sufficiently to make myself understood.   11. Where
abbastanza per

was – your – Italian[3] master[1] born[d]?   12. He
 il vostro d' italiano maestro

was born at Sienna, (a) town famous for the
      a   *famosa*   *la*

purity of its language.   13. Have you asked[e] him[f]
purità della   *gli*

whether he has travelled much in Italy?   14. No;
se   *molto*

---

[a] Obs. 1, p. 98. [b] Obs. 4, p. 98. [c] Imperf. Subj. of *potere*.
[d] Perfect. See Group VII., p. 99. [e] Obs. 1, p. 98.
[f] Note *a* (1), p. 43.

but yesterday I asked him if he had been at Naples.
　　　　　　　　13　　　　　　　　　　　　　*a*

15. And what reply did he make? 16. At first he
　　　 [did he answer you]　　　　*Da prima*

hid his face with his hands, and wept as if he were*
　　　　con le mani　　　　　　*quasi*

overcome by grief; then he began to give me a
　　　　dal dolore poi　　　　 [to make me] *un*

long account of his sufferings in that city. 17. I
lungo racconto dei suoi patimenti　*quella*

hope[b] you did not laugh at his story. 18. I never
laugh at any one[c]. 19. Why have you put on[d] your
gloves? 20. In-order-that my hands may be[f] warmed.
　　　　Perchè[e]

QUESTIONS.

Dove avete messo il piego? 4*.—Come s' è estinta
la lucerna? 9*.—Quali acque si corrompono facilmente?
13*.—A che ora ha acceso la serva nel salotto il fuoco?
1.—Chi ha chiuso la finestra della stanza da mangiare?
5.—Avete letto le opere di Dante? 9.—Avete risposto
alla lettera che riceveste stamane?—Avete chiesto a
vostra madre, se vi lascierà andare al concerto domani?
13.—Dove avete messo il libro?—Sapete dove abbia
vostra sorella nascosto il temperino? 16.—Che cosa vi
mettete quando andate a spasso? 19.—Quando vi met-
terete a fare la traduzione? 16.—Quando avete messo
in sesto le vostre cose? 16*.—Fin a quando avete rimesso la vostra partenza per la campagna? 17*.

ST OF IRREGULAR VERBS IN **ERE** (SHORT) WHICH HAVE TWO FORMS IN EITHER THE PERFECT OR PAST PARTICIPLE, OR IN BOTH, ONE FORM BEING IRREGULAR, AND THE OTHER GENERALLY REGULAR.

LIST OF VERBS.

Infinitive.	Perfect.	Past Participle.	
concedere[1]	concessi or concedei	concesso or conceduto	to grant
connettere[2]	connessi or connettei	connesso or connettuto	to connect, join
difendere	difesi or difendei	difeso or difenduto	to defend
fendere	fessi or fendei	fesso or fenduto	to split
figgere[3] or figere	fissi or fissi	fisso, fitto, or fiso	to fix
fondere[4]	fusi or fondei	fuso or fonduto	to melt
nascondere[5]	nascosi	nascoso or nascosto	to hide
perdere[6]	persi or perdei	perso or perduto	to lose
piovere	piovve or piovè	piovuto	to rain
prendere[7]	presi or prendei	preso	to take
radere	rasi or radei	raso	to shave, scrape [off
redimere	redensi or redimei	redento	to redeem
rendere	resi or rendei	reso or renduto	to give back
rilucere	rilussi or rilucei	No Past Participle	to shine
risolvere[8]	risolsi, risolvei, or risolvetti	risolto or risoluto	to resolve
scernere[9]	scersi or scernei	scerso or scernuto	to discern
vivere[10]	vissi	vissuto or vivuto	to live

OBSERVATIONS.

1. *intercedere*, to intercede, and *succedere*, to succeed, happen, are conjugated like *concedere*. (See Note b, p. 86.)

2. *annettere*, to annex, *sconnettere*, to disjoin, are conjugated like *connettere*.

3. The verb *figgere*, and its compounds *affiggere*, to affix, to attach, post up bills, &c., *configgere*, to fix with nails, *crocifiggere*, to crucify, and *prefiggere*, to prefix, may be spelt with only one *g*, like *figere*, but they take always a double *s*, both in the Perfect and Past Participle, and have only one form in those tenses. The other compounds of *figgere*—*infiggere*, to drive in, *sconfiggere*, to drive out, to defeat, and *trafiggere*, to pierce with a sword, have always two *g*'s in the Infinitive, a double *s* in the Perfect, and two *t*'s in the Past Participle.

4. The compounds of *fondere*, *confondere*, or *sconfondere*, to confound, *diffondere*, to spread, *infondere*, to infuse, *rifondere*, to repay, *trasfondere*, to transfuse, are all conjugated like *fondere*, but have only one form in both the Perfect and Past Participle, and make *confusi*, *confuso*, &c.

5. *ascondere*, to conceal, is conjugated like *nascondere*.

6. *disperdere*, to scatter, has two forms like *perdere*.

7. All the compounds of *prendere* are conjugated like *prendere*, but very seldom admit the regular form in *ei* in the Perfect.

8. *assolvere*, to absolve, and *dissolvere*, to dissolve, are conjugated like *risolvere*.

9. The compounds of *scernere* are conjugated alike.

10. The compounds of *vivere*, as *rivivere*, to revive, *sopravivere*, to survive, &c., are conjugated alike; *vivere* in poetry is often contracted in the Future, Conditional, and Past Participle, and makes *vivrò*, I shall live, &c.; *vivrei*, I should live, &c.; *visso*, lived.

PHRASES.

succedere a uno, to succeed to any one.
concedere una cosa, to grant a thing.
connettere due cose, to connect two things.
difendere la patria, to defend one's country.
fendere un querciuolo, to split a small oak tree.
sconfiggere i nemici, to defeat the enemy.
affiggere al cavicchio qualche cosa, to attach something to a peg.
sconfiggere chiodi, to draw out nails.
figere chiodi, to drive in nails.
fondere campane, to cast bells.
nascondere qualche cosa a uno, to hide something from a person.
radere il muschio (or *moscolo*), to scrape off the moss.
risolversi di fare una cosa, to make up one's mind to do a thing.
vivere a spese di alcuno, to live at the charge of some one.

VOCABULARY.

Papa, pope.	*spaccalegna,* woodcutter.
pezzo, piece.	*scure,* axe.
legno, wood (for building).	*soldato,* soldier.
corpo, body.	*berretta,* cap (boy's or man's).
solo, single.	*parete* (f.), wall of a room.
Greco, a Greek.	*cassa,* case.
assalto, assault.	*giardiniere,* gardener.
Persiano, a Persian.	*vite* (f.), vine tree.

READING EXERCISE.

1. Quando il Papa morì gli[a] successe[b] suo nipote. 2. Mia madre m' ha sempre conceduto tutto quel che[c] le[a] ho chiesto[d]. 3. Se due pezzi di legno sono bene connessi, essi[a] paiono un corpo solo. 4. I Greci hanno difeso la patria dagli assalti dai Persiani. 5. Lo spaccalegna ha fesso un querciuolo colla scure. 6. Ieri i nostri soldati sconfissero i nemici. 7. Io affissi al cavicchio la berretta, prima d' entrare in iscuola[e]. 8. Quando avrete sconfissi[f] tutti i chiodi che sono fitti nelle pareti, me li[g] darete per metterli nella cassa. 9. Le

---

[a] See Pers. Pron., p. 8.   [b] Obs. 1, p. 104.   [c] Note *d*, p. 35.
[d] Obs. 1, p. 98.   [e] Note *a*, p. 85.   [f] Obs. 3, p. 104.
[g] Whether there be one or two conjunctive pronouns in a sentence, the rules respecting the placing of them in relation to the verb are the same; *i.e.,* they will either precede or follow the verb, according to what has been said respecting them (see Obs. 2, and Note *a* (1), p. 43). It must however be observed—(1) that when one conjunctive pronoun immediately follows another in the same phrase, the dative precedes the accusative, and the genitive *ne* generally follows all other pronouns except *loro;* as, *Mi vi racco-*

campane furono fondute. 10. Io non ho nascoso mai nulla alla madre. 11. Il giardiniere ha raso tutto il muschio che si trovava nella vite. 12. Egli si risolvette di partire. 13. Io non ho mai vissuto a spese altrui[a].

VOCABULARY.

to look, *mirare*.
to happen, *succedere*.
to post (bills), *affigere (cartelli)*.
to let people know, *far sapere*.
to grant, *concedere*.
to take, *prendere*.
to lose, *perdere*.
to give back, *rendere*.
to inquire for, *cercare* (active).

to take (carry), *portare*.
to thank one a thousand times, *rendere mille grazie ad uno*.
to resolve, *risolvere*.
to buy, *comprare*.
to rent, *prendere a pigione*.
to live, *vivere* (neuter).
to settle (in a place), *stabilirsi*.

TRANSLATION EXERCISE.

1. Look what (a) crowd there is at the corner-of-
   folla   c'   alla   canto-
the-street; let us go and[b] see what has happened. 2. Oh,
nata   Oh
they are reading a bill which has been posted
   un cartello   che
on the wall this morning. 3. What bill is it? 4. It is
al   muro
only to[c] let people know that the Government has granted
   il   governo
a printer's patent   to — Mr. D. 5. What did
la patente di stampatore   al   Signor
you take[d] at the coffee-house? 6. I took an ice, and
   al   caffè   un sorbetto

---

manda, he recommends you to me; *Non vuol raccomandarvimi*, he will not recommend me to you;—(ii.) That *mi, ti, ci, vi, si* change the *i* into *e* before *lo, la, gli, li, le, ne;* and *gli*, to him, and *le*, to her, become *glie* before *lo, la, li, le, ne;* as, *datemelo*, give it to me; *glielo darò*, I shall give it to him *or* to her.

[a] See Indef. Pron., p. 10.
[b] The conjunction 'and,' used between a verb of motion and another verb in the same tense, person, and number with the former, is rendered by the preposition *a*, and the verb which follows is put in the infinitive; as, I shall come and dine with you, *Verrò a pranzare con voi*.
[c] Note *g*, p. 30.   [d] Note *h*, p. 15.

stayed there all the time that it rained[a].   7. Had you
    colà

not taken your umbrella with you?   8. I lost it yester-
    l' ombrello

day in a shop.   9. But why did not the people
    una bottega   *quelli*

in the shop give[b] it back to you[c]?   10. Because some-
della   *qualcu-*

body who   was   in the shop ha dtaken it[d]
no   *che* [found himself] *nella*

before[e] I went to inquire for it[d].   11. One day I found

a walking-stick which had the owner's name and ad-
un   *bastone*   *che*   *il nome e l' indirizzo del pro-*

dress   on the handle.   So   I took it to him[c],
prietario sul pomo   *Così che*

and he thanked me a thousand times.   12. I have lost

so many umbrellas, that I am resolved – not to buy –
tanti   *di*   *ne[f]*

any more.   13. Have you rented the house you saw
   più

yesterday?   14. Not yet; I shall wait till I have lived

a little longer in this city, to[g] see if I care to settle here.
un poco più questa   [like[h]]

QUESTIONS.

Quando paiono due pezzi di legno un corpo solo? 3*.
—Come si chiama colui[i] che[j] fende le legna? 5*.—Che
fa il ragazzo prima d' entrare in iscuola? 7*.—Che cosa
ha raso il giardiniere? 11*.—Chi ha concesso la patente
di stampatore al Signor D.? 4.—Che avete preso al
caffè? 5.—Che avete perduto? 8.—Che fareste, se qualcuno vi portasse qualche cosa che aveste perso? 11.—
Avete preso a pigione una stanza od una casa? 13.

---

[a] Note *f*, p. 15.   [b] Note *h*, p. 15.   [c] Note *g*, p. 105.
[d] Note *a*, p. 43.   [e] Note *c*, p. 70.
[f] When the name of the object spoken of is not repeated in a
phrase, *ne* (of him, her, it, or them) must be used in its stead.
[g] Note *g*, p. 30.   [h] Note *a*, p. 72; and Note *b*, p. 76.
[i] See Dem. Pron., p. 9.   [j] See Relat. Pron., p. 9

IRREGULAR VERBS—THIRD CONJUGATION.

Obs.—The irregular verbs of the 3rd conjugation are:

apparire, to appear,	*morire*, to die
aprire, to open,	*offrire*, to offer,
cucire, to sew,	*salire*, to ascend,
convertire, to convert,	*seguire*, to follow,
dire, to say,	*seppellire*, to bury,
empire, to fill,	*udire*, to hear,
esaurire, to exhaust,	*uscire*, to go out,
istruire, to instruct,	*venire*, to come,

with some of their derivatives which are conjugated like them.

———

Apparíre, to appear.

[N.B.—This verb is partly conjugated like *parere*, and partly like *finire*.]

Infinitive—*apparíre*, to appear.

Indicative Present.

Singular.	*Plural.*
apparisco or *appáio*, I appear.	*appariámo*, we appear.
apparisci, thou appearest.	*apparite*, you appear.
apparisce or *appáre*, he appears.	*appariscono* or *appáiono*, they [appear.

Imperfect—*appariva*, I appeared.

Perfect *or* Past.

apparíi, *appárvi*, or *appársi*, I [did appear.	*apparímmo*, we did appear.
apparisti, thou didst appear.	*appariste*, you did appear.
appari, *appárve*, or *appárse*, he [did appear.	*apparirono*, *appárvero*, or *appár- [sero*, they did appear.

Future—*appariró*, I shall appear.

Conditional—*apparirêi*, I should appear.

Imperative Mood.

No first person singular.	*appariámo*, let us appear
apparisci, appear (thou).	*apparite*, appear (you).
apparisca or *appáia*, let him [appear.	*appariscano* or *appáiano*, let them [appear.

Subjunctive Present.

ch' io apparisca or *appáia*, that I
    [may appear.

che tu apparisca or *appáia*. that
    [thou mayest appear.

ch' egli apparisca or *appáia*, that
    [he may appear.

che appariámo, that we may
    [appear.

che appariáte, that you may ap-
    [pear.

che appariscano or *appáiano*, that
    [they may appear.

Subjunctive Imperfect—*s' io apparissi*, if I might appear.

Present Participle $\begin{Bmatrix} apparéndo \\ apparénte \end{Bmatrix}$ appearing.

Past Participle—*apparito* or *appárso*, appeared.

COMPOUND TENSES.

Infinitive—*essere apparito*, to have appeared.
    &c.   &c.   &c.

OBS.—*Comparire*, to show one's self, *sparire*, to disappear, with all their derivatives, are conjugated like *apparire*, but they are seldom found with the termination *si* in the Perfect, and *so* in the Past Participle, and some of them have only the terminations *isco*, *isce*, &c., in the Present.

Aprire, to open.

[N.B.—*Aprire*, to open, and its compounds *coprire*, to cover, *sco-prire* or *discoprire*, to discover, &c., may be regular or irregular in the Perfect, must be irregular in the Past Participle, and are con-jugated in the other tenses like *sentire*.]

Infinitive—*aprire*, to open.

Perfect *or* Past.

Singular.

aprii or *apérsi*, I did open.

apristi, thou didst open.

aprì or *apérse*, he did open.

Plural.

aprimmo, we did open.

apriste, you did open.

aprirono or *apérsero*, they &c.

Past Participle—*apérto*, opened

COMPOUND TENSES.

Infinitive—*avere aperto*, to have opened.
    &c.   &c.   &c.

Cucire, to sew.

[N.B.—*Cucire*, to sew, *ricucire*, to sew again, *scucire*, to unsew, *sdrucire* or *sdruscire*, to rip a seam, take an *i*, in order to preserve the soft sound of the *c*, when followed by *a* or *o*.]

Infinitive—*cucire*, to sew.

Indicative Present.

Singular.	*Plural.*
cúcio, I sew.	*cuciámo*, we sew.
cúci, thou sewest.	*cucíte*, you sew.
cúce, he sews.	*cúciono*, they sew.

Indicative Imperfect... *cucíva*, I was sewing.
  „   Perfect...... *cucíi*, I did sew.
  ·,   Future...... *cucirò*, I shall sew.

Conditional—*cuciréi*, I should sew.

Imperative Mood.

No first person singular.	*cuciámo*, let us sew.
cúci, sew (thou).	*cucíte*, sew (you).
cúcia, let him sew.	*cúciano*, let them sew.

Subjunctive Present.

ch' io cúcia, that I may sew.	*che cuciámo*, that we may sew.
che tu cúcia, that thou mayest sew.	*che cuciáte*, that you may sew.
ch' egli cúcia, that he may sew.	*che cúciano*, that they may sew.

Subjunctive Imperfect—*s' io cucíssi*, if I might sew.

Present Participle—*cucéndo*, sewing.
Past Participle—*cucíto*, sewed.

COMPOUND TENSES.

Infinitive—*avere cucito*, to have sewed.
&c.   &c.   &c.

Convertíre, to convert, and *Sovvertíre*, to subvert.

[N.B.—These verbs may be conjugated throughout like *sentire*, or like *finire*, but in the Perfect and Past Participle have also the irregular forms *conversi*, I converted, *sovversi*, I subverted, and *converso*, converted, *sovverso*, subverted.]

Díre, to say.

[N.B.—*Dire*, to say, is often placed by grammarians among the irregular verbs of the 2nd conjugation, because it is contracted from *dicere*, now obsolete, of which it still retains many forms.

Infinitive—*díre*, to say.

Indicative Present.

Singular.	*Plural.*
díco, I say.	*diciámo*, we say.
díci, thou sayest.	*díte*, you say.
díce,[a] he says.	*dícono*, they say.

Imperfect—*dicéva*, I was saying.

Perfect *or* Past.

díssi, I did say, *or* I said.	*dicémmo*, we did say.
dicésti, thou didst say.	*dicéste*, you did say.
dísse, he did say.	*díssero*, they did say.

Future—*dirò*, I shall say.

Conditional—*diréi*, I should say.

Imperative Mood.

No first person singular.	*diciámo*, let us say.
dì, say (thou).	*díte*, say (you).
díca, let him say.	*dícano*, let them say.

Subjunctive Present.

ch' io díca, that I may say.	*che diciámo*, that we may say.
che tu díca, that thou mayest say.	*che diciáte*, that you may say.
ch' egli díca, that he may say.	*che dícano*, that they may say.

Subjunctive Imperfect—*s' io dicéssi*, if I might say.

Present Participle $\left\{ \begin{array}{l} dic\acute{e}ndo \\ dic\acute{e}nte \end{array} \right\}$ saying.

Past Participle—*détto*, said.

COMPOUND TENSES.

Infinitive—*avere detto*, to have said.
    &c.   &c.   &c.

OBS.—*Ridire*, to say again, *contradire*, to contradict, *interdire*, to forbid, *maldire*, to speak ill of, are all conjugated like *dire*. *Benedire*, to bless, *maledire*, to execrate, may be conjugated either like *dire*, or like *finire*, in all the tenses, but not in the Participles, in which the forms of *dire* are always followed.

---

[a] The expression, *Come si dice in italiano ....?* What is the Italian for ....? is used in asking the equivalent of a word or phrase.

Empíre, to fill.

[N.B.—The verbs *empíre*, to fill, *compíre*, to finish, *adempíre*, to fulfil, are also spelt, *empíere*, *compíere*, *adempíere*, and then they may be conjugated according to the 2nd conjugation, dropping the *i* preceding the Infinitive termination *ere*, when followed by another *i*.]

Infinitive—*empíre*, to fill.

Indicative Present.

Singular.	*Plural.*
émpio or *empísco*, I fill.	*empiámo*, we fill.
émpi or *empísci*, thou fillest.	*empíte*, you fill.
émpie or *empísce*, he fills.	*émpiono* or *empíscono*, they fill.

Indicative Imperfect... *empíva*, I was filling.
       ,,   Perfect...... *empíi*, I did fill.
       ,,   Future...... *empirò*, I shall fill.

Conditional—*empiréi*, I should fill.

Imperative Mood.

No first person singular.	*empiámo*, let us fill.
émpi, fill (thou).	*empíte*, fill (you).
émpia, let him fill.	*émpiano*, let them fill.

Subjunctive Present.

ch' io émpia, that I may fill.	*che empiámo*, that we may fill.
che tu émpia, that thou mayest fill.	*che empiáte*, that you may fill.
ch' egli émpia, that he may fill.	*che émpiano*, that they may.

Subjunctive Imperfect—*s' io empíssi*, if I might fill.

Present Participle { *empiéndo* / *empiénte* } fillig.

Past Participle—*empíto*, filled.

COMPOUND TENSES.

Infinitive—*avere empito*, to have filled.
    &c.   &c.   &c.

Esauríre, to exhaust, and *dijeríre*, to digest.

[N.B.—These verbs are conjugated like *finíre*, but have two forms in the Past Participle, *esaurito* and *esausto*, *digerito* and *digesto*.]

Instruíre, to instruct.

[N.B.—*Instruíre* or *istruíre,* to instruct, and all verbs ending in *struíre,* as *costruíre,* to build, &c., are conjugated like *fi iire,* except that they may be either regular or irregular in the Perfect and Past Participle.]

Infinitive—*instruíre,* to instruct.

Perfect *or* Past.

instruíi, or *instrússi,* I did in- *instruímmo,* we did instruct.
instruísti, thou didst &c. [struct. *instruíste,* you did instruct.
instruì or *instrússe,* he did &c. *instruírono* or *instrússero,* they
[did instruct.

Past Participle—*instruíto* or *instrútto,* instructed.

COMPOUND TENSES.

Infinitive—*avere instruíto,* to have instructed.
&c.　　　&c.　　　&c.

Moríre, to die.

Infinitive—*moríre,* to die.

Indicative Present.

Singular. *Plural.*
muóio or *muóra,* I die. *muoiámo* or *moriámo,* we die.
muóri, thou diest. *moríte,* you die.
muóre, he dies. *muóiono* or *muórono,* they die.

Indicative Imperfect... *moríva,* I was dying.
　　　,,　　Perfect...... *moríi,* I did die.
　　　,,　　Future...... *moriró* or *morró,* I shall die.

Conditional—*moriréi* or *morréi,* I should die.

Imperative Mood.

No first person singular. *muoiámo* or *moriámo,* let us die.
muóri, die (thou). *moríte,* die (you).
muóia or *muóra,* let him die. *muóiano* or *muórano,* let them die.

Subjunctive Present.

ch' io muóia or *muóra,* that I may *che muoiámo* or *moriámo,* that we
　　　　　[die. 　　　　　　　　[may die.
che tu muóia or *muóra,* that &c. *che muoiáte,* that you may die.
ch' egli muóia or *muóra,* that &c. *che muóiano* or *muórano,* that &c.

Subjunctive Imperfect—*s' io moríssi,* if I might die.

Past Participle—*mórto*, dead.

$$\text{Present Participle} \left\{ \begin{array}{c} \textit{moréndo} \\ \textit{morénte} \\ \textit{moriénte} \end{array} \right\} \text{dying.}$$

COMPOUND TENSES.

Infinitive—*essere morto*, to be dead.
&c. &c. &c.

OBS.—*Premorire*, to die before, is conjugated like *morire*.

Offeríre or *offríre*, to offer.

[N.B.—Of the two Infinitive forms of this verb, the first is con-jugated like *finire*, and the second like *sentire*. In the Perfect, however, they may be both regular and irregular, but have only one form (irregular) in the Past Participle.]

Infinitive—*offerire* or *offrire*, to offer.

Perfect *or* Past.

Singular.	*Plural.*
offerii, offrii, or *offérsi,* I offered.	*offerímmo* or *offrímmo,* we offered.
offeristi or *offrísti,* thou offeredst.	*offeríste* or *offríste,* you offered.
offerì, offrì, or *offérse,* he offered.	*offerírono, offrírono,* or *offérsero,* [they offered.

Past Participle—*offérto,* offered.

OBS.—*Sofferire* or *soffrire,* to suffer, respectively follow exactly the forms of *offerire* or *offrire,* and have the same irregularities in the Perfect and Past Participle. *Conferire,* to confer, *differire,* to differ, *inferire,* to infer, *preferire,* to prefer, *proferire,* to proffer, *riferire,* to refer, and *transferire,* to transfer, have only one form in the Infinitive, and are conjugated only like *finire* for all tenses.

Salíre, to ascend.

[N.B.—This verb is partly conjugated like *valere*, and partly like *finire*.]

Infinitive—*salíre,* to ascend.

Indicative Present.

Singular.	*Plural.*
sálgo or *salísco,* I ascend.	*saliámo* or *sagliámo,* we ascend.
salí or *salísci,* thou ascendest.	*salíte,* you ascend.
sale or *salísce,* he ascends.	*sálgono* or *salíscono,* they ascend.

Imperfect—*saliva*, I was ascending.

Perfect *or* Past.

sàlsi or *salìi*, I did ascend.	*salìmmo*, we did ascend.
salìsti, thou didst ascend.	*salìste*, you did ascend.
sàlse or *salì*, he did ascend.	*sàlsero* or *salìrono*, they did &c.

Future—*salirò*, I shall ascend.

Conditional—*salirèi*, I should ascend.

Imperative Mood.

No first person singular.	*salidmo* or *sagliàmo*, let us ascend.
sàli, ascend (thou).	*salìte*, ascend (you). [cend.
sàlga or *salìsca*, let him ascend.	*sàlgano* or *salìscano*, let them as-

Subjunctive Present.

ch' io sàlga or *salìsca*, that I may [ascend.	*che salidmo* or *sagliàmo*, that we [may ascend.
che tu sàlga or *salìsca*, that thou &c.	*che sagliàte*, that you &c.
ch' egli sàlga or *salìsca*, that he &c.	*che sàlgano* or *salìscano*, that &c.

Subjunctive Imperfect—*s' io salìssi*, if I might ascend.

Present Participle $\left\{\begin{array}{l}saléndo\\ salénte\\ sagliénte\end{array}\right\}$ ascending.

Past Participle—*salìto*, ascended.

COMPOUND TENSES.

Infinitive—*essere salito*, to have ascended.
    &c.   &c.   &c.

OBS.—*Risalire*, to re-ascend, *assalire*, to assail, &c., are conjugated like *salire*.

Seguíre, to follow.

[N.B.—This verb is partly conjugated like *sentire*, and partly like *sedere*.]

Infinitive—*seguíre*, to follow.

Indicative Present.

Singular.	*Plural.*
séguo or *siéguo*, I follow.	*seguiámo*, we follow.
ségui or *siégui*, thou followest.	*seguíte*, you follow.
ségue or *siégue*, he follows.	*séguono* or *siéguono*, they follow.

Indicative Imperfect...	*seguiva*, I was following.
,, Perfect......	*seguíi*, I did follow.
,, Future......	*seguirò*, I shall follow.

Conditional—*seguirei*, I should follow.

Imperative Mood.

No first person singular.　　　　*seguiámo*, let us follow.
ségui or *siégui*, follow (thou).　　*seguíte*, follow (you).
ségua or *siégua*, let him follow.　*séguano* or *siéguano*, let them &c.

Subjunctive Present.

ch' io ségua or *siégua*, that I may　*che seguiámo*, that we may fol-
　　　　　　　[follow.　　　　　　　　　　　　[low.
che tu ségua or *siégua*, that &c.　*che seguiáte*, that you &c.
ch' egli ségua or *siégua*, that &c.　*che séguano* or *siéguano*, that &c.

Subjunctive Imperfect—*s' io seguíssi*, if I might follow.

Present Participle $\left\{ \begin{array}{l} seguéndo \\ seguénte \end{array} \right\}$ following.

Past Participle—*seguíto*, followed.

COMPOUND TENSES.

Infinitive—*avere seguíto*, to have followed.
&c.　　　　　　&c.　　　　　　&c.

OBS.—*Conseguire*, to obtain, *inseguire* or *perseguire*, to pursue, *proseguire*, to prosecute, to follow on, *susseguire*, to follow immediately after, are conjugated like *seguire*.

Seppellíre, to bury.

[N.B.—This verb is conjugated like *finíre*, but it has two forms of the Past Participle.]

Past Participle—*seppellíto* or *sepólto*, buried.

Udíre, to hear.

[N.B.—This verb is not a compound of *dire*, and its irregularity consists in changing the letter *u* into *o* throughout the singular, and in the 3rd person plural, of the Indicative Present, Subjunctive Present, and Imperative.]

Infinitive—*udíre*, to hear.

Indicative Present.

Singular.　　　　　　　　　*Plural.*
òdo, I hear.　　　　　　*udiámo*, we hear.
òdi, thou hearest.　　　*udíte*, you hear.
òde, he hears.　　　　　*ódono*, they hear.

Indicative Imperfect... *udíva,* I was hearing.
" Perfect...... *udíi,* I heard.
" Future...... *udirò,* I shall hear.

Conditional—*udirái,* I should hear.

Imperative Mood.

No first person singular. *udiámo,* let us hear.
ódi, hear (thou). *udíte,* hear (you).
óda, let him hear. *ódano,* let them hear.

Subjunctive Present.

ch' io óda, that I may hear. *che udiámo,* that we may hear.
che tu óda, that thou mayest &c. *che udiáte,* that you may hear.
ch' egli óda, that he may hear. *che ódano,* that they may hear.

Subjunctive Imperfect—*s' io udíssi,* if I might hear.

Present Participle $\left\{ \begin{array}{l} \textit{udéndo} \\ \textit{udénte} \end{array} \right\}$ hearing.

Past Participle—*udíto,* heard.

COMPOUND TENSES.

Infinitive—*avere udito,* to have heard.
&c. &c. &c.

OBS.—*Riudire,* to hear again, is conjugated like *udire.*

Uscíre, to go out.

[N.B.—This verb has some of its forms derived from the verb *escíre,* to go out, now obsolete.]

Infinitive—*uscíre,* to go out.

Indicative Present.

Singular.	*Plural.*
ésco, I go out.	*usciámo,* we go out.
ésci, thou goest out.	*uscíte,* you go out.
ésce, he goes out.	*éscono,* they go out.

Indicative Imperfect ... *uscíva,* I was going out.
" Perfect ...... *uscíi,* I went out.
" Future ...... *uscirò,* I shall go out.

Conditional—*usciréi,* I should go out.

Imperative Mood.

No first person singular. *usciámo,* let us go out.
ésci, go (thou) out. *uscíte,* go (you) out.
ésca, let him go out. *éscano,* let them go out.

Subjunctive Present.

ch' io ésca, that I may go out.   *che usciámo*, that we may go out.
che tu ésca, that thou &c.   *che usciáte*, that you may go out.
ch' egli ésca, that he may go out.   *che éscano*, that they may go out.

Subjunctive Imperfect—*s' io uscissi*, if I might go out.

Present Participle $\begin{Bmatrix} uscéndo \\ uscénte \end{Bmatrix}$ going out.

Infinitive—*uscito*, gone out.

COMPOUND TENSES.

Infinitive—*essere uscito*, to have gone out.
    &c.   &c.   &c.

OBS.—*Riuscire*, to go out again, to succeed, is conjugated like *uscire.*

Venire, to come.[a]

[N.B.—This verb has the same irregularities as *tenere.*]

Infinitive—*venire*, to come.

Indicative Present.

Singular.	*Plural.*
vengo, I come.	*veniámo*, we come.
viéni, thou comest.	*venite*, you come.
viéne, he comes.	*véngono*, they come.

Imperfect—*veniva*, I was coming.

Perfect *or* Past.

vénni, I came.	*venimmo*, we came.
venisti, thou camest.	*veniste*, you came.
vínne, he came.	*vénnero*, they came.

Future—*verrò*[b], I shall come.

Conditional—*verréi*, I should come.

Imperative Mood.

No first person singular.	*veniámo*, let us come.
viéni, come (thou).	*venite*, come (you).
vénga, let him come.	*véngano*, let them come.

---

[a] *Venire*, used in the 3rd person with the dative of the subject, is Englished by 'to have'; as, *Mi vien voglia*, I have a desire; *Se mi viene il destro*, If I have an opportunity; *Quanto vi viene?* How much have I to pay?   [b] Note *e*, p. 66.

Subjunctive Present.

ch' io vénga, that I may come.	*che veniámo*, that we may come.
che t·*vénga*, that thou &c.	*che veniáte*, that you may come.
ch' egli vénga, that he &c.	*che véngano*, that they may come.

Subjunctive Imperfect—*s' io venissi*, if I might come.

Present Participle $\left\{\begin{array}{l} venéndo \\ veniénte \\ vegnénte \end{array}\right\}$ coming.

Past Participle—*venúto*, come.

COMPOUND TENSES.

Infinitive—*essere venuto*, to have com
&c. &c. &c.

OBS.—*Avvenire*, to happen, *addivenire*, to suit, *convenire*, to become, agree, *divenire*, to become, *invenire*, to find, *pervenire*, to reach, *prevenire*, to anticipate, *provvenire*, to come from, *rivenire*, to come back, *sovvenire*, to assist, and all other compounds of *venire*, are conjugated alike.

PHRASES.

apparire più grande, to appear larger.
scoprire una cosa, to discover a thing.
cucire panni rotti, to mend torn clothes.
mettere toppa, to put on a patch.
convertirsi in vento le speranze d' alcuno, for any one's hopes to be
    scattered to the winds.
contradire una nuova, to contradict a piece of news.
esaurire le forze, to exhaust one's strength.
costruire case, to build houses.
morire per salvare la patria, to die to save one's country
salire scale, to mount stairs
ascendere montagne, to climb mountains.
seppellire nell' obblio le ingiurie, to bury injuries in oblivion.
udire i suoni, to hear sounds.
uscire la notte, to come out by night.
non venire in fama, not to come into notice.
convenire ad uno stare appresso ai savi uomini, to be befitting to seek
    the society of wise men.
venire meno, or *svenire*, to faint.

VOCABULARY.

luna, moon.	*generoso*, generous.
Colombo, Columbus.	*aria*, air.
America, America.	*pipistrello*, a bat (anim.).
rimendatrice, a repairer (f.).	*sotto*, under.
cittadino, citizen.	*coltre* (f.), bed-clothes.
molti, many persons.	

READING EXERCISE.

1. La luna appare più grande delle stelle. 2. Colombo ha scoperto[a] l' America. 3. Le donne che cuciono panni rotti senza mettervi toppa si chiamano "rimendatrici." 4. Tutte le sue speranze si sono converse in vento. 5. La nuova della pace fu contradetta dai giornali. 6. Egli ha esausto tutte le sue forze. 7. Le case in Italia sono ben costrutte. 8. I buoni cittadini muoiono volentieri per salvare la patria. 9. Molti hanno sofferto[b]. 10. Si salgono scale, e si ascendono montagne. 11. Gli uomini generosi hanno sepolto nell' obblio le ingiurie. 12. Senza aria non s' odono i suoni. 13. I pipistrelli non escono che la notte. 14. Non si vien in fama sotto la coltre. 15. Ci convien stare appresso ai savi uomini. 16. Ella vien meno, cioè[c] sviene.

VOCABULARY.

to come, *venire*.	to hear, *udire*.
to tell, *dire*.	to open, *aprire*.
to come again, *rivenire*.	to throw wide open, *spalancare*.
to happen, *avvenire*.	to finish, *compiere* or *compire*.
to die, *morire*.	to be necessary, *convenire* (imp.)
to bury, *seppellire*.	to be contented with, *contentarsi*
to sew, *cucire*.	to offer, *offrire*. [*di.*
to go out, *uscire*.	to agree upon, *convenire*.

TRANSLATION EXERCISE.

1. Is your aunt coming to see   you   the-day-after-
   [Will your aunt come[d] to find]   *pos-*

to-morrow?   2. Yesterday she told – the porter that
domani   *al   portiere che*

she would come again this week.   3. Have you seen
                      questa

– poor Walter? 4. No; what has happened to him?
il povero Gualtiero   [is]

5. His sister Laura is dead.   She was buried yesterday,
Sua

---

[a] N.B., p. 109.   [b] Obs., p. 114.
[c] *cioè* is a compound word of *ciò*, that, and *è*, is.
[d] Note *e*, p. 62.

at – two (o'clock) in-the-afternoon.   6.   I am
alle   *pomeridiane*   [To me of it

very sorry indeed.   7. Joseph, where is the maid-
grieves[a] very much.]   *Giuseppe*   *la came-*

servant?   8. She is in the parlour   sewing.   9. Tell[b]
riera   *nella stanza* [that sews]

   her   to come here.   10. At what time do you go
[to her]   *quà*   [hour]

out (in) the morning?   11. I go out generally at –
       la   *per solito alle*

eleven (o'clock). Will you   go   with me?   12. I can-
                   Pres. Ind.   [come[c]] *meco*
                   of *volere.*

not this morning, because I am going for a ride with
                                   a cavallo

my uncle.   13. Who is coming up-stairs?   I hear
mio   *di sopra*

a footstep.   Oh, it is Joseph.   Well, have you told
un calpestio   *Or bene*

– the servant that I want her?   14. Yes,   ma'am,
alla   *lei*   *signora padrona*

and she said — she would come to you immediately.
        che   *da voi*   *subito*

15. Have you opened all the doors and – windows
                    tutti gli usci   e le finestre

upstairs?   16. I have thrown everything wide open.
di sopra   *tutto*

17. Have you entirely finished – your work?   18. I
           interamente   *il vostro lavoro*

have finished everything.   19. How much have I to
           ogni cosa

pay[d]?   Two   pounds?   20. I must be contented

---

  [a] Note *a*, p. 72, and Note *g*, p. 105.
  [b] Note *b*, p. 76, and Note *a*, p. 43.
  [c] *Venire*, instead of *andare*, must be employed in Italian when
desiring or offering to accompany any one to some place; as, *Volete
venire al teatro meco?* Will you go with me to the theatre?
  [d] Note *a*, p. 118.

with what you have offered me. 20. `Here-is-(for-you)
   quel che   *Eccovi*

what we have agreed upon.

QUESTIONS.

Che fanno le rimendatrici ? 3*.—Da chi fu contradetta
la nuova della pace? 5*.—Chi verrà a trovarvi posdomani ? 1.—Esce tutti i giorni vostra madre ? 11.—A chi
avete detto che voi studiate l'italiano?—Udite voi qualche
suono[a] ?—Quando avete compiuto il vostro lavoro? 17.—
Che si fa per dar aria alle stanze? 15 & 16.—Come si dice
in italiano[b]: "How much have I to pay ?" 18.—Con
chi ci convien stare per imparare ? 15*.—Dove avete
convenuto d' andare a passare l' estate ? 20

DEFECTIVE VERBS.

The following verbs are called Defective, because they
have only those Moods, Tenses, and Persons here
given:—

Algere, to be cold, to be chilled.
    Perfect—*álsi, algésti, álse, algémmo, algésti, álsero,*
        I was cold, &c. (No other tenses.)

Angere, to afflict.
    Indicative Present—*ánge,* he afflicts.

Arrógere, to add.
    Indicative Present...... *arróge,* he adds.
        „   Imperfect... *arrogéva,* he added.
        „   Perfect...... *arróse,* he added; pl. *arrósero,* they
                                   added.
    Present Participle...... *arrogéndo,* adding.
    Past Participle .... *arróso* or *arróto,* added.

---

[a] *Suono* means 'sound,' and may be used for any noise in general.
[b] Note *a*, p. 111.

Calére, to care for.

(This verb is conjugated impersonally, and requires the dative pronouns *mi, ti, gli,* &c., before it.)

Indicative Present...... *mi cále, ti cále,* &c., I care for, thou carest for, &c.

„ Imperfect... *mi caléva,* I cared for.

„ Perfect...... *mi cálse,* I did care for.

Subjunctive Present ... *che mi cáglia,* that I may care for.

„ Imperfect *se mi calésse,* if I might care for.

Present Participle ...... *calóndo,* caring for.

Past Participle .... *calúto,* cared for.

Cápere, to contain.

Indicative Present...... *cápe,* it contains.

„ Imperfect... *capéva,* it contained; and a few other forms.

Chérere, to ask.

Indicative Present...... *chéro,* I ask; *chére,* he asks.

Cólere, to worship, revere.

Indicative Present—*cólo,* I revere; *cóle,* he reveres.

Estóllere, to raise, exalt.

This verb is wanting in the Perfect and Past Participle only; all the other tenses are conjugated like *credere.*

Fiédere, to smite.

Indicative Present...... *fiédo, fiédi, fiéde,* I smite, &c.; pl. *fiédono,* they smite.

„ Imperfect... *fiedéva,* I was smiting.

„ Perfect...... *fiedéi,* I did smite.

Subjunctive Present... *che fiéda, che fiéda, che fiéda, che fiediámo, che fiediáte, che fiédano,* that I may smite, &c.

„ Imperfect *se fiedéssi, se fiedéssi, se fiedésse, se fiedéssimo, se fiedéste, se fiedéssero,* if I might smite, &c.

Present Participle ...... *fiedéndo,* smiting.

Folcíre, to prop up.

Indicative Present...... *fólce,* he props up.

Subjunctive Imperfect *se folcísse,* if he might prop up.

Gíre, to go.

This verb has, in the Indicative Present and the Imperative, *gíte,* you go, go (you); and in the Subjunctive Present *che giámo,* that we may go, and *che giáte,* that you may go. All its other moods and tenses are conjugated like *sentire,* but it has no Present Participle.

Ire, to go.

> Indicative Present...... *ite*, you go.
>   „   Imperfect... *iva, ivi, iva, ivámo, iváte, ivano,*
>   I was going, &c.
>   „   Perfect...... *isti*, thou didst go; *iste*, you did go.
>   „   Future ...... *irémo, iréte, iránno,* we shall go, &c.
> Imperative .... *ite*, go (you).
> Subjunctive Imperfect *isse*, that he might go ; *iste*, that
>   you &c.; *issero*, that they &c.
> Past Participle .... *ito*, gone.

Licere or *lécere*, to be lawful.

> Indicative Present...... *lice* or *léce*, it is lawful.
> Past Participle .... *lícito* or *lécito*, been lawful.

Lúcere, to shine.

> This verb is wanting in the 1st pers. sing. of the Indi-
> cative Present, of the Perfect and of the Past Parti-
> ciple ; all the rest is conjugated like *credere*.

Mólcere, to soothe.

> Indicative Present...... *mólce*, he soothes.
>   „   Imperfect... *molcéva*, he was soothing. (And a
>   few other forms.)

Olíre, to be fragrant.

> Indicative Imperfect... *oliva, olivi, oliva,* I was fragrant,
>   &c. ; pl. *olivano*, they were
>   fragrant.

Pávere, to fear.

> Indicative Present...... *páve*, he fears.

Récere, to be sick.

> This verb has only the Infinitive.

Riédere, to return.

> Indicative Present...... *riédo*, I return ; *riédi*, thou re-
>   turnest ; *riéde*, he returns ;
>   *riédono*, they return.
>   „   Imperfect... *rediva*, he was returning.
>   „   Perfect...... *redì*, he returned, *redirono*, tney &c.
> Subjunctive Present ... *che riéda*, that he may return;
>   *che riédano*, that they may &c.
>   „   Imperfect... *se riedísse*, if he might return.

Sérpere, to creep.

> This verb has only the singular and 3rd pers. pl. of the
> Present and Imperfect Indicative and Present Sub-
> junctive, as well as the Present Participle, conjugated
> like *credere*.

Silére, to be silent.
Indicative Present...... *silli, sile*, thou art silent, &c.

Soffólcere, to support.
Indicative Present...... *soffólce*, he supports.
" Perfect...... *soffólse*, he supported.
(And a few other forms.)

Solére, to be accustomed, to be wont.

Infinitive—*solére*, to be wont.

Indicative Present.

Singular.	Plural.
sóglio, I am wont.	*sogliámo*, we are wont.
suóli, thou art wont.	*soléte*, you are wont.
suóle, he is wont.	*sógliono*, they are wont.

Indicative Imperfect... *soléva*, I was wont.
" Perfect...... *fui sólito*, I was wont.
" Future...... *sarò sólito*, I shall be wont.
Conditional—*saréi sólito*, I should be wont.

(No Imperative Mood.)

Subjunctive Present.

ch' io sóglia, that I may be wont.	*che sogliámo*, that we may &c.
che tu sóglia, that thou &c.	*che sogliáte*, that you may &c.
ch' egli sóglia, that he &c.	*che sógliano*, that they may &c.

Subjunctive Imperfect—*s' io soléssi*, if I might be wont.

Present Participle—*soléndo*, being wont.
Past Participle—*sólito*, been wont.

Stúpere, to be astonished.
Indicative Present...... *stúpe*, he is astonished.

Tángere, to touch.
Indicative Present...... *tánge*, it touches.

Tóllere, to take away.
Indicative Present...... *tólli, tólle*, thou takest away, &c.
Subjunctive Present ... *che tólla*, that he may take away.

Tórpere, to become numb.
Indicative Present...... *tórpo, tórpe*, I become numb, &c.
Subjunctive Present ... *che tórpa, che tórpa, che tórpa*, that
I may &c.

Úrgere, to press.
Indicative Present...... *úrge*, he presses.
" Imperfect... *urgéva*, he pressed; pl. *urgévano*,
they pressed.

Subjunctive Imperfect *se urgésse*, if he might press; pl.
                  se urgéssero, if they might press.
Present Participle...... *urgénte*, pressing.

Vigere, to be vigorous.

     Indicative Present...... *vígo*, he is vigorous.
         „   Imperfect... *vigéva*, he was vigorous.

OBS.—To the above defective verbs must be added *ambire*, to crave, and *ardire*, to dare; which are wanting in the 1st person plural of the Present Indicative and of the Imperative, as well as in the 1st and 2nd persons plural of the Present Subjunctive, because those persons might be confounded with the corresponding forms of the verbs *ambiare*, to amble, and *ardere*, to burn. In the above cases, another verb of similar signification must be employed, or a different form be given to the expression; as, in the case of *ardire*, we would say *osiamo*, we dare, from the verb *osare*, or *abbiamo ardimento*, we are daring; and not *ardiamo*, which means ' we burn.'

N.B.—A few other verbs of the 3rd conjugation are also wanting in certain persons for the reason above given, and the same substitution of words or expressions must be made in their case also.[a]

OBSERVATIONS ON THE ORTHOGRAPHY OF VERBS

1. The 1st and 3rd persons plural of Italian verbs in all tenses (except the 1st person plural of the Perfect and Conditional) may drop the final vowel *o*; as, *parliam*, for *parliamo; parlan*, for *parlano; credevam*, for *credevamo; credevan*, for *credevano; sentiron*, for *sentirono; sentirem*, for *sentiremo; venderebber*, for *venderebbero; sentissim*, for *sentissimo*, &c.

---

[a] At the end of the book will be found an alphabetical list of all the verbs, and a table showing their conjugation.

2. When the 3rd person plural ends in *nno*, the last syllable *no* may be dropped; as, *han*, for *hanno; fan*, for *fanno*, &c.

3. The 3rd person plural of the Perfect of verbs ending in that person in *rono*, may drop the last syllable *no*, or even the last three letters; as, *furo* or *fur*, for *furono; parlaro* or *parlar*, for *parlarono; partiro* or *partir*, for *partirono*, &c.

4. The 2nd person singular of the Imperative of verbs ending in that person in *ni*, may drop the final vowel *i*; as, *tien*, for *tieni; pon*, for *poni*, &c.

5. Many Past Participles of the 1st conjugation ending in *ato* are frequently contracted in these terminations, by suppressing the *at*; as *priv-o*, for *priv-at-o; dest-o*, for *dest-at-o*, &c.

6. The 1st person singular of the Present Indicative of *essere* may drop the final vowel *o*; as, *son*, I am. (See also Obs. 1, p. 126.)

7. *ggi* is sometimes substituted for *d* in certain persons of verbs whose Infinitive ends in *dere*; as, *chieggio*, for *chiedo*, I ask; *riveggia*, for *riveda*, that I may see.

8. The letter *v* of the terminations of the 1st and 3rd persons singular and of the 3rd person plural of the Imperfect Indicative is often omitted in verbs belonging to the 2nd and 3rd conjugations; as, *avea*, for *aveva; credea*, for *credeva; dormiano*, for *dormivano*.

9. A few verbs are spelt with either the Infinitive termination *are* or *ire;* as *impazzare*, or *impazzire*, to go mad, &c. These verbs are differently inflected, each according to the conjugation to which its termination belongs. (See also Note *a*, p. 52; and Note *b*, p. 71.)

PHRASES.

calere di sapere alcuna cosa, to care for knowing anything.
gire a sarchiare il grano, to go to weed the corn.
lucere come la stella,[*] to shine like the sun.
esser tutto oro, to be all gold.
ire a casa, to go home.
olire soavemente, to smell sweet.
estollere la gran fronte, to raise the proud·brow.

---

[*] Poets often call the sun, *stella*, star.

tangere alcuna cosa, to touch anything.
soddisfare il bisogno che urge, to supply a pressing want.
appartenere di ragione, to belong of right.
voler dir la sua, to give one's opinion.
esser buono a dar consiglio, to be able to advise, counsel.

VOCABULARY.

già, already.
ancora, yet.
lucere, to glitter.

anche, also.
miseria, distress.

READING EXERCISE.

1. Non mi cal[a] di saper[b] chi voi siate. 2. Non aveva ancora cinque anni che già egli giva a sarchiare il grano. 3. Lucevan[c] gli occhi suoi più che la stella. 4. Non è tutto oro ciò che luce. 6. Quando irete voi a casa, irem[c] anche noi. 6. Siete ito a casa? 7. Come quelle viole olivano soavemente! 8. Egli la gran fronte estolle. 9. La vostra miseria non mi tange. 10. Quando il bisogno urge, si deve soddisfarlo. 11. Questa cosa m' appartien[a] di ragione. 12. Tutti voglion[c] dir la sua. 13. Tutti siam buoni a dar consiglio.

VOCABULARY.

to go, *ire, gire,* or *andare.*
to care, *calere.*
to smell sweet, *olire soavemente.*
usually (to be accustomed) to spend, *solere (essere solito) passare.*

to be allowed, *licere.*
to pick, *cogliere.*
to return, *tornare.*

TRANSLATION EXERCISE.

1. Where are you going, my friend? 2. I am going to the Crystal Palace. 3. Do you usually spend the
al Palazzo di cristallo

Saturday afternoon at that place? 4. I do not care to
dopopranzo a quel luogo   *di*

go there (on) any other day of the week. 5. Why, I
alcun altro   *della*   [Oh!]

---

* Note *b,* p. 71.   b Note *a,* p. 52.   c Obs. 1, p. 26.

was accustomed to go there, - last summer, every day,
tutti i giorni
and I remember how sweetly the flowers in the garden
i del
smelt. 6. But it is not allowed to pick the flowers.
7. Yes, I know, but I never returned to town
[I know it] [in]
without having* bought some flowers from a gardener.
dei da un

QUESTIONS.

Come si dice in italiano[b]: "It is not all gold that glitters"? 4*.—Dove siete ito oggi? 6*.—Sanno di buono° le viole? 7*.—Che si deve fare quando il bisogno urge? —Che cosa voglion dir tutti? 12*.—Solete ire sovente al Palazzo di cristallo? 3 & 4. — È lecito cogliere fiori nei giardini del Palazzo di cristallo? 6.

POETICAL FORMS OF CERTAIN VERBS.[d]

Essere, besides the forms given at pp. 12 and 13, has also
the poetical forms :—

fóro	for *furono*		fórano	}
fía	„ *sarà*		saríuno[e]	} for *sarebbero*
fíano fíeno	} „ *saranno*		saríeno	}
fóra saría	} „ *sarei*[e] or *sarebbe*		síeno	„ *siano*

E fallo fora *non fare a tuo senno.* (DAN. PAR.)
To distrust thy sense were henceforth error. (CARY.)
Onde fien *l' opre tue nel ciel laudate.* (PET. C.)
And on the holy work heaven's blessing shall descend.
(MACGREGOR.)

---

[a] Note *j*, p. 22.   [b] Note *a*, p. 111.   [c] See VOC., p. 70.
[d] Certain of the above poetical forms are sometimes used also in prose.
[e] The termination *ria* for the 1st and 3rd persons singular, and

G 3

Avere, besides the forms given at pp. 19 and 20, has in the Present Indicative *áve* for *ha.*

> *Soccorri al core omai che langue e posa non* ave. (D. Cas.)
> Help thou my heart that languishes and has no rest.

Fare, besides the forms given at pp. 59 and 60, has :—

fáce	for *fa*	fé	} for *fece*		
féa	„ *faceva*	féo	}		
féano	„ *facevano*	fémmo	„ *facemmo*		
féi	„ *feci*	féste	„ *faceste*		
fésti,	·, *facesti*	férono[a]	} „ *fecero*		
		fénno	}		

> *Italia ! Italia ! O tu cui feo la sorte*
> *Dono infelice di bellezza.* (FIL. S.)
>
> Italia ! O Italia ! thou who hast
> The fatal gift of beauty. (BYRON.)

> *Tolto m' hai, Morte, il mio doppio tesauro ;*
> *Che mi* fea *viver lieto e gire altero.* (PET. S.)
>
> Double the treasure death has torn from me
> In which life's pride was with its pleasure joined. (POTT.)

Potere, besides the forms given at pp. 65 and 66, has :—

puo'	for *puoi*	potè	for *potei*
puóte }		potéo[b]	„ *potè*
póte }	„ *può*	poría	„ {potrei / potrebbe}
potémo	„ *possiamo*		
pónno	„ *possono*	poríano	„ *potrebbero*

> *E, se mie rime alcuna cosa* ponno. (PET. S.)
> And if my verse shall any value keep. (MACGREGOR.)

---

riano or *rieno* for the 3rd person plural of the Conditional, may be used for all verbs instead of *rei, rebbe,* and *rebbero.*

> *.... Infranto*
> Avriano *già del rio tiranno il giogo.* (MAF. M.)
>
> Long since they would have shaken off the yoke of the wicked tyrant.

> *Si* vedria *che i lor nemici*
> *Hanno in sen.* (MET.)
>
> It would be seen that concealed within their breasts they lodge their foes.

[a] The termination *ero* of the 3rd person plural of the Perfect and Conditional has often been changed into *ono* by old writers.

[b] The 3rd pers. sing. Perfect has often a vowel affixed in poetry :
> *E poi che mosso* fue. (DANTE.)
> And when he had moved onward.

Volere, besides the forms given at pp. 66 and 67, has:—

vuóli ⎫			vólsi	for *volli*
vuó ⎬	for *vuoi*		vógli[a]	„ *voglia*
volía	„ *voleva*			

> *E venni a te, così com' ella volse.* (DANTE.)
> I came to thee, thus, as she wished.

OBSOLETE FORMS OF CERTAIN VERBS OFTEN MET WITH IN OLD ITALIAN WRITERS.

Essere—

sémo	for *siamo*		fústi	for	*fosti*
séte	„ *siete*		fússi	„	*fossi*
énno ⎫			séndo	„	*essendo*
én ⎬	„ *sono*		súto	„	*stato*
so' ⎭					

Avere—

ábbo ⎫			avémo	for	*abbiamo*
aggío ⎬	for *ho*		éi	„	*ebbi*
aio ⎭			arò	„	*avrò*
háe	„ *ha*		aggía	„	*abbia*

Fare—

fáci	for *fai*		facía[b]	for	*faceva*
fáe ⎫			faróe[c]	„	*farò*
fáce ⎬	„ *fa*				

Finally, the termination is sometimes changed for the sake of rhyme. Dante uses *venesse* for *venisse.*[d]

> *Ma non sì che paura non mi desse*
> *La vista che m' apparve d' un leone;*
> *Questi parea che contro me* venesse. (DAN. IN.)
> New dread succeeded, when in view
> A lion came 'gainst me, as it appeared. (CARY.)

---

[a] The 2nd pers. sing. of the Present Subjunctive of all verbs of the 2nd and 3rd Conjugations may end either in *i* or in *a*.

[b] The termination *ía* is often used for *ea* or *eva*, in the Imperfect of the Indicative.

[c] We often find the vowel *e* affixed to the 1st and 3rd pers. sing. of the Future.

[d] For further examples of obsolete and erroneous forms, see Delâtre's Teoria dei Verbi italiani.

CHAPTER III.

NOUNS.

In speaking of Nouns, Gender, Number, and Case are to be considered.

GENDER.

The Italian language has two genders only, the *masculine* and the *feminine*.

There being no neuter gender, both nouns of *beings possessing animal life*, and nouns of *things destitute of life*, must, in Italian, be either masculine or feminine. The rules, however, for determining the gender of each of the above two classes of nouns are different.

RULES FOR DETERMINING THE GENDER OF NOUNS OF BEINGS POSSESSING ANIMAL LIFE.

RULE I.—Nouns denoting males are masculine; as, *uomo*, man; *poeta*, poet; *re*, king; *Giovanni*, John; *leone*, lion, &c.

RULE II.—Nouns denoting females are feminine; as, *donna*, woman; *poetessa*, poetess; *regina*, queen; *Maria*, Mary; *leonessa*, lioness, &c.

EXCEPTIONS.

1. *Santità*, holiness; *Maestà*, majesty; *Eminenza*, eminence; *Eccellenza*, excellency; *Signoria*, lordship or ladyship; *guida*, guide; *guardia*, guard, watch; *sentinella*, sentry; *spia*, spy; are always *feminine*, even when denoting a man.

2. All surnames, also as *nipote*, nephew or niece; *erede*, heir or heiress; *tigre*, tiger or tigress; *idiota*, an idiot man or an idiot woman, and a few other nouns, applied alike to both *males* and *females*, are of the common gender, *i.e. masculine* and *feminine*.

3. *Fante*, meaning a 'foot-soldier,' is masculine; when it means a 'maid-servant,' it is feminine.

DISTINCTIONS OF GENDER OF THE ABOVE NOUNS.

There are five ways of distinguishing the masculine from the feminine of nouns of *beings possessing animal life* :—

1. By employing a different word for each gender.

Masculine.	Feminine.
padre, father.	*madre,* mother.
frate, friar.	*monaca,* nun.
re, king.	*regina,* queen.
cané, dog.	*cagna,* bitch.

2. By suffixing a termination.

conte, earl.	*contessa,* countess
guidatore, a male guide.	*guidatrice,* a female guide
imperatore, emperor.	*imperatrice,* empress.
pastore, shepherd.	*pastoressa,* shepherdess.
eroe, hero.	*eroina,* heroine.
gallo, cock.	*gallina,* hen.

3. By merely changing the termination.

ragazzo, boy.	*ragazza,* girl.
sarto, tailor.	*sarta,* dressmaker.
cervo, stag.	*cerva,* hind.
fattore, steward.	*fattora,* stewardess

4. By prefixing a distinguishing word.

Giovanni Colonna, John [Colonna.	*Vittoria Colonna,* Victoria [Colonna.
Signor Tasso, Mr. Tasso.	*Signora Tasso,* Mrs. Tasso.
il giovine, the young man.	*la giovine,* the young woman.
un idiota, an idiot man.	*un' idiota,* an idiot woman.

This class comprises those nouns which are of the common gender. (See Excep. 2, p. 132.)

5. By appending a distinguishing word.

cammello maschio, a male [camel.	*cammello femmina,* a female [camel.
aquila maschio, a male [eagle.	*aquila femmina,* a female [eagle.

VOCABULARY.

come si chiama...? or } what is the name of...?
come si denomina...? }

colui che[a], he who, the man who.
colei che, she who, the woman who.

QUESTIONS.

[N.B.—The words to be used in answering the following questions
have already been given in previous exercises. Should the
student not recollect them, they must be looked for in the
Vocabulary at the end of the book.]

Come si chiama colui che compone versi?.... colui
che fabbrica le case?.... che fa e vende il pane·?....
che guarisce le malattie?.... che conduce al pascolo le
pecore?—Come si chiama il soldato che va a piedi[b]?—
Come si denomina colei che ha cura dei bambini?....
colei che cuoce la minestra, la torta?.... che pulisce le
stanze?

RULES FOR DETERMINING THE GENDER OF NOUNS OF THINGS DESTITUTE OF LIFE.

All nouns in Italian terminate in one or other of the
vowels *a, e, i, o, u*[c]. It is by these terminations that
the gender of nouns of *things destitute of life* can generally be determined.

A.

RULE I.[x]—Nouns ending in *a* are feminine; as, *carta*,
paper; *bottega*, shop, &c.

EXCEPTIONS.

1. Are masculine :—

(i.) Terms of science, in general ending in *ma;*
as, *telegramma*, telegram; *anagramma*, anagram;
prisma, prism, &c.

(ii.) Names of mountains ending in *a;* as, *Etna*,
Etna, &c.

---

[a] See Demons. and Relat. Pron., p. 9.
[b] See Excep. 3, p. 132.
[c] *Lapis*, pencil, *diesis*, semitone, *ribes*, a currant, and a few
other nouns found in Italian ending with a consonant, are foreign
words used in their primitive state. They are masculine, and have
the same termination in both singular and plural.

(iii.) The names of the following three rivers : *Mella, Pescara, Volga,* and of the lake *Ladoga.*

(iv.) All the nouns in the following list :—

baccalà, dried cod.	*poema,* poem.
boa, boa.	*problema,* problem.
Canadà, Canada.	*proclama,* proclamation.
cholera, cholera.	*programma,* prospectus.
clima^a, climate.	*sofà,* sofa, couch.
emblema, emblem.	*sciloma,* a long speech.
falpalà, flounce.	*sistema,* system.
idioma, tongue.	*stemma,* coat of arms.
Panamà, Panama.	*taffetà,* taffety.

2. The nouns *diadema,* diadem, *scisma,* schism, *stratagemma,* stratagem, and the names of the two rivers *Adda* and *Brenta,* are of the common gender.

3. The nouns *dramma, pianeta, tema,* in the signification of 'drama,' 'planet,' 'theme,' are *masculine;* and in the signification of 'drachm,' 'cope,' 'fear,' are *feminine.*

O.

RULE II.—Nouns ending in *o* are masculine ; as, *oro,* gold ; *argento,* silver, &c.

EXCEPTIONS.

1. *Mano,* hand ; which is feminine.

2. *Milano,* Milan, and all names of towns ending in *o,* are of the common gender.

3. *Eco,* echo, is feminine in the singular, and masculine in the plural.

OBS.—*Vorago, Cartago, immago,* and *testudo,* are feminine ; but they are only used in poetry, and are contracted from *voragine,* gulf, *Cartagine,* Carthage, *immagine,* image, *testudine,* tortoise, all feminine nouns.

U.

RULE III.—Nouns which end in *u* are feminine ; as, *gioventù,* youth ; *virtù,* virtue ; *servitù,* the servants, &c.

EXCEPTIONS.

Perù, Peru ; *fisciù,* neckerchief ; *bambù,* bamboo ; *accagiù,* mahogany ; *soprappiù,* overplus ; *meu,* dill (herb) ; are masculine.

---

^a Almost all nouns in the above list ending in *ma* are Greek neuters.

E—I.

Of nouns ending in *e* or *i*, some are masculine and some feminine; as,

Masculine.	Feminine.
fiume, river.	*neve*, snow.
brindisi, toast.	*metropoli*, metropolis.

These being very irregular in regard to gender, the dictionary must be referred to in order to ascertain it. However the following rules will be of some assistance to the student :—

RULE I.—All nouns ending in *zione* and *udine* are feminine ; as, *nazione*, nation; *inquietudine*, disquietude, &c.

RULE II.—The noun *dì*, *day*, and all its derivatives, *lunedì*, Monday, *mezzodì*, mid-day, &c., are masculine.

RULE III.—*Analisi*, analysis ; *diocesi*, diocese ; *ellissi* or *ellisse*, ellipsis ; *parentesi*, parenthesis ; *genesi*, origin, and a few more nouns ending in *i*, are feminine.

RULE IV.—Almost all names of kingdoms and provinces and rivers ending in *e* or *i*, are masculine ; as, *Tamigi*, Thames ; *Piemonte*, Piedmont.

RULE V.—The names of towns ending in *i* or *e*, as *Napoli*, Naples, *Firenze*, Florence, &c., and the nouns *aere*, air, *carcere*[a], prison, *cenere*[a], ashes, *elce*, holm-oak (tree), *fine*[b], end, *folgore*, thunderbolt, *fonte*, fountain, *fronte*[c], forehead, *fune*[c], rope, *gregge*[a], flock, *rovere*, oak-tree, *trave*, beam, *Genesi*, the book of Genesis, *eclissi*, eclipse, are of the common gender.

RULE VI.—*Dimane*, *margine*, in the signification of ‘to-morrow,’ ‘brink,’ are masculine ; but in the signification of ‘the break of day,’ ‘scar,’ are feminine.

OBSERVATIONS ON THE GENDERS OF NOUNS OF THINGS DESTITUTE OF LIFE.

1. With regard to the letters of the alphabet, the

----

[a] *Carcere, cenere, gregge*, in the plural, are feminine only.
[b] *Fine*, in the signification of ‘aim,’ is masculine only.
[c] *Fronte* and *fune* in prose are feminine only.

letters *a*, *e*, *f*, *h*, *l*, *m*, *n*, *r*, *s*, *z* are of the *feminine* gender; all the others are *masculine*.

> Ex.: *Ceno contò dall'* [a] *A fino alla Z ogni cosa*. (Ces.)
> Ceno related everything from beginning to end.

2. Any part of speech converted into a noun is masculine.[b]

> Ex.: *Lo*[a] sprecare *nuoce, contentati* del[a] *poco*. (Pand.)
> Extravagance is injurous; be contented with little.

3. Masculine nouns in *o*, being names of trees, change their termination into *a*, and become feminine, to denote the fruit; as, *pero*, pear-tree, and *pera*, a pear (the fruit), &c. ; excepting however *fico*, fig ; *dattero*, date ; *cedro*, cedar ; and *pomo*, apple ; which do not change, and are always masculine, both when signifying the tree and the fruit. Similar nouns in *e* are masculine when denoting the tree, and feminine when denoting the fruit ; as, *un*[a] *noce*, a nut-tree ; *una*[a] *noce*, a nut ; excepting *limone*, lemon, which is masculine in both instances.

4. Some nouns have two terminations in the singular, one in *o* and another in *a*. In the first case they are masculine, and in the second feminine ; as, *mattino* (mas.) or *mattina* (fem.), morning. Other nouns have either the termination *a* or *e*, and others *o* or *e*. The nouns having the two former terminations are always feminine, and those having the two latter ones are masculine, as, *ala* or *ale*, wing (fem.) ; *pensiero* or *pensiere*, thought (masc.).

[N.B.—The knowledge of the gender of a noun is necessary in order to the correct use of the articles, adjectives, pronouns, and past participles, which have in Italian to agree with the nouns.]

VOCABULARY.

ottavo, eighth.	*oncia*, ounce.
parte, part.	*componimento*, composition.

---

[a] See Articles, p. 8.

[b] Adjectives ending in *e*, cardinal numbers, and some possessive, demonstrative, and indefinite pronouns, when converted into nouns, may be either masculine or feminine, according to the gender of the noun they represent. Examples of these will be given in those chapters of this book, which treat of the above parts of speech.

prezioso, precious.   *maschile,* masculine.
metallo, metal.   *frutto,* fruit.
che nome si da... ? what is called... ?   *melo,* apple.

QUESTIONS.

Come si chiama l' acqua che piove ?....l' ottava parte
d' un' oncia[a] ? — Che componimento è il "Comus" di
Milton[b]?—Come si chiama il più prezioso dei metalli[c] ?—
Che nome si dà a tutti i servi d' una casa[d] ?....a molte
pecore che vanno insieme ?—Quali giorni della settimana sono maschili ?—Come si dice[e] il frutto del melo[f] ?
....del pero ?....del limone ?....del fico ?

NUMBER.

Italian nouns have two numbers, *Singular* and *Plural.*
Both the nouns of *beings possessing animal life* and of
those destitute of life follow the same rules in forming the
plural.

I. Feminine nouns in...**a** form the plural in **e**; as,

	Sing.	Plur.
	sorella, sister ;	*sorelle.*

II. { Masculines in ...... **a** }
    { Masc. and Fem. in **e** } form the plural in **i**; as,
    {   ,,   ,,   **o** }

Sing.	Plur.
poeta, poet ;	*poeti.*
padre, father ;	*padri.*
madre, mother ;	*madri.*
mano, hand ;	*mani.*
fratello, brother ;	*fratelli.*

III. { Masc. and Fem. in **i** }
     {   ,,   ,,   **u** }
     {   ,,   ,,   **ie** } are invariable ; as,
     { Monosyllables......... }
     { Nouns with accented }
     { final vowel .... }

Sing.	Plur.
metropoli, capital ;	*metropoli.*
virtù, virtue ;	*virtù.*
specie, kind ;	*specie.*
re, king ;	*re.*[g]
città, city ;	*città.*

N.B.—Of those nouns which have two terminations in
the singular (see Obs. 4, p. 137), those which end in

---

[a] See Excep. 3, p. 135.   [b] See Excep. 1 (iv.), p. 135.
[c] Rule II., p. 135.   [d] Rule III., p. 135.   [e] Note *a*, p. 111.
[f] See Obs. 3, p. 137.   [g] See Nouns, p. 7.

o and in *a* will have in the plural *i* and *e*; as, *cesto, cesta*, basket; pl. *cesti, ceste*. Those which end in *a* or *e* will have in the plural *e* and *i*; as, *ala, ale*, wing; pl. *ale, ali*. Those which end in *e* and *o* will have only one termination in the plural; as, *cavaliere, cavaliero*, knight; pl. *cavalieri*.

OBSERVATIONS ON THE EUPHONIC MODIFICATION OF PLURAL NOUNS. (See also p. 7.)

1. Nouns ending in *ca* or *ga* form the plural in *che* and *ghe* when feminine, and in *chi* and *ghi* when masculine; as, *monaca*, nun, *monache;* *bottega*, shop, *botteghe;* *monarca*, monarch, *monarchi; collega*, colleague, *colleghi*.

2. Nouns ending in *cia* or *gia* (with *i* not accented) form the plural in *ce* and *ge;* as, *guancia*, cheek, *guance*. This alteration, however, is not made when the accent falls on the *i*; as, *Lucia*, Lucy, *Lucie; bugia*, lie, *bugie*.

3. Nouns ending in *io* form the plural by dropping the final *o*; as, *specchio*, looking-glass, *specchi*. When, however, the accent falls on the *i*, the plural is formed regularly; as, *zio*, uncle, *zii*. The latter mode is employed also in words which might be mistaken for others of a different meaning; as, *tempio*, temple, has *tempii* or *tempj*, to distinguish it from *tempi*, plural of *tempo*, time.

4. Nouns of two syllables ending in *co* or *go* form the plural in *chi* and *ghi;* as, *bosco*, wood, *boschi; lago*, lake, *laghi*. Excepting *porco*, pig, *Greco*, Greek, which in the plural make *porci, Greci.*[*] So *mago*, one of the Magi, makes plural *magi;* but *mago*, a magician, has the plural *maghi*.

5. Nouns of more than two syllables ending in *co* and *go* take *h* in the plural when these terminations are preceded by a consonant; as, *tedesco*, German, *tedeschi*, Germans. When the final syllables *co* and *go* are preceded by a vowel, they form the plural in *ci* and *gi;* as, *amico*, friend, *amici*.

---

[*] When *greco* is used adjectively to qualify *wine*, it takes an *h* in the plural, and we say, *vini grechi*, Greek wines.

The following words are exceptions to the last rule, and take an *h* in the plural:—

abaco, abacus.	*parroco*, curate.
antico,* ancient.	*pedagogo*, pedagogue.
beccafico, fig-pecker.	*pelago*, ocean.
caduco, perishable.	*pizzico*, pinch.
carico, load.	*presago*, diviner.
castigo, punishment.	*prodigo*, prodigal.
catalogo, catalogue.	*prologo*, prologue.
demagogo, demagogue.	*pudico*, chaste.
epilogo, epilogue.	*rammarico*, regret.
fondaco, warehouse.	*ripiego*, expedient.
impiego, employment.	*rogo*, funeral pyre.
incarico, charge.	*risico*, risk.
indaco, indigo.	*sacrilego*, sacrilegious.
impudico, immodest.	*sambuco*, elder-tree.
intrigo, intrigue.	*statico*, hostage.
intrinseco, intrinsic.	*stomaco*, stomach.
lastrico, pavement.	*strascico*, train.
manico, handle.	*traffico*, traffic.
obbligo, obligation.	*ubbriaco*, drunkard.
opaco, opaque.	

Plural *abachi, antichi, beccafichi,* &c.

With the following words the *h* may be either employed or not:—

analogo, analogous.	*filologo*, philologue.
apologo, apologue.	*fantastico*, fantastic.
aprico, sunny.	*idropico*, dropsical.
astrologo, fortune-teller.	*mendico*, mendicant.
bifolco, ploughman.	*pedagogo*, pedagogue.
dialogo, dialogue.	*selvatico*, wild.
dittongo, diphthong.	*zotico*, boorish.
equivoco, mistake.	

These may be in the plural *analogi* or *analoghi, apologi* or *apologhi,* &c.

---

* Adjectives and nouns, in the formation of the plural, follow the same rules. *Cardinal numbers,* however (except *mille* and *milione*), remain invariable in their termination. Some pronouns, which are also used as adjectives, have special forms in the plural, which will be found in the chapters of this book which treat of them.

IRREGULAR PLURALS.

The irregularity in the plural of nouns is of three different kinds, as shown in the following lists (see p. 7):

I. Nouns having anomalous plurals.

Singular.	Plural.
uomo, man.	*uomini.*
dio, god.	*dei.*
bue, ox.	*buoi.*
moglie, wife.	*mogli.*

II. Nouns which, ending in the singular with the masculine termination *o*, become feminine by forming their plural in *a*.

Singular Masc.	Plural Fem.
centinaio, a hundred.	*centinaia.*
migliaio, a thousand.	*migliaia.*
miglio, a mile.	*miglia.*
moggio, a measure of corn equal to a bushel.	*moggia.*
paio, a pair.	*paia.*
staio, a bushel.	*staia.*
suolo, the sole of a shoe.	*suola.*
uovo, an egg.	*uova.*

N.B.—*Donora*, wedding presents, and *tempora*, the four Ember weeks, are the feminine plurals respectively of the masculine nouns *dono* and *tempo*.

III. Nouns in *o* having two terminations in the plural, one regular in *i*, masculine, and an irregular one in *a*, feminine.

Sing. Masc.	Pl. Masc.	Pl. Fem.
anello, ring.	*anelli.*	*anella.*
braccio, arm.	*bracci*[a].	*braccia.*
budello, bowel.	*budelli.*	*budella.*
calcagno, heel.	*calcagni.*	*calcagna.*
carro, cart.	*carri.*	*carra.*
castello, castle.	*castelli.*	*castella.*
ciglio, eyebrow.	*cigli*[a].	*ciglia.*
cervello, brain.	*cervelli.*	*cervella.*
cogno, a wine measure of ten barrels.	*cogni.*	*cogna.*

---

[a] Obs. 3, p. 139.

Sing. Masc.	Pl. Masc.	Pl. Fem.
coltello, knife.	*coltelli*.	*coltella*.
comandamento, commandment.	*comandamenti*.	*comandamenta*.
corno, horn.	*corni*.	*corna*.
dito, finger or toe.	*diti*.	*dita*.
digiuno, fasting.	*digiuni*.	*digiuna*.
fastello, bundle of wood.	*fastelli*.	*fastella*.
fosso, ditch.	*fossi*.	*fossa*.
filo, thread.	*fili*.	*fila*.
fondamento, foundation.	*fondamenti*.	*fondamenta*[a].
frutto, fruit.	*frutti*.	*frutta*[b].
fuso, spindle.	*fusi*.	*fusa*.
gesto, gesture.	*gesti*.	*gesta*[c].
ginocchio, knee.	*ginocchi*.	*ginocchia*.
gomito, elbow.	*gomiti*.	*gomita*.
grido, cry.	*gridi*.	*grida*.
labbro, lip.	*labbri*.	*labbra*[d].
legno, wood.	*legni*.	*legna*[e].
lenzuolo, sheet.	*lenzuoli*.	*lenzuola*.
membro, member.	*membri*.	*membra*[f].
muro, wall.	*muri*.	*mura*[g].
osso, bone.	*ossi*.	*ossa*.
peccato, sin.	*peccati*.	*peccata*.
pomo, apple.	*pomi*.	*poma*.
pugno, fist.	*pugni*.	*pugna*.
quadrello, dart.	*quadrelli*.	*quadrella*.
riso, laugh.	*risi*.	*risa*[h].
sacco, bag.	*sacchi*.	*sacca*.
strido, shriek.	*stridi*.	*strida*.
vestigio, vestige.	*vestigi*.	*vestigia*.
vestimento, raiment.	*vestimenti*.	*vestimenta*.

---

[a] *fondamenti* and *fondamenta*, foundations of a building; for 'fundamental principles,' only *fondamenti* is used.

[b] *frutti*, *frutta*, or *frutte*, the fruit of a tree; *frutti*, the income, interest, or productions of the earth.

[c] *gesti*, gesticulations; *gesta*, exploits.

[d] *labbri* or *labbra*, lips; *labbri*, brim of a cup.

[e] *legni*, ships, coaches, or billets of wood; *legna* or *legne*, firewood.

[f] *membri*, members of a society; *membra*, limbs of the body.

[g] *muri*, the walls of a house; *mura*, the walls of a fortress; but in poetry *mura* is also used for the walls of a house.

[h] *risi* or *risa* laughter; *riso*, rice, has plural *risi* only.

Defective Nouns.

(1.) Some nouns have only the singular, and want the plural; as, *aere*, air; *mane*, morning; *tema*, fear; *mano*, handful of men, &c.

(2.) Other nouns want the singular, being only used in the plural:—

annali (m.), annals.   *moine*, caresses.
carabottole, riff-raff.   *molle*, tongs.
cesoie, shears.   *nozze*, nuptials.
fasti (m.), annals.   *spezie*, spices.
forbici, scissors.   *stoviglie*, crockery-ware.

N.B.—The words in the above list which have not the gender indicated, are feminine.

Plural of Compound Nouns.

1. Some nouns form the plural by inflecting the principal noun, and leaving invariable the word that serves to qualify it; as, *capopopolo*, popular chief; plural, *capipopolo; cassamadia*, a kneading-trough, pl. *cassamadie.*

2. Other compound nouns inflect both compounding words according to the general rules; as, *bassorilievo*, bas-relief, pl. *bassirilievi.*

3. Finally, nouns composed of a verb and a noun generally remain invariable; as, *guardavivande*, pantry, pantries, &c.

Observations on the Orthography of Nouns.

1. Some nouns ending in *l, m, n*, or *r*, followed by a vowel, may drop their final vowel; as, *sal* for *sale*, salt; *don* for *dono*, gift, &c.

2. When the noun ends in *llo*, it drops the final syllable *lo;* as, *agnel* for *agnello*, lamb.

See also Use of Capitals, p. 6.

Vocabulary.

oggetto, object.   *scheletro*, skeleton.
cerchio, ring.   *animale* (m.), animal.
ornamento, ornament.   *melarancio*, orange.

QUESTIONS.

Che fa il muratore?.... il sarto?—Quante dita abbiamo in ciascuna[a] mano?—Con che possiamo noi vedere gli oggetti?—Come si chiamano i cerchi d' oro che si portano in dito per ornamento[b]?—Di che si compone lo scheletro d 'un animale?—Che cosa produce il melarancio[c]?

CASE

Italian nouns are not declined. The prepositions *di*, of, *a*, to or at, *da*[d], from or by, are used to point out the relations between the Subject and Object with the Possessor and indirect Object[e]; as,

> *Ho dato a Luigi il libro di Pietro che è venuto da Parigi,*
> I have given *to* Louis Peter's book which came *from* Paris.

OBS.—There is only one way of expressing in Italian, the possessive case, *i. e.* with the preposition *di*. This preposition denotes also *affinity, source,* and *material;* as,

> *pena di morte,* pain of death ;
> *vino d' Oporto,* port wine ;
> *bottiglia di vino,* bottle of wine.

Di must not to be confounded with *da*, which denotes *use, destination,* and *derivation;* as,

> *bottiglia da vino,* wine bottle ;
> *cavallo da vendere,* horse to be sold ;
> *moda (venuta) da Parigi,* Parisian fashion.

---

[a] See Indef. Pron., p. 10.   [b] III., p. 141.
[c] See Obs. 3, p. 137; Obs. 2, p. 189; and Obs. 2, p. 143.
[d] Note *g*, p. 48.
[e] It is customary with many to speak of Italian nouns as if declined, and then to the terms Nominative &c. the same meaning is given in Italian as in Latin grammar. We do not do so in the case of nouns, because Italian nouns, strictly speaking, are not declined; but we will adopt the above plan with the Personal and Relative Pronouns, which have proper case inflections.

CHAPTER IV.

ARTICLES.

THE Articles are *definite* and *indefinite*.

I. The *definite* article in Italian has different forms for gender and number:—

Il and *lo* (the) for the masculine singular, *la* (the) for the feminine singular. In Italian the definite article agrees in gender and number with the noun with which it is used.

$$\left.\begin{array}{lll}
il \text{ makes in the plural } i \\
lo \quad,, \quad\quad ,, \quad\quad gli \\
la \quad,, \quad\cdot\quad ,, \quad\quad le
\end{array}\right\} \text{ the.}$$

II. The forms of the *indefinite* article are *un, uno* (a *or* an) for the masculine singular; *una* (a *or* an) for the feminine singular.

The indefinite article, of course, has no plural.

RULES FOR THE USE OF THE DEFINITE ARTICLE.

RULE I.—The *masculine il*, pl. *i*, is used before all words beginning with a consonant, except an *s* followed by another consonant:

Ex.:   Il *figliuolo savio fa lieti* i *genitori.* (DA RIP.)
           The wise son makes his parents happy.

EXCEPTIONS.

1. Before the noun *Dei*, plural of *Dio*, God, *gli* is always used:

Ex.:   *I pagani adoravano* gli *dei menzogneri.* (SEGN.)
           Pagans adored lying gods.

2. After the preposition *per*, for, &c., *lo* is more properly used before either a vowel or a consonant:

Ex.:   *Tenendo per* lo *braccio l' infermo.* (Boc.)
           Holding the sick person by the arm.

RULE II.—The *masculine lo*, plural *gli*, is used before words beginning with *s* followed by a consonant, as well as before vowels:

Ex.: Lo *sparviere perseguita* gli *uccelletti*. (SEGN.)
The falcon pursues small birds.
Fuggi gli *oziosi*. (ALB.) Shun idle persons.

EXCEPTIONS.

1. Before *z* or *sci* or *sce*, either *il* or *lo*, and *i* or *gli* may be used; as, *il* or *lo zio*, the uncle; *i* or *gli scellerati*, the wicked.

2. In poetry, and in old writers, we find *li* frequently used instead of *i* or *gli*; as, *li padri*, the fathers, *li scogli*, the sea rocks.

3. Poets very often use *il* and *i*, or *lo* and *gli*, indifferently before any letter:

Ex.: *Il splendido*, the splendid. *Lo giorno*, the day.
Gli rami (DAN.), the branches.

RULE III.—The *feminine la*, pl. *le*, is used before consonants and vowels[*]; as,

Contieni la *lingua, e raffrena* le *mani*. (S. CONC.)
Moderate thy language, and hold thy hands.

OBSERVATIONS ON THE ORTHOGRAPHY OF ARTICLES.

1. The forms *lo, la, le* before vowels are generally spelt *l'*:

Ex.: *Canto l' armi pietose* (TAS.), I sing the pious arms, &c.

2. *Gli* drops the *i* and takes an apostrophe only before another *i*:

Ex.: *Fuggi gl' ingannatori* (ALB.), Shun deceivers.

3. *Il* sometimes takes an apostrophe in place of the *i* after a word ending with a vowel:

Ex.: *E 'l duca a lui* (DAN.), and my leader to him.

OBSERVATIONS.

The combinations of the above forms of the definite article with prepositions have been already given (see p. 8), and we have to add in regard to them the following observations:—

---

[*] See Definite Articles, p. 8.

1. The poets very often use the prepositions separate from the article; in which case the prepositions *di*, of, and *in*, in, become *de* and *ne :*

> Ex.: *Mostra altrui l' error* de *la mogliere.* (ARI.)
> It shows to others the fault of the wife.
>
> *Fece il Romeo chiamar* ne *la sua corte.* (ARI.)
> She had the pilgrim called into her court.

2. *Del, dello, della,* in the singular, and *dei, degli, delle* in the plural, are used as adjectives of quantity for *some, any, a few ;* as,

> *Datemi del pane,* give me some bread.
> *Portatemi dei zolfanelli,* bring me a few matches.
> *Avete delle noci?* have you any nuts?

3. The above adjectives are only employed where it is necessary to convey an idea of quantity. To denote quality in such cases no adjective is used; as, *bevete vino?* do you drink wine?

4. When one substantive in English compound words is used adjectively to qualify another, the order of the words is reversed in Italian, and *del, dello, della,* &c., is sometimes used; as, *la porta della strada,* the street-door (see Obs., p. 144.)

RULES FOR THE USE OF THE INDEFINITE ARTICLE.

RULE I.—The masculine *un* is employed before all words beginning with a vowel or consonant, except *s* followed by another consonant ; as,

> *Un amico è un tesoro,* a friend is a treasure.

RULE II.—The masculine *uno* is used before words beginning with *s* followed by another consonant ; as,

> *Io aveva* uno *specchio,* I had a looking-glass.

EXCEPTIONS.

Before *z*, or *sci*, or *sce*, either *un* or *uno* may be used; as, *uno* (or *un*) *zio*, an uncle.

RULE III.—*Una* is used before words beginning with a consonant, and before a vowel drops the *a* and takes an apostrophe*; as, *dopo una vittoria,* after a victory ; *un' ombra,* a shadow.

---

* See Indef. Article, p. 8.

Obs.—When the preposition *su* precedes the indefinite article, an *r* is affixed to the preposition; as, *sur una porta*, on a door; *sur un pilastro*, on a pillar, &c.

EXERCISE.

Write the nouns given in the exceptions to 'Rules for knowing the gender of nouns of things destitute of life,' at pp. 134, 135, and all the irregular plurals given under I. and II., p. 141, each with its proper *definite* article.

Also write, with the *indefinite* article, those defective nouns which are used only in the singular. (See p. 143.)

RULES FOR DETERMINING THE USE OF THE DEFINITE ARTICLE.

The definite article is employed in Italian according to general rules analogous to those which regulate its use in English. But there are certain cases in which the definite article is required in Italian, though not in English; and others in which it must be used in English, though not in Italian.

Rules for determining when the Definite Article is required in Italian, though not used in English.

RULE I.—The Italian definite article is used before a common noun used to represent an entire class of beings:

Ex.:   L'*uomo propone e Dio dispone.* (PROV.)
              Man proposes and God disposes.

RULE II.—Before any noun taken in a general sense, in both numbers:

Ex.:   *Non è ver che sia* la *morte*
              Il peggior di tutti i *mali.* (MET.)
      It is not true that death is the worst of all evils.

RULE III.—Before any noun preceded by an adjective of quality:

Ex.:   Il *povero Pietro ha perduto la sorella.*
              Poor Peter has lost his sister.

RULE IV.—Before almost all names of countries taken comprehensively:

Ex.:   *Gran torto faceste* alla *Francia e* all' *Italia.* (BEN. C.)
              You would do great wrong to France and to Italy.

If, however, we speak of going to, coming from, or dwelling in, a country, or use the proper name adjectively to characterise something else, the article is to be omitted :

Ex.: *Mi dispiacque di non ritornar in Italia per Francia.* (Ben. C.)
I was sorry at not returning to Italy through France.

Questo giugno di Francia non è quasi altro che un aprile d' Italia. (Ben. C.)
This June of France is hardly anything but an April of Italy.

Rule V.—Before any part of speech converted into a noun:

Ex.: *La donna veggendo che* il *pregare non le valeva.* (Boc.)
The woman seeing that praying was of no use.

Umana cosa è aver compassione degli *afflitti.* (Boc.)
It is a humane thing to have compassion for afflicted persons.

Il bel paese là dove il *si suona.* (Dan.)
The beautiful country where *si* is spoken.

Rule VI.—Before titles and names denoting rank ; as, *regina,* queen, *generale,* general, *padre,* father, &c. ; also *signor,* Mr., *signora,* Mrs., *signorina,* Miss, followed by the proper name of the person of whom we are speaking ; as,

La *regina Vittoria,* Queen Victoria.
Il *generale Garibaldi,* General Garibaldi.
Il *padre Maccario,* Father Maccario.
Il *signor Ferrari,* Mr. Ferrari.
La *signora Monti,* Mrs. Monti.
La *signorina Loti,* Miss Loti.

1. When the above titles, and names denoting rank, are preceded by a demonstrative adjective, as *questo, quello,* &c., or are followed by the proper name (expressed or understood) of a person to whom we speak or write, the definite article is not used before them ; as,

Signor Conte, Sir Count.
Quel generale Garibaldi, that general Garibaldi.

2. Before the following nouns : *sere,* Sir; *messere,* Mr.; *maestro,* Master; *madamigella,* Miss ; *madama,*

Mrs.; *don*, Don; *donna*, Donna; *frate* or *fra*, friar
or brother; *monsignore*, my lord (a dignitary of the
Church); *santo* or *santa*, Saint, followed by a proper noun, the article is not used; as,

> *Messer Pietro*, Mr. Peter.
> *Maestro Adamo*, Master Adamo.
> *Don Giovanni*, Don Juan.
> *Fra Cristoforo*, Brother Christopher.

3. Before *papa*, pope, and *re*, king, followed by
a proper noun, the article may be used or not; as,

> (*il*) *papa Bonifacio*, Pope Boniface.
> (*il*) *re Carlo*, King Charles.

RULE VII.—Before surnames of known characters
(male and female), and christian names of women, when
an adjective is implied;

Ex.:   Del *Correggio lo stil puro e sovrano*.   (TAS.)
   The pure and majestic style of Correggio (meaning *del ce-
   lebre Correggio*).
   Canta ancora la Grisi? Does Madame Grisi still sing?
   La Caterina è partita, Catherine is gone (meaning *la bella
   Caterina*, or *la conosciuta Caterina*, the beautiful, or the
   well-known Catherine).

RULE VIII.—Before the following names of cities:—

il Cairo, Cairo.   *la Roccella*, Rochelles.
la Mirandola, Mirandola.   *l' Aia*, the Hague.

RULE IX.—Before the following names of islands:—

la Sardegna, Sardinia.   *l' Elba*, Elba.
la Corsica, Corsica.   *la Sicilia*, Sicily.
la Capraia, Capraia.   *l' Inghilterra*, England.
la Corgona, Corgona.   *l' Irlanda*, Ireland.

RULE X.—Before the nouns *giorno* or *dì*, day, *settimana*, week, *mese*, month, *anno*, year, and the names of
the seasons, especially when used with an adjective; as,

> *la settimana passata*, last week.
> *l' anno prossimo*, next year, &c.
> *il verno scorso*, last winter.
> *ai dì passati*, a few days ago.

RULE XI.—Generally before possessive pronouns, before some relative and indefinite pronouns, and sometimes before *mille*, thousand; as will be explained in
treating of those pronouns and of numerals.

Rules for determining when the Definite Article is not used in Italian, though required in English.

RULE I.—The Article is not used in Italian before an ordinal number, in sentences like the following :—

    Carlo primo fu re d' Inghilterra,
    Charles *the* First was King of England.

RULE II.—The emphatic use in English of the definite article before *more* in comparative adjective forms, is not admissible in Italian; as, *più studio, più imparo, the* more I study, *the* more I learn.

RULE III.—No article is used in expressions like the following :—

    Stare or *essere in casa, in piazza, in campagna, in città, in giardino,* to live *or* to be in the house, the square, the country, the city, the garden. So *andare in casa,* &c., to go into the house, &c.

    Venire or *uscire di casa, di città, di campagna,* to come from, or go out of, the house, the city, the country.

    Parlare italiano, francese, &c., to speak the Italian (French, &c.) language, &c. &c.

N.B.—The poets often omit the article in cases where it would be necessary in prose, or in conversation.

Ex. :   *Morte ebbe invidia al mio felice stato.* (PET.)
      Death envied my happy condition.

      S'Africa pianse, Italia non ne rise. (PET.)
      If Africa wept, Italy did not laugh.

OBSERVATIONS ON THE USE OF THE DEFINITE ARTICLE.

1. When two or more nouns, or adjectives converted into nouns, follow one another in a sentence, if they are of *different gender* and *number*, or have *meanings very distinct from one another*, the article is repeated before every one.

Ex. :   *Lascia le lagrime e i sospiri.* (GUA.)
      Cease from tears and sighs.
      Dio fa piovere sopra i giusti e gl' ingiusti. (S. CON.)
      God makes the rain fall on the just and unjust.

2. When two or more nouns or adjectives refer to one *subject*, the article must not be repeated.

Ex. :   *Il poco e temperato cibo è utile.* (S. CON.)
      Little and moderate food is useful.

3. When two or more nouns are of *the same gender and number*, the article may be repeated before every one, or only used with the first noun.

Ex.: Il *vino e il frumento allegrano* il *cuor degli uomini, ma sopra amendue si è* la *sapienza e dottrina.*
Wine and corn cheer up the hearts of men, but above both of them is wisdom and goodness.

Rules for determining when the Indefinite Article is not required in Italian, although used in English.

RULE I.—The indefinite article is not used in Italian before nouns employed in the predicate to represent *profession, rank, state,* or *country;* as,

Egli è poeta, he is *a* poet.
È marchese, he is *a* marquis.
È italiano, he is *an* Italian.

RULE II.—Nor before *hundred* and *thousand;*
cento scudi, a hundred crowns.
mille scudi, a thousand crowns.

RULE III.—Nor before a noun used in *apposition* to or *qualifying* another which precedes it; as,
Il Tamigi, fiume che passa per Londra.
The Thames, a river which passes through London.

RULE IV.—Nor before a noun where the connection does not admit of the possibility of a plural number; as,
Ella ha buona voce, She has a good voice.

RULE V.—Nor after *che* and *quale* used as exclamations; as, *Che peccato!* What a pity!
Qual prodigio! What a prodigy!

OBS.—The definite article is used instead of the indefinite in Italian in speaking of measure, weight, or time, in sentences like the following:
Tre lire il *metro,* three lire *a* metre.
Due soldi la *libra,* two soldi *a* pound.
Tre volte il *giorno,* three times *a* day.

READING EXERCISE.

[N.B.—The words in the Anecdotes must be looked for in the Vocabulary at the end of the book.]

Un alchimista, il quale si vantava d' aver finalmente scoperto il gran segreto di far l' oro, chiedeva al Pontefice Leone Decimo una ricompensa. Questi[a] gli fe'[b] presente d' una lunga e larga borsa vuota, dicendogli : " Giacchè sapete far l' oro, voi non avete bisogno d' altro che d' una bella borsa per riporlo[c]."

VOCABULARY.

verb, *verbo.*	to roar, *ruggire.*	teacher, *maestro.*
sound, *suono.*	pig, *porco.*	to draw, *disegnare.*
to express, *esprimere.*	to grunt, *grugnire.*	nephew } *nipote.*
animal, *animale.*	wolf, *lupo.*	niece }
dog, *cane.*	to howl, *urlare.*	egg, *uovo.*
to bark, *abbaiare.*	mouse, *topo.*	bread, *pane.*
to growl, *latrare.*	to squeak, *squittire.*	tea, *tè.*
horse, *cavallo.*	cock, *gallo.*	fruit, *frutta.*
to neigh, *nitrire.*	to crow, *cantare.*	grapes, *uva* (sing.)
ass, *asino.*	bird, *uccello.*	key, *chiave.*
to bray, *ragliare.*	to chirp, *garrire.*	drawer, *tiratoio.*
sheep, *pecora.*	parrot, *papagallo.*	to fetch, *andare a*
goat, *capra.*	to talk, *parlare.*	*prendere.*
to bleat, *belare.*	to prefer, *preferire.*	bunch, *grappolo.*
ox, *bue.*	to teach, *insegnare.*	fig, *fico.*
to bellow, *muggire.*	singing, *canto.*	hothouse, *serra.*
cat, *gatto.*	drawing, *disegno.*	wedding, *nozze* (plur.)
to mew, *miagolare.*	prince, *principe.*	to marry, *sposarsi.*
lion, *leone.*	Alfred, *Alfredo.*	daughter, *figlia.*

TRANSLATION EXERCISE.

SUBJECTIVE and } 1. Charles, tell me — the verbs
OBJECTIVE. }
    quali sono

by which the sounds made by[d] different animals are
con cui   *diversi*

expressed[e]. 2. The dog barks and growls ; the horse neighs[f] ; the donkey brays ; the sheep and the[g] goat bleat ; oxen[h] bellow ; cats mew ; lions roar[i] ; pigs grunt[i] ; wolves howl ; mice[i] squeak[f] ; cocks crow birds sing and chirp[f] ; parrots talk. 3. Quite right, Charles. [It goes well]

---

[a] *Questi,* the latter person. (See Dem. Pron. p. 9.)
[b] See *fare,* p. 130, and Note *d,* p. 129.
[c] *riporlo* a compound word, consisting of *ripor* (= *riporre*) to store, and *lo,* it.   [d] Note *b,* p. 49
[e] Group VI., p. 99.   [f] Obs., p. 39.   [g] Obs. 1, p. 151.
[h] Rule II., p. 149, and I., p. 141.   [i] Obs. 3, p. 139.

4. What does Mr.[a] D. teach ?   5. He teaches singing[b]
and drawing.   {POSSESSIVE CASE and INDIRECT OBJECT.}   6. Is he the teacher of
Prince[a] Alfred ?   7. No; but he taught drawing to
Tennyson's[c] nephew[d] and niece.   8. What will[e] you
have for breakfast ?   9. Some eggs[f], a cup of tea, and
     da
some bread (and) butter.   10. Is this your father's
    imburrato   *questa*
cup ?   No; it is Mr. A.'s.   11. When I was in Italy[g]
I used to eat fruits[h] for breakfast : they do not drink
         da
tea in Italy.   12. I will give you some grapes, if you
prefer it.   John, where is the key of the garden door[i] ?
     lo
13. It is upstairs, sir, in the drawer.   14. Fetch me
    di sopra
two or three bunches of grapes, and a few figs from the
                   [in]
hot-house.   15. Is your brother gone to Paris ?   16. No;
he left yesterday for Edinburgh.   He is invited to the
wedding of Mr. D., who is going to be married to Mr.
                che   [will marry with]
T.'s daughter to-morrow.

QUESTIONS.

Che animali avete in casa ?—Con quali verbi espri-
miamo le voci[j] degli animali domestici ? 2.—Chi in-
segnò il canto a vostra sorella ? 7.—A che ora farete
colazione domani ? 8.—Che vuole vostro fratello da
colazione ? 9.—Che frutta preferite ?—Siete stato alle
nozze del Signor e della Signora T. ? 18.—Che segreto
credeva d' aver scoperto un alchimista[k] ?—Che presente
fece Leone X. all' alchimista ?—Che disse il papa
dandogli la borsa ?

---

[a] Rule VI., p. 149.   [b] Rule II., p. 148.
[c] Obs., p. 144.   [d] Exceptions 2, p. 132, and No. 4, p. 133.
[e] Note *d*, p. 70.   [f] II., p. 141, and Obs., p. 147.
[g] Excep. 1, to Rule IV., p. 149.   [h] Note *b*, p. 142.
[i] Obs. 4, p. 147.   [j] *voce*, sound.   [k] See Reading Ex., p. 153.

CHAPTER V.

ADJECTIVES.

All the adjectives terminate in one or other of the vowels *o, e, i.*

Rules on the Concord of Adjectives.

Rule I.—An Adjective, in Italian, must agree in gender and number with the noun, expressed or understood, which it qualifies.

Rule II.—Adjectives ending in *o* are masculine, and change the *o* into *a* for the feminine; as,

Masculine.	Feminine.
Re benefico,	*Regina benefica.*
a beneficent king.	a beneficent queen.

Rule III.—Adjectives ending in *e* and *i* are of both genders; as,

Masculine.	Feminine.
uomo felice,	*donna felice,*
a happy man.	a happy woman.
orgoglio pari,	*forza pari,*
equal pride.	equal strength.

Rule IV.—When the adjective refers to two or more nouns, it must stand in the plural.

Rule V.—The plural of adjectives is formed in the same manner as that of nouns. Hence,

(i.) The adjectives in *o* have four terminations; as,

	Singular.	Plural.
Masc.	*Re benefico,*	*Re benefici.*
Fem.	*Regina benefica,*	*Regine benefiche.**

(ii.) The adjectives in *e* have only two terminations; as,

	Singular.		Plural.	
Masc.	*uomo*	} *felice,*	*uomini*	} *felici.*
Fem.	*donna*		*donne*	

---

* Note *a*, p. 8.

(iii.) The adjectives in *i* have only one termination ; as,

Singular.		Plural.	
Masc. *orgoglio*	} *pari,*	*orgogli*	} *pari.*
Fem. *forza*		*forze*	

N.B.—The plural adjective *several* is expressed by *parecchi* for the masculine, and by *parecchie* for the feminine ; as,

Masc. *parecchi uomini,*   Fem. *parecchie donne.*

RULE VI.—With two or more nouns of *beings possess-ing animal life* of different gender, the adjective stands in the plural masculine.

Ex.:   *Lo scorpione e la vipera sono* velenosi.
The scorpion and the viper are poisonous.

RULE VII.—With two or more nouns of *things des-titute of life* of different gender, the adjective may be in the plural masculine, or made to agree in gender and number with the noun nearest to it.

Ex.:   *Tornano* utili *il biasimo e la lode.*
Blame and praise become useful.
Il decoro e la modestia ne' giovani è molto lodata.
Propriety and modesty in youth are much praised.   ·

RULE VIII.—With the word *persona,* person, or with *ogni cosa,* everything, the adjective may be in the masculine gender.

Ex.:   *La persona quando è* tribolato.
When a person is in trouble.

RULES ON THE POSITION OF ADJECTIVES.

RULE I.—Adjectives are generally placed after their substantives ; as, *una Signora francese,* a French lady.

EXCEPTIONS.

Adjectives expressing either *quantity* or *size,* numeral adjectives, and a few denoting *beauty, ugliness, goodness,* and *holiness,* generally precede their nouns ; as,

molto pane, much bread.
quanta paura, how much fear.
tanti pericoli, so many dangers.   ·

troppe[a] *pere*, too many pears.
poca[b] *speranza*, little hope.
piccolo libro, small book.
grande casa, large house.
due uova, two eggs.
bello specchio, beautiful looking-glass.
brutto animale, ugly animal.
cattivo ragazzo, bad boy.
buono scolare, good pupil.
Santo Stefano, St. Stephen.

RULE II.—Two or more adjectives qualifying the same noun, may be placed before or after the substantive; as, *varie e diverse novità*, various and different novelties; *con panni larghi e lunghi, e voci umili e mansuete*, with garments full and long, and language humble and meek.

RULE III.—Sometimes they are separated by putting one of them before, and the other or others after the noun, whereby grace and elegance is given to the phrase; as, *nobile giovane e bella*, a noble and beautiful young woman; *nobili vestimenti e ricchi*, rich and elegant clothes.

RULE IV.—There are some adjectives which may be placed either before or after their nouns, but whose position affects the signification; as, *un galant' uomo*, a good, an honorable man; *un uomo galante*, a courteous, a gallant man; *un gentil uomo*, a gentleman, a nobleman; *un uomo gentile*, a civil, gentle, courteous, kind man; *un semplice contadino*, a single (no more than one) countryman; *un contadino semplice*, a simple (inexperienced) countryman.

OBSERVATIONS ON THE ORTHOGRAPHY OF ADJECTIVES.

1. *Bello* makes *bel* before nouns beginning with a consonant (except *s* followed by a consonant), and drops

---

[a] Notice that the quantitative adjectives *molto, tanto, quanto, troppo*, are sometimes adverbs, in which case they are invariable.
[b] After *poco* used substantively the preposition *di* is employed; as, *un poco di pane*, a little bread.

the *o* before nouns beginning with vowels. The plural
of *bello* is *begli;* of *bel, bei;* and of *bell', begli;* as,

Singular.	Plural.
bello specchio,	*begli specchi.*
bell' occhio,	*begli occhi.*
bel libro,	*bei libri.*

Several other adjectives ending in *ello* follow the same
rule.

2. *Grande* and *Santo* before nouns beginning with a
consonant, except *s* followed by a consonant, are shortened by one syllable, and become *gran, San;* as,

gran male, great evil.   *San*[a] *Pietro,* St. Peter.
grande studio, great study.   *Santo Stefano,* St. Stephen.

Before vowels, *grand'* and *Sant'* are used; as,

grand' animo, great spirit.   *Sant' Antonio,* St. Anthony.
Grandi (plural of *grande*) may also lose the final syllable; as,

gran pericoli, great dangers.   *gran richezze,* great riches.

3. *Buono* drops the *o* before nouns beginning with
vowels and consonants, except *s* followed by a consonant; as,

buon uomo, good man.   *buon medico,* good physician.

4. Other adjectives ending in *o* and *e* may sometimes
drop the final vowel before nouns beginning with any
letter except *s* followed by a consonant; as, *Donna è
gentil nel cielo* (DAN.), There is a gentle woman in heaven.

*Nessun maggior dolore
Che ricordarsi del tempo felice nella miseria.* (DAN.)

No greater pain
Than to recall, in wretchedness, the happy days gone by.

READING EXERCISE.

Era stato uno Svizzero della guardia pontificia posto
in sentinella all' ingresso della cappella Sistina in Roma,
coll' ordine di non lasciarvi più entrare alcuno: temendo
forse i prelati che il caldo eccessivo, prodotto dal troppo[b]
gran[c] concorso di gente, non incomodasse il Pontefice

---

[a] Instead of *santo*, the initial *S* is generally used; and for the
plural, *SS.* The above contraction of *santo* does not take place
when that word signifies 'holy.'

[b] Note *a*, p. 157.   [c] Obs. 2, above.

che colà assisteva al divino[a] uffizio. Molte persone si presentarono dopo alla porta, ma in vano; l'irrevocabile parola, "Non si entra," le costringeva a ritirarsi. Un giovine ecclesiastico, cui[b] era ben nota la rigida precisione del soldato svizzero, presentossi anch' egli francamente all' ingresso. "Non si entra," disse lo Svizzero. "Io non entro, ma esco," rispose prontamente l' abatino. Il soldato non avendo alcuna consegna che vietasse di lasciar uscire chi[c] voleva, si ritirò, e l' altro entrò nella cappella, tutto glorioso e trionfante, ridendosi della dabbenaggine dello Svizzero.

VOCABULARY.

to re-) *mutare casa,*	other, *altro.*	furniture, *mobilia.*
move) *sgomberare.*	clean, *pulito.*	to furnish, *mobiliare.*
small, *piccolo.*	forecourt, *cortile* (m.)	piece of furniture, *mobile* (m.)
pleasant, *piacevole.*	to consist, *consistere.*	
neighbourhood, *vicinato.* [nato.	rest, *resto.*	beautiful, *bello.*
new, *nuovo.*	convenient, *conveniente.*	rich, *ricco.*
too, *troppo.*		carpet, *tappeto.*
large, *grande.*	library, *libreria.*	comfortable, *comodo.*
family, *famiglia.*	lofty, *alto.*	couch, *sofà* or *canapè* (m.)
floor, *piano.*	hall, *vestibolo.*	
ground, *terreno.*	wine-cellar, *cantina.*	chair, *sedia* or *seggiola.*
first, *primo.*	cool, *fresco.*	looking-glass, *specchio.*
second, *secondo.*	pantry, *dispensa.*	
attics, *soffitta* (sing.)	ventilated, *ventilato.*	to spare one's self, *risparmiarsi.*
bed-room, *camera.*	wall (of a room), *parete* (f.)	
to look (of a window), *dare.*		trouble, *fastidio.*
	to paper, *tappezzare*	white, *bianco.*
pretty, *bello.*	*di carta.*	black, *nero.*
full, *pieno.*	to paint, *dipingere.*	

TRANSLATION EXERCISE.

1. Oh, what good[d] wind brings you here to-day, Mrs.[e] B.? 2. I have removed, and have taken a small house in - your pleasant neighbourhood; therefore, I
    nel vostro
have come[f] to see you. 3. How do you like[g] - your
    [find]   *la vostra*

---

[a] Exceptions, p. 156.
[b] *Cui* is often used without the preposition *a,* to, which is understood. (See Rel. Pron., p. 9.)   [c] See Ind. Pron., p. 10.
[d] Obs. 3, p. 158.   [e] Excep. 1 to Rule VI., p. 149.
[f] Obs. 3, p. 51, and Note *e*, p. 62.   [g] Note *a*, p. 72.

new house ?   4. I like it, but it is too small for – my
                                                    la mia

large family.   5. How many[a] floors are[2] there[1] ?   6. Four ;
the ground floor[b], the first[a] floor, the second floor, and
the attics.   7. And how many bed-rooms are[2] there[1] ?
8. Four bed-rooms, two of – which look into a pretty[c]
                           delle quali   *in*

garden full of beautiful[c] flowers, and the other two into
a clean fore-court.   9. What[2] does the rest of the house
consist[3] of[1] ?   10. There is a pretty drawing-room, and
      [in]

a convenient library, a lofty hall, a cool wine cellar, and
a[1] well[3] ventilated[4] pantry[2].   11. Are the walls of the
drawing-room papered[d] or painted?   12. They are
papered.   13. Have you bought all the furniture?
14. I have taken the house furnished. There are beautiful pieces of furniture, rich carpets, comfortable
couches and chairs, large tables and looking-glasses,
so-that I have spared myself a-great-deal-of trouble.
sicchè   [much]
15. You have done right; will you have a glass of
                     [well]

wine?   Do you like white or red (wine).   16. I
     [Do you like it[e]]   [black]
prefer red[f] (wine).

QUESTIONS.

Perchè volete mutar casa ? 2 & 4.—Quando sgom-
bererete ? 2.—Quanti piani ha la vostra villa ? 5.—Dove
danno le finestre del salotto ? 8.—Dove si tiene il vino ?
—Che mobili avete nel vostro salotto ? 14.—Chi era
stato posto in sentinella all' ingresso della cappella Sistina ?—Che ordine aveva ricevuto la guardia ?—Che
rispose il giovane ecclesiastico per entrare nella cappella ?

---

[a] Exception 1, p. 156.   [b] Rule 1, p. 156.   [c] Obs. 1, p. 157.
[d] Note *f*, p. 13.   [e] Note *a*, p. 72.   [f] Rule V., p. 149.

DEGREES OF ADJECTIVES.

In Italian, as in English, there are three degrees of adjectives :—the *Positive*—*dotto*, learned ; the *Comparative*—*più dotto*, more learned ; the *Superlative*—*dottissimo*, most learned.

ON COMPARATIVES.

RULE I.—The comparison of *equality* is expressed by—

tanto or *altrettanto*...... ..*quanto ;*

or *così* (or *sì*) ....*come*[a] (or *siccome*) ;

Eng. : ' as' (or negatively ' so')...' as.'

Cesare fu tanto *valoroso* quanto *Pompeo.*
Cæsar was as brave as Pompey.

Avete tanti *libri* quanti *ne ho io.*
You have as many books as I have.

Il fratello non è così *ricco* come *la sorella.*
The brother is not so rich as the sister.

N.B.—*Tanto . . . quanto* are used both for *quality* and *quantity ;* and *così . . . come* only for *quality. Tanto .... quanto,* when used for *quantity,* agree in gender and number with the noun, and remain invariable when used for *quality*[b].

OBSERVATIONS.

1. The *tanto* (*altrettanto,* or *cotanto*) and *sì* or *così,* are frequently omitted, and then *quanto* or *come* alone serves to express the comparison ; as,

Il mio cane è fedele come *il vostro.*
My dog is as faithful as yours.

Essa non è bella quanto *sua sorella.*
She is not so handsome as her sister.

2. *Quanto,* with *tanto* or *altrettanto* following it, serves to express the English *in proportion as . . . so ;* as,

Quanto *il primo era dolce* altrettanto *aspro era il secondo.*
In proportion as the first was gentle, so the second was fierce.

---

[a] The word *come* cannot be rendered in English in expressions like the following :—*La volpe,* come *falsa e micidiale* (PUL.), the fox, false and murderous.   [b] Note *a*, p. 157.

3. The following forms are also frequently met with
in the works of good Italian writers :—

> *Egli è valoroso* al pari *di voi.*
> He is as brave as you.

> *Cesare fu valoroso* non meno che *Pompeo.*
> Cæsar was as brave as Pompey.

> Quale *è il padre* tale *è il figlio.*
> As the father is, such is the son.

4. In translating the expression *the more . . . the more,*
the less . . . the less, the definite article is omitted in
Italian[a], or *quanto* and *tanto* are substituted; as,

> Più *la vedo,* più *mi piace.*
> The more I see her, the more I like her.

> Quanto *si mostra men,* tanto *è più bello.* (TAS.)
> The less it is shown, the more beautiful it is.

5. The expression *as quick as possible* is rendered in
Italian by *il più presto possibile,* or *quanto più presto si
possa.*

RULE II.—The comparison of superiority is expressed
in Italian by placing before the positive the adverb *più,*
more ; as,

> *Le pesche duracine sono più belle che buone.*
> Chingstone peaches are more beautiful than good.

> *È più ricco di Creso.*
> He is richer than Crœsus.

N.B.—The English comparative, formed with the
suffix *er,* is likewise rendered in Italian by *più.*

RULE III.—The comparison of inferiority is expressed
by putting *meno,* less, before the *Positive ;* as,

> *La dieta è una medicina* meno *di tutte cara.*
> Diet is a medicine less dear than any other.

The word *than,* which follows the comparative in
English, is rendered in Italian by *che* or *di,* and sometimes also by *che non* or *di quello che.*

---

a Rule II., p. 150.

RULE IV.—*Che* is used to render *than*, when this word is followed by an *adjective*, a *verb* in the Infinitive, or an *adverb*, or is preceded by the words *rather* or *sooner*; as,

Egli è più buono che *dotto*.
He is more good than learned.

È meglio fare che *dire*.
It is better to do than to say.

È meglio tardi che *mai*.
It is better late than never.

Piuttosto *la morte* che *il disonore*.
Death rather than dishonour.

Gli occhi anzi *grossi* che *piccoli*. (Boc.)
His eyes rather large than small.

RULE V.—*Di*, alone, or in its compounds *del, dello, della, dei, degli, delle*, is used to render *than*, when this word is followed by a *pronoun*, a *numeral*, or a *noun*; as,

Io sono più ricco di lei[a].
I am richer than she.

Quel cavallo è più bello del *vostro*.
That horse is more beautiful than yours.

Ho più di due cavalli.
I have more than two horses.

Giovanni è più dotto di Tomaso.
John is more learned than Thomas.

OBSERVATIONS.

1. When *than* is followed by a verb not in the Infinitive, it is rendered by *che non*, or *di quel che*; as,

Affligge più che *non* (or *di quel che*) *conforta*.
He afflicts more than he comforts.

2. Before *più* or *meno* are often found in Italian the words *assai, molto*, or *vie*, much, *troppo*, too much, and *di gran lunga*, by far, which give greater force to the comparison; as,

---

[a] Notice that *lei* is the inflected form of *ella*, *di* being the sign of the Possessor in Italian.

Vedi Sansone, vie più *forte che savio.* (PET.)
See Sampson, far more strong than wise.

3. 'More' and 'less,' denoting numerical excess, are rendered in Italian by *ancora* or *di più*, and *di meno*; as,

Ho due lezioni di più.
I have two lessons *more.*

Voi n' avrete due di meno.
You shall have two *less.*

4. 'Longer' or 'farther,' in relation to time and distance, is translated by *più*; as,

Non la vedo più.
I see her no longer.

5. *Più* is used adjectively for 'several'; and *manco* is sometimes found instead of *meno*; as, *manco male*, not quite so bad.

ON SUPERLATIVES.

The Superlative is either *absolute* or *relative.*

RULE I.—The *absolute superlative* may be formed in two ways:—

(1.) By translating *very* or *most* by *assai*, or *molto*, or *oltremodo*; as,

Egli è assai (or *molto*) *dotto*, he is very learned.

(2.) By changing the termination of the adjective into *issimo* or *issima*, *issimi* or *issime*; as,

Egli è dottissimo, he is very learned.

N.B.—Adjectives ending in *io* lose these two vowels before the superlative termination *issimo*; as, *saggio*, wise, *saggissimo.*

And adjectives ending in *co* and *go*, *ca* and *ga*, which take an *h* in the plural, take it also before *issimo*; as, *largo*, wide, *larghissimo*; *ricco*, rich, *ricchissimo*, &c.

RULE II.—A few adjectives form the absolute superlative in *errimo*; as,

celebre, celebrated, *celeberrimo.*
salubre, salubrious, *saluberrimo*, &c.

Rule III.—The *relative superlative* is formed by adding the definite article to the Comparative; as,

Egli è il più dotto inglese del secolo.
He is the most learned Englishman of the age.

La meno diligente scolara della scuola.*
The least diligent pupil in the school.

OBSERVATIONS.

1. English superlatives in *est*, as *finest, dearest*, &c., must also be translated according to the above rule— *il più bello, il più caro*, &c.

2. "What do you like best?" is rendered in Italian, *Che vi piace più?*

3. When the relative superlative follows the substantive, no article should intervene; as,

Il soldato più attivo, ⎱ The most active soldier.
Il più attivo soldato, ⎰

OBSERVATIONS.

1. The following modes of forming the superlative are also found in the works of good Italian writers:—

Nella egregia[b] città di Firenza, oltre ad ogni altra *italica* bellissima. (Boc.)
In the illustrious city of Florence, the most beautiful amongst Italian cities.

Basì diventò piccin piccino. (Buonar.)
Basì became very little.

Fammi, che puoi, della sua grazia degno, senza fine o *beata.* (Pet.)
Since thou, O exceedingly blessed, canst make me worthy of his grace.

Amava i denari senza misura. (Manz.)
She loved money above measure.

---

* Observe that this superlative takes generally *di* after it, instead of *in*.

[b] *Egregio*, most celebrated, *esimio*, excellent, are used principally in epistolary style; as, *egregio signore*=worthy sir. But the most common forms in letters are *Pregiatissimo* (or *Stimatissimo*) *Signore* = most worshipful sir.

2. *Stra* or *arci* is sometimes prefixed to the positive; as, *strabello* or *arcibello*, very beautiful.

3. In all languages, the adjectives which express some invariable quality do not admit either the comparative or superlative degree. These are—

(i.) The ordinal adjectives; as, *primo*, first.

(ii.) Adjectives denoting *birth, place, nation,* or *appurtenance;* as,

francese, French. *paterno,* paternal.
romano, Roman. *regio,* kingly.

(iii.) Adjectives like the following: *eterno,* eternal, *immortale,* immortal, &c.

Nevertheless the superlative of *italiano,* Italian, *italianissimo,* and a few others, are admitted by custom.

COMPARATIVES AND SUPERLATIVES WITH PARTICULAR FORMS.

There are some comparatives and superlatives which, besides the usual form, have others derived from the Latin. These are—

COMPARATIVES.

maggiore, or *più grande,* larger.
minore, or *più piccolo,* smaller.
migliore, or *più buono,* better.
peggiore, or *più cattivo,* worse.
superiore, or *più alto,* superior.
inferiore, or *più basso,* inferior.

SUPERLATIVES.

ottimo or $\begin{Bmatrix} molto\ buono \\ buonissimo \end{Bmatrix}$ very good, or best.

pessimo or $\begin{Bmatrix} molto\ cattivo \\ cattivissimo \end{Bmatrix}$ very bad, or worst.

massimo or $\begin{Bmatrix} molto\ grande \\ grandissimo \end{Bmatrix}$ very large, or largest.

minimo or $\begin{Bmatrix} molto\ piccolo \\ piccolissimo \end{Bmatrix}$ very little, or least.

sommo or $\begin{Bmatrix} molto\ alto \\ altissimo \end{Bmatrix}$ very high, or highest.

infimo, *imo,* $\Big\}$ or $\begin{Bmatrix} molto\ basso \\ bassissimo \end{Bmatrix}$ very low, or lowest.

OBSERVATIONS.

Either of the above forms may, generally, be used, but attention must be paid to the following observations :—

1. *Maggiore* and *minore*, *superiore* and *inferiore*, cannot be employed when speaking of the size or height of one object ; in the latter case we must say *più grande*, and *più piccolo ;* as,

> *La vostra mela è più piccola della mia.*
> Your apple is smaller than mine.

2. *Minore* = youngest ; *maggiore* = eldest ; as, *sono il minore*, I am the youngest ; *è la maggiore*, she is the eldest.

3. *Better*, when an adverb, is translated by *meglio ;* and *worse*, when not an adjective, is rendered by *peggio ;* as, *tanto meglio*, so much the better ; *tanto peggio*, so much the worse.

> Meglio *oggi che domani.*
> Better to-day than to-morrow.

4. ' Least,' as adverb, is rendered by *meno ;* ' at least,' by *almeno.*

5. *Most men*, and similar expressions, are rendered by *la maggior parte* degli uomini, &c.

6. The adjectives *maggiore*, &c., preceded by an article, become relative superlatives ; as,

> *Il maggior benefattore è Dio.*
> The greatest benefactor is God.

7. The adjectives *ottimo*, &c., are *absolute superlatives,* but when preceded by the definite article, they become *relative superlatives ;* as,

> *Egli è un ottimo uomo,* he is a very good man.
> *Egli è l' ottimo uomo del mondo,* he is the best man in the world.

READING EXERCISE.

Partii di Parigi verso il mezzo gennajo, in compagnia
di un cavaliere mio paesano, giovine di bellissimo[a]
aspetto, di età circa dieci o dodici anni più avanzato di[b]
me, di un certo ingegno naturale; ignorante, quanto[c]
me; riflessivo assai[d] meno, e più amatore del gran
mondo che conoscitore o investigatore degli uomini.
Egli era cugino del nostro Ambasciatore in Parigi, e
nipote del Principe di Masserano allora Ambasciatore di
Spagna in Londra, in casa del quale[e] egli doveva alloggiare. Benchè io non amassi gran fatto[f] di compagnia
per viaggio, pure per andare a un determinato luogo e
non più[g], mi ci accomodai volentieri. Questo mio nuovo
compagno era di un umore assai lieto[h] e loquace, onde
con vicendevole sodisfazione io taceva e ascoltava, egli
parlava e si lodava. (ALFIERI.)

VOCABULARY.

suburb, *sobborgo.*	picturesque, *pitto-*	Europe, *Europa.*
wonderful, *ammira-*	*resco.*	to try, *cercare di.*
bile.	to expect, *aspettarsi.*	to go up, *ascendere.*
environs, *contorni.*	view, *prospettiva.*	Blanc, *Bianco.*
little, *poco.*	handsome, *bello.*	to go down, *scendere*
far, *lontano.*	to ascend, *salire su.*	*per.*
ancient, *antico.*	high, *alto.*	way, *via.*
to build, *fabbricare.*	mountain *or* mount,	short, *corto,*
	monte	

TRANSLATION EXERCISE.

1. Are the suburbs of Florence as[i] interesting as the
city?   2. Not less[j] wonderful than the city (itself) are
its environs.   Do you see that building a little
[the environs of it]   *quel*
further than[b] the "Forte Belvedere?" It is the very

---

[a] Rule I (2), p 164, and Excep. 1, p. 156.
[b] Rule V., p. 163.   [c] Obs. 1, p. 161.   [d] Obs. 2, p. 163.
[e] See Relat. Pron., p. 9.   [f] *Gran fatto*, much.
[g] Obs. 4, p. 164.   [h] Rule I. (1), p. 164.   [i] Rule I., p. 161.
[j] Obs. 3, p. 162.

ancient^a church of Saint^b Miniato. 3. It seems
[To me seems]

better^c built than the church of the Madonna dell' Im-
pruneta. I find the environs of Florence more picturesque than^d I expected. 4. You will see - finer
                                             dei^e

buildings and^e more beautiful views than these beyoud
                                          queste fuori

- the "Porta al Prato." 5. The more^f I travel in
[of]

Italy, the more I like this country. 6. You will go
                          questo

to visit "La Petraja"^g to-morrow in company with my
[to see]   [of]

younger brother. 7. Are you the eldest?^h I thought
- you were the youngest.^h 8. I am three years olderⁱ
che   [I have]   [more]

than my brother. 9. Is Florence as large as Rome?
10. No, it is not so large as Rome, but it is more handsome. 11. Did you ever ascend the highest mountain
                              mai

in Europe? 12. No, I never tried to go up Mont
Blanc. Would you rather go towards Porta Romana
   (Cond. of *volere*)   *verso*

to-day than^j to-morrow? 13. Better^c to-day than to-
morrow. 14. Very well; then let us go down this
               allora   *questa*

way, which is the shortest.

---

^a Rule I., p. 164.   ^b Obs. 2, p. 158.   ^c Obs. 3, p. 167.
^d Obs. 1, p. 163.   ^e Obs. 2, p. 147.   ^f Obs. 4, p. 162.
^g *Petraja* is the name of one of the royal villas in the environs of
Florence.   ^h Obs. 2 p. 167.
ⁱ Obs. 3, p. 164.   ^j Rule IV., p. 163.

I

QUESTIONS.

Sono i contorni di Firenze molto interessanti? 2.—Siete la maggiore o la minore? 7.—È più grande Roma o Firenze? 10.—Qual' è il più alto monte d' Europa? 12.—Prendete la più corta o la più lunga via, quando andate a casa? 14.—Era più giovane Alfieri od il suo compagno di viaggio?[a]—Di che umore era il compagno di viaggio dell' Alfieri?

CHAPTER VI.

AUGMENTATIVES AND DIMINUTIVES.

Italian nouns, adjectives, and sometimes even verbs and adverbs, may have their original meaning modified by various suffixes. Of these, some denote augmentation, and the words modified by them are therefore called *augmentatives* of their originals; some denote diminution, and serve to form the *diminutives;* others signify contempt, and the words modified by them are called *peggiorativi,* i. e. *depreciatives.*

RULE I.—The suffixes used to form *augmentatives* are three—*one, otto,* and *ozzo.*

(i.) *One* signifies largeness of size; as,

libro, a book;	*librone,*[b] a large book.
casa, a house;	*casone,*[c] a large house.
ubbriaco, drunk;	*ubbriacone,* a great drunkard.

---

[a] See Reading Exercise, p. 168.

[b] Words so modified are curtailed of the final vowel.

[c] The suffix *one* renders the feminine noun masculine. When, however, it is suffixed to an adjective, or a lady's name, it is also used for the feminine gender, changing the final *e* into *a*; as, *vecchia,* old woman; *vecchiona,* a big old woman; *Luigia,* Louisa; *Luigiona,* a big Louisa. For the plural, *oni* and *one* are respectively used; as, *vecchioni,* big old men; *vecchione,* big old women. The rules for *gender* and *number* of all augmentatives and diminutives being the same as those of other nouns.

(ii.) $\left\{ \begin{array}{c} Otto \\ ozzo \end{array} \right\}$ or $\left\{ \begin{array}{c} otta \\ ozza \end{array} \right\}$ signify strength and vigour; as,

giovine, a young man ; *giovinotto,* a strong young man.
forese, a villager ; *foresozza,* a vigorous country girl.

Rule II.—The suffixes which form the diminutives
are :—

(i.) *Cello, cino, etto, icello, icino* or *iccino,* (with their
feminine terminations *cella, cina,* &c.,) signifying smallness of size ; as,

bastone, a stick ;	*bastoncello,* a small stick.
limone, a lemon ;	*limoncino,* a small lemon.
fiume, a river ;	*fiumicello,* a rivulet.
libro, a book ;	*libriccino,* a little book.
uomo, a man ;	*ometto,* a mannikin.

(ii.) *Ino* or *ina,* signifying smallness and prettiness ;
as,

viso, a face ;	*visino,* a pretty little face.
adagio, slow ;	*adagino,* softly.
colle, a hill ;	*collina,* a hillock.

(iii.) *Erello* and *arello,* with their feminine terminations *erella,* &c., signifying tenderness or affection ; as,

vecchio, an old man ; *vecchierello,* a poor old man.
pazza, a mad woman ; *pazzarella,* a poor mad woman.

(iv.) *Ellare, acchiare,* signifying repetition ; as,
saltare, to jump ; *saltarellare,* to jump about.

(v.) *Ello, uccio, uzzo,* and their feminines *ella,* &c.,
which are used with various significations ; as,

capana, a hut ; *capanella,* a little hut.
femmina, a female ; *femminella,* a little worthless female.
cappello, a hat ; *cappelluccio,* a little worthless hat.

Obs.—There are other diminutives, which have a form
peculiar to themselves ; as,

cane, a dog ;	*cagnolino,* a little dog.
casa, a house ;	*casipola,* a small rickety house.
acqua, water ;	*acquerugiola,* drizzling rain.

RULE III.—Words with the following suffixes are *peggiorativi* :—

Accio or *accia, ardo* or *arda, attolo* or *attola, onzolo* or *onzola, azzo* or *azza, astro* or *astra, aglia, ame, ume, uolo* or *uola, icciuolo* or *icciuola, icciatto* or *icciatta,* all which suffixes signify contempt, ugliness, badness ; as,

donna, a woman ;	*donnaccia,* a wicked woman.
bianco, white ;	*biancastro,* whitish.
gente, people ;	*gentame,* a mob.
&c.	&c.

OBSERVATIONS.

1. Sometimes a compound diminutive is used, as *vecchierellino,* meaning *a poor and agreeable little old man.*

2. To a diminutive another suffix is often added, which gives to the word, besides a meaning of smallness, another of ugliness or badness ; as, *stanza,* a room ; *stanzucciaccia,* a small and disagreeable room.

3. To an augmentative suffix may be added a diminutive one ; as, *ladro,* a thief ; *ladroncello,* a great young thief ; *one* serving to denote a great propensity of the person to steal, and *cello* the tender age of the person.

4. The adjectives *piccolo, grande,* may be employed before a diminutive or an augmentative, although they give the same signification as the terminations ; as,

piccola coserella, a little thing of no great value.
gran cavallone, a very big horse.

5. Almost all the above augmentatives, diminutives, and depreciatives being extremely arbitrary, they ought to be used sparingly, especially by foreigners. The student, however, would do well to study their various significations in the above given examples, in order to understand, in the perusal of Italian works, the exact import of the words which will be found modified by them.

CHAPTER VII.

NUMERALS.

THE numerals are divided into cardinal and ordinal numbers.

CARDINAL NUMBERS.

1 *uno.*	14 *quattordici.*	70 *settanta.*
2 *due.*	15 *quindici.*	80 *ottanta.*
3 *tre.*	16 *sedici.*	90 *novanta.*
4 *quattro.*	17 *diciassette.*	100 *cento.*
5 *cinque.*	18 *diciotto.*	200 *duecento* or
6 *sei.*	19 *diciannove.*	*dugento.*
7 *sette.*	20 *venti.*	300 *trecento,*&c.
8 *otto.*	21 *vent' uno.*	1,000 *mille.*
9 *nove.*	&c.	1,100 *millecento.*
10 *dieci.*	30 *trenta.*	2,000 *due mila.*
11 *undici.*	40 *quaranta.*	100,000 *cento mila.*
12 *dodici.*	50 *cinquanta.*	1,000,000 *un milione.*
13 *tredici.*	60 *sessanta.*	2,000,000 *due milioni.*

RULE I.—Cardinal numbers are not inflected, except *uno*[a], which has the feminine *una;* as, *uno scudo,* a crown; *una libbra,* a pound (weight). *Mille* and *milione,* when preceded by a number higher than *one,* are spelt *mila* and *milioni:*

EX.: *Cristo con cinque pani, saziò cinque mila persone.* (SEGN.)
Christ with five loaves satisfied five thousand persons.

RULE II. — *Cento, duecento,* &c., when followed by another numeral adjective of more than two syllables, may lose the final syllable *to;* as, *cenquattordici,* one hundred and fourteen; *ducenquaranta,* two hundred and forty.

OBSERVATIONS.

1. In Italian the unit is always placed after the ten;

[a] Obs. 5, p. 50.

as, *trenta due*, two-and-thirty; *quaranta tre*, three-and-forty, &c.

2. A noun used with *ventuno*, *trentuno*, &c., is put in the singular when following the numeral, and in the plural when preceding it; as, *quarantuna lira*, or *lire quarantuna*, 41 *lire*. See No. 5, p. 84.

3. No indefinite article is used before either *cento* or *mille*, and no conjunction is required between numbers; as, *mille trecento ventuno*, one thousand three hundred *and* twenty-one.

4. To render in Italian eighteen hundred, twelve hundred, &c., we must say, *mille ottocento*, *mille duecento*, &c.

5. When speaking of a thousand years after the Christian era, it is necessary to put the definite article before *mille*. Thus we must say either *nel mille ottocento settanta*, or *il mille ottocento settanta*, in eighteen hundred and seventy.

6. The preposition *in*, which precedes a number or an adjective of quantity followed by a noun denoting time, is rendered in Italian by *fra* or *entro*, whenever referring to the future; as,

Tornerò entro sei giorni, I will return in six days.
Vi scriverà fra pochi dì, he will write to you in a few days.

7. The preposition 'within,' referring to past time, is rendered by *a* in sentences like the following:

Ai dì passati, within the last few days.

Ordinal Numbers.

1st *primo*.	11th *undecimo*, or *decimo primo*.	
2nd *secondo*.	12th *duodecimo*, or *decimo secondo*.	
3rd *terzo*.	13th *tredicesimo*, or *decimo terzo*.	
4th *quarto*.	14th *quattordicesimo*, or *decimo quarto*.	
5th *quinto*.	15th *quindicesimo*, or *decimo quinto*.	
6th *sesto*.	&c.	&c.
7th *settimo*.	20th *ventesimo*, or *vigesimo*.	
8th *ottavo*.	21st *ventesimo primo*.	
9th *nono*.	22nd *ventesimo secondo*, &c.	
10th *decimo*.	30th *trentesimo*, &c.	
	100th *centesimo*.	
	1000th *millesimo*.	last, *ultimo*.

RULE I.—All the ordinal numbers, both simple and compound, are subject to all the variations of other adjectives ending in *o*; so we must say—

Il primo giorno, the first day.
I primi giorni, the first days.
La ventesima prima volta, the twenty-first time.
Le ventesime prime volte, the twenty-first times.

RULE II.—Ordinal numbers are used after the names of monarchs, popes, &c., as well as when speaking of the volumes of a work, or chapters of a book, as in English; but the article which precedes the number is omitted in Italian; as,

Enrico ottavo, Henry the Eighth.
Libro primo, capitolo sesto, book *the* first, chapter *the* sixth.

RULE III.—For the dates of the month the cardinal numbers must be used in Italian, except for the first day, which is expressed in the same way as in English; as,

Il tre marzo, 1860, on[a] the 3rd of March, 1860.
Ai dieci or *i dieci d' agosto*, on the tenth of August.
Il primo d' aprile, on the first of April.

EXCEPTION.

If the word *giorno* or *dì*, day, is expressed, the ordinal number may be used.

Ex.: *Il dì nono di settembre* (1494) *Carlo ottavo entrò in Asti.* (GUIC.)
On the ninth of September (1494) Charles VIII. entered Asti.

DISTRIBUTIVE AND COLLECTIVE NUMBERS.

La metà (mezzo)[b],	the half.
Il doppio,	the double.
Il triplo, il quadruplo, &c.	the triple, &c.
Una coppia,	a couple.

---

[a] Observe that the preposition *on*, used in English before numbers of dates or days, is never expressed in Italian.

[b] When *mezzo*, half, is used collectively, it is indeclinable; as, *una libbra e mezzo di castrato*, one pound and a-half of mutton; but when it is an adjective it agrees with the noun; as, *mezza libbra*, half-a-pound. (See Rule IV., p. 152.)

Un paio[a],	a pair, a couple.
Una decina,	half a score, 10.
Una dozzina (una serqua)[b],	a dozen.
Una ventina,	a score.
Una trentina, quarantina, &c.	a batch of 30, 40, &c.
Un centinaio,	a hundred.
Un migliaio,	a thousand.
Trimestre,	three months.
Triennio,	three years.
Lustro,	five years.

N.B. — After distributive numbers, the preposition *di*, of, must be used ; as,

  Un paio di *stivali,* a pair of boots.
  Una ventina di *noci,* a score of nuts.

Commit to memory the following idioms :—

1. *Vanno* $\begin{cases} ad\ uno\ ad\ uno, \\ a\ due\ a\ due,\ \&c. \end{cases}$	They walk $\begin{cases} \text{one by one,} \\ \text{two by two,}\&c. \end{cases}$
2. *Una lira (sterlina) per testa,*	A pound each.
3. *Son morti tutti e due, tutti e tre, tutti e quattro, &c.,*	They are both, all three, all four, &c., dead.
4. *Che ora è ? A che ora ?*	What o'clock is it ? At what o'clock ?
5. *È l' una precisa,* or *È il tocco preciso,*	It is just one o'clock.
6. *Sono le*[c] *tre e mezzo in punto,*	It is exactly half-past three.
7. *Arrivò alle cinque e venti,*	He arrived at twenty minutes past five.
8. *Sono le dieci meno un quarto,*	It is a quarter to ten o'clock.
9. *Il vostro oriuolo avanza ; mancano venti minuti alle dieci,*	Your watch is fast ; it wants twenty minutes to ten.

----

[a] *Paio* is also used in speaking of time ; as, *un paio di giorni,* a couple of days.

[b] *Serqua*, instead of *dozzina*, is used in speaking of eggs or fruit only ; as, *una serqua di pere,* a dozen pears ; *una serqua di uova,* a dozen eggs.   [c] Note *b*, p. 137.

10. *No; il vostro sta in dietro (or è in ritardo di) cinque minuti,* — No; yours is five minutes slow.

11. *Sono le dodici,* — It is twelve o'clock.

12. *È la mezzanotte,* — It is midnight.

13. *Mezzogiorno (mezzodì) è appena suonato,* — It has just struck twelve.

14. *Sono le otto antimeridiane,* — It is eight o'clock A.M. (or, in the forenoon).

15. *Sono le cinque pomeridiane,* — It is five o'clock P.M. (or, in the afternoon).

16. *Dalle due alle* tre,* — From two to three o'clock.

17. *Sei moltiplicato per cinque fa trenta,* — Five times six makes thirty.

18. *Levando sei da nove rimarrà tre,* — Deducting six from nine remains three.

19. *Divedete l' otto per quattro,* — Divide eight by four.

20. *Cercate quante volte sta il* sei in tredici,* — See how many times six is contained in thirteen.

21. *Vi sta due volte e uno di avanzo,* — It is contained twice, with remainder one.

22. *Tre via tre fa nove,* — Three times three are nine.

23. *Due e due fanno quattro,* — Two and two make four.

24. *Oggi a otto partirò da Londra,* — I shall leave London this day week.

25. *Oggi a quindici la vedrò,* — I shall see her this day fortnight.

26. *Lo vedrò entro quindici giorni (or, in una quindicina di giorni),* — I shall see him in a fortnight.

27. *Quando fu l' ultima volta che vedeste vostro fratello?* — When did you see your brother last?

28. *Vi avvertii cento volte e cento,* — I have warned you hundreds of times.

29. *Egli lo visitò da tre volta in su,* — He visited him three times altogether.

30. *Sono pochi giorni che sono qui,* — I have been here but a few days.

---

* Obs. 2, and Note *b*, p. 137.

31. *Vi sono* (or, *mancano*) *due giorni a Natale,*	It wants two days to Christmas.
32. *Esco due giorni di seguito quando fa bel tempo, ed un giorno sì e l' altro no quando fa freddo,*	I go out two days running when it is fine weather, and every other day when it is cold.
33. *Quanti anni avete?*	How old are you?
34. *Ho vent' anni,*	I am twenty years of age.
35. *Quanti ne abbiamo* (or, *ai quanti siamo*) *del mese?*	What is the day of the month?
36. *È il sei* (or, *ne abbiamo sei,* or *siamo ai sei*),	It is the sixth.
37. *La fattura ammonta* (or, *ascende*) *a lire cento quaranta, per la qual somma vi ho fatto tratta a tre mesi data dal cinque maggio,*	The invoice comes to one hundred and forty pounds, for which sum I have drawn upon you at three months' date from May the 5th.
38. *Ho ricevuto la vostra lettera del due corrente,*	I have received your letter of the 2nd instant.
39. *Riferendovi alla mia del venti scorso* (*passato*),	Referring you to my letter of the 20th ultimo.
40. *Vi mando un vaglia postale per lire dieci,*	I forward you a post-office order for ten pounds.
41. *Accluso troverete un ordine a vista per due lire sterline,*	Enclosed you will find a cheque for two pounds sterling.
42. *Trovò una cedola* (or, *lettera di cambio*) *per cento lire sterline,*	He found a bill of exchange for £100.
43. *Dante morì nel secolo decimo quarto* (or, *nel trecento*[a]),	Dante died in the fourteenth century.

---

[a] In literature the Italians generally count by hundreds, beginning to reckon from the thousandth year after the Christian era, because they count the progress of learning from the revival of letters and arts after the Middle Ages. A writer of the fourteenth century is called *trecentista*.

44. *Siamo nel secolo decimo nono* (or, *nell' otto cento*),	We are in the nineteenth century.
45. *La Divina Commedia di Dante è scritta in terza rima,*	Dante's Divine Comedy is written in "terza rima."[a]
46. *Boccaccio ha inventato l' ottava rima,*	Boccaccio invented the "ottava rima."[b]
47. *Un sonetto è una poesia di 14 versi, in italiano divisi in due stanze di quattro versi ed in due di tre,*	A sonnet is a piece of poetry of fourteen lines, divided in Italian into four verses, two of four lines, and two of three.

Reading Exercise.

Nel 1187[c], fu presa Gerusalemme dal Saladino. Urbano III[d] (successore già ad Alessandro III, morto nel 1181, e a Lucio, morto nel 1185) ne morì, dicono di dolore; e succedettero Gregorio VIII per un mese, e poi Clemente III, che concitò la Cristianità al gran riacquisto. (Balbo.)

Vocabulary.

waiter, *cameriere.*
mail coach, *posta (diligenza).*
way, *via.*
porter, *facchino.*
to fetch, *prendere.*
trunk, *baule.*
luggage, *bagaglio.*

far, *lontano, distante, lungi.*
place, *luogo.*
coach, *vettura.*
mile, *miglio.*
bill, account, *conto.*
the amount, *il montante.*

to forward, *inviare.*
to leave a message, *fare un' ambasciata.*
receipt, *quittanza.*
mail, *corriere.*
to send, *mandare.*
address, *indirizzo (recapito).*

Translation Exercise.

1. Waiter, I shall leave Florence to-morrow. At what o'clock[e] does the mail-coach start for Rome?

---

[a] Rhyming every other line.
[b] A verse of eight lines of eleven syllables, rhyming the first with the third and fifth, the second with the fourth and sixth, and the two last together.
[c] Read the numbers as if they were written in words.
[d] Rule II., p. 175.   [e] No. 4, p. 176.

2. The one that goes by the way of Siena leaves at a
   Quella   che   per

quarter[a] to seven in the forenoon[b], and that which goes
                                  quella   che

by the way of Perugia leaves exactly at noon[c]. 3. I

will go by the way of Siena; I wish to be called to-
                              (Cond. of *volere*)

morrow morning at twenty-five minutes past five[d].

4. Very well. . . . . . Sir, it has struck[e] five o'clock; the
   [It goes well]   [are]

coach will start in an hour[f]. 5. Has the porter come to
                                        [Is]

fetch – my two trunks? 6. He will be here in[f] five
        i miei

minutes to fetch all – your luggage. 7. How[l] far[3]
                 tutto il vostro   *Quanto*

is[2] it (to) the place where the coach starts? 8. Half[g]-
a-mile. The day after to-morrow you will be at Rome.

9. Where are you going now? Bring me the bill.

10. Here is – your account; it comes[h] to twenty pounds
    Ecco   il vostro

sterling. 11. Very well; I will forward you a post-

office order[i] for the amount this day week[j]. 12. Is Mr.

M. here? 13. He was here half[g]-an[k]-hour ago, but

he has left for Rome, where he will stay a fortnight[l];

have you any message to leave? 14. I only[2] wanted[1]
              qualche

to give him a receipt for twenty-one pounds[m]. 15.

Leave it here; I will forward it to his address in Rome
   (active)   *al suo*

to-morrow at noon. 16. He is gone by the mail-coach

---

[a] No. 8, p. 176.	[b] No. 14, p. 176.
[c] No. 6, p. 176, and 13, p. 177.	[d] No. 7, p. 176.
[e] No. 13, p. 177. [f] Obs. 6, p. 174.	[g] Note *b*, p. 175.
[h] No. 37, p. 178. [i] No. 40, p. 178.	[j] No. 24, p. 177.
[k] Rule IV., p. 152. [l] No. 26, p. 177.	[m] Obs. 2, p. 174.

after the custom of the eighteenth century, and will
secondo   uso
arrive at Rome on the twenty-first instant.[a] By the
railway *via* Ancona, which was finished in 1864,[b] the
letter will reach Rome before - him.
prima di lui

QUESTIONS.

A che ora fate colazione?—Avanza o sta in dietro il
vostro oriuolo[c]?—Va bene l' orologio della stanza da
mangiare?—Come si chiama colui che viene a prendere il bagaglio per portarlo alla diligenza od alla strada
ferrata? 5.—Quando aspettate vostra zia?—È un pezzo
che studiate l' italiano?—In che secolo morì Dante?—
In qual genere di rima è scritta la Divina Commedia?
—Chi ha inventato l' ottava rima?—Che genere di poesia
è un sonetto?—Quando fu presa Gerusalemme dal Saladino[d]?—Chi concitò la Cristianità al riacquisto?

CHAPTER VIII.

PRONOUNS.

THERE are different classes of pronouns. They are
generally divided into *Personal, Possessive, Demonstrative,
Relative, Interrogative,* and *Indefinite.*

PERSONAL PRONOUNS.

Italian personal pronouns undergo declension.[e] They
have both disjunctive and conjunctive forms; *i. e.,* some
forms which cannot be joined to the verb, and others
which must always stand next to the verb and are often
joined to it. Before proceeding to give special rules on
personal pronouns, we call the attention of the student
to the following table, showing the inflections of these
pronouns:—

---

[a] No. 38, p. 178.   [b] Obs. 5, p. 174.
[c] See Nos. 9 & 10, pp. 176, 177.   [d] See Read. Ex., p. 179.
[e] Note *e*, p. 144.

TABLE OF PERSONAL PRONOUNS, DISJUNCTIVE AND CONJUNCTIVE.

First Person.

		Singular. Disjunctive.	Conjunctive.		Plural. Disjunctive.	Conjunctive.
Nom.	I	io		we	noi	
Gen.	of me	di me		of us	di noi	
Dat.	to me	a me		to us	a noi	
Acc.	me	me	mi	us	noi	ci or ne[b]
Abl.	from me	da me		from us	da noi	ci or ne
	with me	con me or meco	mi	with us	con noi	
	in me	in me		in us	in noi	
	on me	su me		on us	su noi	
	for me	per me		for us	per noi	
	between me	tra or fra me[b]		between us	tra or fra noi	

Second Person.

		Singular. Disjunctive.	Conjunctive.		Plural. Disjunctive.	Conjunctive.
Nom.	thou	tu		you or ye	voi	
Gen.	of thee	di te		of you	di voi	
Dat.	to thee	a te		to you	a voi	
Acc.	thee	te	ti	you	voi	vi
Abl.	from thee	da te	ti	from you	da voi	vi
	with thee	con te or teco		with you	con voi	
	&c.	&c.			&c.	

Third Person Masculine.

		Singular. Disjunctive.	Conjunctive.		Plural. Disjunctive.	Conjunctive.
Nom.	he (it)	egli, or ei, or e'[c], or esso[d]	ne	they	eglino, or ei, or e', or essi	ne
Gen.	of him	di lui or d' esso	gli	of them	di loro or d' essi	loro[l]
Dat.	to him (it)	a lui or ad esso	lo° or il	to them	a loro or ad essi	li° or gli[i]
Acc.	him (it)	lui or esso		them	loro or essi	
Abl.	from him (it)	da lui or da esso		from them	da loro or da essi	
	with him (it)	con lui or con esso or secco[f]		with them	con loro or con essi or seco	
	&c.	&c.			&c.	

Third Person Feminine.

Nom.	she (it)	ella or essa		they	ella or elleno[k] or esse	
Gen.	of her (it)	di lei or d' essa		of them	di loro or d' esse	
Dat.	to her (it)	a lei or ad essa	ne[h]	to them	a loro or ad esse	ne
Acc.	her (it)	lei or essa	le	them	loro or esse	loro
Abl.	from her (it)	da lei or da essa	la	from them	da loro or da esse	le
	with her (it) &c.	con lei or con essa or seco &c.		with them &c.	con loro or con esse or seco &c.	

REFLECTIVE PRONOUNS FOR BOTH GENDERS AND NUMBERS.

No Nominative.

Gen.	of oneself, himself, herself, itself, or themselves .	di sè[l].
Dat.	to oneself, " " " .	a sè
Acc.	oneself, " " " .	sè
Abl.	from oneself, " " " .	da sè.
	with oneself, " " " .	con sè or se-o.

si } conjunctive.
si }

[a] Da me, da te, d.t sè, da lui, da lei, da noi, da voi, mean also 'by myself,' or 'alone,' &c., when the subject is in the same person with the pronoun which follows da (as, L'Italia farà da sè. Italy will do by herself), the words stesso or medesimo, pl. stessi and medesimi, self or selves, being used with all personal pronouns; as, io stesso, tu stesso, d.t me stesso, &c.; but only in cases where the English 'self' is intended to be emphatic. (See Note b, p. 43.)—N.B. The word da, answering to the French chez, da me, da noi, &c., may mean also 'at,' 'in,' or 'to my house'; 'to me,' 'to us,' or 'amongst us,' &c., when the subject is not in the same person with the pronoun which follows da.

[b] Fra me stesso or medesimo, and meco meco stesso, are also used for 'within,' or 'in myself,' 'to myself.'

[c] Ei and è' are both abbreviations of egli and egino; è' is only used in poetry.

[d] See Note a, p. 11.

[e] See Note a (2) and (3), p. 43.

[f] Seco, meco, teco, and the other forms of con and the pronoun, are sometimes found used together; as, con meco, seco lui, seco lei, &c. Meco and voeco are used by poets for con noi and con voi.

[g] Esso, essa, &c., with d before them, means the person himself, &c.; and are used after the verbs essere and parere; as, è dessa, it is herself, i.e. la persona di essa. Esso is also used uninflected after some prepositions, as follows:—con esso me, con esso lui, or con esso loro, &c., with myself, &c. We find used by good writers, con esso le mani, with the hands.

[h] Nè (with the e accented) means 'neither' or 'nor,' and must not be confounded with ne, of it, him, them, &o., and ne, us, to us. The latter ne, us, to us, is poetical.

[i] Gli for loro, to them, is generally used in conversation. Loro generally follows the verb, and is not joined to it.

[k] Lì in old writers is found used for the dative singular gli.

[k] Ella. ella, or elleno are often contracted into la, le.

[l] Sè, pronoun, is accented, to distinguish it from the conjunction se, if.

RULES FOR THE USE OF PERSONAL PRONOUNS WITH DISJUNCTIVE AND CONJUNCTIVE FORMS.

RULE I.—Italian personal pronouns may be either expressed or understood in the nominative case.[a] When they are expressed, they generally stand in the same place in the sentence, as would the noun or nouns they represent; as,

> *Egli [il conte] avea l'anello assai caro per alcuna virtù ch' egli [l'anello] avea.* (Boc.)

He held the ring very dear on account of some virtue which it possessed.

RULE II.—The personal pronouns which are the subjects of the verb,[a] may, like the nouns they represent, either precede or follow the verb; as,

> *S' io fossi nella via come è egli.*
> If I were in the way, as he is.

EXCEPTIONS.

The pronominal subject follows the verb:

1. When a question is asked,[b] without an interrogative pronoun in the nominative case; as,
> *Siete voi solo?* Are you alone?

2. With the imperative mood; as,
Mangi egli del suo, Let him eat what he has.

3. In introducing the parts of a dialogue; as,
> *Perchè? diss' io,* Why? said I.

4. In a narrative sentence, in speaking of the doing or saying of a person; as,
> *Io non piangeva, piangevan elli[c].* (Dan.)
> I did not weep, they wept.

RULE III.—*Disjunctive* pronouns (see p. 182) commonly follow the verb. In the cases in which there are both disjunctive and conjunctive forms (viz., in the dative and accusative, as well as the genitive of the 3rd person), the disjunctive form is generally employed—

---

[a] See p. 11.   [b] Note *a*, p. 14.   [c] Obs. 3, p. 193.

(i.) When there are two *genitives*, two *datives*, or two *accusatives* in the same phrase relating to different persons; as,

> *Parlo* di lui *e non* di lei, I speak of him and not of her.
> *Parlerò* a voi *ma non* a lui, I shall speak to you, but not to him.
> *Invitate* lui *e* lei, Invite him and her.

(ii.) When we wish to lay particular stress on the pronoun; as,

> *Parlo* a voi, *signore*, I am talking to you, Sir.

RULE IV.—*Conjunctive* pronouns (see p. 182) sometimes precede 'and sometimes follow the verb, precisely in the same way as reflective pronouns.* They are generally employed when there is one *genitive*, one *dative*, or one *accusative* only in the same phrase; as,

> *Egli ne parlò ieri*, he spoke of it yesterday.
> *Quando* mi *porterete il cappello?* when will you bring me the hat?
> *La vide*, la[b] *conobbe*, he saw and recognised her.
> *Verro a vedervi domani*, or Vi[c] *verrò a vedere domani*, I will come and see you to-morrow.

N.B.—It is to be noticed that the rules given for the placing of the pronoun, at 2, p. 37, are generally observed in common conversation; but writers, and especially the poets, frequently place the conjunctive pronouns not only after the Infinitive, the Participles, and the Imperative, but also after other parts of the verb. Thus, *pregovi*, I beg you; *parlavale*, he spoke to her; *raccontasi*, it is related; are used for *vi prego, le parlava, si racconta.*

EXERCISES.

Substitute a proper personal pronoun for the nouns in italics, in the following sentences (see N.B., p 152):—

L'avaro s'affattica pazzamente ad ammassare ricchezze; *le ricchezze all' avaro* punto non giovano, perchè *l' avaro*

---

* Obs. 2, p. 43.
[b] When two or more verbs govern the same pronoun, the latter is repeated with each verb.
[c] When a verb is used with an Infinitive after it, the pronoun may either precede the first verb, or follow the Infinitive.

delle ricchezze mai non gode.—La pace non è per l' empio
l' empio cerca *la pace, la pace* fugge *l' empio.*—Ho veduto
vostro fratello, ed ho parlato *con vostro fratello;* diedi *a
vostro fratello* quattro pere, *vostro fratello* parve rimanere
lieto e contento *delle quattro pere.*—Vedrò i vostri amici,
e darò *a' vostri amici* novelle di voi.

RULES ON DOUBLE CONJUNCTIVE PRONOUNS.

RULE I.—When one conjunctive pronoun immediately
follows another in the same phrase in Italian, the dative
precedes the accusative, and the genitive *ne* generally
follows all other pronouns except *loro;* as,

> *Mi* (to me) *vi* (you) *raccomanda*, he recommends
> you to me.
> *Non vuol raccomandarvimi,*[a] he will not recommend
> me to you.

OBSERVATIONS ON THE ORTHOGRAPHY OF CONJUNCTIVE PRONOUNS.

The joining of the pronouns to one another gives rise
to the following changes in their terminations:—

1. *mi, ti, ci, vi, si* change their *i* into *e* before either
lo, la, gli, li, le or *ne;* as,

me lo	or	*melo*			it to me.
te la	,,	*tela*			it to thee.
ce gli	,,	*cegli*	*darà*, he will give	them to us.
ve li	,,	*veli*		them to you.
se le	,,	*sele*		them to himself.
se ne	,,	*sene*		some to himself.

2. *gli*, to him, and *le*, to her, both become *glie* before
lo, la, li, le, ne, and join with them; as,

> *glielo* or *gliela darò*, I shall give it to him *or* to her.
> *glieli* or *gliele darò*, I shall give them to him *or* to her.
> *gliene*[b] *darò*, I shall give some to him *or* to her.

---

[a] When two conjunctive pronouns follow the verb, they join together, and form but one word with the verb. If they precede the
verb, they are never united to it, but are often joined to one another.

[b] For the dative feminine *le* also may be used before *ne.* See
also Note *g*, p. 105.

3. The *o* of *lo*, and the *e* of *ne*, are frequently dropped before a consonant, except *s* followed by a consonant, when joined to one of the other pronouns; so, *mel, tel, sel, cel, vel, gliel, men, ten, sen, cen, ven, glien,* are used instead of *melo, telo,* &c. We find also *nol* for *non lo,* and *avendol* for *avendolo.*

EXERCISE.

Substitute the proper pronouns for the nouns in italics in the following sentences (see N.B., p. 152) :—

Io ho promesso un libro a Pompeo, e darò *quel libro a Pompeo.*—Voi avete un libro di quel fanciullo, rendete *codesto libro a questo fanciullo.*—Quella ficaia è bassa, potete da terra cogliere *i frutti di quella ficaia.*

OBSERVATIONS ON THE ORTHOGRAPHY OF CONJUNCTIVE PRONOUNS WHEN JOINED TO THE VERB OR THE WORD *ecco.*

1. When the pronoun is joined to the verb, if the latter is in the Infinitive, it drops the final *e* or the syllable *re,* if it ends in *rre;* as, *parlarle,* to speak to her; *condurvi,* to conduct you.

2. When the verb is of one syllable, and ends with a vowel; as, *dà,* he gives, or give thou; *ho,* I have; *è,* he is,— or has the accent on the final vowel; as, *parlò,* he spoke; *sentirò,* I shall hear,—then the consonant of all pronouns joined to it, except the *g* of *gli,* is doubled, and the accent suppressed; as, *dammelo,* give it to me; *hotti,* I have thee; *emmi,* to me is; *parlerolle,* I shall speak to her.

3. When the verb ends with *m* or *n* or *r,* followed by a vowel, the latter is dropped; thus we find *domandaronle* for *le domandarono,* they asked her; *dividiamle,* let us divide them; *ebberlo caro,* they held him dear. Sometimes in similar cases the letters *m* and *n* are changed; as in

Viemmi dietro, for *vienmi dietro,* follow me.
Amianci, for *amiamci,* let us love one another*.

---

* See Reciprocal Verbs, p. 46.

4. The pronouns which follow the word *ecco*, 'here is, there is, here are, there are,' are in the accusative, and joined to it; as,

> *eccomi, eccoti, eccolo, eccola*, here I am, here thou art, &c.
> *eccoci, eccovi, eccoli, eccole, eccone*, here we are, &c.

It is also said—

> *eccotelo, eccovelo*, &c., here it is before or for thee, here it is for you, &c.; as,
> *Eccotel* pronto* (Gua.), here it is ready for thee.
> *Eccoti il nappo* (Gua.), here is the cup for thee.

And likewise it is often said, *eccomi quì, eccovi quà, eccolo lì, eccola là*, &c.; the words *quì, quà*, here, and *lì, là*, there, being expletives[b].

———

Observations on some Peculiar Uses of · Personal Pronouns, and the words *ci, vi, ne*.

1. The words *mi, ti, ci, vi, si, egli, ella, la, le, gli, ne*, are very often found used as expletives[b]; as,

> *Io medesimo non so quel ch' io mi voglio.* (Pet.)
> I myself do not know what I want (myself).

> *Amor, che meco al buon tempo ti stavi.* (Pet.)
> Thou, love, who wast (thyself) with me in prosperous times.

> *In un lettuccio assai piccolo si dormiva.* (Bem.)
> He was sleeping (himself) in a very small bed.

> *Andatevene[c] pei fatti vostri.*
> Go (yourselves off) about your business.

———

* Obs. 3, p. 187.

b An expletive is a word the using of which makes a sentence more full of words than is necessary; *quì, quà, lì, là*, might be dispensed with in the above examples, for *ecco* means 'here is' and 'there is.'

c *Ne* is often idiomatically used with *mi, ti*, &c., in conjugating certain verbs. Notice the following model:—

Egli è grave a dismettere le usanze. (SEGN.)
It is hard to leave off habit.

Dovè poi mangiarsel senza sale. (PUL.)
He was obliged to eat it afterwards without salt.

2. *Ci* and *vi* signify sometimes 'of it,' 'to it,' 'for or about it,' 'in it,' 'at it,' 'upon it,' or 'to them,' &c.; and then they answer to the French *y*; as,

Ora che ci penso, now that I think of it.
Riflettetevi bene, reflect on it well.
La necessità lo costrinse a consentirvi, necessity constrained him to consent to it.
Metteteci sopra la mano, put your hand upon it.

3. *Lo* or *il*[a] is employed to render the English word 'so' which follows a verb; as,

Fatelo, do so. *Lo credo,* I think so.

4. *Mi, ti, ci, vi, si*[b], when used with the verbs *salutare* or *riverire,* to salute or present one's compliments, *abbracciare,* to embrace, *baciare,* to kiss, have sometimes the meaning of the English possessive pronoun *my, thy;* sometimes *for me, for you,* &c.; as,

Addio, mio caro, salutatemi gli amici.
Good-bye, my dear, give my compliments to our friends.

Non ho dimenticato di riverirvi il Signor B
I have not forgotten to give many compliments for you to Mr. B.

Infinitive—*andarsene,* to go away.
Indicative Present.

me ne vado, I am going away.	*ce ne andiamo,* we are going away.
te ne vai, thou art &c.	*ve ne andate,* you are &c.
se ne va, he or she is &c.	*se ne vanno,* they are &c.

And so in all the other moods and tenses. Several verbs may be conjugated in the above manner; as, *starsene,* to remain; *partirsene,* to depart, &c.

[a] *Il* for *lo* is more commonly used in poetry; it can neither follow the verb, nor be used before a verb beginning with a vowel or with *s* followed by a consonant.

[b] For other meanings of *si,* see Obs., pp. 42, 46, and 49.

5. *Ci* and *vi* are also used adverbially in the sense of
'here' or 'there'; as,

Se voi andrete a Parigi, v' *andrò anch' io.*
If you go to Paris, I shall go there too.

Io sto a Londra perchè mi ci[a] *trovo bene.*
I remain in London because I am well here.

6. Used as adverbs, *ci* means 'here,' and *vi,* 'there';
but *vi* is often used for 'here,' and *ci* for 'there,' to
avoid the coming together of *ci,* here, with *ci,* us; and
vi, there, with *vi,* you; as,

Voi ci vi chiamaste, you called us here.
Chi vi ci[b] *mandò?* who sent you there?

7. *Ci* and *vi* are used with third persons of the verb
essere, in the same way that 'here' and 'there' are used
in English; as,

c' *è,* or *v' è,* here is, *or* there is; *ci sono,* or *vi sono,*
here are, *or* there are.

c' *era,* or *v' era,* here was, *or* there was; c' *erano,* or
v' erano, here were, *or* there were, &c.

In Italian, however, *ci* or *vi* may be often omitted[b]; as,

Erano in quel tempo tre papi, Gregorio, Benedetto, e
Giovanni (MAC.)
There were at that time three popes, Gregory,
Benedict, and John.

8. *Ci* and *vi* are often found with *avere;* as,

Non ci *ha uomo il quale non ami d' esser felice*
There is no man that does not love to be happy

In questo tempo v' ebbe in Roma diverse mutazioni.
(G. VIL.)
At this time there were in Rome divers com-
motions.

N.B.—The verb *avere,* when thus employed, must be

---

[a] The place of *ci* and *vi,* when adverbs, in relation to the verb
with which they are used, is the same as when these words are
pronouns. The adverb, however, is generally near the verb.

[b] *Ci* and *vi* are never used before *essere* when this verb refers to a
present or past time, and is followed by a quantitative or numeral
adjective preceding a noun expressing time; but if the verb refers
to a future time, *ci* and *vi* may be used. (See No. 30 and 31, pp. 177
and 178.)

in the singular number, whilst *essere*, when used in the same capacity, agrees in number with the noun.

9. *Ci*, *si* and *la* are used idiomatically with certain verbs, to which they give a new meaning; *entrare*, to enter, *entrarci*, to have to do; *mettere*, to put, *metterci*, to take (time); *avere*, to have, *averla*, to be angry; *passare*, to pass, *passarsela*, to get on (in life); as,

> *Io non c' entro*, I have nothing to do with this.
> *Ci ho messo un' ora a venire quì.*
> It has taken me an hour to come here.
> *Con chi l' avete ?*   With whom are you angry ?
> *Come ve la* passate ?*   How do you get on ?

10. *Ne* means also 'some,' 'any,' 'a few,' 'about it,' 'for it,' 'from it,' answering to the French *en;* as,

> *Me ne rincresce*, I am sorry for it.

11. *Ne* must be used when the accusative is not repeated; as,

> *Avete delle pere ?   Non* ne *ho.*
> Have you some pears ?   I have none.
> Ne *volete ?* Do you want some ?

OBSERVATIONS ON THE CONCORD OF PERSONAL PRONOUNS.

1. When the personal pronoun represents more than one singular noun of the same gender, it must be in the plural number, and agree in gender with the nouns; as,

> *La vipera e la vespa mordono chi* le *stuzzica.* (SEGN.)
> The viper and the wasp bite those who molest them

2. When the personal pronoun represents more than one noun of different genders, it must be in the plural masculine; as,

> *Onorate il* padre *e la* madre; *se non fossero stati* eglino, *voi non sareste.*
> Honour your father and mother; without them you would not have existed.

See also Note *b*, p. 185.

---

* *La*, like *ne*, is used with *mi*, *ti*, &c., in conjugating certain verbs (see Note *c*, p. 188).

3. The accusative pronoun, instead of the nominative, must be employed in Italian—

(i.) After the verb *essere*, and the verbs *credere*, to believe, and *stimare*, to suppose, in a dependent sentence, when these verbs imply an idea of transmutation; as,

> *Credendo ch' io fossi* te (Boc.), thinking that I was thee.

(ii.) In apostrophizing, in phrases similar to the following:—*Oh felice lei!* O happy she! *Beato lui!* blessed he!

(iii.) When used as a *predicate* after the verb *essere;* as,

> *L' amico è un altro* me, my friend is another I.

4. The person of the verb *essere* is different in Italian and in English in phrases such as the following:—*Sono io*, it is I; *sei tu*, it is thou; *siete voi*, it is you, &c.

5. After the *di* which follows a comparative, the genitive is used in Italian; as,

> *Io sono più pigro di* lei,[a] I am more lazy than she.

6. *Lui, lei,* and *loro*, instead of *egli, ella, eglino* or *elleno*, are used after *come* or *siccome*, as *or* like, *quanto*, so much *or* as, when the verb, of which they might be the subjects, is not expressed; as,

> *Costoro ch' erano* come lui *maliziosi* (Boc.), those who were like him malicious.

OBSERVATIONS ON POETICAL AND POPULAR LICENSES.

1. In common conversation *lei* is used instead of *ella*, and *loro* instead of *elleno*, and *lui* instead of *egli;* as,

> *Come sta lei ?*[b] How is she?
>
> Lei è *giovine*, ma lui è *vecchio*.
>
> She is young, but he is old.
>
> *Vedono* loro *il lume ?* Do they see the light?

2. The people in Tuscany, and the poets, often use *i* for *io;* as, *i non so*, I do not know.

> Ex.:   *I non so ben ridir com' io v' entrai*. (DAN.)
> How I entered there I cannot tell.

---

[a] Note *a*, p. 163.

[b] When we use the contracted forms of *ella* or *elle*, we say, *come la sta*, and *le vedono il lume*. (See Note *j*, p. 183.)

3. The poets use

nui, vui, ello, elli or *egli,*

for *noi, voi, egli, eglino.*

Ex.: *Il cavalier ch' era con* nui. (ARI.)
The knight who was with us.

Noi uderemo e parleremo a vui. (DAN.)
We shall hear and speak to you.

Ed ello *abbia quella (la rendita) del mulino.* (SAC.)
And let him have that (the revenue) of the mill.

Piangevan elli (DAN.), they wept.

Perchè egli *stanno* (MAC.), because they remain.

4. *Ella* is used by poets in other cases besides the nominative; thus Ariosto has *memoria d' ella,* memory of her.

5. *Elle* has been used by Dante instead of *loro.*

Ex.: *E suon di man con* elle, and sound of hands with them.

6. *Gli* is employed in the dative plural, instead of *loro.*

Ex.: *Tutto il paese che il Soldano* gli *avea renduto.* (G. VIL.)
All the country which the Sultan had restored to them (the Saracens).

7. *Li* has been used instead of *gli* in the dative singular masculine, meaning, 'to him.' (See Note *j*, p. 183.)

Ex.: *Domandolli poi se via c' era.* (ARI.)
He then asked him if there was any way.

8. *Lui* and *lei* are found in old writers used in the dative case without the preposition before them, where *gli* and *le* should have been used.

Ex.: *Risposi* lui *con vergognosa fronte.* (DAN.)
I answered him with a blushing countenance.

Ond' io risposi lei (DAN.), therefore I replied to her.

READING EXERCISE.

Narrano le antiche cronache ch' egli fu già* in Portogallo un uomo dabbene, il quale avea un suo unico figliuolo da lui caramente amato: e vedendo ch' egli era

---

* Formerly.

K

di animo semplice e inclinato al ben fare, stavagli[a] sempre con gli occhi addosso, temendo che non gli[b] fosse guasto da' corrotti costumi di molti altri. Di che spesso gli[b] tenea[c] lunghi ragionamenti, e gli[b] diceva che si guardasse molto bene dalle male compagnie; e gli facea[c] in quella tenerella età comprendere chi facea male, e perchè facea male. Il fanciullo udia le paterne ammonizioni; ma pure una volta gli disse: "Di che volete voi[d] temere? Io son certo che non mi si appiccherà mai addosso vizio veruno, e spero che avverrà il contrario, ch' essi[e] ad esempio di me diverranno virtuosi." Il buon padre, conoscendo che le parole non faceano[c] quel frutto ch' egli avrebbe voluto, pensò di ricorrere all' arte; ed empiuta una cestellina delle più belle e più vistose pere che si trovassero, gliene[f] fece un presente. Ma riconosciuto a certi piccoli segnali che alcune poche di esse eran vicine a guastarsi, quelle mescolò con le buone. Il fanciullo si rallegrò, e come si fa in quell' età, volendo egli vedere quante e quali fossero le sue ricchezze, mentre che le[g] novera e mira, esclama, "Oh, padre! che avete voi[d] fatto? A che avete voi mescolate queste che hanno magagna con le sane?"

"Non pensar[h], figliuol mio, a ciò[i]," risposegli[a] il padre; "queste pere sono di tal natura, che le sane appiccano la salute loro alle triste." "Voi[j] vedrete," ripigliò il fanciullo, "che sarà fra pochi giorni il contrario." Sì sarà, non sarà; il padre lo[b] prega che le lasci per vederne[b] la sperienza. Il figliuolo, benchè a dispetto, se ne[k] contenta[l]. La cestellina si chiude in una cassa, il padre prende le chiavi. Il putto gli era di tempo in tempo intorno perchè riaprisse; il padre indugiava. Finalmente gli disse: "Questo è il dì, ecco le chiavi." Appena potea il fanciullo attendere che la[m] si voltasse nella toppa. Ma appena fu la cestellina aperta, che non vede più pere, le quali erano tutte coperte di muffa e guaste.

---

[a] N.B., p. 185.   [b] Rule III., p. 184.   [c] Obs. 8, p. 127.
[d] Excep. 2, p. 184.   [e] Note a, p. 11.
[f] Rule I., and Obs. 2, p. 186.   [g] Rule IV., p. 185.
[h] Note c, p. 14.   [i] That.   [j] Rule I., p. 184.
[k] Rule I., and Obs. 1, p. 186.
[l] The present is used instead of the past in a narrative, in order to bring the action more vividly before the reader.
[m] Note k, p. 183.

"Oh ! nol[a] diss'io," grida egli[b], "che così sarebbe stato ?
Non è forse avvenuto quello ch'io dissi ? Padre mio,
voi l'[c] avete voluto." "Non è questa cosa che ti debba
dare tanto dolore, rispose il padre baciandolo[c] affettuosa-
mente. Ma tu[d] ti lagni ch' io[d] non abbia voluto credere
a te[e] delle pere. E tu[d] qual fede prestavi a me[e] quando
io[d] ti dicea che la compagnia dei tristi guasta i buoni ?
Credi tu ch' io non possa compensarti di queste poche
pere che hai perdute ? Ma io[d] non so chi potesse com-
pensar me, quando tu mi fossi guasto e contaminato."

(GOZZI.)

VOCABULARY.

host (landlord), *alber-gatore.*
to want, *avere bisogno di.*
to wish, *bramare.*
to wish to know, *desiderare sapere.*
to charge, *fare pagare a.*
courier, *corriere.*
to pardon, *scusare.*
master, *padrone.*
to hear from, *ricevere nuove di* or *da.*
tailor, *sarto.*

to show in, *far entrare.*
to send for, *mandare a chiamare.*
to take the measure for, *prendere la misura di.*
coat, *vestito.*
fashion, *moda.*
shoemaker, *calzolaio.*
shoe, *scarpa.*
to show, *mostrare, far vedere.*
to try on, *provarsi.*
tight, *stretto.*

to take, carry back, *riportare.*
to take off, *cavarsi.*
boot, *stivale* (masc.)
hat, *cappello.*
to accompany, *accompagnare.*
guide-book, *guida.*
to deprive, *privare.*
compliment, *complimento.*
brother in law, *cognato.*
favour, *favore.*
to ask for, *domandare* (act.)

TRANSLATION EXERCISE.

Rules I., II., III.} 1. How shall we go to Tivoli to-day?
2. You[d] shall walk[f], and I[d] will ride. Waiter! 3. Do
you want me, Sir? 4. I do not want you, but I want
(use *volere*)
to speak to the host, because I wish to know why he
siccome
charges me and – my courier more than[g] he ought for
(dative) *al mio* (Cond. of *dovere.*)

---

[a] Obs. 3, p. 187.   [b] Excep. 4, p. 184.   [c] Rule IV., p. 185.
[d] See p. 11.   [e] Rule III., p. 184.
[f] See Phrases, p. 62.   [g] Obs. 1, p. 163.

K 2

everything — we take. 5. I beg your pardon, Sir,
   tutto   *ciò che*   [Pardon, Sir]

but we charge you and him the same that we do
              (dative)   (dative) [as much as we charge]

others.   6. Tell – your master to[a] come to me[b]
agli altri   *al*

at once; I do not wish to speak to you, but to him.
subito   (use *volere*)

7. He is gone out, Sir.

   Rule IV.} 8. Well-then, I will speak to him another
          Allora   (Fut. of *parlare*.) *un' altra*

time. 9. Courier, have you heard from your brother?
10. I[c] write to him often, but he[c] does not answer me.
11. Sir, the tailor wishes to see you. 12. Show him
            (use *desiderare*)

in. 13. Good morning, Sir. 14. I have sent for
you, as   I wish   you to take my
    siccome (use *volere*) [that you may take to me the]

measure for a coat. 15. How do you wish it made?
                   (Pres. of *volere*.)

16. Make it (according) to the latest fashion. 17. Very
                        ultima

well, Sir, you shall have it.   Good day. 18. Sir, the
      [you will be served]

shoemaker — has brought your shoes.
     [to you]   [the]

   Rule I.
Obs. 1 & 2, p. 186.} 19. Show them to me; I will try them
on. He has[3] made[4] them[2] too[5] tight[6] for me[1]. Take
                     [to me]

them back to him, and tell him to make me —[d] another
                       un altro

pair. 20. Take them off, and I will carry them back
to him immediately.
    subito

---

[a] Note *b*, p. 76.   [b] N.B., p. 183.
[c] See p. 11.   [d] Obs. 11, p. 191.

^{Oss. 4.}_{p. 188.}} 21. Waiter! 22. Here I am. 23. Where have you put – my boots? 24. There they are.
 i miei

25. And where is – my hat? 26. There it is on the
 il mio

table. 27. Have – my friends come? 28. Here they
 [Are] *i miei*

are. 29. Oh! here you are, at last. 30. How do you
 al fine.

do? We are late; are we not? 31. It does not
 [is it not true]

matter. 32. Is – your courier in his room?
 il *nella sua*

^{Oss. 5 & 6,}_{p. 190.}} 33. I do not know. Waiter, go and see if he
is there. 34. He was there only just now. 35. Have
 [now now]
 or ora

you been to Tivoli before? 36. I have not yet been
 avanti *ancora*

there. 37. I shall be happy to accompany you there.
38. Have you a guide-book?

^{Rules and}_{Oss. 10 & 11, p. 191.}} 39. I have² none¹. 40. Would you
like to have one? Take this. 41. I do not wish to
 questa

deprive you of it. 42. I have two, so I can give you
 così

one. Here it is for you.

^{General Rules}_{and Observations.}} 43. No, thank you, I know that my
sister has one. Here is my courier, I will tell him *to*
 (dative)

go to² her and ask her to lend it me. John, go to² my
sister's; tell her that   I should be glad   if she
 (dative)   [she would do me a favour]

would   lend me – her guide to the environs of Rome.
(use *volere*)   *la sua guida* [of]

N.B., p. 183.

Give my compliments[a] to my brother-in-law, and if you see any roses in the garden, ask him for some. 44. I am going immediately.

     [I go]   20

QUESTIONS.

Come andrete in città domani? 2.—Quanto vi ha fatto pagare l' albergatore per una stanza? 5.—Quando avete scritto a vostro fratello?—Vi ha egli risposto?—Si è vostra zia fatta prender la misura d'una mantiglia o d' un vestito? 14.—Come se lo farà fare? 16.—Vi vanno bene le scarpe? 19.—Dove è la penna?—Ne avete una da prestarmi?—Dove siete?—Dove sono i vostri guanti?—Quanti cavalli avete? 42.—Avete detto al servo di venire da me? 6.—Che disse una volta il figlio al padre?[b]—Che presente fece il padre al figlio?—Come trovò le pere il figlio quando aperse la cassa?

POSSESSIVE PRONOUNS.

There are in Italian six possessive pronouns, viz. :—

mio, my.	*nostro*, our.
tuo, thy.	*vostro*, your.
suo, his, her, its.	*loro*, their.

RULE I.—These pronouns are generally preceded by the definite article. They are used also as adjectives, and vary according to gender and number, as follows :—

Singular.		Plural.			
Masc.	Fem.	Masc.	Fem.	As Adj.	As Subst.
il mio,	*la mia,*	*i miei,*	*le mie,*	my,	mine.
il tuo,	*la tua,*	*i tuoi*[c],	*le tue,*	thy,	thine.
il suo,	*la sua,*	*i suoi*[c],	*le sue,*	{ his, her, its.	his, hers, its.
il nostro,	*la nostra,*	*i nostri,*	*le nostre,*	our,	ours.
il vostro,	*la vostra,*	*i vostri,*	*le vostre,*	your,	yours.
il loro,	*la loro,*	*i loro,*	*le loro*[d],	their,	theirs.

RULE II.—The above pronouns agree in person with

---

    [a] Obs. 4, p. 189.   [b] See Read. Ex., p. 194.

    [c] The poets often use *tui* and *sui* for the sake of rhyme, instead of *tuoi* and *suoi*.   [d] Observe that *loro* is invariable.

the *possessor*, and in gender and number with the thing *possessed*; as,

> *Ho la* sua *penna*, I have his pen.
> *Ho il* suo *libro*, I have her book.
> *Abbiamo le*.sue *carte*, we have her papers.
> *Abbiamo i* suoi *libri*, we have his books.

OBSERVATIONS.

1. Possessive pronouns are used without the article—

(i.) In addressing a person and in exclamations; as,

> *Come state, amico mio?* how do you do, my friend?
> *Oh, miei figli, che fate?* oh, my sons, what are you doing?

(ii.) Generally when immediately followed in the singular by the words—

Signoria { lordship, ladyship.	*nipote*, nephew, niece.
	figlio, figlia, son, daughter.
Eccellenza, excellency.	*fratello, sorella*, brother, sister.
Eminenza, eminence.	*cognato*, brother-in-law.
Altezza, highness.	*cognata*, sister-in-law.
Maestà, majesty.	*cugino, cugina*, cousin.
Santità, holiness.	*nonno*, grandfather.
marito, husband.	*nonna*, grandmother.
moglie, wife.	*suocero, suocera*, father-in-law,
padre, father.	mother-in-law.
madre, mother.	*genero, nuora*, son-in-law,
zio, zia, uncle, aunt.	daughter-in-law.

> Ex.: *Favellando col Re diremo, vostra Maestà.* (CAS.)
> Speaking with the king, we will say, Your Majesty.
> *Tristo chi abbandona* suo *padre.* (SEGN.)
> Wicked the man who abandons his father.

N.B.—The article (as well as the pronoun) must be used with any word in the above list—

> In the plural, or in a diminutive form.

> When the pronoun follows the noun; or is preceded by *signor*, Mr., *signora*, Mrs., *signorina*, Miss, or by an adjective.

> Also when, instead of the above nouns of relations, the corresponding words—*sposo, sposa*, bridegroom, bride; *consorte*, husband or wife; *genitore, genitrice*, father, mother; *germano, ger-*

mana, brother, sister ; *avo* or *ovolo*, grand-father ; *ava* or *avola*, grandmother—are used.

Ex. :
Sono le Signorie[a] vostre pronte ?
Are your Ladyships ready ?

È in casa il vostro fratellino ?
Is your little brother at home ?

È in casa il fratello vostro ?
Is your brother at home ?

Come sta il suo consorte ?
How is your husband ?

Come sta la vostra signora madre ?
How is your mother?

Dov' è la vostra bella sorella ?
Where is your pretty sister ?

Il mio genitore è morto.
My father is dead.

(iii.) When the pronoun precedes a substantive used in apposition with a former noun.

Ex. :
Villani scrisse la storia di Firenze, sua patria.
Villani wrote the history of Florence, his native city

L' ho detto a Carlo, mio servitore.
I have told it to Charles, my servant.

(iv.) Generally in answering a question.

Ex. :
Di chi è questo libro ? È mio[b].
Whose book is this ? It is mine.

(v.) When relating to a noun before mentioned, or followed by a noun taken in an indefinite sense.

Ex. :
Questo cavallo è mio, this horse is mine.

Spero di ricevere presto vostre lettere.
I hope to receive a letter from you soon.

(vi.) In the following idiomatic expressions :—

1. *È persona di* mia *cono-scenza,*	He is well known to me.
2. *Salutatelo da parte* mia, or *in nome* mio,	Give my compliments to him.
3. *Sta in* vostro *potere,*	It is in your power.
4. *Per* mio *avviso,*	In my opinion.
5. Vostro *danno se non ve-nite,*	So much the worse for you if you do not come.

---

[a] Possessive pronouns may precede or follow the noun in Italian; in the plural, however, when referring to titles, they must follow the noun.

[b] *È il mio* may be used, but then the expression becomes emphatic, or implies contrast; as, *Non è il mio, è il vostro.*

6. *Lo farò* suo *malgrado,*⎫
7. *Lo farò a* suo *dispetto,*⎭   I shall do it in spite of him.

8. *Parlerò io con* vostra *licenza,* or *con* vostra *grazia,*   I shall speak with your permission.

9. *Questo* mio[a] *cappello è inutile,*   This hat of mine is useless.

10. *Vado a casa* mia,   I go to my own house.
11. *Egli sta in casa* sua,   He stays in his own house.
12. *Vado io in* sua *vece,*   I am going in his stead.
13. *Casa* mia *è casa* vostra,   Dispose of my house as if it were your own.

14. *In vita* mia,   In all my life.
15. *Farò a modo* suo,   I shall do as he pleases.
16. *Fate a modo* mio,   Do as I tell you.
17. *È di* mio *gusto,*   It is to my taste.
18. *È colpa* vostra,   It is your fault.
19. *Fa tutto a* suo *capriccio, a* sua *voglia* or *a* suo *piacere, a* suo *senno, a* suo *talento, a* suo *agio* or *comodo, di* sua *testa, per amor* mio,   He does everything according to his whim, his will, his mind, his fancy, at his leisure *or* convenience, his imagination, for my sake.

20. *Sono a* vostra *disposizione,*   I am at your disposition.
21. *Comprate a conto* mio,   Buy on my account.

N.B.—The following expressions admit of a double form :—

Un mio amico me lo disse, or⎫
Uno dei miei amici me lo disse,⎭   A friend of mine told it to me.

Un suo servitore v' andò, or⎫
Uno dei suoi servitori v' andò,⎭   One of his servants went there.

Molti miei amici v' erano, or⎫
Molti dei miei amici v' erano,⎭   Many of my friends were there.

Alcuni⎫
Alquanti⎬ *miei amici* (or *dei miei*⎫
Parecchi⎭ *amici*) *son morti,*⎭   Several friends of mine are dead.

4. *Proprio*[b] or *propio, propria* or *propia,* answering to

---

[a] Observe that the possessive pronoun never takes the article, when immediately preceded by a demonstrative pronoun.

    In answering a question in the affirmative, *proprio* is an adverb, and means 'exactly.'

K 3

the English word 'own,' are generally used with the article, and without the possessive pronoun before them.

> Ex.: *Abbandonarono* la propria *città è* le proprie *case*. (Boc.)
> They abandoned their own city and their own houses.

5. *Mio, tuo, suo, nostro, vostro*,[a] *loro*, with their feminines *mia*, &c., and *miei, tuoi, suoi*, with their feminines *mie*, &c., are often used substantively with the article before them, without reference to a noun previously mentioned. In these cases, a noun is understood; viz., in the singular masculine, *avere*, property, in the singular feminine, *lettera*, letter; and in the plural masculine, *compagni*, companions, *soldati*, soldiers, *parenti*, relations, or *concittadini*, countrymen, &c.; in the plural feminine, *lettere*, letters, *grazie*, thanks, &c.

> Ex.: *Spendo il* mio *in metter tavola*. (Boc.)
> I spend my *wealth* in keeping open table.
>
> *Uscirono dalla città con molti dei* suoi. (Dav.)
> They went out of the city with many of his *soldiers*.
>
> *Ricevo la* sua *graziosissima dei* 12. (Leop.)
> I have just received your very kind *letter* of the 12th.

6. When the pronoun refers to an object not belonging to the nominative, *di lui* and *di lei* must be used instead of *suo, sua, suoi, sue*, to avoid ambiguity.

> Ex.: *Tito ama Cesare e i figli* di lui (or, *i* di lui *figli*).
> Titus loves Cæsar and *his* children (meaning Cæsar's children).
>
> *Sono* di lei *servo*, I am *her* servant.

7. In Italian, the possessive pronoun is left out, and the definite article substituted for it, when the noun which follows refers to the subject of the sentence.[b]

> Ex.: *Il giovane udendo le parole* della *madre*. (Boc.)
> The youth hearing the words of *his* mother.

8. The dative personal pronoun is substituted for the possessive with nouns which refer either to the members of the body, or any part of the dress.

---

[a] In familiar style, *nostro* and *vostro* are used to denote the person who remains in one's house to dine; as,
Per oggi vi contenterete ch' ella sia nostra.
For to-day you will be content that she should dine with us.

[b] Note *i*, p. 17.

Ex. : *Ambo le mani per dolor* mi *morsi.* (DAN.)
I bit both *my* hands for grief.

Squarciossi i panni e si percosse il vis (ARI.)
She tore *her* clothes and struck *her* face.

9. In old writers and poets, the pronouns *mio, mia ; tuo, tua ; suo, sua,* are occasionally found changed into *mo, ma ; to, ta ; so, sa,* and suffixed to the words *fratello,* brother, *sorella* or *suora,* sister, *moglie,* wife, *signore,* master.

Ex. : *Sarei udito da* fratelmo *s' io l' aprissi.* (Boc.)
I should be heard by *my* brother if I opened it.

Allora disse la suorsa *alla reina.* (FIOR.)
Then said *his* sister to the queen.

Ragazzo aspettato da signorso. (DAN.)
A boy expected by *his* master.

MODES OF ADDRESS[a].

In Italian there are three ways of addressing a person ; viz.,

In the 2nd person singular, *tu,* thou, which is named,
dar del tu, to use *thou.*

„ 2nd person plural, *voi,* you, which is named,
dar del voi, to use *you.*

„ 3rd person singular feminine, *ella* or *lei,* named,
dar del lei, to use *she.*

1. *Tu,* thou, is employed in cases of the greatest intimacy and nearest connection ; in speaking to children ; in authoritative and elevated style ; by way of anger or scorn ; and in poetry.

Ex. : *Dove sei tu ?* or *dove sei ?* where art thou ?

2. *Voi,* you, is employed when speaking in a familiar way, and towards servants or dependants. It is usual also in commerce.

Ex. : *Dove siete andato ?* where have you gone ?

3. *Ella* or *lei,*[b] representing *vostra signoria,*[c] or *la*

---

[a] Note *g,* p. 16.   [b] Obs. 1, p. 192.
[c] For *vostra signoria* we may write the initials only, *V.S.* It is often contracted into *vossignoria.*

signoria vostra, your lordship, or your ladyship, *vostra
maestà*, your majesty, &c., is used towards persons
superior in rank, age, or office to the speaker, and also
as a matter of politeness in speaking to a gentleman
or lady with whom the speaker is not on terms of intimacy.

In this mode of address, the speech is supposed to be
directed, not to the person spoken to, but to the title
vostra signoria, represented by *ella*. This title being
feminine, any adjective or past participle qualifying it
must be likewise feminine. The possessive pronouns
referring to the subject *ella*, must also be in the third
person ; as,

È ella stata in Francia? have you been in France ?
          literally, has she been in France ?

Come sta ella? or *come sta?* how do you do ?
          literally, how does she do ?

È contenta del suo maestro?
          are you satisfied with your master ?
          literally, is she satisfied with her master ?

4. The same form of address is used in the 3rd person plural feminine, when speaking to more than one
person, with *elleno* or *loro*, which represent *le signorie
vostre*, your lordships, or your ladyships ; or *loro signori,
loro signore*, you gentlemen, you ladies ; as,

      Come stanno elleno? how do you do ?
          literally, how do they do ?

N.B.—In order to acquire a facility in employing the
polite mode of address in the 3rd person singular feminine, *ella*, the pupil should take up the former translation exercises in this book one by one, and turn them
from the 2nd person plural into the 3rd singular
feminine, taking care to commit again to memory the
verb or verbs which precede each exercise. This will
afford an opportunity for reviewing all that has been
done, and will increase the pupil's facility in employing
the verbs.

The success of the pupil in mastering the language of
Italian conversation will depend very much on the strict
application of the above direction.

We subjoin a Model for the 1st Translation Exercise (See p. 16) :—

ENGLISH.	DANDO DEL VOI.[a]	DANDO DEL LEI.[b]
1. Are you a native of Italy ?	1. *Siete italiano* (or *italiana*) *?*	1. *È italiano* (or *italiana*) *?*
3. Of what country is your uncle ?	3. *Di che paese è vostro zio ?*	3. *Di che paese è suo zio ?*
5. How long have you been in Italy ?	5. *È un pezzo che siete in Italia ?*	5. *È un pezzo che è in Italia ?*
7. Where were you two years ago ?	7. *Dov' eravate due anni sono ?*	7. *Dov' era due anni sono ?*
9. Were you in that country a long time ?	9. *Siete stato in quel paese un pezzo ?*	9. *È stata in quel paese un pezzo ?*
14. Is it true that your parents are in the country ?	14. *È vero che i vostri genitori sono in campagna ?*	14. *È vero che i suoi genitori sono in campagna ?*

READING EXERCISE.

Al Conte Leonardo Trissino.

Recanati, 26 gennaio, 1821.

Veneratissimo[c] Signor Conte,

Ricevo la sua[d] graziosissima dei 12. Le mie[d] de' 13 e 23 di ottobre che rispondevano alle sue[d] pregiatissime de' 6 e dell' ultimo di settembre non so se le sieno state recapitate. Ma V.S.[e] mi contrista dicendo che non mi scrive frequentemente per non darmi noia. S' Ella non mi creda incapace di ogni retto giudizio e gusto[f], non dee pensare ch' io non desideri il com-

---

[a] In the above Model, those sentences of the Exercise which require no change have of course been left out.

[b] In some parts of Italy the above mode of address is seldom used; but in Florence, which is the capital of Italy, the polite way, viz. *ella*, is constantly employed in addressing a lady or a gentleman with whom the speaker is not intimately acquainted. It will be unnecessary for the pupil to practise the other way of address, *tu*, thou, as a foreigner has very seldom occasion to employ it.

[c] When we write to a friend or a relation, the forms used in letters are—*caro amico*, dear friend, or *caro padre*, dear father; but in writing to some person superior in rank, age, or office, several other forms are used. (See Note *b*, p. 165.)

[d] Obs. 5, p. 202.   Note *c*, p. 203.   [f] Rule I.I., p. 157.

mercio delle sue[a] lettere quanto si possa dire.　Sebbene
le obbligazioni che ho con V.S. sono già grandissime,
tuttavia saranno maggiori quanto[b] le sue[a] lettere saranno
più frequenti.　V.S. non mi dà notizia veruna della salute
sua ; spero che sia conforme al mio desiderio.　Della
mia non ho cagione di lamentarmi più dell' ordinario
anzi forse alquanto[c] meno.　I voti ch' io fo per la felicità
di V.S. desidero che sieno adempiuti molto più di quello
ch' io brami l' adempimento dei suoi benevoli desideri
intorno alla felicità'mia.　E ringraziandola ed abbraccian-
dola riverentemente coll' animo, resto suo

Devotissimo servitore ed amico,

LEOPARDI.

VOCABULARY.

welcome, *benvenuto.*	to have at heart, *pre-*	brother-in-law, *co-*
kindness, *bontà.*	*mere di.*	*gnato.*
noise, *romore.*	welfare, *felicità.*	lately, *ultimamente.*
drum, *tamburo.*	kind, *cortese.*	to squander away,
to be surprised, *mara-*	box, *scatola.*	*scialacquare.*
vigliarsi.	to mistake, *sbagliare.*	to support, *mantenere.*
to enquire after, *do-*	to leave in charge of,	to mind, *badare.*
mandare di.	*lasciare in consegna*	to walk, *camminare.*
family, *famiglia.*	*a.*	to hurt, *far male a.*

TRANSLATION EXERCISE.

[Dialogue between two Gentlemen addressing each other in
the 3rd person singular feminine, *ella.* (See 3, p. 203.)]

1. Oh! welcome, my dear Mr.[d] D.; give me your[e]
hand; I am glad to see you.　2. I am obliged to you
for your kindness.　3. How does your wife　do?
[of]　　　　　　　　　　　　　　　　　　　　　　　　[stand]

4. Very well, thank you; she told me to give you her
　　　　　　　　　　　　　　　　　　　　　　　　　　di

compliments.[f]　5. And your little daughter,[g] how　is
　　　　　　　　　　　　　　　　　　　　　　　　　　[stands]

(she)?　6. She is very well also.　7. And your little

---

[a] Rule I., p. 198.　　　[b] Obs. 1, p. 161.　　　[c] Somewhat.
[d] Excep. 1 to Rule VI., p. 149.　　　[e] Obs. 7, p. 202.
[f] No. 2, p. 200.　　　[g] N.B., p. 199.

son, does he continue to make a great noise with his
   [does he[a] always make]

drum? 8. Yes, as usual. 9. Do not be surprised
             come il solito

if I inquire after all your family, because I have your

welfare and   that   of all your people[b] much at heart.[c]
          di quella

10. You are very kind indeed. 11. Have you taken

my trunk with you? 12. Your trunk will arrive to-

gether with mine. I have left all my boxes at the
            [to]

railway station in charge of Joseph, my servant. Here

are your keys. 13. Thank you; are these mine?
                         queste

14. Oh, no! wait a moment; I have given you the
                   [I have mistaken

wrong keys. Those are mine; here are yours. 15. Yes,
   keys]   *Quelle*

you are right.   Have you heard   from your
             [Have you received news]

brother-in-law lately? 16. Yes, he has squandered

away all his property[b]; and now he does not know how

to support his wife and children. 17. I am sorry to

hear it. 18. But it is his fault[d]; he would never do as

I told him.[e] Instead of listening (to) my advice, he

did everything according to his own fancy[f]; and now

he is reduced to this (condition). So much the worse
             questo

for him.[g] 19. I will go and see what my servant is

doing. 20. I will put on my hat[h] and coat, and will

---

[a] Excep. 1, p. 184.   [b] Obs. 5, p. 202.   [c] Note *d*., p. 86.
[d] No. 18, p. 201.   [e] No. 16, p. 201.   [f] No. 19, p. 201.
[g] No. 5, p. 201.   Obs. 8, p. 202.

go[a] with you; but mind, I cannot walk fast, I have a
          presto
boot that hurts my foot[b]: '21. Oh, here is my servant;
   we need not go out.   22. You will dine
[it is not necessary that we go out]
with us[c] to-day.

QUESTIONS.

Come sta Ella?—Ha salutato sua sorella da parte
mia? 4.—A chi lascerà in consegna il bagaglio quando
arriverà a Parigi? 12.—Andò la Signorina B. al teatro
col fratello o colla madre?—Ha sbagliato via nell' andare
dalla Signora D.?—Come stanno i suoi? 9.—A quali
lettere rispose il Leopardi il 26 gennaio, 1821?—Come
finisce la lettera del Leopardi?—Come comincia la
lettera?

N.B.—The pupil should put the questions following
former Exercises to the master, addressing him with
Ella. (See N.B., p. 204.)

DEMONSTRATIVE PRONOUNS.

RULE I.—Demonstrative pronouns cannot be preceded
by any article.

Some demonstrative pronouns are employed adjectively both for persons and things, and substantively
for things only. Others can only be used substantively
for persons.

Demonstrative pronouns used adjectively and substantively
for things.

	Singular.			Plural.	
Masc.	Fem.		Masc.	Fem.	
questo	questa[d]	this.	questi	queste	these.
cotesto	cotesta	} that.	cotesti	coteste	} those.
quello	quella		quelli	quelle	

---

[a] Note *c*, p. 121. [b] Obs. 8, p. 202. [c] Note *a*, p. 202.

[d] The poets use *esto, esta,* &c., for *questo, questa,* &c.; as,
 D' esto secolo gli amici (BET.), the friends of this century.

RULE II.—*Questo, questa,* &c., are used to point out objects near the speaker; as,

> *Questo cappello è mio,* this hat is mine.
> *Con queste penne non posso scrivere,* I cannot write with these pens.

RULE III.—*Cotesto, cotesta,*[*] &c., are employed to denote objects near the person addressed; as,

> *Prendete questo libro, e portatemi cotesto.*
> Take this book, and bring me that one (meaning that near you).

RULE IV.—*Quello, quella,* &c., are used to point out objects distant both from the speaker and the person addressed; as,

> *Andatemi a prendere quello specchio,* go and fetch me that looking-glass (meaning the looking-glass distant alike from you and me).

N.B.—The two last rules are disregarded in conversation, *quello* being used to indicate both the object near the person spoken to, and the one distant both from the speaker and the person to whom he speaks.

ORTHOGRAPHY OF *Quello,* &c.

Quello, quelli are used before *s* followed by a consonant, or *z,* and at the end of the sentence. Before any other consonants, *quel* for the singular, and *quei* for the plural, must be employed; and before vowels *quell'* and *quegli;* as,

Singular.	Plural.
Quello *specchio è rotto.*	Quegli *specchi sono rotti.*
That looking - glass is broken.	Those looking - glasses are broken.
Quell' *amico mio.*	Quegli *amici miei.*
That friend of mine.	Those friends of mine.
Quel *libro è mio.*	Quei *libri sono miei.*
That book is mine.	Those books are mine.

---

* *Cotesto, cotesta,* are frequently spelt *codesto, codesta,* &c.

OBSERVATIONS.

1. *Questo* and *quello* are used substantively for 'this thing' and 'that thing,' or 'this one' and 'that one'; as,

> *Fate questo, non fate quello*, do this thing, do not do that.

2. *Ciò* is a word which means the same as *questo* and *quello;* but it is invariable, and can only be used substantively; as,

> *Chi ha fatto ciò?* who has done this (*or* that) thing?

3. *Questo* is found used alone, in some peculiar sentences, with a noun understood; as,

> *In* questo (*momento* understood) *ella sopravvenne.*
> At this (moment) she came up.
> *Io son venuto a* questo (*fine, stato*).
> I am come to this (end, condition).

4. *Quello* and *questo* are used as relative pronouns in the sense of 'the former' and 'the latter,' or 'the one' and 'the other'; as,

> *Scegli fra la fortuna e la virtù;* quella *può farti ricco,* questa *solo felice.*
> Choose between fortune and virtue; the former can make thee rich, the latter alone happy.

Demonstrative pronouns, used substantively for persons only.

	Singular.		Plural.
Masc.		**Fem.**	**Masc. & Fem.**
questi } *costui* } this man.		*costei*, this woman.	*costoro* { these men. { these women.
cotesti } *cotestui* } that man.		*cotestei*, that woman.	*cotestoro* { those men. { those women.
quegli or *quei* } or *que'* } that man. *colui* }		*colei*, that woman.	*coloro* { those men, { those women.

OBSERVATIONS.

1. Instead of the pronouns under II., we may use, *questo signore, questo uomo*, this gentleman, this man; *quella*

signora, quella donna, that lady, that woman, &c. (See also Rules 1, 2, 3, p. 191.)

2. *Quegli* or *quei* or *que'*, and *questi*, may also be used for 'the former' and 'the latter' (see Obs. 4, p. 210) ; as,

> *Dante e Milton furono due grandi poeti :* quegli *fu italiano e* questi *inglese.*

Dante and Milton were two great poets : the former was an Italian and the latter an Englishman.

3. In conversation, *costui, colui, costei, costoro, coloro,* convey a meaning of contempt; as, *Chi è costui,* who is this fellow ? In poetry, however, they are used in the sense of highest admiration. Thus Dante, speaking of Virgil, says, *Quando io vidi* costui *nel gran diserto,* when I saw this man in the great forest.

4. The above pronouns are found applied to anything, when the object is personified. Thus Dante, speaking of a lion, says, *Questi parea che contra me venesse,* this lion seemed coming to meet me.

READING EXERCISE.

Leggesi del Re Currado che, quando era garzone, si[a] avea in compagnia dodici garzoni di sua etade. Quando lo[b] Re Currado fallava, li[c] maestri che gli erano dati a guardia non lo batteano, ma batteano questi garzoni suoi compagni[d]. E que'[e] dicea : Perchè battete voi costoro ? Rispondeano li maestri : Per li falli tuoi. E que' dicea : Perchè non battete voi me, chè[f] mia è la colpa ? E li maestri rispondeano : Perchè tu se' nostro Signore. Ma noi battiamo costoro[g] per te. Onde[h] assai ti dee dolere se tu hai gentil cuore, ch' altri porti pena delle tue colpe. E perciò si dice che lo re Currado si guardava molto di fallire per la pietà di coloro[g]. (NOVELLINO, 13th century.)

---

[a]. Obs. 1, p. 188.   [b] Excep. 3, p. 146.   [c] Excep. 2, p. 146.

[d] The above mode of punishment existed in England even at the time of King James I., it was called the "whipping-boy."

[e] Obs. 2, above.

[f] *Chè,* with the *è* accented, means 'because.'

[g] See p. 210.   [h] So that.

VOCABULARY.

jeweller, *gioielliere.*   a piece of twenty necklace, *collana.*
ring, *anello.*   francs, *un napo-* shop, *bottega.*
window (of a shop), *leone d' oro.*   cheap, *a buon mercato.*
  vetrina.   water, *acqua.*   article, *articolo.*
to set, *montare.*   dear, *caro.*   customer, *avventore.*
stone, *pietra.*   plain, *semplice.*   chain, *catena.*
to cost, to be worth, jewel, *gioiello.*   to deceive, *ingannare.*
  valere.   to buy, *comprare.* earring, *orecchino.*
diamond, *diamante*(m.) bracelet, *braccialetto.* brooch, *spillone* (m.)

TRANSLATION EXERCISE.

[Dialogue between a lady and a jeweller.]

N.B.—The lady addresses in the 2nd person plural, and the
jeweller in the 3rd person singular.

1. I should like to see some of those rings - you
  (conditional of *volere*)   *alcuni*   *che*

have in your window. 2. Yes, madam; would you like
one of these rings set in precious stones ? They are now
in fashion. 3. What is the price of this one[a] ? 4. That
                [How much costs]

one is worth forty twenty-franc pieces; as you see, the
diamond is of the finest water. 5. It is too dear. Show
me   —   one of those plain (ones). 6. These are
  [of them]

each[3] worth ten[1] twenty-franc pieces[2]. 7. You sell
[the one]

your jewels very dear. I once bought a bracelet and a
necklace in that shop opposite, and they did not charge
            dirimpetto

me so much. 8. Those who sell their things cheap
           che

cannot give good articles to their customers. Where
did you buy that watch and that chain ? 9. The man[b]

---

[a] Obs. 1, p. 210.   [b] Obs. 3, p. 211.

who sold me these* has deceived me. This* watch does
che

not go. 10. You see, then, madam, that it is as I tell
     dunque   *che*

you. Which will you have of these two? 11. I shall
  Quale

take this one. 12. Would you like a pair of those ear-
rings, or one of these brooches? 13. Not to-day, thank
you.

QUESTIONS.

Dove ha comprato il suo oriuolo? 7.—Quanto vale
il suo spillone? 12.—L'ᵇha pagata cara la sua catena?
8.—Che regaloᶜ farà a sua sorella?—Come farà montare
il suo braccialetto? 2.—Quanti garzoni avea in compagnia il Re Currado?—Chi battevano i maestri quando
il re fallava?—Che faceva il Re Currado per la pietà dei
garzoni che aveva in compagnia?

RELATIVE PRONOUNS.

The relative pronouns are *che, cui, il quale,*ᵈ who, that,
which; and all of them are applied both to persons and
things. They are declined as follows :—

	M. & F.	Masc.	Fem.	
			SINGULAR.	
Nom.	*che,*	*il quale,*	*la quale,*	who, that, which.
Gen.	*di cui,*	*del quale,*	*della quale,*	of whom, that, which.
Dat.	*a cui,*	*al quale,*	*alla quale,*	to whom, that, which.
Acc.	*che, cui,*	*il quale,*	*la quale,*	whom, that, which.
Abl.	*da cui,* *in* *per* *con* &c. }*cui,*	*dal quale,* *nel* *pel* *col* &c. }*quale,*	*dalla quale,* &c.	from whom, that, which. &c.
			PLURAL.	
Nom.	*che,*	*i quali,*	*le quali,*	who, that, which.
Gen.	*di cui,*	*dei quali,*	*delle quali,*	of whom, that, which.
Dat.	*a cui,*	*ai quali,*	*alle quali,*	to whom, that, which.
Acc.	*che, cui,*	*i quali,*	*le quali,*	whom, that, which.
Abl.	*da cui,* &c.	*dai quali,* &c.	*dalle quali,* &c.	from whom, that, which. &c.

---

* Rule III., p. 209.   ᵇ Obs. 1, p. 188.
ᶜ Present.   ᵈ See p. 9.

Rule I.—*Che* is invariable, and is chiefly used in the nominative and accusative; but it is sometimes found used in other cases, instead of *cui*, when it relates to things.

> Ex.:   *La materia di* che *parlate.* (DAV.)
> The subject you are speaking of.

N.B.—The relative pronoun must always be expressed in Italian, even where it is understood in English; as,

> *La lettera* che *scrivo*, the letter I write.

RULE II.—*Cui* is never employed in the nominative, and very seldom in the accusative. In the genitive and dative cases, when it precedes the noun to which it relates, it is generally used without the preposition, and often stands between the article and the noun.

> Ex.: *Si scontrò in un gentiluomo, il* cui *nome era Torello.* (Boc.)
> He met a gentleman whose name was Torello.
>
> *Voi* cui *fortuna ha posto il freno.* (PET.)
> You on whom fortune has placed the bridle.

RULE III.—*Quale*, as a relative pronoun, is always preceded by the definite article. It is used in all cases, and, as it agrees with the noun to which it relates, ought to be employed instead of *che* or *cui* when necessary for the clearness of the sentence.

> Ex.:   *Filomena* la quale *discretissima era.* (Boc.)
> Filomena who was very prudent.

OBSERVATIONS ON *Onde, Dove* OR *Ove, Donde.*

1. *Onde* is a word which includes within itself the preposition and the pronoun, and it has the same sense as that of *del quale, di cui, dalla quale, da cui, in cui, per cui, con cui*, relating to things.

> Ex.: *Di lor progenie discese il buon e cortese Re Artù,* onde *i romanzi brettoni fanno menzione.* (VIL.)
> Of their lineage descended the good and courteous King Arthur, of whom the British romances make mention.

2. *Dove* or *ove* may be used for *a cui, da cui, per cui*, and *donde* for *da cui*, when the antecedent denotes place.

> Ex.: *L' ellera se non avesse un muro* dove *attenersi e* donde *sugar l' alimento cadrebbe a terra.* (BART.)
> If ivy had not a wall to which to cling, and whence to draw nutriment, it would fall to the ground.

3. *Onde* and *donde* are also adverbs, and mean 'whence,' or 'from where'; as, *Donde venite?* whence do you come? *Onde* means also 'wherewith'; as, *Ho molti debiti, e non ho onde soddisfarli,* I have many debts, and I have not wherewith to pay them.

Various meanings of the words *Che* and *Quale*.

1. *Che,* used substantively with or without the definite article before it, means, '*which thing.*'

Ex.: *Convien che i dotti siano modesti,* il che *forma la loro maggior gloria.*
It is necessary that learned men should be modest, *a thing which* forms their greatest glory.

Bisogna esser docili, senza che *non avrem pace.*
We must be obedient, without *which* we shall have no peace.

2. *Che,* used substantively with the indefinite article *un,* means, 'something.'

Ex.: *Mi sento* un *non so* che.
I feel a 'something,' I know not what.

3. *Che,* preceded by the demonstrative pronoun *quello* or *quel,* or *ciò,* is used to render 'that' or 'what' in the sense of 'that which.' (See Note, p. 17.)

4. *Che,* or *di cui, del quale, a cui,* &c., preceded by the demonstrative pronoun *quello* or *quella, colui* or *colei,* is used to render 'the one who,' 'which,' or 'that'; 'the one of whom,' or 'to whom,' 'which,' &c.

Ex.: *Che libro volete dire?* Quello che *mi regalaste.*
What book do you mean? The one that you gave me.

Parlo di quella a cui *diedi un fiore.*
I speak of the one to whom I gave a flower.

5. *Che* has also the meaning of *in cui* or *nel quale,* 'in which.'

Ex.: *Mi trovai in una selva oscura* che *la diritta via era smarrita.* (Dan.)
I found myself in a dark forest in which the straight way was lost.

6. *Che*, with or without a grave accent on the *e*, is used in the sense of *perchè*, 'because' or 'for.'

Ex. : *Comandatemi*, che *io desidero servirvi*.
Command me, *for* it is my wish to serve you.

7. *Che*, when coming after a verb conjugated negatively, means 'nothing' or 'but,' in the sense of 'only.'

Ex. : *Non avete* che *un cavallo*, you have but one horse.
Non ho che *fare*, I have nothing to do.

8. *Chè*, with an accent on the *e*, is used as an interjection expressing denial; it may also be used as the interrogative 'why.'

Ex. : Chè ! *non credete niente*, No ! do not believe anything.
Chè *non andate ?* why do you not go ?

9. *Che*, used to express comparison, means the same as the word 'than.' (See Rule IV., p. 163.)

10. *Che* is used as a conjunction in the sense of 'that,' and it is often expressed in Italian in cases where it is not necessary in English.

Ex. : *Credete* che *sia tardi ?* Do you think it is late ?
Spero che *mi scriverete*, I hope you will write to me.

11. *Che*, when immediately preceded by the negative *non*, answers the purpose of the English conjunctions, 'much more,' 'much less,' 'as well as.'

Ex. : *Spero trovar pietà*, non che *perdono*. (PET.)
I hope to find pity, as well as pardon.

Un volume non basterebbe, non che *una lettera*. (BEN.)
A volume would not be enough, much less a letter.

12. *Che* sometimes stands for 'as,' or 'when.',

Ex. : *Un giorno* che *veniva a visitarci*.
One day as he was coming to visit us.

13. *Che* has the meaning of 'whether' in sentences like the following :—Che *veniate o no*, whether you come or no.

14. *Qual* or *quale* has sometimes the meaning of 'some,' and sometimes of 'such as,' or 'like.'

Ex. : *E* qual *lasciò ferito e* qual *ucciso*. (ARI.)
And some he left wounded and some dead.

Quale *i fioretti dal notturno gelo*, &c. (DAN.)
Like the young flowers by the nightly frost, &c.

INTERROGATIVE PRONOUNS.

The interrogative pronouns are *chi?* who? *che?* what?[a] *quale?* pl. *quali?* which? as,

Chi *siete ?* who are you?
Di chi *è la colpa ?* whose[b] fault is it?
Che *volete ?* what do you want?
Quale[c] *di queste penne è la vostra ?*
Which of these pens is yours?

OBSERVATIONS.

1. *Che*, as an interrogative, always means 'what'; *quale* may mean 'which,' 'what,' or 'who'; and *chi* has always the sense of 'who' or 'whom.'

2. *Che* and *quale* are used in an exclamatory way in the sense of 'what,' in which case no indefinite article is used in Italian[d]; as,

Ex.: Che *bella donna !* what a beautiful woman!

3. *Chi* is also used as a singular indefinite pronoun in the sense of 'he who,' 'she who,' 'the one who,' 'any person who,' 'some person who,' 'whoever,' 'whosoever.'

Ex.: Chi *va lontan dalla sua patria.* (ARI.)
He who goes far from his own country.

Chi *ha la sanità è ricco.* (PROVERB.)
Whoever enjoys health is rich.

Nè sarà in Italia chi *vi s' opponga.* (GUI.)
Nor will there be anyone in Italy who will oppose himself to it.

N.B.—'He who,' 'she who,' 'the man who,' 'the one

---

[a] *Che cosa* may be used to render 'what'; as,
Che cosa *è sonno se non immagine di morte ?*
What is sleep but the image of death?

[b] Notice that the word 'whose' must be rendered in Italian by *di chi,* when it has an interrogative sense; and by *di cui* or *del quale* when used in a relative sense; as,
Di chi *son queste carte ?* whose papers are these?
Una donna la di cui *virtù è celebre.*
A woman whose virtue is celebrated.

[c] *Quale* takes the definite article before it only when it is used as a relative pronoun. [d] Rule V., p. 152.

wl,o,' &c., may likewise be rendered in Italian by *colui che*, or *colei che*.

> Ex.: *Vidi l' ombra di* colui che *fece per viltate il gran rifiuto.*
> (DAN.)
> I saw the shade of him who through cowardice made the great denial.

See also 4, p. 215.

___

OBSERVATIONS ON THE ORTHOGRAPHY OF THE WORDS
Che, Quale, Quali, Dove, and *Onde.*

1. The relative pronoun *che*, when not referring to the word immediately preceding it, must have a comma before it.

> Ex.: Quegli *non ama Dio,* che *si parte da' suoi comandamenti.*
> (S. GREG.)
> He who does not keep the commandments does not love God.

2. *Che* is found in poetry spelt *c'* before the third person singular and plural of the present indicative of the verb *avere,*

> Ex.: *Una palude fa c' ha nome Stige.* (DAN.)
> It makes a swamp which is named Styx.

3. *Quali*, plural of *quale*, before any letter except *s* followed by a consonant, may be spelt *quai* or *qua'*.

> Ex.: *Alle* qua' *lettere io mi rimetto.* (CAS.)
> To which letters I refer.

4. *Dove* or *ove* and *onde* before vowels drop the final *e* and take an apostrophe; as, *Dov' eravate?* where were you? (See also Note *c*, p. 13, and Note *g*, p. 18.)

READING EXERCISE.
A Giulia Lunga.

Cara Giulia,
    Ho veduto volentieri la tua lettera, per la quale* ti rallegri meco del mio ritorno; e più volentieri vedrò te, se verrai quì, come scrivi, insieme con tuo marito; il quale* saluterai a nome mio. Madama Cecilia e la Morosina, le quali* ho salutate con la tua lettera, ti

___

* Rule III., p. 214.

risalutano. Elleno stanno bene, e ti aspettano con desiderio. Salutami[a] tuo cognato e tua[b] cognata; e ve-
nitevene[c] per questi bei tempi.

Agli 11 di marzo 1530, di Padova.

P. BEMBO.

VOCABULARY.

intimate, *intimo*.	card, *biglietto di vi-*	paradise, *paradiso*.
countess, *contessa*.	*sita*.	to belong, *appartenere*.
to marry, *sposare*	to laugh, *ridere*.	lady, *signora*.
(active).	to mean, *voler dire*.	Venetian, *veneziano*.
gentleman, *signore*.	edition, *edizione*.	binding, *legatura*.

TRANSLATION EXERCISE.

[Dialogue between two intimate friends. (See 1, p. 203.)]

1. Who knocks at the door? 2. It is I[d] who knock.
3. Oh! come in, John; you know that I am always
glad to see you. 4. Is it your sister who is playing (on)
the harp? 5. No, it is the daughter of the countess
whose[e] brother is going to marry my aunt. 6. Oh! the
[will marry]
gentleman to whom I gave my card yesterday. 7. No, not
the one[f] you gave your card to, but the gentleman who
made us laugh. 8. I know whom you mean now.
What a[a] beautiful edition of Milton's Paradise Lost you
have here, Charles; to whom does it belong? 9. It
belongs to the lady with whom we dined yesterday, and
at whose[e] house I made your acquaintance. 10. You
may as well say, the house I come from[h], and in which
anche
I live. This edition is better than the one that[f] I have
at home. 11. Which do you mean? 12. The one[f] with
the Venetian binding, which I showed you yesterday.

[a] Obs. 4, p. 189.	[b] Obs. 1 (ii.), p. 199.	[c] Note *c*, p. 188.
[d] Obs. 4, p. 192.	[e] Note *b.* p. 217.	[f] 4, p. 215.
[g] Obs. 2, p. 217.	[h] Obs. 3, p. 215.	

L 2

QUESTIONS.

A chi ha scritto stamane ?—Donde[a] viene la sua serva?
—Chi sposò la sua amica? 5.—Crede che sia vero quel che
dice suo fratello ?—Può darmi l' indirizzo del signore la
cui[b] figlia vidi ieri sera da lei ?—Ha dato il suo biglietto
di visita a quella signora che cantò od a quella che suonò
l' arpa ? 7.—Dove fece la conoscenza della signora che
incontrai in casa sua ? 9.—Di che si rallegrava Giulia
Lunga in una sua lettera al Bembo.—Quale invito fa il
Bembo a Giulia Lunga nella sua lettera degli 11 marzo
1530 ?

INDEFINITE PRONOUNS.

Indefinite Pronouns may be divided into four classes :—

    I. Those used substantively for *persons*.
    II.   „   „   substantively for *things*.
    III.   „   „   substantively for *persons and things*.
    IV.   „   „   adjectively for *persons and things*[c].

CLASS I.

RULE.—The indefinite pronouns used substantively
for *persons* take no article before them.

> Ex.: *Chi avrà misericordia di altrui, altri l' avrà di lui.*
> Who has pity for another, others will have it for him.

N.B.—The word *altrui*, meaning ' property,' takes the
article ; as,

> *Non toglier l' altrui.*
> Do not take the property of others.

OBSERVATIONS.

1. *Altri* has no plural, is employed in the nominative
and accusative cases only, and is sometimes used in the
sense of ' some persons,' with the verb in the singular.

> Ex.: Altri *cade*, altri *fugge*, altri *s' appiatta*. (ARI.)
> Some fall, some flee, some crouch down.

2. In a familiar style, *altri* is used after *noi* and *voi*,
as an expletive.

> Ex.: Noi altri *fiorentini siamo ricchi*.
> We Florentines are rich.
> Voi altri *siete pazzi*, you are madmen.

---

[a] Obs. 3, p. 215.   [b] Rule II., p. 214.   [c] See p. 10.

3. *Altrui* is used both for the singular and plural, has no nominative, and in the genitive and dative is often employed without a preposition.

Ex.: *Non fare* altrui *ciò che per te non vuoi.*
Do not do to others that which you do not wish for yourself.

4. *Chi*, like *altri*, is used for 'some,' with the verb in the singular.

Ex.: *A chi piace la cherca, a chi la spada.* (ARI.)
Some prefer the church, some the army.

5. *Cui* is sometimes used for *chi*.

Ex.: Chi *a sè è rio, a* cui *può esser buono ?* (CAS.)
Who is cruel to himself, to whom can he be good?

6. *Tutti* takes the verb in the plural.

Ex.: Tutti *lo dicono,* everybody says so.

7. *Chiunque, chicchessia,* and *chisivoglia* all mean the same; but *chiunque* is only used in the singular, whilst the two other pronouns have also the plural *chicchessiano* and *chisivogliano.* *Chicchessia* and *chisivoglia* are seldom used; but when employed they are followed by the conjunction *che,* and take the verb in the subjunctive, like *chiunque*[a]. (See Note c, p. 70.)

8. For the different meanings of *si*, see Obs. 3, p. 49.

CLASS II.

RULE.—Of the indefinite pronouns used substantively for *things, tutto,* all, *nulla* or *niente,* nothing, are found used with or without the article before them.

Ex.: *E quel savio gentil che* tutto *seppe.* (DAN.)
And that mild sage who knew all.

Quel Dio che vede il tutto. (DAV.)
That God who sees all.

Tutto questo è un niente, all this is nothing.

Dio creò il mondo dal nulla.
God created the world from nothing.

OBSERVATIONS.

1. *Nulla* and *niente* mean 'something,' 'anything,'

[a] What has been said about *chiunque, chicchessia,* and *chisivoglia,* is applicable also to *checché, checchessia, checchesivoglia,* indefinite pronouns used for things.

when they come after a verb not preceded by the negative *non*. (See Note *e*, p. 22.)

> Ex.:   *Volete* niente ? do you want anything ?
>
>   *Direte* nulla *in mio favore ?*
>
>   Will you say something in my favour ?

2. *Nulla* and *niente*, when followed by an adjective,
take the preposition *di*, and when followed by a verb,
the preposition *da*.

> Ex.:   *Non avete* niente di *buono*, you have nothing good.
>
>   *Non ho* nulla da *fare*, I have nothing to do.

Class III.

RULE.—Of the indefinite pronouns used substantively
for *persons and things*, *uno* is used in contrast with *altro*,
takes the definite article, and can then also be employed in the plural.

> Ex.:   *Perfida* l' una *e* l' altro *è traditore.* (ARI.)
>
>   The one is perfidious, and the other a traitor.
>
>   Gli uni *e* gli altri *son mille.* (TAS.)
>
> literally,   The ones and the others are a thousand.
>
>   *Non conosco nè* l' uno *nè* l' altro.
>
>   I know neither the one nor the other.

Observations.

1. *Altro* is used to render ' else.'

> Ex.:   *Datemi qualche cosa* altro.
>
>   Give me something else.
>
>   *Non lo trovo in nessun* altro *luogo.*
>
>   I find him nowhere else.
>
>   *La troverete in qualche* altro *luogo.*
>
>   You will find her somewhere else.

2. *Altro*, repeated in the same sentence, signifies ' one
thing' and 'another thing.'

> Ex.: Altro *è parlar di morte*, altro *è morire.* (MAF.)
>
>   It is one thing to talk of death, another thing to die.

3. *Altro* has often the meaning of 'something else,'
'anything else'; and when following a verb conjugated
negatively, it means 'nothing else.'

> Ex.:   *Avete* altro ? have you anything else ?
>
>   Non *ho* altro, I have nothing else.

4. *Per altro* signifies 'on the other hand,' 'however.'

Ex.: *È d' un temperamento collerico*, per altro *ha buon cuore.*
He is of an irritable temper; however he has a good heart (is generous).

5. *Senz' altro* means 'undoubtedly.'

Ex.: *Egli verrà* senz' altro, he will come undoubtedly.

6. *Tutt' altro* has the signification of 'quite the contrary'; and *altro* is sometimes an interjection used in answering a question, and then means 'very.'

Ex.: *Siete* tutt' altro *di quel ch' eravate.*
You are quite the contrary of what you were.

È ricco il vostro amico ? Altro!
Is your friend rich? Very!

7. *L' un l' altro* are used to express 'each other' or 'one another.' (See Note *a*, p. 46.)

Class IV.

Rule.—Of the indefinite pronouns used adjectively for *persons* and *things*, *stesso* or *medesimo*, self, only can take the article before them.

Ex.: *Egli fa sempre lo stesso sbaglio.*
He always makes the same mistake.

Observations.

1. *Ogni*, every, *qualche*, some, and *qualunque*, any, are always followed by a singular noun; the word *Ognissanti*, All Saints' Day, and the nouns following cardinal numbers, excepted

Ex.: *Ogni beltà ha qualche neo*, every beauty has some fault.

2. *Tutto*, all, the whole,[a] preceding a noun, is always followed by the definite article.

Ex.: *Tutto* il *mondo è sossopra*, the whole world is upside-down.
Tutte le *donne sono angeli*, all women are angels.

N.B.—*Tutto*, used after the verb, and referring to the subject of the sentence, has no article.

Ex.: *Erano* tutti *uomini*, they were all men.

---

[a] 'The whole,' taken substantively, is rendered by *il tutto.* (See Rule, p. 221.)

3. *Tutto* is often followed by the word *quanto*, and the expressions *tutto quanto* or *tutta quanta*, plural *tutti quanti* or *tutte quante*, are used to signify 'the whole without exception.'

Ex.: *Perirono tutti quanti*, all perished without exception.

4. *Tutti* and *tutte*, followed by a cardinal number, take the conjunction *e*.

Ex.: *Erano tutte e due morte*, both the women were dead.
Tutti e quattro perirono, all four perished.

5. *Tutti* and *tutte* are not followed by any preposition in such expressions as the following:—

tutte voi, all of you; *tutti noi*, all of us.

6. *Tuttodì, tutto giorno*, are adverbial phrases which express 'continually.'

Ex.:   *Queste cose si vedono tuttodì.*
These things are seen continally.

7. *Tutto tutto* or *tututto* is found used emphatically by writers for 'all.'

Ex.:   *L' anima mia* tututta *gli apro.* (Boc.)
I open to her all my mind.

8. *Tale*, 'such,' *medesimo* or *stesso*, 'same,' are found used substantively.

Ex: *È un* tale *che mi tormenta*, he is a person who torments me.
Avete veduto quel tale? have you seen that so-and-so?
Non sono gli stessi, they are not the same persons.

N.B.—We say also, *un certo tale, un certo Tedesco*, a certain person, a certain German.

9. *Tale* with *quale* is used to form a comparison. (See Obs. 3, p. 162.)

10. *Ambo, entrambi*, &c., 'both,' when preceding a noun, are followed by the definite article, but as the subject of a verb they are used without the article.

Ex.:   Ambo le *mani per dolor mi morsi.* (Dan.)
I bit both my hands for grief.
Furono entrambi *condannati*, they were both condemned.

11. *Both* is sometimes expressed in Italian by repeating the conjunction *e*, and.

Ex.:   *Essi sono* e *tristi* e *ostinati.*
They are both wicked and obstinate.

ORTHOGRAPHY OF INDEFINITE PRONOUNS.

1. *Tutto*, all, and *si*, one, they, people, may drop their final *o* and *i* before vowels, the elision being marked by an apostrophe.

Ex.: *Non è tutt' oro quel che luce.*
It is not all gold that glitters.

2. Those ending in *un*, *uno*, or *una*, are subject to the same elisions as the definite article. (See p. 8.)

3. For *tale*, *cotale*, and *quale*, see page 10.

READING EXERCISE.

La lucciola.

Non ho io, diceva ad alta voce una[a] lucciola, questo foco di dentro che risplende? Ora che fo io quì in terra? Chè non volo sulle sfere a ruotare questi miei nobilissimi raggi dal levante al ponente, e a formare una nuova stella fra le altre mie sorelle del cielo? Amica, le disse un vermicello che udì i suoi vantamenti, finchè con quel tuo splendido focherello stai fra le zanzare e le farfalle, verrai onorata; ma se sali dove tu di', sarai nulla.[b]

Questa favoletta ammonisca me e molti altri.[c]

GOZZI.

VOCABULARY.

to spend (of time), *passare*.	world, *mondo*.	to be abroad, *viaggiare*.
play, *commedia*.	appetite, *appetito*.	
party, *serata*.	royal, *reale*.	library, *libreria*.
theatre, *teatro*.	sure, *certo*.	relation, *parente*.

TRANSLATION EXERCISE.

[Dialogue between an English and an Italian gentleman. They will address each other in the polite way.]

Class I. of Indef. Pron. } 1. How do people[d] spend the evening in Milan? 2. Everybody[e] goes out to enjoy himself; some[f] go to the opera, some to the play, and others to a party. 3. Is it true that "La Scala" is the largest theatre in the world? 4. Everybody[e] says so. Have

---

[a] See p. 8.   [b] Rule, p. 221.   [c] See p. 10.
[d] Obs. 3, p. 49.   [e] Obs. 6, p. 221.   [f] Obs. 4, p. 221.

L 3

you not seen it yet? Whoever[a] comes to Milan
should   go to see it. 5. Do you know anybody
use the Cond. of *dovere*.)
                                              alcuno

who could   take me there[b]? 6. I know nobody.
(Subj. of *potere*.) (use *condurre*.)

Did you not meet some one you know at Mrs. B.'s yesterday? 7. Nobody. A certain person spoke to me in
Italian; but I could not understand him. 8. Was there
no one who could speak English? 9. Nobody.

Class. II. of }
Indef. Pron. } 10. Have you had anything this morn-
                                  [taken]

ing? 11. I have eaten nothing yet. 12. Do you want
anything? 13. No, thank you; whatever you may give
me, I have no appetite. 14. Have you everything you
want? 15. Everything.

Class III. of }
Indef. Pron } 16. Did you see any of your brothers
yesterday? 17. I have seen neither (of them). 18. Are
you sure that one of your two sisters will come to Italy
next year? 19. Yes; either the one or the other will
come undoubtedly[c]. 20. Does your eldest[d] sister know
many languages? 21. Yes, she knows several[e] modern
languages; however[f], she does not speak them fluently,
because she has not been abroad. 22. After – she
                                          che

has been in Italy, will she go somewhere else[g]? 23. She
will go nowhere else next year. 24. Do you think
your brother is better now than he was?
(use *stare*)
                                          [stood]

25. Quite the contrary[h]; he is very poorly indeed, and
always talks of death. 26. It is one thing to talk of
death, and another[i] to die.

---

[a] Obs. 7, p. 221.   [b] Note *a*, p. 190.   [c] Obs. 5, p. 223.
[d] Obs. 2, p. 167.   [e] N.B., p. 156.   [f] Obs. 4, p. 223.
[g] Obs. 1, p. 222.   [h] Obs. 6, p. 223.   [i] Obs. 2, p. 222.

CLASS IV. OF INDEF. PRON.
AND THE THREE OTHER CLASSES. } 27. Have you any[a] books here?
28. Yes, I have a few[a]. Should you like to read any,
here is all my library. 29. Have you any[b] guide-book
for Italy? 30. Yes, here is one.

QUESTIONS.

Come sogliono passare la sera i Milanesi? 2.—Qual è
il più gran teatro del mondo? 3.—Conosce Ella alcuno
in Firenze? 5.—Non è venuto nessuno a trovarla oggi?
—Chi le parlò alla serata della Signora B.?—Ha bisogno
di niente? 12.—Che cosa ha?—Occupa Ella una parte o
il tutto di questa casa?—Conosce Ella meglio Roma o
Napoli[c]?—Andrà in qualche luogo domani? 23.—Che
disse un vermicello alla lucciola?

CHAPTER IX.

ADVERBS.

ADVERBS are not inflected in Italian. They are used
to limit or modify the meaning of verbs, adjectives, and
other adverbs; as,

Ella canta bene, she sings well.

Il tenere il capo troppo caldo, fa assai male.
Keeping the head too hot, is very hurtful.

RULE.—Many adverbs are formed by adding *mente*
to the feminine adjective of quality ending either in *a* or
e; as,

generosa, generosamente... generous, generously.
felice, felicemente .... happy, happily.

N.B.—Adjectives ending in *le* or *re* drop the final *e*
in forming the adverb; as,

facile, facilmente......... easy, easily.
regolare, regolarmente... regular, regularly.

---

[a] See p. 10. [b] Obs. 1, p. 223. [c] Rule, p. 222.

Different Classes of Adverbs.

Adverbs are classified according to their signification, as follows :—

Adverbs of Place.

1. The following adverbs denote locality in a manner corresponding with the three classes of demonstrative pronouns[a] :—

(i.) Where the speaker or writer is.

ci[b], *qui, quà,* here.

(ii.) Where the person addressed is.

costì, cotestì $\left\{ \begin{array}{l} \text{'there,' referring to} \\ \text{a fixed place.} \end{array} \right.$

costà, cotestà $\left\{ \begin{array}{l} \text{'there,' less deter-} \\ \text{minately.} \end{array} \right.$

(iii.) Distant from both the speaker and person addressed.

$\left. \begin{array}{l} li, colì \\ là, colà \\ vi^b, ivi, quivi \end{array} \right\}$ there.

2. Other adverbs of place denote—

(i.) Rest in a place; as,

dove or *ove,* where; *vicino,* near; *su,* up; *sopra,* upon, above; *giù,* down; *sotto,* under, below.

(ii.) Motion to or from a place; as,

di lì or *di là,* thither; *di qui* or *di quà,* hither; *indi,* thence; *quindi* or *quinci,* from thence; *costinci,* from thence, where you are; *onde* or *donde,* whence.

(iii.) Place in a variety of relative positions; as,

entro or *dentro,* within; *fuori* or *fuora,* without, outside; *avanti,* before; *dietro,* behind; *allato, accanto,* or *accosto,* aside, near; *attorno* or *intorno,* around; *rimpetto,* opposite; *lungi* or *lontano,* far; *oltre,* beyond; *altrove* or *altronde,* elsewhere; *dovunque* or *ovunque*[c], wherever.

---

[a] See p. 209.   [b] Obs. 6, p. 190.

[c] *Unque* answers to the English 'ever,' in compound pronouns and adverbs.

EXERCISE.

N.B.—Translate the following sentences, and point out the adverbs contained in them, giving their exact signification:—

Monsignor quì non c' è, ma ci siamo ben noi.—Scrivetemi e ditemi se il Giordani sia o no costì.—Il mercante che va di quà e di là portando la sua mercanzia si chiama merciaiuolo.—Dove non è pace vi è guerra.— Sedete accanto a me.—L'uomo adirato tutto si muta dentro e di fuori.

Adverbs of Time.

1. Adverbs of Time may refer to different relations of time.

(i.) Present; as,

ora, adesso, or *mo,* now; *testè,* just now; *oggi,* to-day; *ancora* or *tuttora,* still; *subito,* immediately.

(ii.) Past; as,

dianzi, innanzi, prima, or *pria,* before; *ieri,* yesterday; *allora,* then; *altrevolte,* once; *già,* already, in time past.

(iii.) Future; as,

tosto, soon; *presto,* quick; *poi, indi, dopo, poscia,* or *appresso,* afterwards; *domani,* to-morrow.

(iv.) Duration or repetition; as,

sempre or *ognora,* always, ever; *mai* or *giammai,* never; *spesso* or *sovente,* often; *talvolta* or *talora,* sometimes; *adagio,* slow; *per tempo,* early; *tardi,* late; *intanto* or *frattanto,* in the meantime; *mentre,* whilst; *alfine,* at last.

EXERCISE. (See N.B., above.)

Vi ho detto ove sono, ora intendete che faccio.—Oggi voglio esser migliore di ieri.—Egli non ride mai.—Andate subito e tornate tosto.—A rivederci domani, intanto vi saluto.

Adverbs of Quantity and Quality.

1. These adverbs denote manner of degree and

quality, and are:—*più*[a], more; *meno, manco,* less; *molt)
assai,* much; *bene,* well; *male,* badly; *troppo,* too much;
guari, not much; *tanto,* so much; *poco,* little; *affatt),*
any, at all; *fino* or *sino,* till.

EXERCISE. (N.B., p. 229.)

Chi assai parla spesso falla.—Oggi non sto affatto
bene.—Chi troppo vuole spesso perde anche il poco.

---

*Adverbs of Affirmation and Negation, Doubt, Choice,
and Interrogative Adverbs.*

Sì, yes; *già,* indeed; *certo,* certainly; *bene,* well;—*no,*
no; *non,* not; *mai, giammai,* never; *mica, punto, affatto,*
not at all;—*forse,* perhaps; *circa,* about; *davvero, difatti,*
indeed, truly, in truth; *appunto,* exactly so; *pure,* yet;
presso, about; *quasi,* almost;— *anzi, prima,* rather;
piuttosto, piupresto, sooner; *ecco,* behold; *eccoli*[b], there
is;—*ove?* where? *dove?* whither? *donde?* whence?
quando? when? *che?* come? how? *perchè?* why?
quanto? how much?

EXERCISE.—Read the Exercise at page 15, and point
out all the adverbs contained in it.

OBSERVATIONS.

1. The difference between *no* and *non* is, that *no*
stands by itself, *non* is used to form a negative sen-
tence.

Ex.:   No; non *posso permetterlo.* No; I cannot allow it.

2. *Mai*[c] and *giammai,* employed negatively, mean
never,' and are used with *non,* except when they stand
by themselves in answer to a question.

Ex.:   *Non l' avete* mai *visto?* Giammai (*or* mai).
        Have you never seen it? Never.

3. Employed interrogatively, and in conditional or

---

[a] Some of the above adverbs are used in comparison. (See
pp. 161, 162, and 163.)
[b] See Obs. 4, p. 188.
[c] *Mai* is sometimes found used as an expletive with *sempre, sì,
no;* as,

Giace mai sempre in ghiaccio. (PET.)
It lies for ever amidst the ice.

doubtful phrases, *mai* and *giammai* are used without *non*, and mean 'ever.'

Ex.: *L' avete* mai *veduta ?* have you ever seen her ?
Se mai *la vedessi*, if ever I were to see her.

4. *Già*, certainly, already; *bene*, well; *punto*, at all; *mica* or *miga*, no; are often employed as expletives.

Ex.: *Non* già *che l' ami*, not that I love her.
Non è mica *da scherzo*, it is not for a joke.

5. Some adjectives are sometimes used as adverbs, and, as such, are of course invariable. The following is a list of the principal adjectives thus used:

chiaro, clear.	*sodo*, firm.
aperto, open.	*felice*, happy.
schietto, free.	*sano*, healthy.
dolce, sweet.	*sommesso*, submissive, low.
giusto, just.	

Ex.: *Parlate chiaro*, speak plainly.
Vivete felice, live happily.

6. Some words are sometimes adverbs and sometimes adjectives; such as,

alto, high, or highly.	*basso*, low, lowly.
caro, dear, dearly.	*spesso*, frequent, frequently.
diritto. straight.	*presto*, quick, quickly.
piano { smooth, smoothly. slow, slowly.	*troppo*, too-much, too.
	vicino, near.
rado, rare, rarely.	*lontano*, far.
solo, alone, only.	*sicuro*, certain, certainly.

Ex.: *Avete pagato* caro *il vostro capriccio*.
You have paid dearly for your whim.

Dove siete, cara *sorella ?* where are you, sister dear ?

7. Some adjectives and nouns become adverbs by the addition of a preposition.

Ex.: *Avviene di rado*, it happens seldom.
L' ho fatto in fretta, I have done it hurriedly.
È fatto alla francese, it is done after the French fashion.

DEGREES OF ADVERBS.

RULE I.—Adverbs formed from an adjective of quality (see Rule, p. 227) admit of the comparative and su-

perlative degrees, which are expressed in the same manner
as the degrees of adjectives; as,

Comparative of Superiority: *più facilmente*, more easily.
      „   Inferiority: *meno facilmente*, less easily.
Superlative {Relative: *il più facilmente*, the most easily.
           {Absolute: *facilissimamente*, very easily.

Notice that the absolute adverbial superlative is expressed by adding *mente* to the feminine superlative adjective.

RULE II.—The following adverbs have particular forms
in the comparative and superlative:

> *male, peggio, pessimamente;* bad, worse, worst.
> *bene, meglio, ottimamente;* well, better, best.
> *poco, meno, minimamente;* little, less, least.

OBSERVATIONS ON THE ORTHOGRAPHY OF ADVERBS.

1. The adverbs, *bene*, well, *male*, bad, *ora*, now,
talora, sometimes, *ognora*, always, *ancora*, still, *meno*,
less, *fino*, till, *pure*, yet, *solo*, only, *davvero*, indeed,
piano, slow, *alfine*, at last, may lose their final vowel
before any consonant, without taking an apostrophe; as,

> *Chi mal fa male aspetti.* (PROV.)
> Who does harm may expect harm.

2. *Quando*, when, *dove* or *ove*, where, *quanto*, how
much, drop their final vowel, and take an apostrophe
before vowels; as,

> *Dov' era andata*, where she had gone.

ADVERBIAL EXPRESSIONS MOST COMMONLY IN USE.

(To be committed to memory by the pupil.)

in appresso, } afterwards,		*da che,* }	
di poi, } then*.		*da poi,* } since.	
fin d' allora, } since then,		*d' allora in poi,* }	
d'allora in quà, } since.		*d' ora in avanti,* henceforth.	

---

* 'Then,' in the sense of 'therefore,' is rendered by *dunque*,
quindi, perciò.

da quando in quà, since when.

da due mesi in quà, two months since.

da non molto, not long since.

da quì innanzi,
da quà innanzi, } from this
da questo punto } time
in poi, } forth.
da indi innanzi.

d' altronde, besides.

abbastanza, enough.

altrimenti, otherwise.

appena, scarcely, hardly.

attorno, circa,
in circa, all' incirca, } { about, round about.

bel, bello, softly, gently.

per l' avvenire, in future.

a bocca,
a voce, } by word of mouth.

cioè,
cioè a dire, } { that is, that is to say.

pur dianzi,
poco fa,
poc' anzi,
non molto fa, } { not long ago, a little while ago.

molto tempo fa, long ago.

pochi giorni passati, a few days ago.

fra poco, shortly, presently.

in fatti, in effect, in fact.

di fatto, really.

finora,
fino,
infino ad ora } { up to the present time, till now.

in fine,
in somma, } in short.

fin dove, how far.

a fondo, thoroughly.

quaggiù, down there.

da basso, down stairs.

di sopra, up stairs.

non guari, not long.

laggiù, } below (there),
lassù, } above (there).

quassù, (here) above.

di gran lunga, by far.

in quel mentre, just then.

niente affatto, not at all.

a destra or
a mano destra, } { on or to the right hand.
a diritta,

a manca or
a mano manca, } on the left.
a sinistra,

presso a poco,
a un dipresso, } { nearly,
pressochè, } almost,
quasi, } thereabouts.

di mano in
mano, } { by degrees,
a poco a poco, } gradually.

ad onta, in spite of.

per lo passato,
per l' addietro, } formerly.
altre volte,

piano, pian piano, slowly.

di quando in
quando,
quando...quando,
tratto tratto or } { now and then.
di tratto in tratto,
di tanto in tanto,
di tempo in tempo

a minuto, in detail.

all' improvviso, suddenly, unexpectedly.

subito dopo, soon after.

tosto che, as soon as.

ad un tratto,
su due piedi, } at once.

per tutto,
da per tutto, } everywhere.

da banda,
da parte, } aside.

a buon mercato, cheap.

da solo a solo, } *a quattr' occhi,* } tête-à-tête.

in un batter } *d' occhio,* } in a moment. *in un attimo,* }

per esempio, for instance.

da prima, } *in prima,* } first, at first.

il più presto possibile, as soon as possible.

a bello studio, } *apposta,* } on purpose.

ultimamente, lately.

da senno, truly, indeed.

volentieri, } *di buona voglia,* } { willingly, with pleasure. }

malvolentieri, } *di mala voglia* } unwillingly.

per tempo, } *di buon ora,* } early.

da capo, } *di nuovo,* } again.

invece, instead, on the other hand.

per ischerzo, } *da burla,* } in jest.

di fretta, hurriedly.

alla fin delle fini, last of all.

READING EXERCISE.

Sono pochi giorni passati[a] che andò un uomo alla bottega d' un caffettiere che sta a . . . e dissegli: Subito[b] quattro caffè alla tal casa, chè io attendo qui[c] fuori[d]; e nominò un casato degno di rispetto. Mentre[e] che il caffè bolliva, metteva di quando in quando[a] il capo dentro[d] e dicea, Fate tosto per amor del cielo. Quando ogni cosa fu all' ordine, esce il giovane dalla bottega con una guantiera di metallo e quattro belle chicchere e un vaso di zucchero di porcellana, e trova l' uomo fuori, il quale gli dice: Il tè dov'[f] 'è ? Risponde il giovane: Io non udii di tè. Oh sordi ! grida l' altro ; io vado di fretta[g] e qui si ha ancora ad indugiare. Tosto fa un tè e dà a me quello ch' è fatto, che io vado avanti. Così detto, prende la guantiera e dicea: Io ti prego, spicciati e col tè viemmi[h] dietro. Il giovane rientra, si sbriga, va alla casa, non trova ordine alcuno ; che l' uomo aveva ordinato per sè e non per altri.—GOZZI.

VOCABULARY.

kind, *cortese.*
already, *già.*
regular, *regolare.*
manner, *modo.*
volume, *volume* (m.)
reading, *lettura.*

through, *per.*
passage, *corrittio.*
to go abroad, *andare all' estero.*
a country seat, *villeggiatura.*

to stay at a country seat, *villeggiare, fare villeggiatura.*
vintage, *vendemmia.*
to be over. *esser passato.*

---

[a] See p. 233.
[d] (iii.), p. 228.
[g] See above.

[b] (i.), p. 229.
[e] I. (iv.), p. 229.
[h] Obs. 3, p. 187.

[c] I. (i.), p. 228.
[f] Obs. 2, p. 232.

TRANSLATION EXERCISE.

[Dialoguo between an Italian and an English lady. They will
address each other in the 3rd person singular, *Ella*.]

1. How do you do, Madam? You have done well to
come early.[a] 2. Thank you; I have brought you back
the book which you kindly[b] lent me the last time —
[that]
I was here. 3. Have you already finished – reading
[of]
it? 4. I finished it long ago. 5. How have you ever[c]
been able to read all that so quickly? 6. Lately I read
regularly for three hours every evening, and in this
manner I can read nearly[d] three volumes in about[3] a[1]
week[2]. 7. And I, on the other hand,[a] can scarcely[d]
read one volume in a month. 8. Will you come down
now into the dining-room? 9. With pleasure. 10. I
will go before. Go slowly[d] through the passage, because
it is rather dark here. This is the dining-room. 11. The
windows look into the street, so whilst we dine we can
see the people pass. 12. Let us sit near each other, that
we may talk while we dine. How long[d] have you been
[Since when] [are you]
in this country? 13. — two years. 14. Have you
[Since]
never been to Italy since then[e]? 15. I go to see my
country now and then.[d] 16. Do you like England?
17. At first I did not like it, but gradually I became
accustomed to it. 18. Do Italians go abroad in the
summer? 19. They seldom go out of their country.
The rich have their country-seats; they go there to stay
through the summer, and return to town as soon as
[in]
the vintage is over.

---

[a] See p. 234.   [b] Rule, p. 227.   [c] Obs. 3, p. 230.
[d] See p. 233.   [e] See p. 232.

Tornerà a casa presto stassera? 1.—Che ha riportato alla Signora B. l' ultima volta che andò a trovarla? 2.— È già arrivato suo fratello? 3.—Da quando in quà studia l' italiano?—Va sua sorella malvolentieri alla scuola?— V' era molta gente alla serata della Signora D.?—Chi abita dirimpetto a casa sua?—Che faceva Ella mentre suo fratello leggeva?—Dove passano la state gl' Italiani ricchi?—Quando andò un uomo alla bottega d'un caffettiere?—Che disse egli?—Che faceva mentre il caffè bolliva?—Che aveva il giovine quando uscì dalla bottega?

CHAPTER X.

PREPOSITIONS.

THE Preposition is an uninflected part of speech.

We have already given, at page 8, all the prepositions which may be joined in one word with the definite article, and explained the use of *di*, *a*, *da*, in relation with the noun (p. 144) ; we will now point out the Italian prepositions most commonly in use.

Prepositions are classified according to their significations, as follows :—

I. PLACE.—Under place we have—

(i.) Rest in (the 'where'); as, *in*, in; *a*, at; *appo* or *appresso*, among, with ; *per*, by.

(ii.) Motion with direction (the 'whence' and the 'whither') ; as, *a*, to or unto; *in*, into, to ; *oltre*, beyond ; *verso*, *alla volta*, or *incontro*, towards ; *a seconda*, in the direction of; *da*, from.

OBSERVATIONS.

1. The preposition *a* is employed to express tendency

towards a person or thing, whether the motion be commenced, or ended, or merely implied; as,

Vado a *Roma,* I am going to Rome.
Avvicinatevi a *me,* come near me.

2. *A* is used to connect the word expressing the motive power with that expressing the object set in motion, and is also found in many adverbial expressions; as,

Un mulino a *vento,* a wind-mill.
Una macchina a *vapore,* a steam-engine.
È dipinto a *meraviglia,* it is painted wonderfully well.

(See also Note *c,* p. 62.)

3. *In* is used instead of the English *to,* before a name of a place, excepting that of a town, in speaking of going or having been to that place; as,

Quando andrete in *Italia?* when will you go *to* Italy?
Siete stato in *chiesa?* have you been *to* church?

(iii.) Place and direction:—*Sopra* or *sovra, su,* on, over, above; *di su, di sopra,* up;—the opposites of these are *sotto,* under, beneath; *di sotto, giù,* down, below. *Per,* through (idea of passage); *lungo* or *lunghesso,* along; *rasente,* close to; *avanti, davanti,* or *prima,* before (with or without proximity);—opposed to these are *apresso, dietro,* after; *di dietro,* behind. *Fra, tra, infra,* between *or* among; *in mezzo, entro,* amidst, as opposed to *fuori, di fuori,* without. *Attorno,* round; *intorno, d'intorno, circa,* about; *presso* or *vicino,* near (in proximity to); *lungi, lontano,* or *discosto,* far; *contra, di contro,* or *rincontro,* close by; *rimpetto* or *a fronte,* opposite.

OBSERVATIONS.

1. *Per* is used to express 'motion *through* a place,' 'the reason *why,*' 'the cause *by* which,' 'the manner *in* which,' and 'the purpose *for* which,' a thing is accomplished; as,

Entrò per *la finestra,* he entered through the window.
Scrivo per *compiacervi,* I write to please you.
Per *le continue pioggie,* because of the continual rains.
Viaggio per *la posta,* I am travelling by post.
È per *amor vostro,* it is for your sake.

2. *Per*, followed by an infinitive after the verbs *stare*
and *essere*, signifies 'to be about,' 'to be on the point
of'; as,

Sto per *partire*, I am about to depart.

Io era per *partire*, I was on the point of departing.

(See also Note *g*, p. 30, and Note *b*, p. 49.)

EXERCISE.

Translate the following sentences, and point out the
prepositions of *place* contained in them:—

Le stelle si veggono in cielo.—Appo⁴ gl' Italiani si fa
multo uso di caffe.—Ogni acqua va al mare.—Sul mare
canta il nocchiero.— Fra l' armi dorme il guerriero.—
Una pecora perduta fuor dell' ovile va belando per i
campi.

II. TIME :—*Da*, since ;˙*fin*, *fino* or *sino*, till, until; *dopo*,
after ; *durante*, during.   Many prepositions of place
may be applied to time by governing a noun of time;
as, *in*, in, *prima*, before, *da*, by, &c.

OBSERVATIONS.

1. *In* is used in phrases denoting passing from one
time to another; as,

L' aspettiamo di giorno in *giorno*.

We expect him from day to day.

2. *In* is elegantly used before *su* by good writers.

Ex.:   *Gli parve in su*lla *mezzanotte sentire d'* in sul *tetto*, &c. (Boc.)
He thought he heard at midnight, on the roof, &c.

III. AGENCY, END, and MANNER :—*Con*, with; *da*, by ;
per, for, by ; *affine*, for the sake of ; *di*, of, from ; *a modo*,
a guisa, or *alla foggia*, after the manner, according to.

IV. ORIGIN, SEPARATION, and EXCLUSION : — *Di*, of;
da, from ; *senza*, without ; *salvo*, save ; *eccetto* or *tranne*,
except.

OBSERVATIONS.

1. *Di* is found in many elliptical phrases; as,

Fu punito di *morte*
(i.e., colla pena *di morte*).   He was punished with death.

See I. (i.), p. 236.

Dare del *lei a uno*
(i.e., il titolo *di lei*). } To address one with *lei*.

2. *Di* is often used instead of *da*, after verbs expressing separation or removal, when the noun has no article; as,

È uscito di *casa*, he is gone out of the house.

Levatevi di *tavola*, leave the table.

Mi cade di *mano la penna*, the pen falls out of my hand.

N.B.—If the noun is preceded by the article, *da* is generally used; as, *Levatevi* dalla *tavola*. But examples occur in good writers of the use of *di*, even with the article.

Ex.: *Cacciata avea il sole* del *cielo già ogni stella.* (Boc.)
The sun had already chased every star from the heavens.

3. *Di* is found in phrases in which 'in,' 'by,' 'to,' 'at,' 'with,' or 'on,' are used in English; as,

Abbondante di *ricchezze*, abounding *in* riches.

Viaggio di *giorno*, di *notte*, I travel *by* day, *by* night.

Egli è segretario del *re*, he is secretary *to* the king.

Mi meravigliai di *vederlo*, I was surprised *at* seeing him.

Sono contento di *voi*, I am satisfied *with* you.

Egli vive di *solo pane*, he lives *on* bread alone.

(See also p. 144, and Note *b*, p. 76.)

4. *Da* expresses a relation of dependence, origin, or departure; as,

Dipende da *voi*, it depends on you.

Leonardo da *Vinci*, Leonardo from Vinci.[a]

È partito dalla *villa*, he has left the country-seat.

5. *Da* is used to indicate the agent; as,

È tormentato da *mille timori*, he is tormented by a thousand fears.

Fu fatto da *Pietro*, it was done by Peter.

(See also Note *b*, p. 49; p. 144; and N.B. above.)

V. INCLINATION, CONFORMITY, and SUBSTITUTION:—*Per*, for; *secondo*, according to; *invece*, instead of; *in cambio*, or *in luogo*, in place of, &c.

N.B.—Some words are both prepositions and adverbs.

---

[a] *Vinci*, a castle near Florence, was the birth-place of *Leonardo*.

A preposition is known by its governing a noun, or a
phrase corresponding to a noun; as, *al suo arrivo a casa*,
on his arriving at home.

EXERCISE.

Translate the following sentences, and point out the
prepositions contained in them :—

Dalla luna d' ottobre a quella di gennaio si potano
gli alberi.—Le piante nascono da semi.—L' involto si
lega collo spago.—Il padre è amato dal figlio.—Morirono
tutti tranne due.—Tutta la terra è circondata dall' aria.

OBSERVATIONS ON THE ORTHOGRAPHY OF PREPOSITIONS.

The prepositions *sino* or *fino*, till, *fuori*, beside,
senza, without, may be spelt *sin, fin, fuor, senz'*.
(See also p. 8, and Obs., 1, p. 147.)

GOVERNMENT OF PREPOSITIONS.

Most Italian prepositions govern the noun or phrase
(see above) by another preposition which follows them;
other prepositions are used alone; others, again, may
govern the noun indifferently by any one out of two or
more different prepositions; whilst others may or may
not take another preposition.

I. The prepositions which require *di* after them are—
alla volta, towards; *a seconda*, in the direction of; *prima*,
before; *a modo* or *a guisa*, after, in manner of; *invece*,
in cambio, or *in lungo*, instead of, in place of.

Ex.: *Egli ride invece* di *piangere*, he laughs instead of weeping.

II. Those which require *a* after them are—*accanto* or
allato, near, by the side of; *dietro*, behind; *presso* or
attorno, about; *sino, fino*, as far as; *rimpetto*, opposite;
rincontro, against.

Ex.: *Accanto* al *bene ci sta il male.* (SEGN.)
Good and evil go side by side.

III. Those which require *da* after them are—*di quà*,
this side; *di là*, that side; *lungi*, far; *in fuori*, besides.

Ex.: *State lungi* dai *cattivi compagni.*
Keep far from bad companions.

IV. The following prepositions require no other prepositions after them :—*eccetto, salvo,* or *tranne,* except; *lunghesso* or *rasente,* close to, or along; *mediante,* by means; *per,* for; *in,* in; *tra* or *fra,* between; *su,* on; *giusto* or *secondo,* according.

Ex.: *Sono per le vie e* sui *ponti della città.*
They are about the streets and on the bridges of the city.

V. The following prepositions may take either *di* or *a* after them :—*a rispetto* or *per rispetto,* on account of; *a lato,* aside; *a rincontro,* against; *vicino,* near; *attorno,* round.

Ex.: *Sedete vicino* di (*or* a) *me,* sit near me.

VI. The following may take either *a* or *da* :—*di dietro,* behind; *discosto,* distant from.

Ex.: *Trovasi due miglia discosto* dalla (*or* alla) *città.*
It is two miles distant from the city.

VII. The following may take either *di,* or no preposition at all :—*verso* or *inverso,* towards; *salvo,* except; *senza,* without.

Ex.: *Non fanno niente senza* dél (*or* il) *padre.*
They do nothing without the father.

VIII. The following may take either *a,* or no preposition at all :—*di contra,* or *addosso,* on, against; *entro,* into, within; *anzi,* before; *dirimpetto,* opposite.

Ex.: *Non andate entro* (a) *quella stanza.*
Do not go into that room.

IX. The following may take either *di, a,* or *da :—di fuori,* without; *di lungi,* from far. ·

Ex.: *Erano di fuori* dalla (*or* della, *or* alla) *città.*
They are without the city.

X. The following may take *di* or *a,* or no preposition: — *appo,* with *or* among; *oltre,* beyond; *appresso* or *dopo,* after; *sopra* or *sovra,* upon; *contra* or *contro,* against; *lungo,* along; *circa,* about; *presso* or *accosto,* near.

Ex.: Appo *noi non si fa uso di tè,* with us tea is not used.

XI. The following may take *a, da,* or no preposition : —*di costa,* close; *dietro,* after, behind; *dianzi* or *innanzi,* before.

Ex.: *Egli era innanzi a noi,* he was before us.

M

XII. Lastly, the following prepositions may take either *di*, *a*, or *da*, or no preposition :—*avanti*, forward, before; *intorno*, around; *dentro*, within, inside; *di sotto*, under; *di sopra*, upon, above; *fuori*, outside.

Ex.: *Essi erano avanti di noi*, they were before us (*or* in advance).

READING EXERCISE.

Carlo di Valois, brutto[a] di[b] tanti delitti, al principio del 1302 andò a[c] Roma per aver consiglio del Papa, e gli chiese danari. Bonifazio rispose che mandandolo a Firenze lo avea messo nella[d] *fonte dell' oro*. Risposta che bene spiega la qualità delle sue intenzioni. Dai fatti che seguitarono apparisce che allora fu stabilito definitivamente l'esilio de' Bianchi. In effetto Carlo tornò a Firenze, e sapendo che ivi era la *fonte dell' oro*, saziò a quella fonte le bramose voglie[e], fece altre rapine, dette sentenze di morte pubblicò i beni e arse le case ad alcuni che falsamente e con empio artifizio furono accusati di aver cospirato per[f] ucciderlo. Poi per mezzo del Potestà (aprile, 1302) procedè alle condanne del bando, ed esiliò oltre a 600 cittadini delle principali casate dei Bianchi che si sparsero per[f] Toscana e l'Italia, e fecero causa comune coi Ghibellini. Fra questi esuli fu anche Dante che, citato a comparire per essere stato dei Bianchi e per aver contrastato alla venuta dello straniero, non si presentò, ed ebbe arse le case, confiscati i beni, e condanna di morte.—VANNUCCI.

VOCABULARY.

bonnet, *cappellino*.	chaplain, *cappellano*.	the break of day, *lo*
straw, *paglia*.	to come near, *avvici-*	*spuntar del giorno*.
to ask after one, *do-*	*narsi*.	as far as, *fino*.
mandare di uno.	boat, *battello*.	opposite, *dirimpetto*.
to take away, *con-*	steam, *vapore*.	behind, *dietro*.
durre via.	Christmas, *Natale*.	near, *vicino*.
glass, *vetro*.		origin, *origine* (f.)

---

[a] Obs. 5, p. 127.   [b] Obs. 3, p. 239.
[c] Obs. 1, p. 236.   [d] I. (i.), p. 236.
[e] Like the *lupa* (wolf) of Dante, Inf. c. I., v. 98.   [f] Obs. 1, p. 237.

TRANSLATION EXERCISE.

[Dialogue between two young ladies.—They will address each
other in the 3rd person with *Ella.*]

ᴾᴿᴱᴾᴼˢᴵᵀᴵᴼᴺ} 1. Where is your straw[a] bonnet? 2. It is
in my sister's[a] room. 3. Is your brother gone out of[b] the
house? 4. Yes; Mr. D. came to ask after him, and
took him away. 5. How did you break the glass of your
gold watch? 6. It fell out of[b] my hands. 7. Did you
travel by[c] day or by night, when you came to London?

a

8. I travelled by night: we were three friends; the
daughter of Mr. B., chaplain to the Queen, Mrs. D.'s
niece, and myself.

[I]

ᴾᴿᴱᴾᴼˢᴵᵀᴵᴼᴺ
ˢ.} 9. Is your room on[d] the ground floor or on
the first floor? 10. It is on the third floor. 11. Where
will you go next summer? 12. I shall go to Leghorn.[e]
13. How will you go — ? 14. I shall go to Liverpool,

[there]

and thence by steam-boat to Leghorn. 15. Will you

per

be able to make yourself understood when you are at
Leghorn? 16. I hope so. 17. When did you begin to
learn Italian? 18. Last year, at Christmas.

ᴾᴿᴱᴾᴼˢᴵᵀᴵᴼᴺ
ᵈᵃ.} 19. From whom do you learn Italian?
20. From an Italian gentleman.

ᴾᴿᴱᴾᴼˢᴵᵀᴵᴼᴺˢ
ᴳᴱᴺᴱᴿᴬᴸᴸʸ.} 21. When do you start for France?

[will]

22. To-morrow morning at day-break. 23. And when
will you arrive at Paris? 24. Before[e] night. 25. I have
been in France twice, but I never went so far as[f] Paris

---

[a] Obs., p. 144.	[b] Obs. 2, p. 239.	[c] Obs. 3, p. 239.
[d] I. (i.), p. 238.	[e] I., p. 240.	[f] II., p. 240.

M 2

26. Who lives opposite to[a] your house ?   27. I do not
know; but I am well acquainted with the lady who lives
behind[b] my house; she has been in Italy, and says that
the country near[c] Florence is beautiful. Not far from
the city, out[d] of "Porta San Gallo," is Fiesole, (a) town
from which Florence had its origin.

QUESTIONS.

Che cappello porta Ella d' estate ? 1.—Chi è venuto a
domandare di suo fratello ? 4.—Quando le piace viaggiare ? 8.—Di chi è segretario il Signor B.? 8.—Che
mulini si usano in Inghilterra[e] ?—Dove fa conto di andare
la state prossima ?—Quando arrivò a Londra suo zio ?—
Come andrà a casa sua ?—Chi fu fra gli esuli fiorentini
esiliati nel 1302 ?—Perchè fu Dante citato a comparire ?
—Che cosa gli fecero ?

CHAPTER XI.

CONJUNCTIONS.

I. CONJUNCTIONS are uninflected. They join together
sentences and single words; as,

> *Francesco ama la virtù* e *odia il vizio.*
> Francis loves virtue and hates vice.
> *Pietro* e *Paolo*, Peter and Paul.

II. Conjunctions are divided into—*copulative, augmentative* or *adjunctive, negative, alternative, conditional,
arrestive, exceptive, adversative,* and *causal.*

---

[a] VIII., p. 241.   II., p. 240.   [e] V., p. 241.
[d] XII., p. 242.   Obs. 2, p. 237.

1. *Copulative* conjunctions unite sentences or clauses, and are—

e, ed, (et[a]*),* and.   *anco* or *ancora,* also, even,
anche, also, as well as.   likewise.

as,   *Il tempo passa, e non torna più.*
     Time passes, and returns no more.

OBS.—The conjunction *e* is sometimes omitted, and then it is understood; as,

     Cerca il bene, dispregia il male.
     Seek after the good, and despise the evil.

2. The *Adjunctive* are conjunctions which, in connecting sentences, give especial emphasis to the union; these are—

di più,   *in oltre* or *innoltre,*   *d' altronde,* } besides.   *non solo,* not only.

oltrechè } besides this *oltracciò* } or that.
ancora, again.
pure or *altresi,* also.

as,   *La modestia oltrechè è virtù è pure bellezza.*
     Modesty, besides being a virtue, is also grace.

3. The *Negative* conjunctions place the second sentence or clause in some kind of opposition to what precedes; they are—

no, not.   *non già,* not at all.   *anzi,* on the contrary.   *nè, ned*[b]*,* nor, neither.

neppure[c]*,* *nemmeno,* *tampoco,* *nettampoco,* } neither.

as,   *Non ispargere disuguali nè troppo spesse le sementi dei grani.*
     Do not scatter unequally, neither too thick, the seeds of corn.

4. *Alternative* conjunctions unite contrary sentences or words; they are—

---

[a] *e* is used before any consonant; *ed* before vowels; *et* is obsolete.
[b] *ned* is seldom used for *nè.* See Note *h,* p. 183.
[c] *neppure,* &c., are conjunctions compounded of *ne* and *pure,* &c.; so also we can say *eppure,* instead of *e* and *pure.*

o, ossia, or *ovvero,* or.

anzi,

innanzi,

meglio, } sooner.

piuttosti,

più presto,

anzichè,

prima, first.

nè, nor, neither.

anzi che no, rather than.

più volentieri, more willingly.

OBS.—*o,* or *ossia,* sometimes expresses a mere alternative name or synonym ; as,

> *Le pecchie traggono dalla citronella o citragine mele delicatissimo.*
> Bees extract from mint very sweet honey.

5. *Conditional* conjunctions express that a thing is stated, not absolutely, but under a certain condition or supposition ; they are—

se, if.

se mai, } if, if even.

se pure, }

posto che, supposing that.

dato che, granting that.

ancorchè, even although.

a meno che, unless.

ogni volta che, } any time

tutte le volte che, } that.

purchè, provided.

con patto che, }

con questo però, } on condition.

a condizione che, }

ove, dove, or *quando,* when.

quand' anche, even when, whenever.

solamente che, only that.

> as, *Sarete sano se sarete sobrio.*
> You will enjoy good health if you are sober.

6. The *Arrestive* and *Exceptive* conjunctions suggest a pause to hear what is to be said by way of exception or opposition to what precedes ; they are—

ma or *però,* but.

pure, still, even (only).

nondimeno, yet.

nulladimeno, however.

tuttavia, nevertheless.

tuttavolta, notwithstanding.

con tutto ciò, } for all that,

ciò non ostante, } in spite of

ciò non dimeno, } that.

non per questo, notwithstanding this.

salvo,

eccetto,

tratto,

tranne,

fuori, } save or except.

in fuori,

fuor di,

fuorchè,

se non, } if not,

se non che, } otherwise, but.

as, *Gli onori ti possono esser tolti, ma la virtù mai ti può esser tolta.* (DA RIP.)

Honour can be taken from you, but of virtue you can never be deprived.

OBSERVATIONS.

(1) *Ma,* used as correlative to *non solo, non che,* means 'still,' 'also'; as,

La cicala non solo canta, ma nel cantare è importuna.
The grasshopper not only chirps, but also annoys by its chirping.

(2) *Pure* is often used in the signification of 'only'; as,

Natura non aveva ivi pur dipinto.
Nature had not only painted there.

7. *Causal* conjunctions express *end, reason,* and *purpose;* and are—

chè,	for,	*sicchè,*	so.
perchè,	because.	*di manierachè,*	
poichè,	because, since.	*di modo che,*	so that.
posciachè,	since, after.	*in guisa che,*	
perciò,	therefore.	*perocchè,*	because.
perciocchè,	for which reason,	*imperocchè,*	
imperciocchè,	because,	*per tanto,*	for which
conciossiachè,	as.	*per la qual cosa,*	reason.
dunque,	then.	*in somma,*	in short.
adunque,		*in fine,*	in conclusion.
cosichè,	wherefore.	*per fine,*	
chè,		*che*,*	that.

as, *Ogni giorno riceviamo da Dio benefizi, dunque ogni giorno noi dobbiamo ringraziarlo.*

Every day we receive benefits from God, therefore every day we must thank Him.

N.B.—For the conjunctions which require the subjunctive mood after them, see Note *c,* page 70.

---

* For the different meanings of *che,* see pp. 215, 216.

OBSERVATIONS ON THE ORTHOGRAPHY OF CONJUNCTIONS.

1. The conjunctions *e*, *o*, followed by a word beginning with a vowel, often take a *d* after them; as,

Dure ed aspre battaglie, hard and severe battles.

2. *Pure, eppure, oppure, almeno, nemmeno, ora, ancora*, followed by a consonant, drop the last vowel; as,

Che il cuor mi preme già pur pensando.
Which to think of, oppresses my heart.

READING EXERCISE.

La monarchia cristiana è popolare, in quanto mira al bene del popolo e* specialmente delle classi più numerose ed infelici, nelle quali, ad esempio di Cristo suo institutore, essa pone il suo affetto e* le sue compiacenze. L' aristocrazia, nei regni bene ordinati, è un semplice mezzo, di cui il popolo, e sovratutto la plebe, è l' ultimo fine. La plebe è la parte più sacra delle nazioni, perchè[b] è la più degna insieme e la più misera; la più degna, perchè i suoi sudori alimentano tutto lo stato, e senza di essi il potente, il nobile, il ricco non potrebbero vivere non che[c] oziare e godere; la più misera perchè a lei tocca un minimo frutto delle sue fatiche.

VOCABULARY.

cabman, *vetturino.*
to drive, *condurre.*
comfortable, *comodo.*
sitting-room, *stanza di ricevere.*
crown, *scudo.*
to breakfast, *far colazione.*
table d' hôte, *tavola rotonda.*
to show, *condurre.*
to show in, *fare entrare.*

sofa, *sofà* (m.)
arm chair, *poltrona.*
to inquire after, *domandare di.*
to take, *condurre.*
to play an opera, *dare un' opera.*
ticket, *biglietto.*
pit, *platea.*
box, *palco.*
overture, *sinfonia.*
curtain, *sipario.*
scenery, *decorazioni.*

splendid, *splendido.*
tenor, *tenore.*
sweet, *dolce.*
melodious, *melodioso.*
duet, *duetto.*
to have success, *incontrare.*
act, *atto.*
ballet, *ballo.*
to fail, *far fiasco.*
to drop, *calarsi.*
to be over, *esser finito.*

TRANSLATION EXERCISE.

[Arriving at an Hotel.]

1. Cabman, drive me to the best hotel. 2. This is the best hotel, sir. 3. Tell the host — I want two

[that]

---

[a] 1, p. 245. [b] 7, p. 247. [c] Obs. 11, p. 216.

good rooms. 4. Yes, sir; here is the host. 5. Have
you a comfortable bed-room and a sitting-room? 6.
Yes, sir. 7. How much do you charge (by) the
week? 8. Ten crowns. 9. Very well; I will breakfast at ten o'clock, and dine at the table d' hôte.
10. How long will you stay here, sir? 11. I shall
stay about a month. Show me to my rooms. 12. These
  circa
are your rooms, sir. 13. Have you a sofa to put in my
          da
sitting-room? 14. No; but I can give you an arm-chair.
15. Let me also have a writing-table. 16. A gentleman
has come to inquire after you, sir. 17. Show him in.
18. Oh! how do you do, Mr. D.? 19. Very well, thank
you: I have come to take you to the theatre. 20. To
what theatre shall we go? 21. Where you like.
22. Let us go to the opera. 23. What opera do they
play this evening? 24. The new opera, "L'Africaine."
25. They say it is a good opera. 26. Let us take
tickets for the pit. 27. We will go into my box.
28. What a number of people! How do you like this
   Quanta gente!
theatre? 29. I like it very much: I like it more than
any I have seen. 30. What a good orchestra! This
overture is very beautiful. 31. The curtain is rising.
32. The scenery is very splendid. 33. Who is the
tenor? 34. It is Signor A.; have you ever heard him? !
35. I have not yet heard him. 36. He sings very well.
37. Who is the prima donna? 38. It is Signora B.;
you will hear what (a) beautiful voice (she has).
39. What (a) sweet and melodious voice the soprano
has! 40. Now she will sing a duet with the prima
donna. 41. This duet is very beautiful. 42. I never

heard such a beautiful voice. 43. She is the best Italian
soprano. 44. The first act is over. 45. It is very warm
here; let us go out for a few minutes. 46. We shall
come back again before the second act; before the ballet.
47. This opera has great success. 48. The ballet has
failed. 49. The curtain is dropping. 50. The opera is
over; let us go. 51. To-morrow evening I am invited
to a ball at Mrs. C.'s. 52. I am invited there also.
53. Good-bye, then, till to-morrow evening. 54.
Till we see each other again.

[To see each other again]
A

QUESTIONS.

Dove vuole che il vetturino la conduca? 1.—A che
ora farà colazione domani?—Vorrebbe qualche cos' altro nella sua stanza da ricevere? 15.—In che parte del
teatro andò suo fratello? 27.—Le piacque la sinfonia del
Guglielmo Tell quando l' udì la prima volta?—Aveva
la prima donna bella voce?—A che ora si alzò ed a che
ora si calò il sipario? 31.—Come le piacquero le decorazioni? 32.—Ha fatto fiasco il tenore? 48.—Al bene
di quali classi di popolo mira la monarchia cristiana?

CHAPTER XII.

INTERJECTIONS.

INTERJECTIONS are classified according to their meaning,
as follows:—

Of Grief and Surprise:

oh! \
ahi! } oh!

aimè or ahime! } alas!
oimè or ohime!

ah! oh!

lasso! \
lasso me! } alas!
ahi lasso!

povero me! poor me!
misero me! wretched me!

Of Joy:

ah ah! ha ha! *oh!* oh!
bene! well! *O che allegrezza!* oh what
buono! good! joy!

Of Desire and Beseeching:

deh! ah!
pure! yet! *di grazia!* { pray! I beseech
oh se! oh if! you!
mercè! mercy! if you please.
non più! enough! *per carità!* for charity's
sake!

Of Anger, Aversion, and Indignation:

doh! oh! *puh!* pooh!
oh! oh! *via!* away!
eh! eh! *oibo!* fye!
deh! pshaw!

Of Approbation:

sì! yes! *buono!* good!
così! } *bravo!* bravo!
già! } yes certainly. *viva!* }
bene! ebbene! well! *evviva!* } well done!

Of Admiration:

o! oh! oh! *capperi!* } aye! hey day!
come! why! *cappita!* }
bello! fine! *poffare!* } marry!

Of Encouragement:

sù! } *animo!* } courage!
orsù! } come! *coraggio!* } cheer up!
via! } *fate cuore!* }

Of Warning:

guai a voi! woe to you! *piano!* } slowly.
badate! } take care! *adagio!* }
state all' erta! } mind! *fermati olà!* } hold!
state fresco! you are in *ferma! ferma!* } hold!
a fine predicament. *dalli! dalli!* }

Of Calling :

oh! oh !	*ehi!* } oh hey !
chi è di là? who is there ?	*ola!* } ho there !

Of Silencing :

zi! hist !	*silenzio!* silence !
zitto! hush !	*tacete!* peace then !
cheto! be still !	*basta!* enough !

Of Cheering :

Viva l' Italia! Long live Italy !	*evviva il Re!* hurrah for the King !

OBS.—The same interjection may express different affections. The event which it precedes determines its signification.

> Ex. :   Oh *qual soave incanto nelle virtù si chiude!*
> Ah! what sweet enchantment there is in virtue!
> Oh *quanto male sta il cuor dell' empio!*
> Ah! how wretched is the heart of the wicked!

CHAPTER XIII.

EXPLETIVES, ELLIPSIS, COLLOCATION OF WORDS.

The different *expletives* have been already mentioned. See Obs. 1 and Note *b*, p. 188; Note *c*, p. 230; and Obs. 4, p. 231.

Italian admits also of many *ellipses*. Of these, the most remarkable are : —

1. The omission of the personal pronoun in the nominative ; as,

Sono felice di vedervi, I am happy to see you.

2. The suppression of the present participle of the auxiliary verb in sentences which relate the occurrence of events following in immediate succession ; as,

Vedutala l' amò, having seen her, he loved her.

3. The omission of the relative pronoun *che* or *il quale*, and the auxiliaries *essere* and *avere* when used in the indicative mood, the past participle agreeing with the subject; as,

> *Non so le cose* dette *o* fatte; i. e., *le cose* che son state *dette o fatte;* I do not know the things *which have been* said or done.

4. The omission of *che* before the verb of a dependent sentence, after *temere*, to fear, *dubitare*, to doubt, *sperare*, to hope, and *volere*, to wish (see Note *b*, p. 34); as,

> *Spero non sia vero*, I hope it is not true.

See also Obs. 1 to Class IV., p. 238, and Obs., p. 245.

But what renders the Italian language most difficult to foreigners is the great freedom used, especially by the poets, in the *collocation of words*. There are no unvarying rules for the order of words in a sentence; but by observation of good authors, and accurate analysis of sentences, the student will soon master the difficulties of Italian construction.

Read the following passage by MONTI :—

Ottimo divisamento degli antichi saggi fu quello di consecrare con monumenti di pubblica e religiosa riconoscenza la memoria di tutti coloro che furono di un' arte, comunque giovevole, ritrovatori, o che, mediante lo scoprimento di alcun segreto della natura, la ragione umana aiutarono, e somma gloria a se stessi e alla patria partorirono ; reputando essi quegli uomini sapientissimi, niuno potersi rendere della patria più benemerito che colui, il quale di utili ritrovati la vantaggiasse, e splendor le crescesse fra le nazioni. Perciò niun pittore in Atene ebbe iscrizioni più onorevoli d' Apollodoro, solo perchè trovò egli l' arte di comporre i colori e cavarne le ombre; e fecero di un zoppo e povero fabbro nulla meno che un Dio, perchè primo foggiò il ferro in servigio dell' uomo; e concessero divini onori a Trittolemo, artefice dell' aratro ; e infinite ammirabili cose favoleggiarono di Mercurio, inventore della grammatica e della musica, e di Prometeo, scopritore del fuoco, e di Atlante, primo contemplatore del cielo.

CHAPTER XIV.

MAXIMS AND FIGURES OF SPEECH.

Andare a monte un affare,
To go to a mountain a business.

To be broken off (of an engagement).

Andare col calzare di piombo,
To go with a leaden boot.

To be cautious.

Andare a fronte scoperta,
To go with one's brow uncovered.

To have nothing to be ashamed of.

Andar colla testa nel sacco,
To go with the head in the bag.

To rush into anything blindly.

Non aver da far cantare un cieco.
Not to possess enough to make a blind man sing.

Not to have enough to buy salt for one's porridge.

Aver grilli in capo,
To have grasshoppers in the head.

To be whimsical.

Aver il cuore in bocca,
To have the heart in the mouth.

To be sincere.

Avere gusto (or caro),
To have taste (*or* dear).

To be glad.

Avere voglia,
To have will.

To desire, long.

Avere fumo,
To have smoke.

To be proud.

Aver la testa altrove,
To have the head somewhere else.

To think of other things.

Aver la testa dura,
To have a hard head.

To be thick-headed.

Non aver sale in zucca,
To have no salt in the head.

To be weak-minded.

Battersi la guancia,
To smite one's own cheek.

To repent.

Cascare il cacio sui maccheroni,
To have cheese falling on the maccaroni.

To be unexpectedly fortunate.

Cercare il pelo nell' uovo,
To seek for hair on an egg.

To be very particular in everything.

Ci va la vita,
It concerns life.

Life is at stake.

Comprarsi brighe a denari contanti,
To buy troubles with cash.

To make one's own troubles.

Dar la voce ad uno,
To give the voice to one.

To call anyone aloud.

Dare il capo d'anno,
To give the head of the year.

To wish a happy new year.

Darsi della scure sul piede,
To cut one's own foot with the axe.

To bite one's own nose off.

Essere l' occhio dritto di uno,
To be the right eye of anyone.

To be the favourite of anyone.

Essere di buona (or *larga*) *bocca,*
To be of a good (*or* large) mouth.

To have a good appetite.

Essere benveduto,
To be well seen.

To have a good reputation.

Essere malveduto,
To be badly seen.

To be of ill repute.

Essere in grado di,
To be in condition of.

To be able to.

Essere a buon porto,
To be at a good harbour.

To be nearly out of trouble.

Essere a cavallo,
To be on horseback.

To be out of danger.

Non vi è caso,
There is no chance.

It is impossible.

Non esser pane pei denti di qualcuno,
Not to be bread for one's teeth.

To be out of one's reach.

Essere una cosa da dozzina,
To be a thing by the dozen.

To be something very common.

Farla pagare con usura,
To exact payment with usury.

To make one pay dearly for an injury.

Far tanto di cuore,
To make so big a heart.

To rejoice greatly.

Fare la gatta morta,
To play the dead cat.

To pretend to be quiet.

Fare il dottore,
To play the doctor.

To lay down the law in company.

Farsi caso (or specie),
To make to oneself a case.

To be astonished.

Farsi cuore (or animo),
To make to one's self heart (or mind).

To take courage.

Fare una cosa a pennello,
To do a thing with a brush.

To do a thing perfectly.

Fare uno sproposito,
To make a blunder.

To do something rash.

Guardare colla coda dell' occhio,
To look with the tail of the eye.

To cast sheep's eyes.

Inarcare le ciglia,
To arch the eyebrows.

To be dumbfoundered.

Lasciar la lingua a casa,
To leave the tongue at home.

To remain silent.

Lavorare sott' acqua (or sotto mare),
To work under water.

To work underhand.

Mettersi nei panni di uno,
To put oneself in anyone's clothes.

To put oneself in another's place.

Mettersi la mano al cuore,
To place one's hand on one's heart.

To consult one's conscience

Misurar tutto collo stesso braccio,
To measure everything with the same arm.

Not to allow any distinction.

Non vedo l' ora di partire,
I do not see the hour of leaving.

I long to leave.

Pagare di cattiva moneta,
To pay in bad money.

To be ungrateful.

Parlar sotto voce,
To speak under voice.

To whisper.

Pensare alla pelle,
To think to the skin.

To have regard to one's life.

Perder d' occhio qualcuno,
To lose some one from the eye.

To lose sight of one.

Perder la bussola,
To lose the (mariner's) compass.

To be at a loss.

Piantare alcuno,
To plant anyone.

To leave anyone suddenly.

Portare acqua al mare,
To bring water to the sea.

To carry coals to Newcastle.

Promettere mari e monti,
To promise seas and mountains.

To be prodigal of promises.

Salvare la capra e i cavoli,
To save both the goat and the cabbage.

To have one's cake and eat it too.

Sapere di latino.
To know of Latin.

To be a Latin scholar.

Son tanto occupato, che non so da che parte voltarmi,
I am so busy, I do not know which way to turn.

I have so many things to do, that I do not know how to commence.

Stare colle mani in mano,
To stand with the hands in hand.

To stand idle.

Stare alla larga,
To stand at a great distance.

To keep aloof.

Studiare il passo,
To study the pace.

To quicken one's pace.

Tenere a bada alcuno,
To keep any one at bay.

To keep in uncertainty.
To delay giving an answer.

Tenere uno sulla corda,
To keep one on the rope.

To keep anyone in a state of suspense.

Tenere uno in croce,
To keep one on the cross.

To torture one with anxiety.

Tirare per le lunghe,
To draw by long ways.

To delay anything, to make slow work of anything.

Toccare una cosa con mano,
To touch a thing with one's own hand.

To see a thing with one's own eyes.

Toccar sempre lo stesso tasto,
To play always the same note.

To harp on the same string.

Un luogo fuor di mano,
A place out of hand.

A remote place.

Voltare le spalle,
To turn the shoulders.

To withdraw, to retreat.

Il fine corona l' opera,
The end crowns the work.

All's well that ends well.

1st *F VERBS IN ERE* (short) *which have two forms*
ther the Perfect or Past Participle, or ⚫ *both; one form*
AN*g irregular and the other generally regular.* (p. 104.)

ive.	*Perfect.*	*Past Participle.*
e	concessi *or* concedei	concesso *or* conceduto
re	connessi *or* connettei	connesso *or* connettuto
p	difesi *or* difendei	difeso *or* difenduto
	fessi *or* fendei	fesso *or* fenduto
figcre	fissi *or* fisi	fisso, fitto, *or* fiso
	fusi *or* fondei	fuso *or* fonduto
re	nascosi	nascoso *or* nascosto
	persi *or* perdei	perso *or* perduto
	piovve *or* piovè	piovuto
	presi *or* prendei	preso
	rasi *or* radei	raso
	redensi *or* redimei	redento
	resi *or* rendei	reso *or* renduto
	rilussi *or* rilucei	*No Past Participle.*
	{ risolsi, risolvei, *or* } { risolvetti }	risolto *or* risoluto
	scersi *or* scernei	scerso *or* scernuto
	vissi	vissuto *or* vivuto

3rd Conjugation.

E.—*Pres. Ind.* apparisco *or* appaio, apparisci, appa-
or appare, appariamo ᵃ, ᶜ, ⁽, ʰ, ⁾. *Perf.* apparii *or* ap-
or apparsi. *Past Part.* apparito *or* apparso.

—*Perf.* aprii *or* apersi. *Past Part.* aperto.

—*Pres. Ind.* cucio, cuci, cuce, cuciamo.

IRE *and* SOVVERTIRE.—*Perf.* conversi *and* sovversi.
FA*Part.* converso *and* sovverso.

Pres. Ind. dico*, dici, dice, diciamo. *Imperf.* diceva.
dissi. *Past Part.* detto. *See Note e, p.* 32.

—*Pres. Ind.* empio *or* empisco, empi *or* empisci,
o *or* empisce, empiamo.

E *and* DIGERIRE.—*Past Part.* esaurito *or* esausto,
ito *or* digesto.

E.—*Perf.* instrussi *or* instruii. *Past Part.* instrutto
struito.

—*Pres. Ind.* muoio *or* muoro, muori, muore, muoi-
or moriamo.

E *or* OFFRIRE.—*Perf.* offerii *or* offrii *or* offersi. *Past*
offerto.

—*Pres. Ind.* salgo *or* salisco, sali *or* salisci, sale *or*
e, saliamo *or* sagliamo. *Perf.* salii *or* salsi.

.—*Pres. Ind.* seguo *or* sieguo, segui *or* siegui, segue
gue, seguiamo.

IRE.—*Past Part.* seppellito *or* sepolto.

—*Pres. Ind.* odo, odi, ode, udiamo.

—*Pres. Ind.* esco, esci, esce, usciamo.

ST*is conjugated like* tenere.

ALPHABETICAL LIST OF IRREGULAR VERBS.

N.B.—The verbs in parentheses are the models of conjugation.

FIRST CONJUGATION.

VERBS OF THE SECOND CONJUGATION IN *ERE* (*long.*)

VERBS OF THE SECOND CONJUGATION IN *ERE* (*short*).

N.B.—In this List are comprised also the verbs in *ere* short which differ from *credere* in the formation of the Perfect and Past Participle.

	Page		Page
Accendere, to light, I.	98	*Apporre*, to put to (*porre*),	
Accingersi, to prepare one-		(Obs.)	92
self, II.	98	*Ardere*, to burn, I.	98
Accogliere or *accorre*, to make		*Arrendersi*, to give oneself up,	
welcome (*cogliere*), (Obs.)	90	I.	98
Accorgersi, to perceive, II.	98	*Arridere*, to smile, I.	98
Accorrere, to run to (*correre*), I.	98	*Ascendere*, to ascend, I.	98
Acorescere, to increase (*cre-*		*Ascondere*, to hide, (Obs. 5)	104
scere), VII.	98	*Ascrivere*, to ascribe, III.	99
Addurre (or *adducere*), to bring.	87	*Aspergere*, to besprinkle, II.⁴	98
Affigere, to fix, (Obs. 3)	104	*Assistere*, to assist, VII.⁸	99
Affligere, to afflict, II.	98	*Assolvere*, to absolve, (Obs. 8).	104
Aggiungere, to add, II.	98	*Assorbere*, to absorb, VII.	99
Alludere, to allude, I.	98	*Assumere*, to undertake, V.	99
Ammettere, to admit (*mettere*),		*Astergere*, to rub clean, II.	98
VI.	98	*Astrarre* or *astraere*, to abstract	
Ancidere, to kill, I.	98	(*trarre*), (Obs.)	95
Annettere, to annex, (Obs. 2).	104	*Astringere*, to constrain, II.	98
Anteporre, to prefer (*porre*)	92	*Attendere*, to attend, I.	98
Appendere, to hang, I.	98	*Attingere*, to draw water, II.	98

VERBS OF THE THIRD CONJUGATION IN *IRE*.

N

DEFECTIVE VERBS.

VOCABULARY.

ABBREVIATIONS.

act. ... active.	imp. ...... impersonal.	p. .... page.
adj. ... adjective.	ind. ...... indefinite.	pl. .... plural.
adv. ... adverb.	m. .... masculine.	pron. ...... pronoun.
conj.... conjunction.	No. ...... number.	sing. ...... singular.
f. ...... feminine.	n. .... noun.	v. .... verb.
	neut. .... neuter.	

I. ENGLISH-ITALIAN.

A.

A, *un, uno, una, un'*. See p. 145.

Abandon (to), *abbandonare*.

Able (to be), *potere*.

About, *circa, all' incirca;* (= concerning), *intorno a*.

Abroad (adj.), *in viaggio*.

Abroad (to be *or* go), *viaggiare*.

Accompany (to), *accompagnare*.

According to, *secondo*.

Account, *informazione;* (= bill), *conto;* (= story), *racconto*.

Accustom oneself to (to), *abituarsi a, avvezzarsi a*.

Accustomed (to be), *esser solito, solere*.

Ache (to), *dolere*. See Note *e*, p. 79.

Acquaint (to), (act.), *far conoscere a,* or *sapere a*.

Acquaintance, *conoscenza*.

Acquainted with (to be), *conoscere, sapere*. See Note *b*, p. 68.

Act, *atto*.

Add, *aggiungere*.

Address, *indirizzo, recapito*.

Admiral, *ammiraglio*.

Adonis, *Adone*.

Adorn (to), *adornare*.

Advice, *avviso, consiglio*.

Afraid (to be), *avere paura, temere*.

After, *dopo;* afterwards, *in appresso, poi;* (= according to), *secondo*.

Afternoon, *dopopranzo*.

Again, *ancora, da capo, di nuovo*.

Ago, *fa*.

Agree (to), *convenire*.

Air, *aria*.

Albert, *Alberto*.

Alfred, *Alfredo*.

All, *tutto, -a;* ind. pron., *tutto* (for things), *tutti* (for persons).

Allowed (to be), *licere*.

Almost, *quasi, pressochè*.

Already, *già*.

Also, *anche*.

Always, *sempre*.

Amount, *montante* (m.).

Amuse (to), *divertire*.

Amusement, *divertimento*.

Ancient, *antico, -a*.

And, *e*. Obs. 1, p. 248.

Animal, *animale* (m.).

Another, *un altro, un' altra.*

Answer (to), *rispondere* (neut.).

Anteroom, *anticamera.*

Any (indef.), *alcuno, qualche, qualunque;* (partitive), *del, dei,* &c.

Any body, any one, *alcuno, -a; qualcuno, -a.*

Any thing, *niente, nulla.*

Apartment, *stanza.*

Appear (to), *parere.*

Appetite, *appetito.*

Apple, *mela.*

Architecture, *architettura.*

Armchair, *poltrona.*

Arrive (to), *arrivare, giungere.*

Art, *arte* (f.).

Article, *articolo.*

As, *come, siccome.* See p. 161.

As far as, *fino a.*

As if, *quasi.*

As much...as, *tanto...quanto.*

As soon as, *tosto che.*

Ascend (to), *salire su.*

Ashamed (to be), *avere vergogna, vergognarsi.*

Ask (to), *chiedere, domandare a;* ask after, *domandare di;* ask for, *domandare* (act.).

Aspect, *aspetto.*

Ass, *asino.*

Assist (to), *aiutare, assistere.*

Astronomer, *astronomo.*

At, *a;* at Paris, *in Parigi;* at what o'clock, *a che ora;* at seven o'clock, *alle sette* (ore) ; at all, *punto.*

At first, *in prima, da prima;* at last, *al fine.*

At least, *almeno.*

At once, *subito.*

At present, *adesso, ora.*

At the, *al,* &c. See p. 8.

Attic, *soffitta.*

Aunt, *zia.*

Autumn, *autunno.*

Awake (to), *svegliare* (act.); to awake one's self, *svegliarsi.*

Axe, *scure* (f.).

B.

Bad, *cattivo, -a;* badly, *male.*

Baker, *fornaio.*

Ballet, *ballo.*

Baptism, *battesimo.*

Bark (to), *abbaiare, latrare.*

Bat (anim.), *pipistrello.*

Be, *essere;* to be afraid, *temere, avere paura.* In idioms, *stare,* &c. See Voc., p. 63 ; to be off, *partire;* to be over, *esser passato, finito.*

Beat (to), *battere.*

Beautiful, *bel,* &c. (see p. 157); *vago;* beautifully, *vagamente, a meraviglia.*

Beauty, *bellezza.*

Because, *perchè.*

Become accustomed (to), *avvezzarsi.*

Bed, *letto.*

Bee, *ape* (f.).

Before (of time), *avanti, prima;* (of place), *davanti, dinanzi.*

Begin (to), *cominciare, mettersi a.*

Behave well (to), *diportarsi bene.*

Behind, *dietro.*

Believe (to), *credere.*

Bellow (to), *muggire.*

Belong, *appartenere.*

Berlin, *Berlino.*

Besides (conj.), *e poi, d' altronde.*

Best, *il migliore, ottimo.*

Better (adj.), *migliore;* (adv.) *meglio;* I am better, *sto meglio.*

Beyond, *al di là, fuori, oltre.*

Bid (to) (=command), *imporre a.*

Bill (=account), *conto, cartello.*

Binding, *legatura.*

Bird, *uccello.*

Black, *nero.*

Blanc (white), *bianco;* Mont Blanc, *Monte Bianco.*

Bleat (to), *belare.*

Blow (to), *soffiare, spirare.*

Boast (to), *vantarsi.*

Boat, *battello.*

Boil (to), *bollire.*

Bone, *osso,* (pl. m.) *ossi,* (pl. f.) *ossa.*

Bonnet, *cappellino.*

Book, *libro.*

Boot, *stivale* (m.).

Born (to be), *nascere.*

Both, *ambo, -e; ambeduo, -e; l'uno e l' altro; tutti e due; entrambi.*

Box, *scatola;* (of a theatre), *palco.*

Boy, *ragazzo.*

Bracelet, *braccialetto.*

Bray (to), *ragliare.*

Bread, *pane* (m.).

Break (to), *rompere.*

Break of day, *spuntar del giorno.*

Breakfast, *colazione;* to breakfast, *far colazione.*

Bride, *sposa.*

Bridegroom, *sposo.*

Bring (to), *portare.*

Brooch, *spillone* (m.).

Brother, *fratello;* brother-in-law, *cognato.*

Build (to), *fabbricare.*

Builder, *muratore, mastro muratore.*

Building, *fabbricato, edifizio.*

Bunch, *grappolo.*

Burn (to), *abbruciare;* to burn down the house, *abbruciare la casa.*

Bury (to), *seppellire.*

Business, *affare* (m.).

But, *ma, però.*

Buy (to), *comprare.*

By (denoting agent, and after passive participle), *da, con;* denoting means, *per;* by sight, *di vista.*

By the bye, *a proposito.*

C.

Cabman, *vetturino.*

Café, *caffè* (m.).

Cake, *focaccia.*

Call (to), *chiamare;* to call on a person, *passare da uno.*

Can (I), *posso.* See p. 65.

Cap (man's), *berretta.*

Capital, *capitale* (f.).

Capitol, *Campidoglio.*

Card (visiting), *biglietto di visita.*

Care (to), *calere.*

Carpet, *tappeto da (pavimento).*

Carriage, *carrozza;* in a carriage, *in carrozza.*

Carry (to), *portare;* to carry back, *riportare.*

Carve (to), *intagliare;* to carve at table, *trinciare.*

Carved, *intagliato.*

Case, *cassa.*

Castle, *castello*

Cat, *gatto.*

Cathedral, *cattedrale* (f.); the cathedral of St. Peter's at Rome, *la basilica di San Pietro di Roma;* Milan cathedral, *il duomo di Milano.*

Celebrated, *celebre.*

Central, *centrale.*

Century, *secolo.*

Certainly, *certamente.*

Chain, *catena.*

Chaplain, *cappellano.*

Charge (to), *fare pagare a.*

Charge, *consegna;* to deliver into the charge of, *dare in consegna a.*

Charles, *Carlo, Carlino* (dim.).

Cheap, *a buon mercato.*

Cheerfulness, *ilarità.*

Chest, *petto.*

Chiefly, *principalmente.*

Child, *fanciullo, figlio, bambino.*

Chirp (to), *garrire.*

Christmas, *Natale* (m.).

Church, *chiesa.*

Citizen, *cittadino.*

City, *città.*

Clean, *pulito.*

Clear, *chiaro.*

Clever, *bravo.*

Climate, *clima* (m.).

Cloth, *panno.*

Clothes, *vestiti* (pl.); linen clothes, *pannilini;* bed clothes, *coltre* (f. sing.).

Cluck (to), *chioociare.*

Coach, *vettura* ; mail-coach, *posta, diligenza.*

Coat, *vestito.*

Cock, *gallo.*

Coffee, *caffè* (m.); coffee-house, (*bottega di*) *caffè.*

Cold (to be), *aver freddo* ; to be cold weather, *far freddo* ; to have a cold, *avere un' in-freddatura.*

Cold (adj.), *freddo, -a* ; a cold, *un' infreddatura* (n.).

Come (to), *venire* ; to come again, *rivenire* ; to come near, *avvicinarsi di* ; to come to, *ammontare* ; come in, *avanti.*

Comfit, *confetto.*

Comfort, *comodo.*

Comfortable, *comodo, -a.*

Commence (to), *cominciare, prin-cipiare.*

Commerce, *commercio.*

Company, *compagnia.*

Complain (to), *lagnarsi.*

Compliment, *complimento.*

Comply with anyone's request (to), *contentare uno.*

Compose (to), *comporre.*

Concert, *concerto.*

Confuse (to), *confondere.*

Connoisseur, *conoscitore.*

Consist (to), *consistere.*

Consul, *console.*

Contain (to), *contenere.*

Contented (to be), *contentarsi.*

Continent, *continente* (m.).

Continual, *continuo.*

Contrary (on the), *anzi.*

Convenient, *conveniente.*

Convince (to), *convincere, per-suadere.*

Coo (to), *tubare.*

Cool, *fresco, -a.*

Coral, *corallo.*

Cord, *spago.*

Corn, *grano.*

Cost (to), *valere.*

Could. See *potere*, p. 65.

Count, *conte* ; countess, *con-tessa.*

Country, *paese, campagna, pa-tria* ; countryman, *contadino* ; country seat, *villeggiatura.*

Courier, *corriere.*

Cover (to), *coprire.*

Cow-keeper, *vaccaro.*

Cross (to), *varcare, attraversare.*

Crow (to), *cantare.*

Crowd, *folla.*

Crown, *corona* ; (money), *scudo.*

Crystal, *cristallo.*

Cup, *tazza, chicchera.*

Curious, *curioso, -a.*

Curtain, *tenda* ; (of a theatre), *sipario.*

Custom, *costume* (m.); *uso.*

Customer, *avventore.*

Cut (to), *tagliare* ; cut off (in surgery), *amputare.*

D.

Daisy, *margheritina.*

Dark, *buio, oscuro* ; to get dark, *farsi buio.*

Daughter, *figlia, figliuola.*

Day, *giorno.*

Dear, *caro, -a.*

Deaf, *sordo, -a*

Death, *morte* (f.).

Deceive (to), *ingannare.*

Decisive, *assoluto, -a.*

Decorate (to), *decorare.*

Decorated, *adorno, -a.*

Delay, *indugio.*

Depart (to), *partire.*

Deposit (to), *depositare.*

Deprive (to), *privare.*

Derive (to), *ricavare.*

Describe (to), *descrivere.*

Description, *descrizione.*

Deserve (to), *meritare.*

Diamond, *diamante* (m.).

Die (to), *morire.*

Different, *diverso, -a.*

Difficult, *difficile.*

Diligent, *diligente.*

Dine (to), *desinare, pranzare.*

Dining-room, *stanza da man-giare.*

Dinner, *pranso.*

Directly, *subito.*

Dish, *piatto ;* earthen pie-dish, *tegghia.*

Dislocate (to), *dislogare.*

Disobey (to), *disubbidire.*

Distress, *miseria.*

.Do (to), *fare ;* (of health), *stare ;* as auxiliary, not translated.

Doctor, *medico.*

Dog, *cane* (m.).

Door, *porta, uscio.*

Doubt, *dubbio.*

.Dove, *colomba.*

Down, *giù, da basso.*

Drachm, *dramma.*

Draw (to), *disegnare ;* to draw out, *tirare, estrarre.*

Drawer, *tiratoio.*

Drawing, *disegno.*

Drawing-room, *salotto.*

Dress, *abito, vestito.*

Dress oneself (to), *vestirsi.*

Drink (to), *bevere, bere.*

.Drive (to), *condurre, guidare, andare in carrozza.*

Drop. (fo), *calarsi, cadere.* See No. 16, p. 54.

Drum, *tamburo.*

Duet, *duetto.*

During, *durante.*

E.

Each, *ogni, ciascuno, -a.*

Early, *per tempo, di buon mattino.*

Ear-ring, *orecchino.*

Earth, *terra.*

Easy, *facile.*

Eat (to), *mangiare.*

Eclipse, *ecclissi.*

Edinburgh, *Edimburgo.*

Edition, *edizione* (f.).

Egg, *uovo.* (m.); pl. *uova* (f.).

Eight, *otto.*

Eighteenth, *decimo ottavo.*

Either, *o l' uno o l' altro.*

.Eldest (of brothers or sisters), *maggiore.*

Eleven, *undici.*

Else, *altro ;* elsewhere, *altrove.*

Embroidered, *ricamato, -a.*

Enduring, *perenne.*

Enemy, *nemico.*

England, *Inghilterra.*

English, *inglese ;* an Englishman, (un) *Inglese ;* an Englishwoman, (una) *Inglese.*

Enjoy (to), *godere di ;* to enjoy oneself, *divertirsi.*

Enough (to be), *bastare ;* enough! *basta ! abbastanza !*

Enquire after (to), *domandare di.*

Entertainment, *trattamento.*

Entirely, *interamente.*

Environs, *contorni, dintorni.*

Eternal, *eterno, -a.*

Europe, *Europa.*

Even (conj.), *anche.*

Evening, *sera ;* this evening, *stassera.*

Ever, *mai.*

Every, *ogni ;* everybody, *ognuno, tutti ;* everything, *tutto ;* everywhere, *da per tutto.*

Exactly, *a pennello, precisamente ;* exactly so, *per l' appunto ;* it is exactly three o'clock, *sono le tre precise.*

Excepting (adv.), *salvo, tranne.*

Excuse (to), *scusare ;* to be excused a thing, *esser dispensato di una cosa.*

Exercise, *tema* (m.); *esercizio.*

Expect (to), *aspettarsi.*

Express (to), *esprimere.*

Exterior, *esterno.*

Eye, *occhio.*

F.

Face, *volto.*

Fail (to), *mancare ;* (of an undertaking), *far fiasco.*

Fall (to), *cadere ;* to fall asleep, *addormentarsi.*

Family, *famiglia.*

Famous, *famoso, -a ; rinomato, -a.*

Far, *lontano, distante, lungi.*

Farm, *podere* (m.).

Fashion, *moda.*

Fast, *presto.*

Father, *padre ;* father-in-law, *suocero ;* fatherly, *paterno.*

Favour, *favore* (m.).

Fear, *paura ;* to fear, *temere.*

Feed (to), *pascolare* (neut.); *pascere* (act.).

Feel (to), *sentire ;* well or unwell, *sentirsi bene o male.*

Fetch (to), *andare a prendere,* or *prendere ;* to come to fetch, *venire a prendere.*

Fever, *febbre* (f.).

Few (a), *pochi, -e ; alcuni, -e, dei, delle.*

Field, *campo.*

Fifty, *cinquanta.*

Fig, *fico ;* (tree), *ficaia.*

Find (to), *trovare.*

Fine, *bello, -a ;* the fine arts, *le belle arti.*

Finish (to), *finire.*

Finger, *dito* (m.); pl. *dita* (f.).

Fire, *fuoco, incendio.*

First, *primo, -a.*

Five, *cinque.*

Flee (to), *fuggire.*

Flock, *gregge* (m. & f.).

Floor (in elevation), *piano ;* (as a surface), *pavimento, spazzo.*

Florence, *Firenze.*

Flow (to), *scorrere.*

Flower, *fiore* (m.).

Fluently, *correntemente.*

Fond of (to be). See *piacere,* Note *a,* p. 72.

Foot, *piede* (m.); on foot, *a piedi ;* footstep, *calpestío ;* foot soldier, *fante.*

For, *per, perchè, siccome.*

Forenoon, *antimeridiane.*

Forget (to), *dimenticare.*

Forecourt, *cortile* (m.).

Foreigner, *forestiero.*

Former (the), *quello, -a.* See pp. 210 and 211.

Formerly, *altre volte, già.*

Fortnight, *quindici giorni.*

Forty, *quaranta.*

Forward (to), *inviare, mandare.*

Found (to), *fondare.*

Four, *quattro.*

Franc, *franco, lira ;* twenty-franc piece, *napoleone d' oro.*

France, *Francia.*

Freeze (to), *gelare.*

Fresh, *fresco, -a.*

French, *francese ;* a Frenchman, (un) *Francese ;* a Frenchwoman, (una) *Francese.*

Friday, *venerdì.*

Friend, *amico.*

From, *da, di.*

Fruit, *frutta.*

Full, *pieno, -a.*

G.

Gain (to), *guadagnare.*

Garden, *giardino.*

Gardener, *giardiniere.*

Gather (to), *cogliere.*

General, *generale.*

Generally, *per solito.*

Generous, *generoso.*

Genius, *genio.*

Genoa, *Genova.*

Gentleman, *signore.*

German, *tedesco, -a ;* pl. *-chi, -che.*

Germany, *Germania.*

Get ready (to), *allestirsi ;* — angry, *adirarsi ;* — tired, *stancarsi ;* — ill, *ammalarsi.*

Get up (to), *alzarsi, levarsi.*

Girl, *ragazza.*

Give (to), *dare ;* to give back, *rendere.*

Glad (to be), *rallegrarsi di ;* glad, *contento, -a.*

Glass, *vetro ;* a glass of water, *un bicchier d' acqua ;* wine-glass, *bicchierino.*

Glitter (to), *lucere.*

Glove, *guanto.*

Go (to), *andare ;* go abroad, *andare all' estero, viaggiare ;* go down (a street), *scendere per ;* go in, *entrare ;* go out, *andar fuori, uscire ;* go up, *salire su, ascendere ;* go, *venire* (see Note *c,* p. 121) ; go for a ride, *an-*

dare a cavallo ; to go to rest, *coricarsi.*
Goat, *capra.*
Gold, *oro.*
Good, *buono, -a ;* good morning, *buon giorno ;* good-bye, *addio.*
Gradually, *a poco a poco.*
Grandfather, *nonno, avo, avolo.*
Grandmother, *nonna, ava, avola.*
Grammar, *grammatica.*
Grant (to), *accordare, concedere.*
Grapes, *uva* (f. sing.)
Grass, *erba.*
Great deal, *molto.*
Greek, *greco, -a.*
Greenhouse, *serra.*
Grief, *dolore* (m.).
Grieve (to), *dispiacere.*
Ground, *terreno.*
Grunt (to), *grugnire.*
Guide, guide-book, *guida.*

H.

Hail (to), *grandinare* (of weather).
Half, *mezzo.* See Note *e,* p. 175.
Hall, *vestibolo.*
Hand, *mano* (f.) ; on the other hand, *invece.*
Handsome, *bello, -a.*
Hang (to), *appendere* (act.) ; to have hung, *fare appendere.*
Happen, *avvenire, accadere, succedere, nascere.*
Happy, *felice, contento, -a.*
Harp, *arpa.*
Haste, *fretta ;* make haste ! *fate presto !*
Hat, *cappello.*
Have (to), *avere ;* to have at heart, *premere di ;* see Note *d,* p. 86 ; to have success, *incontrare.*
He, *egli, ei, esso.*
Head, *testa, capo ;* headache, *mal di capo.*
Health, *salute* (f.).
Hear (to), *sentire, udire ;* hear from, *ricevere nuove di* or *da ;* hear of *sentire parlare.*

Help (to), *aiutare, assistere.*
Hen, *gallina.*
Here, *qui, quà, ci, vi ;* here is..., *ecco...* Obs. 4, p. 188.
Hide (to), *nascondere.*
High, *alto, -a ;* highly (to mark absolute superlative), *moltissimo, sommo.*
Hill, *colle* (m.).
Him, *lo,* &c. See p. 183.
His, *suo,* &c. See p. 198.
Home (at), *a casa ;* to go home, *andar a casa.*
Honey, *miele* (m.).
Hope (to), *sperare.*
Horse, *cavallo.*
Host, *albergatore.*
Hot, *caldo, -a.*
Hotel, *albergo.*
Hothouse, *serra.*
Hour, *ora.*
House, *casa.*
How, *come ;* how much, *quanto, -a ;* how many, *quanti, -e ;* how far is it ? *quanto è distante ?* how do you do ? *come state ?*
However, *per altro, tuttavia.*
Howl (to), *urlare.*
Hundred, *cento.*
Hunger, *fame* (f.).
Hungry (to be), *aver fame.*
Hurry, *fretta ;* to hurry a person, *far fretta a uno.*
Hurt (to), *far male a.*
Husbandman, *agricoltore.*
Hush ! *zitto !*

I.

Ice (to eat), *sorbetto.*
If, *se.*
Ill, *ammalato, -a ; malato, -a.*
Immediately, *subito.*
Impose (to), *imporre a.*
In, *in ;* in the, *nel,* &c. (see p. 8) ; after superlatives, *di ;* in addition to, *oltre a ;* in short, *insomma ;* in the meantime, *intanto, frattanto.*
Indeed ! *davvero !*

India, *India.*
Inform (to), *informare.*
Information, *informazione.*
Inhabitant, *abitante.*
Ink, *inchiostro.*
Inkstand, *calamaio.*
Inquire after (to), *domandare di ;*
to inquire for, *cercare.*
Instead, *invece.*
Institute (to), *istituire.*
Intend (to), *far conto di.*
Interest (to), *interessare.*
Interesting, *interessante.*
Interpreter, *interprete.*
Intimate, *intimo, -a.*
Into, *in.*
Introduce (to), *introdurre.*
Invite (to), *invitare.*
It. See p. 182.
Its. See p. 198.
Italian, *italiano, -a.*
Italy, *Italia.*

J.

Jewel, *gioiello.*
Jeweller, *gioielliere.*
John, *Giovanni.*
Joseph, *Giuseppe.*
Journey, *viaggio.*
Just, *appunto.*

K.

Keep (to), *tenere ;* (preserve,
nourish), *mantenere.*
Key, *chiave* (f.).
Kind, *genere* (m.).
Kind (adj.), *cortese, gentile.*
Kindness, *bontà.*
Kindly, *cortesemente.*
Knock (to), *battere.*
Know (to), *sapere, conoscere.*
See Note *b,* p. 68.

L.

Lady, *signora.*
Lamb, *agnello.*
Language, *lingua.*
Large, *grande.* See p. 158.

Last, *fine* (m. and f.).
Last (adj.), *passato, -a ; scorso,*
-a ; last night, *ieri sera ;*
(=latest), *ultimo.*
Lately, *finalmente.*
Late, *tardi ;* to be late, *esser in*
ritardo.
Lately, *ultimamente.*
Latest, *ultimo.*
Latin, *latino.*
Latter, *questo, -a.*
Laugh (to), *ridere.*
Laundress, *lavandaia.*
Laura, *Laura.*
Lay (to), *porre ;* to lay the
cloth, *apparrechiare la tavola.*
Lead (to), *condurre.*
Learn (to), *imparare.*
Least (at), *almeno.*
Leave (to), *lasciare* (act.); to
leave in charge of, *lasciare in*
consegna a ; to leave (neut.),
partire ; leave off, *tralasciare.*
Left, *sinistro, -a.*
Lemon, *limone* (m.).
Lend (to), *prestare.*
Less, *meno.*
Lesson, *lezione* (f.).
Let (to) people know, *far sapere*
a uno.
Letter, *lettera ;* a man of letters,
un dotto.
Lewis, *Luigi.*
Library, *biblioteca, libreria.*
Lie down (to), *giacere.*
Light (to), *accendere.*
Like (to), *piacere.* See Note *a,*
p. 72.
Likely, *probabile.*
Lion, *leone.*
Listen (to), *ascoltare.*
Little, *poco, -a ;* (=size), *pic-*
colo, -a ; a little, *un poco.*
Live (to), *vivere ;* (= reside),
abitare, dimorare, stare di
casa.
Lofty, *alto, -a.*
London, *Londra.*
Long, *lungo, -a ;* a long time,
un pezzo, molto tempo, molto.
Longer, *più.*
Look (to), *guardare, mirare ;*

the window looks on the gar-
den, *la finestra dà sul giar-
dino.*
Looks, *cera* (sing.).
Lose (to), *perdere.*
Luggage, *bagaglio.*
Lupercal, *Lupercale.*

M.

Madam, *signora.*
Mæcenas, *Mecenate.*
Magnificence, *magnificenza.*
Magnificent, *magnifico, -a;* pl.,
ci, ce.
Maid-servant, *serva.*
Maintain (to), *preservare.*
Mail, *corriere;* mail-coach, *posta,*
diligenza.
Make (to), *fare.*
Mamma, *mamma.*
Man, *uomo;* a man of letters,
un dotto; man-servant, *servo.*
Manner, *modo.*
Manuscript, *manoscritto.*
Many, *molti, -e.* See 'much.'
Marble, *marmo.*
Marquis, *marchese.*
Marry (to), *sposare;* marry
with, *sposarsi con.*
Mason, *muratore.*
Master, *maestro, padrone.*
Match, *zolfanello, fiammifero.*
Matter (to), *importare;* it does
not matter, *non importa, non
fa niente.*
May. See *potere,* p. 65.
May, *maggio.*
Me. See p. 182.
Mean (to), *voler dire.*
Means (the), *i mezzi.*
Measure, *misura;* to take the
measure for, *prendere la mi-
sura di.*
Mediterranean, *Mediterraneo.*
Meet (to), *incontrare.*
Melodious, *melodioso, -a.*
Message (to leave a), *fare
un' ambasciata.*
Messiah, *Messia.*
Mew (to), *miagolare.*

Michael Angelo, *Michelangelo.*
Midst, *mezzo.*
Mile, *miglio* (m.); pl. *miglia* (f.).
Milk, *latte* (m.).
Mind (to) (=beware), *badare.*
Mine. See p. 198.
Milan, *Milano.*
Million, *milione.*
Minute, *minuto.*
Mischief, *male* (m.); to do mis-
chief, *far del male.*
Misfortune, *disgrazia.*
Mistake, *sbaglio;* to mistake,
sbagliare.
Moderate, (of climate), *tempe-
rato, -a.*
Modern, *moderno, -a.*
Monday, *lunedì* (m.).
Money, *danaro.*
Monkey, *scimia.*
Month, *mese* (m.).
Monument, *monumento.*
Moon, *luna.*
More, *più;* (=further), *di più.*
Morning, *mattina, mattino;* this
morning, *stamane;* good
morning, *buon giorno.*
Mosaic, *mosaico.*
Most (the), *il più.*
Mother, *madre.*
Mount, mountain, *monte* (m.).
Mouse, *topo, sorcio.*
Mr., *Signor;* Mrs., *Signora.*
Much, *molto, -a; assai.* See
'many.'
Music, *musica.*
Must. See *dovere,* p. 67.
My. See p. 198.

N.

Name, *nome* (m.).
Naples, *Napoli.*
Native, *nativo, -a;* a native of
Italy, *Italiano, -a;* — of Eng-
land, *Inglese.*
Near, *vicino, vicino a.*
Nearly, *presso a poco, a un di-
presso, quasi.*
Necessary, *necessario, -a;* to be
necessary, *bisognare.*
Necklace, *collana.*

Need, *bisogno.*
Neigh (to), *nitrire.*
Neighbour, *vicino.*
Neighbourhood, *vicinato.*
Neither...nor, *nè...nè.*
Neither (pron.), *nè l' uno nè l' altro.*
Nephew, *nipote.*
Net, *rete* (f.).
Never, *mai, giammai,* with *non* before verbs.
New, *nuovo, -a.*
News, *nuove* (pl.).
Newspaper, *giornale* (m.).
Next, *prossimo, -a ; venturo, -a ;* the next day, *il giorno dopo.*
Niece, *nipote.*
Night, *notte* (f.); last night, *ieri sera.*
Nine, *nove.*
No, *no ;* I have no books, *non ho libri.*
Nobody, no one, none, *nessuno, niuno, veruno.*
Noise, *romore* (m.).
None. See 'nobody.'
Noon, *mezzodì.*
Nor, *nè ;* nor even, *neppure.*
North wind, *vento di tramontana.*
Not, *non ;* ...or not, *...o no ;* I think not, *credo di no ;* not at all, *punto.*
Note, *annotazione ;* to take notes, *far annotazioni.*
Nothing, *niente, nulla.*
Now, *adesso, ora ;* now and then, *di quando in quando, tratto tratto.*
Nowhere else, *in nessun altro luogo.*
Nursemaid, *bambinaia.*

O.

Object, *cosa, oggetto.*
Obliged (to be), *esser tenuto, obbligato.*
O'clock. See p. 176.
Of, *di ;* of it, *ne ;* of course *certamente.*

Offer (to), *offrire.*
Officer, (strictly), *uffiziale ;* (commonly), *militare.*
Often, *spesso.*
Oh, *oh.*
Old, *vecchio, -a ;* how old is he? *quanti anni ha ?*
On, *su, sopra ;* on account of, *per.*
Once, *una volta ;* (=formerly), *altre volte.*
One, *un, uno, -a.* See p. 145.
Only (adv.), *solamente, soltanto, solo, non...che ;* only just now, *or ora.*
Opera, *opera ;* opera-glass, *occhialetto ;* to play an opera, *dare un' opera.*
Opinion, *opinione* (f.).
Opposite, *dirimpetto a.*
Oppression, *oppressione* (f.).
Or, *o, oppure.*
Orange, *arancia.*
Oratorio, *oratorio.*
Orchestra, *orchestra.*
Order (to), *commandare, ordinare.*
Origin, *origine* (f.), *principio.*
Ornament, *ornamento.*
Other, *altro, -a.*
Ought. See *dovere,* p. 67.
Our. See p. 198.
Out, *fuori, fuora ;* outside, *fuori.*
Overcome (to), *opprimere.*
Overture, *sinfonia.*
Owe (to), *dovere.*
Owner, *proprietario.*
Ox, *bue ;* pl., *buoi.*

P.

Page (of book), *pagina.*
Paint (to), *dipingere.*
Pair, *paio* (m.) ; pl. *paia* (f.).
Palace, *palazzo.*
Patent, *patente* (f.).
Palatine, *Palatino.*
Pantry, *dispensa.*
Papal, *papale.*
Paper, *carta ;* wall-paper, *tappezzeria ;* to paper (walls), *tappezzare di carta ;* a sheet of paper, *foglio.*

Papa, *babbo.*
Paradise, *paradiso.*
Parents (one's), *i genitori.*
Parlour, *stanzino.*
Paris, *Parigi.*
Party (evening), *serata.*
Pardon (to), *scusare.*
Parrot, *papagallo.*
Pass (to), *passare.*
Passage (of a building), *corritoio.*
Passport, *passaporto.*
Patron, *protettore.*
Pay attention (to), *badare*; to pay a visit, *fare una visita.*
Pear (tree), *pero*; fruit, *pera.*
Pen, *penna.*
Penknife, *temperino.*
People, *gente* (sing. f.).
Perhaps, *forse.*
Persian, *Persiano.*
Person, *persona*; personally, *di persona*; persons (collectively), *gente*; a certain person, *taluno.*
Peter, *Pietro.*
Physician, *medico.*
Pick (to), *cogliere*; pick up, *raccogliere*; pick out, *scegliere.*
Picture, *quadro, pittura.*
Picturesque, *pittoresco, -a.*
Piece, *pezzo*; piece of furniture, *mobile* (m.).
Pig, *porco.*
Pit (of a theatre), *platea.*
Place, *luogo,* pl. *-ghi*; to place, *porre.*
Plain, *semplice.*
Plant, *pianta.*
Play, *commedia*; to play (of music), *suonare*; (of opera), *dare.*
Pleasant, *piacevole*; pleasantly, *piacevolmente.*
Please (to), *piacere*; will you please to..., *favorite di...*; if you please, *per favore,* or *di grazia.*
Pleasure, *piacere* (m.); with pleasure, *con piacere, volentieri.*
Poem, *poema* (m.).

Poet, *poeta* (m.).
Poor, *povero, -a.*
Poorly (to be), *essere indisposto.*
Pope, *papa.*
Port, *porto di mare.*
Port wine, *vino d' Oporto.*
Porter, *facchino*; (in a house), *portiere.*
Portuguese, *portoghese.*
Post, *posta*; to post up, *affigere.*
Pound (sterling), *lira sterlina.*
Pour out (to), *mescere, versare.*
Pray (to), *pregare.*
Precision, *esattezza.*
Precious, *preziosa, -a.*
Prefer (to), *preferire.*
Present, *presente* (adj.); present (n.), *regalo, presente* (m.); to present, *presentare*; to present anyone with..., *regalare...ad uno.*
Pretty, *bello, -a*; *gentile.*
Pretend to be ..., *fare il ...*; to pretend to be deaf, *fare il sordo.*
Prevent (to), *impedire.*
Prince, *principe.*
Principal, *principale.*
Price, *prezzo.*
Priest, *prete.*
Printer, *stampatore.*
Probable, *probabile.*
Produce (to), *produrre.*
Prolong (to), *prolungare.*
Proper, *adatto, -a.*
Promise, *promessa.*
Property, *proprietà.*
Pule (to), *pigolare.*
Put (to), *mettere, porre*; to put out a light, *spegnere un lume*; to put on a coat, *mettersi un vestito.*

Q

Quarter, *quarto.*
Question, *domanda.*
Quick, quickly, *presto.*
Quietly, *tranquillamente.*
Quite (adv.), *tutto*; quite the contrary, *tutt' altro.*

R.

Railway, *strada ferrata*.
Rain, *pioggia;* to rain, *piovere*.
Rare, *raro, -a*.
Rather, *piuttosto*.
Reach (to), *giungere*.
Read (to), *leggere*.
Reading, *lettura*.
Ready, *pronto, -a*.
Receive, *ricevere*.
Receipt (to a bill), *quittanza*.
Recollect (to), *rammentarsi*.
Reduce (to), *ridurre*.
Re-establishment, *ristabilimento*.
Regimen, *igiene* (f.).
Regular, *regolare;* regularly, *regolarmente;* regularity, *regolarità*.
Relation, *parente*.
Remain (to), *restare, rimanere*.
Remarkable, *singolare*.
Remember (to), *ricordarsi di*.
Remove (to), *mutar casa, sgomberare;* to remove from, *toglier via*.
Renowned, *rinomato, -a*.
Rent (to), *prendere a pigione*.
Repose (to), *riposarsi*.
Repairer (f.), *rimendatrice*.
Reputation, *fama*.
Require (to), *aver bisogno di*.
Reside (to), *abitare, dimorare, stare di casa*.
Residence, *soggiorno*.
Resolve (to), *risolvere*.
Rest, *riposo;* the rest, *il resto;* to rest, *riposarsi;* to go to rest, *coricarsi*.
Restorer, *ristauratore*.
Return (to), *tornare, ritornare, riedere*.
Rich, *ricco, -a*.
Ride (to), *andare a cavallo, cavalcare*.
Right, *ragione* (f.).
Right (to do), *far bene;* to be right (of something done), *andar bene;* you are right, *avete ragione*.
Ring, *anello;* to ring, *suonare*.
Rise (to), *alzarsi, levarsi*.

River, *fiume* (m.).
Roar (to), *muggire*.
Rock, *rupe* (f.).
Roman, *Romano*.
Rome, *Roma*.
Romulus, *Romolo*.
Room, *stanza, camera*.
Rose, *rosa*.
Round, *intorno a*.
Royal, *reale*.
Ruin, *rovina;* to ruin, *rovinare*.

S.

Salute (to), *salutare*.
Same, *stesso, -a;* *medesimo, -a*.
Saturday, *sabbato*.
Saucepan, *pentola*.
Say (to), *dire*.
Scarcely, *appena;* scarcely ever, *quasi mai*.
Scenery (of a theatre), *decorazioni*.
School, *scuola*.
Sculpture, *scoltura*.
Sea, *mare* (m.).
Season, *stagione* (f.).
Seat, *sedile* (m.).
Second, *secondo, -a*.
See (to), *vedere, mirare;* to see home, *condurre a casa;* come and see me, *venite a trovarmi;* to see again, *rivedere*.
Seed, *seme* (m.).
Seam (to), *parere*.
Seldom, *di rado*.
Select (to), *scegliere*.
Self, as sign of reflective pronoun. See Reflective Pronouns, p. 183. As intensive, *stesso, -a*.
Sell (to), *vendere*.
Send (to), *mandare;* to send for, *mandare a chiamare, mandare per*.
Sentence, *frase* (f.).
Servant, *servo, serva;* maid-servant, *cameriera;* all the servants of a house, *servitù*.
Serve (to), *servire*.

Set a jewel (to), *montare un gioiello.*

Settle (to), *fissare ;* to settle in a place, *stabilirsi.*

Seven, *sette.*

Several, *parecchi* (m. pl.), *parecchie* (f. pl.).

Sew (to), *cucire.*

Shame, *vergogna.*

Shepherd, *pastore, pecoraio.*

Sheep, *pecora.*

Shilling, *scellino.*

Shine (to), *splendere.*

Shoe, *scarpa.*

Shoemaker, *calzolaio.*

Shop, *bottega.*

Short, *corto, -a.*

Should (implying obligation). See *dovere*, p. 67.

Shoulder, *spalla.*

Show (to), *mostrare, far vedere ;* to show in, *far entrare ;* to show to, *condurre a.*

Shut (to), *chiudere.*

Sibyl, *Sibilla.*

Side, *parte* (f.).

Sienna, *Siena.*

Sight, *vista.*

Silent (to be), *tacere.*

Since, *da che ;* since then, *d' allora in poi ;* since when, *da quando in quà.*

Sing (to), *cantare ;* to sing out of tune, *stuonare.*

Singer, *cantante.*

Singing, *canto.*

Single (adj.), *solo, -a.*

Sir, *signore.*

Sister, *sorella.*

Sit (to), *sedere ;* sit down, *accomodarsi, sedersi.*

Sitting-room, *stanza da ricevere.*

Situation, *situazione* (f.).

Sixty, *sessanta.*

Sleep, *sonno ;* to sleep, *dormire.*

Slowly, *piano, adagio.*

Small, *piccolo, -a.*

Smell sweet (to), *olire soavemente.*

Snow (to), *nevicare.*

So, *così, tanto ;* so much, *tanto, -a ;* so many, *tanti, -e.*

Sofa, *sofà* (m.).

Sojourn, *soggiorno.*

Soldier, *soldato ;* foot-soldier, *fante.*

Some, *ne, qualche* (followed by sing. noun), *alcuno ;* (partitive) *del ;* sometimes, *qualche volta, alcune volte, delle volte.*

Somebody, some one, *alcuno qualcuno, qualcheduno.*

Sometimes. See 'some.'

Something, *qualche cosa.*

Somewhere, *in qualche luogo ;* somewhere else, *in qualche altro luogo.*

Son, *figlio, figliuolo.*

Song, *canzone* (f.).

Soon, *subito, presto.*

Soprano, *soprano.*

Sorry (to be), *rincrescere.* See Note *a*, p. 72.

Sound, *suono.*

Soup, *minestra.*

Speak (to), *parlare, favellare.*

Spend (to), *passare* (of time); to spend money, *spendere danaro.*

Spill (to), *spandere.*

Splendid, *splendido, -a.*

Splendour, *splendidezza.*

Spring (the), *la primavera ;* a spring (of water), *una sorgente.*

Squander away (to), *scialacquare.*

Square, *piazza.*

Squeak (to), *squittire.*

Stagnant, *fermo.*

Stairs, *scala ;* upstairs, *di sopra.*

Stand (to), *stare ;* to stand up (rise), *alzarsi.*

Start (to), *partire* (neut.).

Station, *stazione* (f.).

Statue, *statua.*

Stay (to), *stare, rimanere ;* to stay in one place, *trattenersi ;* to stay at one's country seat, *villeggiare, fare villeggiatura.*

Steam, *vapore* (m.).

Steeple, *campanile* (m.).

Stem, *stelo.*

Step into (to), *entrare.*

Stick (for walking), *bastone* (m.).
Still (adv.), *ancora.*
Stone, *pietra.*
Stop (to), *fermarsi.*
Straightness, *dirittura.*
Straw, *paglia.*
Street, *via, strada ;* street-door, *porta della strada.*
Stroll, *passeggiata ;* to take a stroll, *fare una passeggiata.*
Strike (of a clock), *suonare.*
Study to), *studiare.*
Suburb, *sobborgo.*
Such, *tale ;* such a one, *taluno.*
Suffer (to), *soffrire.*
Sufficiently, *abbastanza.*
Summer, *state* (f.), *estate* (f.).
Sun, *sole* (m.).
Sunday, *domenica* (f.).
Superior(= excellent), *buono, -a.*
Support (to), *mantenere.*
Suppose (to), *supporre.*
Sure, *certo, -a.*
Surgeon, *chirurgo.*
Surprised (to be), *maravigliarsi di.*
Swallow up (to), *inghiottire.*

T.

Table, *tavola ;* tablecloth, *tovaglia ;* to set the table, *apparecchiare ;* to sit properly at table, *stare composto a tavola ;* to leave the table, *andar giù di tavola ;* table d'hôte, *tavola rotonda.*
Tailor, *sarto, sartore.*
Take (to), *prendere, portare ;* to take any one home, *condurre uno a casa ;* to take back, *riportare ;* to take off (one's hat, &c.), *cavarsi ;* to take away, *toglier via, condurre via ;* to take one's leave, *salutare ;* to take place, *avere luogo.*
Talk (to), *parlare.*
Tap (to), *bussare.*
Tapestry, *arazzo.*

Tarpeian, *Tarpeo, -a.*
Tart, *torta.*
Taste, *gusto.*
Tea, *tè* (m.).
Teach (to), *insegnare.*
Teacher, *maestro.*
Tear up (to), *svellere.*
Tell (to), *dire.*
Temple, *tempio.*
Ten, *dieci.*
Tenor, *tenore.*
Than, *di, che.* See p. 163.
Thank (to), *ringraziare.*
Thanks, thank you, *grazie.*
That (pron.), absolutely, *ciò ;* as demonstrative, *quello.* See p. 208 ; as relative, *che, quel che.*
That (conj.), *che.*
Thaw (to), *digelare.*
The. See p. 145.
Theatre, *teatro.*
Their. See p. 198.
Them. See p. 183.
Then, *allora ;* (= therefore), *dunque ;* (= afterwards), *poi, dopo.*
There, *vi, ci, colà, là, lì.*
There ! *ecco !* there goes..., *ecco che passa....*
Therefore, *perciò, quindi, dunque.*
Thing, *cosa.*
Think (to), *credere ;* I think not, *credo di no ;* what do you think ? *che vi pare ?*
Third, *terzo.*
Thirst, *sete* (f.).
Thirsty (to be), *aver sete.*
Thirty, *trenta.*
This, *questo, -a.* See p. 208.
Those, *quelli.* See p. 208.
Thousand, *mille ;* preceded by a number higher than one, *mila.*
Three, *tre.*
Through, *per,* sometimes *in.*
Throw wide open (to), *spalancare.*
Thunder (to), *tuonare.*
Thursday, *giovedì* (m.).
Ticket, *biglietto.*
Tight, *stretto, -a.*
Till, *che, fino a.*

Time, *tempo;* (= turn), *volta;* sometimes, *delle volte.*

Tired, *stanco, -a;* (= out of breath), *sfiatato, -a.*

To, *a;* to the, *al,* &c.; before names of country, *in;* implying necessity, *da;* before infinitives (frequently), *di;* to me, *da me.* See N.B., p. 183.

To-day, *oggi.*

Together, *insieme.*

Tomb, *tomba.*

To-morrow, *domani;* day after to-morrow, *posdomani.*

To-night, *stassera.*

Too, *troppo.*

Tooth, *dente* (m.); toothache, *mal di denti.*

Touch (to), *toccare.*

Towards, *verso.*

Town, *città.*

Trace, *traccia.*

Train, *treno.*

Translate (to), *tradurre.*

Translation, *traduzione* (f.).

Travel (to), *viaggiare.*

Tree, *albero.*

Trouble (to), *disturbare.*

True, *vero, -a.*

Trunk, *baule* (m.).

Try (to), *cercare di;* to try on, *provarsi.*

Tuesday, *martedì* (m.).

Turin, *Torino.*

Turn, *giro.*

Tuscany, *Toscana.*

Twelve, *dodici.*

Twice, *due volte.*

Twenty, *venti.*

Two, *due.*

U.

Ugly, *brutto, -a.*

Umbrella, *ombrello.*

Uncle, *zio.*

Under, *sotto.*

Understand (to), *capire;* I understand, *ho capito* (continued perfect); to make oneself understood, *farsi capire.*

Undoubtedly, *senz' altro, senza dubbio.*

Unexpected, *imprevisto, -a.*

University, *università.*

Unwell (to be), *star male.*

Usual (to be), *esser solito;* as usual, *come il solito.*

V.

Valuable, *prezioso, -a.*

Vatican, *Vaticano.*

Venice, *Venezia.*

Venetian, *veneziano, -a.*

Ventilated, *ventilato, -a.*

Verb, *verbo.*

Very, *molto, assai.*

Victory, *vittoria.*

View, *prospettiva, vista.*

Villa, *villa.*

Vine, *vite* (f.).

Vintage, *vendemmia.*

Violet, *viola.*

Virgil, *Virgilio.*

Visit (to), *visitare.*

Vivacity, *spirito.*

Voice, *voce* (f.).

Volume, *volume* (m.), *tomo.*

W.

Wait (to), *aspettare.*

Waiter, *cameriere.*

Walk, *passeggiata; passeggio;* to take a walk, *fare una passeggiata;* go for a walk, *andare a spasso.*

Walk (to), *camminare, andare a piedi;* to walk into, *entrare in.*

Wall, *muro;* wall (of a room), *parete* (f.).

Walter, *Gualtiero.*

Want (to), *aver bisogno di, bramare, volere, desiderare.*

War, *guerra.*

Warm, *caldo, -a;* to be warm (of a person), *avere caldo;* (of weather), *far caldo;* to warm up, *riscaldare.*

Warn (to), *avvertire*.
Wash oneself (to), *lavarsi*.
Watch, *oriuolo*.
Water, *acqua*; waterfall, *cascata
d' acqua*.
Way, *via*.
Weather, *tempo*; fine weather,
bel tempo; bad weather, *cat-
tivo tempo*; to be ... weather,
far...tempo.
Wear (to), *portare*.
Wedding, *nozze* (f. pl.)
Wednesday, *mercoledì*.
Week. *settimana*.
Weep (to), *piangere*.
Welcome, *benvenuto, -a*.
Welfare, *felicità*.
Well, *bene*; to be well, *star
bene*; well then! *allora!*
Went. See 'Go.'
What, *che* (=that which), *quel
che*; what a number, *quanti*;
what? *che?* or *che cosa?*
Whatever, *checchè*.
When, *quando*.
Where, *dove*.
Whether, *se*.
Which, *quale che, il quale, cui*.
See Relat. Pron., p. 213.
While, whilst, *mentre*.
White, *bianco, -a*.
Who, *che*; who? *chi?*
Whoever, *chiunque*.
Whole, *tutto, -a*.
Why? *perchè?*
Wife, *moglie*; pl. *mogli*.
Will (to), be willing, *volere*.
Wind, *vento*.
Window, *finestra*; to look out
of window, *stare alla finestra*;
shop-window, *vetrina*.
Wine, *vino*; wine-cellar, *can-
tina*.

Winter, *inverno, verno*.
Wipe (to), *tergere, asciugare*.
Wisdom, *giudizio*.
Wish (to), *bramare, desiderare,
volere*; — something to any
one, *augurare*.
With, *con*; with pleasure, *vo-
lentieri*; with me, *meco*.
Without, *senza*.
Wolf, *lupo*.
Wonder, *meraviglia*; to wonder,
maravigliarsi.
Wonderful, *ammirabile*.
Wont (to be), *solere*.
Wood, *legno*.
Woodcutter, *spaccalegna*.
Word, *parola*.
Work, *opera*.
World, *mondo*.
Would (as principal verb). See
volere, p. 66.
Wound (to), *ferire*.
Worth (to be), *valere, meritare*;
not to be worth a straw, *non
valere un' acca*.
Wrap up (to), *imbacuccare*.
Write, *scrivere*.
Writing-book, *quaderno*.
Wrong, *torto*.
Wrong (to be), *andar male* (of
a thing done); I am wrong,
ho torto.

Y.

Year, *anno*.
Yes, *sì*.
Yesterday, *ieri*.
Yet, *pure, ancora*.
Yield (to), *cedere*.
You. See p. 182.
Young, *giovine*.
Your. See p. 198.

II. ITALIAN-ENGLISH.

A.

A, to, at. See p. 144, & p. 237.
Abatino, young priest (clerk in holy orders).
Abbagliare, to dazzle.
Abbandonare, to abandon.
Abbastanza, enough.
Abbracciare, to embrace.
Abbrucciare, to burn down.
Abitante (m. & f.), inhabitant.
Abituarsi, to accustom oneself.
Abusarsi, to take advantage of.
Accadere, to happen.
Accanto, near.
Accendere, to light, to kindle.
Accoglienza, reception.
Accogliere, to receive.
Accomodarsi a, to put up with, to accommodate oneself to.
Accompagnare, to accompany.
Accusare, to charge, to accuse.
Acqua, water.
Adattare, to accommodate.
Addio, good-bye.
Addormentarsi, to fall asleep.
Addosso, on, upon any one's back.
Adeguato, proper.
Adempimento, fulfilment.
Adempire, to fulfil.
Adesso, now, at present.
Adirarsi, to get angry.
Adirato, -a, angry.
Adunque, therefore.
Affare (m.), business.
Affaticarsi, to struggle.
Affetto, love, attachment.

Affettuoso, affectionate.
Affiggere, to attach, to post up (bills).
Aggiungere, to add.
Agnello, lamb.
Agosto, August.
Agricoltore, husbandman.
Aiutare, to assist.
Al, to the. See p. 8.
Albergatore (m.), host.
Albero, tree.
Alchimista, alchemist.
Alcuno, some one, somebody.
Alimentare, to nourish, to feed.
All', to the. See p. 8.
Alla, to the. See p. 8.
Allagare, to inundate.
Allegro, merry.
Allestirsi, to get ready.
Alloggiare, to lodge.
Allungare, to lengthen.
Alpi (pl. f.), Alps.
Alterarsi, to get excited.
Alto, high, lofty.
Altro, other, else; *un altro*, another.
Alzarsi, to rise, get up.
Amare, to love.
Amatore, lover.
Ambasciata, message.
Ambasciatore, ambassador.
Amico, -a, friend.
Ammalarsi, to get ill.
Ammalato, ill, unwell; *un ammalato*, a patient.
Ammassare, to hoard.
Ammirabile, wonderful.
Ammiraglio, admiral.

Ammonire, to admonish, to teach.

Ammonizione, admonition (f.).

Anche, even.

Ancora, yet.

Andare, to go; — *a piedi*, to walk; — *a spasso*, to go for a walk; — *in collera*, to put oneself in a passion; — *in carrozza*, to ride in a carriage; — *bene* (of a thing done), to be right; (of a garment), to fit; — *male*, to be wrong; — *a cavallo*, to go on horseback; — *carponi*, to go on all fours; — *in barca*, to go in a boat; — *giù di tavola*, to leave the table; — *a caccia*, to go a-hunting; — *d' accordo*, to agree; — *per vapore*, to go by steamboat; — *per strada ferrata*, to go by railway; — *a trovare*, to go to see.

Anello, ring.

Animale (m.), animal.

Animo, mind.

Annali, annals. See p. 143.

Anno, year.

Annottare, to become night.

Anticamera, ante-room.

Antico, ancient.

Anzi, on the contrary.

Apertura, opening.

Apparecchiare la tavola, to lay the cloth.

Apparire, to appear.

Appartenere, to belong.

Appena, scarcely; — *che*, as soon as.

Appiccare, to give, to impart.

Appiccarsi, to become contaminated.

Appo, among, with.

Aprile (m.), April.

Aratro, plough.

Arazzo, tapestry.

Ardere, to burn.

Aria, air.

Aristocrazia, aristocracy.

Armi (pl. f.), arms.

Arpa, harp.

Arrabiarsi, to get angry.

Arrivare, to arrive.

Arte (m.), art, artifice.

Artefice, maker, artisan.

Artificio, artifice, cunning.

Ascendere, to climb.

Ascoltare, to listen.

Aspettare (act.), to wait for, to await, to expect.

Aspetto, aspect, look.

Assai, much.

Assalto, assault.

Assistere, to assist, to attend.

Assurdo, -a, absurd.

Astronomo, astronomer.

Atene, Athens.

Atlante, Atlas.

Attendere, to wait.

Attorno a, about; *esser attorne a uno*, to torment one.

Autunno, autumn.

Avanti, forward, first.

Avanzare (of a watch), to gain.

Avanzato, -a, advanced, old.

Avaro, miser.

Avere, to have; *aver bisogno di*, to want; — *buona cera*, to look well; — *cal lo*, to be warm; — *fame*, to be hungry; — *freddo*, to be cold; — *giudizio*, to be wise; — *luogo*, to take place; — *paura*, to be afraid; — *ragione*, to be right; — *sete*, to be thirsty; — *sonno*, to be sleepy; — *torto*, to be wrong; — *vergogna*, to be ashamed; (followed by *da*), to be obliged, must; *che avete?* what is the matter with you?

Avvenire, to happen, to take place.

Avventore (m.), customer.

Avvertire, to warn, to tell.

Avvezzarsi a, to accustom oneself to.

Avviso, advice.

B.

Babbo, papa.

Bacchiare le noci, to bring nuts down with a stick.

Baciare, to kiss.
Badare, to mind.
Bagaglie, luggage.
Bambinaia, nursemaid.
Bambino, -a, child.
Bando, banishment.
Basilica, cathedral.
Basso, low.
Bastare, to be enough.
Bastone (m.), walking-stick.
Battaglia, battle.
Battere, to beat, knock, thrash.
Battesimo, baptism.
Baule (m.), trunk.
Bellezza, beauty.
Bello, beautiful, fine.
Benché (conj.), although.
Bene, well ; (n. m.), good, welfare.
Benemerito, well merited.
Berlino, Berlin.
Berretta, (man's) cap.
Bevere, to drink.
Bianco, -a, white.
Bicchiere (m.), drinking-glass.
Biglietto, ticket ; — *di visita*, card (visiting).
Bisognare, to be necessary.
Bisogno, want.
Bollire, to boil.
Bonifazio, Boniface.
Bontà, kindness.
Borsa, purse.
Bottega, shop.
Braccialetto, bracelet.
Bramare, to wish.
Bramoso, desirous.
Bruttare, to stain.
Buca, hole, letter-box.
Buono, -a, good.

C.

Cadere, to drop.
Caffè (m.), coffee, café.
Caffettiere, coffee-house keeper.
Cagione (f.), reason ; *a* —, in consequence.
Calarsi, to be lowered.
Caldo, -a (adj.), warm ; (n. m.), heat.

Calere, to care for.
Calpestio, footstep.
Calzolaio, shoemaker.
Camera, bed-room.
Cameriera, maid-servant.
Cameriere, waiter.
Campagna, country (out of town).
Campana, bell.
Campo, field.
Canapè (m.), couch.
Candela, candle.
Cane, dog.
Cantante (m. & f.), singer.
Cantare, to sing.
Cantina, wine-cellar.
Canto, singing.
Cantonata, street-corner.
Canzone (f.), song.
Capire, to understand.
Capitale (f.), capital.
Capo, head.
Cappella, chapel.
Cappello, hat.
Carlino, Charles (dimin.).
Carlo, Charles.
Caro, -a, dear ; (adv.) dearly.
Carozza, carriage.
Carta, paper ; — *sugante*, blotting-paper.
Cartello, bill (to post up).
Casa, house.
Casato or *Casata*, (noble) family name.
Cassa, case, box.
Catena, chain.
Cattivo, bad.
Causa, cause.
Cavaliere, knight.
Cavallo, horse.
Cavare, to draw ; *cavarsi*, to take off.
Cavicchio, peg.
Cento, a hundred.
Cercare, to search, to enquire for.
Cerchio, ring.
Certamente, certainly.
Certo, certain.
Cestellina, basket (dim.).
Ceto, class.
Che ? or *che cosa ?* what ? *che*, who, that, which.

Che (after a comparative adjective), than ; (after a verb conjugated negatively), nothing but ; *chè*, because.

Chi ? who ?

Chiamare, to call.

Chiaro, -a, clear.

Chiave (f.), key.

Chicchera, cup.

Chiedere, to ask, to claim.

Chiesa, church.

Chiodo, nail.

Chitarra, guitar.

Chiudere, to shut, to shut up.

Chiunque, whosoever.

Ci, here.

Cielo, heaven, sky.

Cinquanta, fifty.

Cinque, five.

Circa, about.

Circondare, to surround.

Citare, to summon.

Città, town, city.

Cittadino, citizen.

Classe (f.), class.

Cogliere, to gather.

Cognato, brother-in-law; *cognata*, sister-in-law.

Colà, there.

Colazione (f.), breakfast.

Colla, with the. See p. 8.

Colombo, Columbus.

Colpa, fault.

Coltre (f. sing.), bed clothes.

Colui, that man, the man.

Combattere, to fight.

Come ? how ? *come si dice in italiano...?* what is the Italian for...?

Cominciare, to begin, commence.

Commendabile, commendable.

Commercio di lettere, correspondence.

Comodo, -a, comfortable.

Compagnia, company.

Compagno, companion.

Comparire, to appear.

Compensare, to compensate.

Compiacenza, delight.

Compiacersi, to be pleased.

Compiere, compire, to finish.

Componimento, composition.

Comporre, to compose ; — *la faccia*, to set one's countenance.

Comprare, to buy.

Comune, common.

Comunque, however.

Con, with.

Concedere, to grant, to bestow.

Concorso, concourse.

Concerto, concert.

Condanna, condemnation, sentence.

Condolersi, to condole.

Condurre, to conduct, to take.

Confiscare, to confiscate.

Conforme a, in keeping with.

Connettere, to connect.

Conoscenza, acquaintance, knowledge.

Conoscere, to know.

Conoscitore (m.), connoisseur.

Consecrare, to consecrate.

Consegna, charge, watchword.

Considerare, to consider.

Consiglio, advice.

Console, consul.

Contadino, countryman.

Conte, count.

Contemplatore, observer.

Contenere, to contain.

Contentarsi, to be contented.

Contessa, countess.

Continuo, -a, continual.

Conto, bill, account ; *far — di*, to intend.

Contorni (pl.), environs.

Contradire, to contradict.

Contrario, contrary.

Contrarre, to contract.

Contrastare, to oppose.

Contristare, to distress.

Convenire (v. neut.), to suit, agree; (v. impers.) to be necessary.

Convertirsi in vento, to turn into nothing.

Copernico, Copernicus.

Coprire, to cover.

Corallo, coral.

Coricarsi, to go to rest.

Corpo, body.

Correggiato, flail.

Correntemente, fluently.

Corriere (m.), mail.

Corrispondere a, to repay.
Corrompersi, to go bad, to be spoiled.
Corrotto, -a, corrupt.
Corto, -a, short.
Cosa, thing.
Così, thus.
Cospirare, to conspire.
Costare, to cost.
Costì, here.
Costringere, to compel.
Costume (m.), custom, manner.
Cotesto, that.
Credere, to believe ; *credersi*, to be believed.
Crescere, to increase.
Cristallo, crystal.
Cristo, Christ.
Cristiano, Christian.
Cronaca, chronicle.
Cucire, to sew.
Cugino, -a, cousin.
Cui, whom, that, which.
Cuocere, to cook.
Cuore (m.), heart.
Cura, care.
Currado, Conrad.

D.

D', of. Note *b*, p. 15, and Obs. p. 239.
Da, by, from. See p. 239.
da me, to me = at, to, or in my heuse.
Dabbenaggine (f.), obtuseness.
Dai, by the. See p. 8.
Dal, by the. See p. 8.
Danaro, coin ; *danari*, money.
Dare, to give ; — *da mangiare*, to give something to eat ; — *da bere*, to give something to drink ; — *da cena*, to give some supper ; — *in giardino* (of a window), to look into the garden ; — *un' opera*, to play an opera ; — *retta*, to give heed.
Davvero, indeed.
Debito, debt.
Dicembre (m.), December.

Decorare, to adorn.
Decorazioni, scenery.
Definitivo, -a, definite.
Degno, -a, worthy.
Del, dell', della, dello, of the. See p. 8.
Delitto, crime, misdeed.
Deludere, to disappoint.
Dentro, in, within.
Derelitto, destitute.
Desiderare, to wish.
Desiderio, desire, anxiety.
Destarsi, to awake.
Di, of ; (after a comparative), than ; *di sopra*, upstairs.
Dì, day.
Dicianove, nineteen.
Diciasette, seventeen.
Diciotto, eighteen.
Dieci, ten.
Dietro, behind.
Difendere, to defend.
Difficile, difficult.
Digelare, to thaw.
Diligente, diligent.
Dimenticare, to forget.
Dimorare, to reside.
Dio, God.
Dipingere, to paint.
Diportarsi, to behave.
Dire, to say ; — *da senno*, to speak in earnest.
Dirimpetto, opposite.
Disgrazia, misfortune.
Dispensa, pantry.
Dispetto — a dispetto, reluctantly.
Dispiacere, to be sorry. See Note *a*, p. 72.
Distinguere, to distinguish.
Dito, finger ; *a mena* —, at one's fingers' ends.
Divenire, to become, to grow.
Divertimento, amusement.
Divertirsi, to enjoy oneself.
Divisamento, device.
Divorare, to devour.
Dodici, twelve.
Dolere, to ache See Note *e*, p. 79.
Dolersi, to complain.
Dolore (m.), pain, grief.
Domanda, question.
Domandare, to ask.

Domani, to-morrow.
Domenica, Sunday.
Domestico, domestic.
Donde, whence.
Dopopranzo, afternoon.
Dormire, to sleep.
Dove, where.
Dovere (n. m.), duty.
Dovere (v. act.), to owe, be obliged.
Due, two.
Duello, duel.
Durante, during.

E.

E, and; *è,* is.
Eccessivo, -a, excessive.
Ecclesiastico, ecclesiastic.
Ecclissi (m. & f.), eclipse.
Ecco, here is, here are.
Edifizio, building.
Edimburgo, Edinburgh.
Edizione (f.), edition.
Effetto, effect; *in —,* in fact.
Egli, he, it. See p. 182.
Eletto, choice.
Ella, she, it. See p. 183.
Empio, wicked, malicious.
Empire, to fill.
Entrare, to enter.
Erba, grass.
Esame (m.), examination.
Esattezza, precision.
Esclamare, to exclaim.
Esempio, example, instance.
Esercizio, exercise.
Esigere, to require, to exact.
Esiliare, to banish.
Esilio, exile.
Espellere, to eject.
Esprimere, to express; *esprimersi,* to be expressed.
Esso, -a, he, she, it; *essi, -e,* they. See p. 183.
Essere, to be; *— infreddato, -a,* to have a cold; *— solito, -a,* to be accustomed.
Estate (f.), summer.
Esterno, exterior.
Estollere, to raise, extol.
Estrarre, to draw, extract.
Esule (m.), an exile.

Età (etade), age.
Europa, Europe.
Evangelio, Gospel.

F.

Fabbricare una casa, to build a house.
Fabbro, smith.
Faccenda, business.
Facchino, porter, carrier.
Fallare, to commit a fault.
Fallo, fault.
Falso, -a, false.
Fama, reputation; *venir in —* or *in nome,* to come into notice.
Famiglia, family.
Famoso, -a, famous.
Fanciullina, little girl.
Fanciullo, child.
Fare, to do, make; (of weather), to be; (of a profession), to exercise, practise; *—freddo,* to be cold; *— colazione,* to breakfast; *— una passeggiata,* to take a walk; *— una visita,* to pay a visit; *— il sordo,* to pretend to be deaf, *far conto di,* to intend; *far del bene,* to do good; *far del male,* to do mischief; *fare buona accoglienza,* to give a kind reception; *far entrare,* to show in; *far fare,* to have made; *far fiasco,* to fail; *far montare,* to have set; *far pagare,* to charge; *far prendere,* to have taken; *farsi fare,* to have made for oneself, *farsi capire,* to make oneself understood; *come si fa,* as is usual.
Farfalla, butterfly.
Fastidio, trouble.
Fatica, labour.
Fatto, fact.
Fattura, invoice.
Favola, fable.
Favoleggiare, to report.
Favoletta, little story.
Favore (m.), favour; *per —,* if you please.

o

Febbraio, February.
Febbre (f.), fever.
Felice, happy.
Fendere, to split.
Ferire, to wound.
Fermarsi, to stay.
Fermezza, firmness.
Fermo, stagnant (water).
Ferro, iron.
Ficaia, fig-tree.
Fico, fig.
Figere, to drive in.
Figlia, daughter.
Figlio, son.
Figliolanza, children.
Figliuolo, little son.
Fin, *fino*, until ; *fin dove*, how far, as far as.
Finalmente, at last.
Finchè, until, so long as.
Fine (m. & f.), end.
Finestra, window.
Fingere, to pretend.
Finire, to finish.
Fiore (f.), flower.
Fiorire, to flower, to flourish.
Firenze, Florence.
Fiume (m.), river.
Focherello, fire (dimin.).
Foco, fire.
Foggiare, to form.
Foglio, sheet of paper.
Folla, crowd.
Fondare, to found.
Fondere, to cast.
Fondo, end, bottom.
Fonte (f.), source ; — *d'oro*, mine of gold.
Forestiero, foreigner.
Formare, to form.
Fornaio, baker.
Forse, perhaps.
Forza, strength.
Fra, among.
Francese, French.
Francia, France.
Franco, free, open.
Fratello, brother.
Freddo, cold.
Fresco, fresh.
Fretta, haste, hurry.
Fronte (f.), brow, forehead.

Frutto, fruit.
Fuggire, to flee.
Fuoco, fire.
Fuori, outside, beyond.

G.

Garzone, a youth.
Gas, *gasse* (m.), gas.
Gelare, to freeze.
Generalmente, generally.
Genere (m.), kind.
Generoso, generous.
Genio, genius.
Genitore, father.
Genitori (pl.), parents.
Gennaio, January.
Genova, Genoa.
Gente (f.), people.
Gentile (adj.), kind.
Germania, Germany.
Ghibellini, Ghibellines.
Ghiotto, greedy.
Già, already, formerly.
Giacchè, since, as.
Giacere, to lie.
Giardiniere, gardener.
Giardino, garden.
Giocare, to play.
Gioielliere, jeweller.
Giornale (m.), newspaper.
Giorno, day.
Giovane (m. & f.), a youth.
Giovanni, John.
Giovare, to be useful.
Giovedì, Thursday.
Giovevole, useful.
Giovine, young man.
Girare, to revolve.
Gire, to go.
Giro, turn.
Giudizio, judgment.
Giugno, June.
Giungere, to arrive.
Giusta, according to.
Giustizia, justice.
Gli, the (pl.). See p. 8.
Godere, to enjoy.
Grammatica, grammar.
Gran, *grande*, large, great.
Grandinare, to hail.

Grano, corn.
Gratitudine (f.), gratitude.
Greco, Greek.
Gridare, to cry out.
Guadagnare, to gain.
Guantiera (*vassoio* at Florence), tray.
Guardarsi di, to take care of, to guard against, to keep aloof from.
Guardia, guard, watch.
Guanto, glove.
Guarire, to recover, cure.
Guastare, to spoil.
Guerra, war.
Guerriero, warrior.
Guglielmo, William.
Guizzare, to shoot.
Gusto, taste, tact.

I.

I, the (pl.). See p. 8.
Ieri, yesterday ; — *l'altro*, the day before yesterday.
Igiene (f.), regimen.
Ignorante, ignorant, ignoramus.
Il, the. See p. 8.
Ilarità, cheerfulness.
Immergere, to plunge.
Impaccio, trouble, embarrassment.
Imparare, to learn.
Impedire, to prevent.
Imperocchè, since.
Imporre, to impose.
In, in, into, to ; *in viaggio*, abroad.
Inaridire, to wither.
Incapace, incapable.
Inchiudere, to enclose.
Incirca, *all'*—, about.
Inclinare, to incline.
Incomodare, to incommode, to disturb.
Incontrare, to meet ; (of a performance), to succeed.
Inoutere spavento, to strike terror.
Indegno, unworthy.
Indirizzo, address.
Indugiare, to tarry.

Indugio, delay.
Inezie (pl. f.), trifling.
Infelice, unhappy.
Informazione (f.), information.
Infreddato, -a, (essere), to have a cold.
Infreddatura, a cold.
Ingegno, genius.
Inghilterra, England.
Inghiottire, to swallow.
Inglese, English.
Ingresso, entrance.
Insegnare, to teach.
Insieme, together.
Inst1tutore (m.), founder.
Intanto, in the mean time.
Intendere, to hear.
Intenzione (f.), intention.
Interamente, entirely.
Interessante, interesting.
Interessare, to interest.
Intorno, about.
Introdurre, to introduce.
Invece, instead.
Inverno, winter.
Inviare, to send, forward.
Invitare, to invite.
Involto, parcel.
Ire, to go.
Iscrizione (f.), inscription.
Italia, Italy.
Italiano, Italian.
Ivi, there.

L.

L', the (see p. 8) ; her, it, him.
La, the (see p. 8) ; her, it.
Là, there.
Laborioso, industrious.
Lagnarsi, to complain.
Largo, wide.
Lasciare, to let, leave ; — *in consegna*, to have in charge.
Latte (m.), milk.
Lavandaia, laundress.
Lavarsi, to wash oneself.
Lavoro, work.
Le, the (see p. 8) ; them, to her, to it (see p. 183).
Legare, to tie.
Leggere, to read.

Leggersi, to be related.
Legno, wood.
Lettera, letter.
Letto, bed.
Levante (m.), East.
Levarsi, to rise, get up.
Lezione (f.), lesson.
Libreria, library.
Libro, book.
Licere, to be allowed.
Lieto, glad, joyful.
Limone, lemon.
Lingua, tongue, language.
Lira, pound; — *sterlina*, pound sterling. *Lira* = franc in money.
Livorno, Leghorn.
Lodare, to praise.
Londra, London.
Loquace, talkative.
Lucciola, glow-worm.
Luce (f.), light.
Lucere, to shine, to glitter.
Luglio, July.
Luna, moon.
Lunedì, Monday.
Lungi, far.
Lungo, long.
Luogo, place.
Lupo, wolf.

M.

Ma, but.
Madre, mother.
Madrid, Madrid.
Maestro, teacher.
Magagna, speck.
Maggio, May.
Maggiore, eldest (of brothers and sisters).
Mai, never.
Mal di capo, headache.
Mal di denti, tooth-ache.
Malattia, illness.
Male or *mal* (m.), pain, illness.
Malo, bad.
Malvolentieri, unwillingly.
Mancanza, want.
Mandare, to send.
Mangiare, to eat.
Mano (f.), hand.

Mantenere, to keep.
Mantiglia, mantle.
Maravigliarsi, to wonder.
Marchese, marquis.
Mare (m.), sea.
Margheritina, daisy.
Marito, husband.
Martedì, Tuesday.
Marzo, March.
Maschile, masculine.
Mattina or *mattino*, morning; *di buon* —, early in the morning.
Meco, with me.
Mediante, by means of.
Medicina, medicine.
Mediterraneo, Mediterranean.
Meglio (adv.), better.
Mela, apple; *melo*, apple-tree.
Melarancia, an orange.
Memoria, memory.
Meno, less.
Mentre che, while.
Mercante, tradesman.
Mercanzia, goods, merchandise.
Merciaiuolo, pedlar.
Mercoledì, Wednesday.
Mercurio, Mercury.
Mescere, to pour out (wine).
Meschino, miserable.
Mescolare, to mix.
Mese (m.), month.
Mesto, sad.
Metallo, metal.
Mettere, to put; *mettersi*, to put on; *mettersi a*, to set about; *mettere in sesto*, to arrange properly; *mettere alte strida*, to scream loudly.
Mezzi, means.
Mezzo, middle, means.
Miele (m.), honey.
Mietere, to reap.
Migliore, better.
Milano, Milan.
Milanese (m. & f.), Milanese.
Militare, officer.
Miltone, Milton.
Minestra, rice-soup.
Minore, youngest (of brothers and sisters).
Mirare, to look; — *a*, to have for one's object.

Miseria, distress.
Misero, wretched.
Misura, measure.
Mobigliare, to furnish.
Mobile (m.), piece of furniture.
Mobiliare (m.), furniture.
Moda, fashion.
Molto, much.
Monarchia, monarchy.
Mondo, world.
Monsignor, My Lord (a dignitary of the Church).
Montagna, mountain.
Montare (of jewels), to set.
Monte (m.), mountain; *Monte Bianco,* Mont Blanc.
Morire, to die.
Morte (f.), death.
Mosaico, mosaic.
Moscolo, moss.
Mulino, mill.
Muffa, mildew.
Muratore, mason.
Muro, wall.
Muschio, moss.
Musica, music.
Mutare casa, to change residence.
Mutarsi, to change.

N.

Napoli, Naples.
Narrare, to relate.
Nascere, to be born, (of vegetation) to grow.
Nascondere, to hide.
Ne, of it, of him, of her, of them, some. See p. 183.
Necessario, necessary.
Negligere, to neglect.
Nemico, enemy.
Nero, black.
Nessuno, nobody.
Nevicare, to snow.
Niente, nothing.
Nipote, nephew, niece.
Niuno, no one.
No, no.
Nobile, noble.
Nocchiero, pilot.
Noia, trouble.

Nominare, to name, to state.
Non, not; — *che,* much less.
Nonna, grandmother.
Nonno, grandfather.
Notizia, intelligence.
Noto, known.
Notte (f.), night.
Novanta, ninety.
Nove, nine.
Novembre (m.), November.
Noverare, to count.
Nozze, wedding. See p. 143.
Nulla, nothing.
Numero, number.
Numeroso, numerous.
Nuova, news.

O.

O, or.
Obbedire, to obey.
Obblio, oblivion.
Occhio, eye.
Occorrere, to want.
Offrire, to offer.
Oggetto, object.
Oggi, to-day; — *a otto,* this day week; — *a quindici,* this day fortnight.
Ogni, every.
Olire, to smell.
Oltre a, upwards of.
Ombra, shadow.
Ombrello, umbrella.
Oncia, ounce.
Onorare, to honour.
Onorevole, honorable.
Opera, work, opera.
Ora (n. f.), hour; *che* — *è?* what time is it? *a che* — *?* at what time; *ora* (adv.), now.
Oratorio, oratorio.
Ordinare, to order.
Ordine (m.), order.
Orecchino, ear-ring.
Origine (f.), origin.
Oriuolo, watch.
Ornamento, ornament.
Oro, gold.
Orologio, clock.
Ossa, bones. See p. 142.

Ottanta, eighty.
Ottenere, to obtain.
Ottimo, superl. of *buono*.
Otto, eight.
Ottobre (m.), October.
Ove, where.
Ovile (m.), sheep-fold.
Oziare, to be inactive, to loiter.

P.

Pace (f.), peace.
Padre, father.
Padrone, master.
Paese (m.), country.
Paesano, fellow-countryman.
Paga, payment.
Pagare, to pay.
Pagina, page.
Paio, pair.
Paluzzo, palace.
Pane (m.), bread.
Panni, clothes.
Pannilini, (linen) clothes.
Papa, pope.
Parecchie, several.
Parente (m. & f.), relation.
Parere, to seem.
Parete (f.), wall of a room.
Parigi, Paris.
Parlamento, parliament.
Parlare, to speak; *parlarsi*, to be spoken.
Parola, word.
Parte (f.), part.
Partire, to leave, depart, start.
Partorire, to produce.
Pascere, to feed.
Pascolo, pasture.
Passaporto, passport.
Passare (of time), to spend; *passare da uno*, to call on a person.
Passato, last.
Passeggiata, walk.
Pastore, shepherd.
Patente (m.), patent.
Paterno, fatherly.
Patimento, suffering.
Patria, country.
Paura, fear; *avere* —, to be afraid.

Pavimento, floor.
Pazzamente, foolishly.
Pecora, sheep.
Pel, for the. See p. 8.
Pena, punishment.
Penna, pen.
Pensare, to think; *non* — *a*, not to trouble one's mind about.
Pensiero, thought.
Pentire, to repent.
Pentola, saucepan.
Per, for; — *tempo*, early.
Pera, pear; *pero*, pear-tree.
Perche? (adv.), why? (conj.), because.
Perciò, therefore.
Perdere, to lose; — *il tempo in inezie*, to lose one's time in trifling.
Perdita, loss.
Pericolo, danger.
Perla, pearl.
Però, however.
Persiano, Persian.
Persona, person.
Persuadere, to persuade.
Pervertire, to pervert.
Pezzo, piece; *un* —, a long time.
Piacere, to like, to be fond of. See note *a*, p. 72.
Piacevolmente, pleasantly.
Piangere, to weep.
Piano, floor, story.
Pianoforte (m.), piano.
Pianta, plant.
Piazza, square.
Piccolo, small.
Piego, parcel.
Pieno, full.
Pietà, piety, compassion.
Pietro, Peter.
Pietroburgo, St. Petersburg.
Pigliare, to catch, take.
Pioggia, rain.
Piovere, to rain.
Pipistrello, bat.
Pittore, painter.
Più, more; *il* or *la* —, the most.
Plebe (f.), the working classes.
Poc' anzi, a short time ago.
Poco, little; *pochi, -e*, few.

Poco lungi, not far.
Poeta, poet.
Pomeridiano, in the afternoon.
Pomo, handle of a stick.
Pompeo, Pompey.
Ponente (m.), West.
Pontefice, Pontiff.
Ponteficio, papal.
Popolare, popular.
Popolo, people.
Porcellana, porcelain, china.
Porre, to place ; — in campo pre-
    testi, to bring forward ex-
    cuses.
Porsi in capo, to take into one's
    head.
Porta, door.
Portare, to carry, bring, wear ;
    — in tavola, to serve up din-
    ner.
Portiere, porter.
Portogallo, Portugal.
Possedere, to possess.
Posta, post.
Potare, to prune.
Potente, powerful.
Poter e,to be able ; non ne — più,
    to be very tired.
Potestà, chief magistrate.
Povero, poor.
Pranzare, to dine.
Pranzo, dinner.
Prato, meadow.
Precetto, precept.
Preferire, to prefer.
Pregare, to beg.
Pregiare, to value.
Prendere, to take.
Presentarsi, to appear.
Presente (m.), a present ; (adj.)
    present.
Prestare, to lend ; — fede, to
    believe.
Presto, soon, early, quickly.
Prezioso, precious.
Prigione (f.), prison.
Prima che, before.
Prima di, before.
Primavera, spring.
Primo, first.
Principale, principal.
Principe, prince.

Principiare, to begin, com-
    mence.
Principio, beginning, commence-
    ment.
Procedere, to proceed.
Prometeo, Prometheus.
Promessa, promise.
Pronto, ready.
Proprio, his, her own.
Prospettiva, view.
Prossimo, next.
Provvedere, to foresee, to provide.
Pubblicare, to publish ; — i beni di,
    to confiscate the property of.
Pulire, to clean.
Pure, yet, however.
Putto, boy.

Q.

Quà, here.
Quadro, picture.
Qualche, some, any (followed by
    sing.).
Quale or qual' (sg.) } which.
Quali (pl.)   }
Qualità, quality, character.
Qualunque, any.
Quando, wher. ; di — in —, ever
    and anon.
Quante (f.) } how many.
Quanti (m.) }
Quanti anni ? how old ?
Quanto, how much ; quanto
    tempo, how long.
Quaranta, forty.
Quattordici, fourteen.
Quattro, four.
Quel, quello, that ; quello che,
    that which, what, or that.
Querciuolo, small oak.
Questi, this man.
Questo, questa, this.
Qui, here.
Quindici, fifteen.

R.

Raccogliere, to pick up.
Racconto, account, story.

Radere, to scrape.
Ragazzo, -a, boy, girl.
Raggio, ray, beam.
Ragionamento, conversation.
Ragione (f.), reason, right.
Rallegrarsi, to be glad.
Rapina, rapine, robbery.
Regalare, to present.
Regalo, a present.
Regno, kingdom, state.
Rendere, to give back.
Restare, to stay.
Resto, rest.
Rete (f.), net.
Retto, right, correct.
Riaprire, to open again.
Riavere, to have back.
Ricapitare, to forward to one's address.
Ricchezza, wealth, riches.
Ricco, -a, rich.
Ricevere, to receive; — *nuove di*, to hear from ; — *con bella grazia uno*, to receive a person kindly.
Ricompensa, reward.
Riconoscenza, gratitude.
Riconoscere, to recognize, to notice.
Ricordarsi, to remember.
Ricorrere a, to recur, to resort to.
Ridere, to laugh.
Ridersi di, to laugh at.
Riedere, to return.
Rientrare, to go in again.
Riflessivo, thoughtful.
Rimanere, to stay ; — *colla lettura*, to leave off reading.
Rimendatrice (f.), repairer.
Rimettere, to put off.
Rimuovere, to remove.
Rincrescere (impers.), to be sorry.
Ringraziare, to thank.
Rinomato, -a, renowned.
Ripetere, to repeat.
Ripigliare, to rejoin.
Riporre, to put in, to place.
Riportare, to carry back.
Riposare, to rest.
Riprodurre, to reproduce.
Riputare, to consider, to look upon.

Riscaldare, to warm up.
Risolversi, to make up one's mind.
Risparmiarsi, to spare one's self.
Rispetto, respect.
Risplendere, to light, to glitter.
Rispondere, to answer.
Ritirare, to withdraw.
Rito, rite.
Ritorno, return.
Ritrovare, to discover.
Ritrovatore, discoverer.
Rivedere, to see again.
Riverente, respectful.
Rivolgersi a, to apply to.
Roba, goods; things in general, from the smallest trifle to the most costly object.
Roma, Rome.
Rompere, to break.
Rosa, rose.
Rovina, ruin.
Ruotare, to roll about, to parade.

S.

Sabbato, Saturday.
Sacro, -a, holy, sacred.
Sala, drawing-room.
Salire, to rise, to ascend.
Salotto, drawing-room.
Salutare, to salute; *salutate da parte mia vostro fratello*, give my compliments to your brother.
Salute, health.
Salvare, to save.
Sano, healthy, sound.
Sapere, to know, to smell ; — *a mente*, to know by heart; — *di buono*, to have a good smell ; — *dire*, to be able to tell.
Sapiente, wise.
Sarchiare, to weed.
Sarto, tailor.
Savio, -a, wise.
Saziare, to satiate.
Sbagliare, to mistake.
Sbaglio, mistake.
Sbrigarsi to hurry.

Scacchi, chess.
Scarpa, shoe.
Scheletro, skeleton.
Sconfiggere, to defeat.
Scoprimento, discovery.
Scoprire, to discover.
Scorrere, to flow.
Scordarsi, to forget.
Scrivere, to write.
Scuola, school.
Scure (f.), axe.
Sdegnato, -a, angry.
Se, if.
Secolo, century.
Secondo, second, according to.
Secreto, secret.
Sedere, to sit.
Sedia, chair.
Sedici, sixteen.
Seggiola, chair.
Segnale (m.), sign, mark
Segretario, secretary.
Segreto, secret.
Seguire, to follow.
Sei, six.
Seme (m.), seed.
Semplice, simple.
Sentenza, sentence ; — *di morte*, death warrant.
Sentinella, sentry.
Sentire, to hear, feel ; —*parlar di*, to hear of.
Senza, without.
Seppellire, to bury.
Sera, evening.
Serata, evening party.
Serva, maid servant.
Servigio, service.
Servire, to serve.
Servo, man servant.
Sessanta, sixty.
Sete (f.), thirst.
Settanta, seventy.
Sette, seven.
Settembre (m.), September.
Settimana, week.
Sfera, sphere, globe.
Sgarbato, rude.
Sgomberare, to remove.
Signor, Mr.
Signora, Mrs., lady.
Signore, gentleman.

Signorina, Miss.
Sinfonia, overture.
Singolarissimo, very remarkable.
Sipario, curtain of a theatre.
Soave, sweet.
Sobborgo, suburb.
Sobrio, -a, sober
Sofà, couch.
Soffitta, attics.
Soggiacere, to succumb.
Soggiorno, residence.
Soldato, soldier.
Sole (m.), sun.
Solere, to be accustomed.
Solo, -a, alone.
Sommo, highest.
Sonare, to play.
Sopra, above, on ; *di* —, upstairs.
Sorbetto, ice.
Sordo, -a, deaf.
Sorella, sister.
Sorte (f.), lot.
Sortire, to sally out.
Sostenere, to bear.
Sottrarre, to subtract.
Sovente, often.
Sovratutto, above all.
Sovvertire, to subvert.
Spaccalegna, wood-cutter.
Spagna, Spain.
Spago, cord.
Spalancare, to throw wide open.
Spargersi, to spread.
Spavento, terror.
Spazzo, floor.
Specchio, looking-glass.
Speciale, especial.
Specie (f.), species.
Spegnere, to put out, to quench.
Speranza, hope.
Sperienza, experience; *veder la* —, to make the experiment.
Spesa, charge.
Spesso, often.
Spicciarsi, to make haste.
Spiegare, to explain.
Spillone (m.), brooch.
Splendere, to shine.
Sposare, to marry.
Sposarsi con, to marry, to get married to.

Sposo, bridegroom.
Sprecare, to waste.
Spregiare, to despise.
Stabilire, to establish, to determine on.
Stabilirsi, to settle.
Stagione (f.), season.
Stamane } this morning.
Stamattina }
Stampatore, printer.
Stancarsi, to get tired.
Stanza, room, apartment; — *da mangiare*, dining-room; — *da ricevere*, sitting-room.
Stare (of health), to be, do; (of residence), to live; *star bene*, (of a dress), to fit; *stare in dietro* (of a watch), to lose; *stare composto*, to sit properly.
Stassera, this evening.
State (f.), summer.
Stato, state.
Statua, statue.
Stazione (f.), station.
Stella, star.
Stelo, stem.
Stimare, to consider.
Stivale (m.), boot.
Storia, history.
Straniero, stranger.
Studiare, to study.
Subito, immediately.
Succedere, to succeed, to happen.
Sudore (m.), sweat, labour.
Suggerimento, advice.
Suo, sua, his. See p. 198.
Suoi, his. See p. 198.
Suonare, to ring, play music.
Suono, sound.
Svegliarsi, to awake.
Svenire, to faint.
Sventura, misfortune.
Sventurato, -a, unfortunate.
Svizzero, Swiss.

T.

Tacere, to be silent.
Tale, such a one, such or such a.
Tangere, to touch.
Tanto, so much.

Tappeto, carpet.
Tappezzare, to paper the wall·
Tardi, late.
Tè, tea.
Teatro, theatre.
Tedesco, German.
Tegghia, earthen pie-dish.
Tema (m.), exercise.
Temere, to fear.
Temperino, pen-knife.
Tempo, time, weather; *per* —, early; *sprecare il* —, to waste one's time.
Tenere, to keep; — *dozzina*, to keep a boarding-house; — *per galantuomo*, to believe (one) to be honest; — *conto di*, to take care of.
Tenerello (speaking of age), young (dim.).
Tergere, to wipe.
Terra, earth.
Terreno, ground.
Ti, thee, to thee.
Titolo, right, title.
Toccare ad uno, to be one's turn, to come to.
Toppa, patch, key-hole.
Tornare, to return.
Torta, tart.
Tosto, soon, quick.
Tovaglia, table-cloth.
Tra, amongst.
Traccia, trace.
Tradurre, to translate.
Traduzione (f.), translation.
Tralasciare, to leave off.
Tranne, except.
Trarsi d' impaccio, to get out of trouble.
Trattenersi, to stay.
Tredici, thirteen.
Treno, train.
Trenta, thirty.
Trinciare, to carve.
Trionfare, to triumph.
Tristo, bad.
Trittolemo, Triptolemus.
Trovare, to find; *andare a* — *uno*, to go to see a person; *trovarsi*, to be found.
Tu, thou.

Two, thy.
Tuonare, to thunder.
Tuttavia, still, nevertheless.
Tutto, all, the whole, every-thing. See p. 223.

U.

Uccello, bird.
Uccidere, to kill.
Udire, to hear.
Uffizio, office; — *divino*, divine service.
Ultimo, *-a*, last.
Umano, human.
Umore (m.), humour.
Un, *uno*, *una*, a, an, one. See p. 145.
Undici, eleven.
Uomo, man; — *dabbene*, a good man.
Urgere, to be urgent.
Usare, to use.
Uscire, to go out.
Uso, use; *fare uso*, to use.
Utile, useful.
Uva, grapes.

V.

Vaccaro, cow-keeper.
Valere, to be worth.
Vano, vain.
Vantaggiare, to profit.
Vantamento, boasting.
Vantarsi, to boast.
Varcare, to cross.
Vaso, pot.
Vaticano, Vatican.
Vedere, to see; *vedersi*, to be seen.
Veli, to you, them. See p. 186.
Velo, to you, it. See p. 186.
Vendere, to sell.
Venezia, Venice.
Venerdì, Friday.
Venire, to come; —*meno*, to faint.
Venti, twenty.
Venuta, arrival.

Verbo, verb.
Vergogna, shame; *aver vergogna*, *vergognarsi*, to be ashamed.
Vermicello, worm (dimin.).
Vero, true.
Versare, to pour out.
Verso (prep.), towards, about.
Veruno, any; *non*—, no.
Vestibolo, hall.
Vestire, to dress.
Vestito, dress, coat.
Vettura, coach.
Vetturino, cabman.
Vi, there; *vi* (conj. pron.), you, or to you; (reflec. pron.) to yourself, yourself or selves.
Via, way.
Viaggiare, to travel; —*a piedi*, to travel on foot; — *in carrozza*, to travel in a carriage.
Viaggio, journey.
Viale, avenue.
Vicendevole, mutual.
Vicinato, neighbourhood.
Vicino, near, neighbour.
Vienna, Vienna.
Vietare, to forbid.
Villa, country-seat, house.
Vino, wine; — *d' Oporto*, Port wine.
Viola, violet.
Virtuoso, virtuous.
Visita, visit.
Vispo, lively.
Vista, sight.
Vistoso, striking to the sight, splendid.
Vite (f.), vine.
Vizio, vice.
Voce (f.), voice; *ad alta* —, aloud.
Voglia, desire, longing.
Voi, you.
Volare, to fly.
Volentieri, with pleasure.
Volere, to wish, will, want; — *dire*, to mean; — *bene*, to be fond of, to love; *si vuole*, it is believed; *volete una mela ?* will you have an apple?
Volgere le spalle a, to turn one's back on.

Volta, time; *altre volte*, formerly.
Voltarsi, to turn.
Volto, face.
Vostro, -a, (pl.) *-i, -e*, your. See p. 198.
Voto, wish.
Vuoto, empty.

Z.

Zanzara, gnat, mosquito.
Zia, aunt.
Zio, uncle.
Zoppo, lame.
Zucchero, sugar.

C. F. HODGSON & SON, Printers, Gough Square, Fleet Street, E.C.